MARKET
LIBERALISM

MARKET LIBERALISM

A Paradigm for the 21st Century

edited by
David Boaz and Edward H. Crane

CATO INSTITUTE
Washington, D.C.

Second Printing: May 1993
Third Printing: January 1994

Library of Congress Cataloging-in-Publication Data

Market liberalism : a paradigm for the 21st century / edited by David
  Boaz and Edward H. Crane.
      p.   cm.
    Includes bibliographical references.
    ISBN 0-932790-98-4 (cloth) : $25.95.—ISBN 0-932790-97-6 (pbk.) :
  $15.95
      1. United States—Politics and government—1993- 2. Liberalism—
  United States. 3. Free enterprise—United States. I. Boaz, David,
  1953- . II. Crane, Edward H., 1944- .
  E885.M37   1993
  320.5'1—dc20   92-42550
                                                                  CIP

Cover Design by Colin Moore.

Printed in the United States of America.

CATO INSTITUTE
1000 Massachusetts Ave., N.W.
Washington, D.C. 20001

Contents

1. Introduction: The Collapse of the Statist Vision

David Boaz and Edward H. Crane

The history of the West is largely a history of liberty. Antigone, Jesus, the emergence of pluralism and independent cities, the Magna Carta, the Renaissance, Martin Luther, the Enlightenment, the American Revolution, the repeal of the Corn Laws, the abolition of slavery, all mark continued progress toward the liberation of the individual from the coercive power of the state.

The 19th century seemed the culmination of that progress, a time when, according to the *Nation* in 1900, "Freed from the vexatious meddling of governments, men devoted themselves to their natural task, the bettering of their condition, with the wonderful results which surround us." But at the end of that great century of peace, progress, and industrial revolution in Europe, when the triumph of liberty seemed almost complete, many liberals saw the *ancien régime* returning in a new guise. Herbert Spencer warned of "the coming slavery," and the *Nation* worried that "before [statism] is again repudiated there must be international struggles on a terrific scale." The liberals' fears were realized; the 20th century has been a century of war and statism on an unprecedented scale. Totalitarian ideologies gave the state a legitimacy it had lost, and technology enabled governments to practice mass murder. Great Britain and the United States were spared the horrors of Nazism and communism, but some of the same nationalist, technocratic, and statist impulses lay behind the growth of the welfare-warfare state in those countries.

To be sure, the 20th century has not been an unmitigated disaster. The promises of the Declaration of Independence, the Constitution, and the Civil War Amendments were at last extended to all Americans, and in many ways Americans have more choices available to them than any other people in history. Though the federal government grew to be the wealthiest entity in human history, and its

1

tax collectors and regulators sought to intrude in our economic lives in a detailed way never before imagined, still the productive powers of the marketplace steadily raised all Americans to an unprecedented standard of living.

Yet by the late 20th century, in the West and elsewhere, governments had become huge, stultifying institutions—bureaucratic socialism in Russia and Eastern Europe, autocracy in Latin America, totalitarian despotism in Asia, kleptocracy in Africa, and tax-and-spend welfare states in the West.

Then, by the last quarter of the century, just as liberals might have despaired of ever returning to the path of progress toward liberty that had characterized Western history until this century, the trend began to turn. Many countries in Latin America threw out their military rulers, established democratic governments, and began privatizing state enterprises and opening protected industries to global competition. The rulers of China noticed how prosperous the Chinese people were becoming in every society but their own and quietly began to privatize agriculture in the world's most populous country, setting in motion one of the world's fastest growing economies. Great Britain privatized hundreds of state enterprises large and small and introduced an element of competition into the stodgy bureaucracies of health and education. Mikhail Gorbachev opened the Pandora's box of glasnost and was no doubt surprised at what he eventually discovered inside. His tentative reforms led rapidly to the most significant change of the late 20th century, the collapse of European communism and the still-in-progress liberation of the people of Russia and Eastern Europe. Even in Africa, a generation after the end of colonialism, the first steps toward democracy and markets are beginning to be seen. In other corners of the world, from Pretoria to Auckland, from Stockholm to Taipei, a liberal revolution is once again bringing free markets and human rights to the people of the world.

And yet it seems that after a few tentative steps toward deregulation in 1978 and tax reduction in 1981, the free-market revolution in the United States has failed to stop the inexorable growth of the omnivorous federal government. In 1940 the federal government spent $13 billion, or about $100 billion in 1990 dollars; today the figure is $1.5 trillion, an increase of over 1,000 percent (see Figure 1.1). Thomas Jefferson said 200 years ago that "the natural progress of things is for liberty to yield

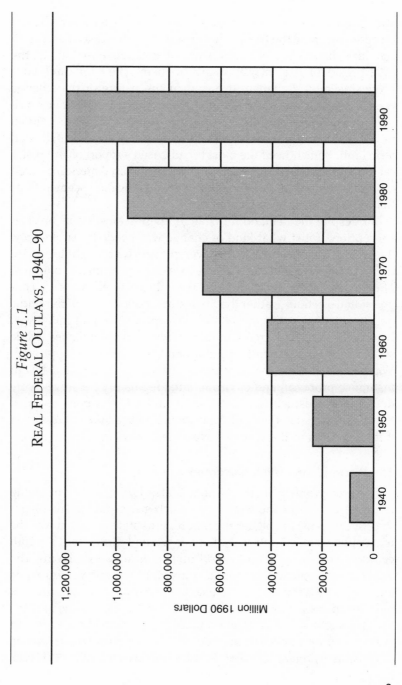

Figure 1.1
REAL FEDERAL OUTLAYS, 1940–90

and government to gain ground," and today's Jeffersonians are recognizing anew the truth of his observation. It's clear that Americans are dissatisfied with the state of their government. In the 1992 presidential primaries many of them voted for candidates promising radical change, even when the nature of that change wasn't clear. Despite a reelection system that had seemed impervious to challenge, an unprecedented number of congressional incumbents either retired under pressure or were defeated, and term limitation showed the most broad-based support of any political movement in a generation. Almost 20 million Americans voted for a presidential candidate whose chief qualification seemed to be that he had never been in politics.

But despite the demand for change, there seemed to be no clear conception of just what kind of change was needed. People knew the system wasn't working; they weren't sure what ought to replace it, but the trend clearly was against seeking government solutions. The 93 percent reelection rate for incumbents in November's congressional elections, rather than being an endorsement of the status quo, seemed to justify the 14-state sweep of term limit initiatives. Nine of 10 state tax increase initiatives went down in flames, while six of eight tax or spending limitation measures were approved. Voters in California overwhelmingly rejected a mandated health insurance proposal, and environmental regulatory initiatives were defeated in Massachusetts and Ohio. Indeed, exit polls revealed that a substantial majority of Americans preferred lower taxes even if it meant less in the way of government services.

The World Is Too Much Governed

The real problem in the United States is the same one being recognized all over the world: too much government. The bigger the government, the bigger the failure; thus state socialism was the most obvious failed policy. As liberals warned throughout the 20th century, socialism faced several insurmountable problems: the totalitarian problem, that such a concentration of power would be an irresistible temptation to abuse; the incentive problem, the lack of inducement for individuals to work hard or efficiently; and the least understood, the calculation problem, the inability of a socialist system, without prices or markets, to allocate resources according to consumer preferences. For decades liberals such as F. A. Hayek and Ludwig von Mises insisted that socialism simply couldn't work, couldn't effectively utilize all the resources and knowledge of a great society to serve consumers. And for decades social democrats in the West sneered that not only was Soviet communism surviving, the USSR's economy was growing faster than the economies of the West. The social democrats were wrong, in many ways. First, some scholars have argued that the Soviet Union gave up true Marxist socialism in 1921, after the devastating failure of the War Communism years, and thereafter operated a crude kind of market economy with massive government intervention.[1] Second, though the clumsy Soviet economy could produce large quantities of steel, it never managed to produce anything that consumers wanted. By the late 1980s the Soviet economy was not two-thirds the size of the U.S. economy, as the CIA estimated; it did not "make full use of its manpower," as John Kenneth Galbraith said; it was not "a powerful engine for economic growth," as Paul Samuelson's textbook told generations of college students. It was, in fact, about 10 percent the size of the U.S. economy, as nearly as such disparate things can be compared, and it made grossly inefficient use of the educated Soviet workforce. A failure in the industrial age, it was a dinosaur in the information age, a fact obvious to everyone—except Western intellectuals—who visited the USSR.

Similarly obvious were the gross human rights abuses and economic inefficiencies of apartheid in South Africa and the stagnation of the coddled, debt-ridden economies of Latin America and New Zealand. Because our own government never amassed as much power as did those foreign regimes, the failure of big government here at home was never as clear. Still, the U.S. government has become a Leviathan that Thomas Jefferson would never recognize. No institution in history has ever commanded as much wealth as the U.S. government. As recently as 1920 government spending at all levels amounted to just 10 percent of national income. By 1950 that percentage had soared to 26 percent. Today the figure is about

---

[1]See Paul Craig Roberts, *Alienation and the Soviet Economy* (Albuquerque: University of New Mexico Press, 1971); Don Lavoie, *Rivalry and Central Planning: The Socialist Calculation Debate Reconsidered* (Cambridge: Cambridge University Press, 1985); Paul Craig Roberts and Karen LaFollette, "The Original Aspirations and the Soviet Economy Today," in *Meltdown: Inside the Soviet Economy* (Washington: Cato Institute, 1990).

44 percent, and government spending rose faster under President Bush than it had under any president in a generation. Government employment rose from 3.9 million in 1933 to 18.4 million in 1992. Government is by far the biggest employer and the biggest landlord in our society. A visit to any state capital—not just Albany or Sacramento but Richmond or Frankfort—will confirm that state governments, too, have become massive, costly enterprises.

The cost of all this government can be measured, imprecisely to be sure, in economic terms. In 1950 the average family paid only 2 percent of its income to the federal government; today the same family pays 25 percent. Government expenditures at all levels amount to about $20,000 per household. Taxes add about 70 percent to the price of the goods we buy. As William Niskanen points out in chapter 5 of this volume, regulation costs the economy about $600 billion a year in lost output. The growth of taxes and regulation over the past generation and the declining quality of government schools have given us 20 years of slow economic growth—a burden that is more easily borne by the upper middle class than by people still struggling to achieve a comfortable standard of living.

But the cost of government should not be measured exclusively in economic terms. Democratic governments today presume to regulate more aspects of our lives more closely than even the autocratic governments of the *ancien régime* ever did. Governments in the United States assign our children to schools and select the books they will learn from, require us to report our most intimate economic transactions, demand 80 permit applications if we want to start a business in Los Angeles, restrict whom we may sleep with and what we may read, prescribe the number and gender ratio of toilets in buildings open to the public, tell us whom we must hire and whom we may fire, bar our most efficient businesses from high-tech markets, regulate the size of the oranges we may buy, deny terminally ill patients access to pain-relieving and life-saving drugs, strangle our financial institutions with archaic rules, prosecute investors for crimes that have never been defined, and devote 19,824 words to a directive on the U.S. peanut program. And, though it rarely comes to this in civilized modern societies, it should be remembered that behind every ridiculous regulation stands the government's willingness to enforce it with violence if necessary.

Thus, the cost of government must finally be measured in freedom. Regulations—from drug laws to anti-discrimination laws to occupational licensing—restrict our freedom to make our own choices. Anti-pornography ordinances, hate-speech codes, and government entanglement in the arts limit our freedom of expression. Compared with the long-suffering people of Russia, or South Africa, or Peru, or China, Americans enjoy a great deal of freedom—but if Thomas Jefferson returned to Washington in 1993 he would surely say that, like George III, our government today has erected a multitude of new offices and sent hither swarms of officers to harass our people and eat out their substance.

Tocqueville warned us of what might happen.

> After having thus successively taken each member of the community in its powerful grasp and fashioned him at will, the government then extends its arm over the whole community. It covers the surface of society with a network of small, complicated rules, minute and uniform, through which the most original minds and the most energetic characters cannot penetrate, to rise above the crowd. The will of man is not shattered, but softened, bent, and guided; men are seldom forced by it to act, but they are constantly restrained from acting. Such a power does not destroy, but it prevents existence: it does not tyrannize, but it compresses, enervates, extinguishes, and stupefies a people, till each nation is reduced to nothing better than a flock of timid and industrious animals, of which the government is the shepherd.[2]

Charles Murray has examined the way the welfare state takes over the responsibilities of individuals and communities and in the process takes away much of what brings satisfaction to life. If government is supposed to feed the poor, then local charities aren't needed. If a central bureaucracy downtown manages the schools, then parents' organizations are less important. If government agencies manage the community center, teach children about sex, and care for the elderly, then families and neighborhood associations feel less needed. As Murray puts it, "When the government takes away a core function [of communities], it depletes not only the

[2]Alexis de Tocqueville, *Democracy in America*, part 2 (1840), book 4, chap. 6, "What Sort of Despotism Democratic Nations Have to Fear."

source of vitality pertaining to that particular function, but also the vitality of a much larger family of responses."[3] If the citizen knows that government will feed the hungry if the local church doesn't, he's less likely to get involved in the church project. Soon "let the government take care of it" becomes a habit. Today's communitarians sense that problem, though they tend too often to envision communities' working through government rather than through voluntary efforts.

A New Vision for America

To make sense of the American people's dissatisfaction with the present state of affairs, we need a new vision for American government, a vision rooted in the principles of our Founders and suited to the challenges of the 21st century. In this book we propose such a vision, one that we call *market liberal*. Today people in the United States and around the world who believe in the principles of the American Revolution—individual liberty, limited government, the free market, and the rule of law—call themselves by a variety of terms, including conservative, libertarian, classical liberal, and liberal. We see problems with all those terms. "Conservative" smacks of an unwillingness to change, a desire to preserve the status quo. Only in America do people seem to refer to free-market capitalism—the most progressive, dynamic, and ever-changing system the world has ever known—as conservative. In addition, many contemporary American conservatives favor state intervention in trade, in our personal lives, and in other areas. "Libertarian" is an awkward and misinterpreted neologism that has become too closely tied to a particular group of activists.

"Classical liberal" is closer to the mark, but the word "classical" connotes a backward-looking philosophy all the tenets of which have been carved in stone. Finally, "liberal" may well be the perfect word in most of the world—the liberals in societies from China to Iran to South Africa to Argentina are supporters of human rights

[3]Charles Murray, *In Pursuit: Of Happiness and Good Government* (New York: Simon & Schuster, 1988), p. 274.

and free markets[4]—but its meaning has clearly been corrupted by contemporary American liberals.

"Market liberal," by modifying liberal with an endorsement of the free market, thus strikes us a solid description of a philosophy that is rapidly gaining adherents throughout the world. It is a forward-looking philosophy, comfortable with a changing world, tolerant, and enthusiastic about the market process and individual liberty.

The market-liberal vision brings the wisdom of the American Founders to bear on the problems of today. As did the Founders, it looks to the future with optimism and excitement, eager to discover what great things women and men will do in the coming century. Market liberals appreciate the complexity of a great society, recognizing that socialism and government planning are just too clumsy for the modern world. It is—or used to be—the conventional wisdom that a more complex society needs more government, but the truth is just the opposite. The simpler the society, the less damage government planning does. Planning is cumbersome in an agricultural society, costly in an industrial economy, and impossible in the information age. Today collectivism and planning are outmoded, backward, a drag on social progress.

Market liberals have a cosmopolitan, inclusive vision for society. We reject the bashing of gays, Japan, rich people, and immigrants that contemporary liberals and conservatives seem to think addresses society's problems. We applaud the liberation of blacks and women from the statist restrictions that for so long kept them out of the economic mainstream. Our greatest challenge today is to extend the promise of political freedom and economic opportunity to those who are still denied it, in our own country and around the world.

As visionaries such as Warren Brookes and George Gilder have pointed out, we stand today at the dawn of a new era in history. Gilder writes, "Capital is no longer manacled to machines and places, nations and jurisdictions. Capital markets are now global and on line twenty-four hours a day. People—scientists, workers,

---

[4]Michael Dobbs reported from Moscow in the *Washington Post* on September 1, 1992, that "liberal economists have criticized the government for failing to move quickly enough with structural reforms and for allowing money-losing state factories to continue churning out goods that nobody needs."

and entrepreneurs—can leave at the speed of a 747. . . . Companies can move in weeks. Ambitious men need no longer stand still to be fleeced or exploited by bureaucrats. Geography has become economically trivial."[5] (Richard McKenzie and Dwight Lee described an extreme example of that: about half a billion dollars was *faxed* out of Kuwait City on the afternoon of August 2, 1990, as the Iraqi army approached.)[6] National boundaries are becoming irrelevant, increasingly ineffective obstacles to trade among entrepreneurs in different parts of the world. The successful economies of the 21st century will be those of countries that liberate their people. Human capital—knowledge, creativity, and entrepreneurship—is the key to prosperity in the information age.

One of the exciting results of the information age, as Jerry Taylor points out in chapter 21, is that our more productive, high-tech economy uses far fewer natural resources to provide a higher standard of living. Tiny silicon chips have replaced bulky vacuum tubes and transistors, and fiber optics and satellites are replacing thousands of miles of copper cable. That's one reason natural resources are 20 percent less expensive today than they were in 1980, 50 percent cheaper than in 1950, and 80 percent cheaper than in 1900.[7]

As central governments become larger, more intrusive, more impervious to political change, and more irrelevant to economic progress, people in many parts of the world—Quebec, Croatia, Bosnia, northern Italy, Scotland, and much of Africa, not to mention the 15 new republics of the old Soviet Union—are challenging the nation-states that they find themselves in. Governments respond to dissatisfaction by trying to set up a new world order or a unified Europe. The European Community, which began as an attempt to

[5]George Gilder, *Microcosm: The Quantum Revolution in Economics and Technology* (New York: Simon & Schuster, 1989), pp. 355–56. See also Floyd Norris, "Why Currencies Move Faster Than Policies," *New York Times*, September 23, 1992, p. D1: The exchange-rate turbulence of mid-September "provided a bitter reminder to central bankers and finance ministers around the world that the power of governments to control economies and currencies has eroded."

[6]Richard B. McKenzie and Dwight R. Lee, "Government in Retreat," National Center for Policy Analysis Policy Report no. 97, June 1991, p. 4. See also Richard B. McKenzie and Dwight R. Lee, *Quicksilver Capital: How the Rapid Movement of Wealth Has Changed the World* (New York: Free Press, 1991).

[7]Stephen Moore, "So Much for 'Scarce Resources,'" *Public Interest* no. 106 (Winter 1992): 98.

make trade flow freely throughout the Continent, now pays five times the world market price to rich European farmers and regulates the content of cheese and the size of condoms.

What the world needs instead of greater centralization is further progress toward free trade and devolution of government decision-making to smaller units. The ideal arrangement for many parts of the world might be very small nations linked by open borders and in some cases by federal governments organized for defense and the protection of individual rights. The United States and Switzerland provide imperfect models for such a structure, which would give maximum opportunity for individuals to vote with their feet and force local communities to bear the costs of their own decisions. Scotland and Slovakia have both demanded more subsidies for their uncompetitive industries from the more productive English and Czechs; chances are an independent Slovakia will soon realize the advantages of Czech prime minister Vaclav Klaus's free-market reforms when the Slovaks have to pay all the costs of doggedly trying to stay semisocialist. An independent Scotland might well discover the same thing. As a sort of thought experiment, one might even speculate about what kinds of policies an independent South Central Los Angeles might pursue. Rep. Maxine Waters can declare her constituents victims—as they are, to some extent, as David Boaz argues in chapter 11—and demand more money from taxpayers in Kansas and Connecticut; President Maxine Waters just might be forced to try free markets in order to create wealth right there in her independent republic. One of the most important checks on the power of wrong-headed governments is open borders for capital, goods, and people.

The market-liberal order requires a stable rule of law that protects private property rights, as Roger Pilon points out in chapter 2. In a culture that sanctions legal plunder and rewards individuals for being irresponsible, there will be a general lack of respect for law, liberty, and justice. Public policies supportive of private property and the rule of law, in turn, rest on cultural values. It is therefore essential for leaders in all fields—not just public officials but teachers, lawyers, journalists, filmmakers, businesspeople, and parents—to affirm our commitment to the moral and cultural values that underlie political freedom: honesty, self-reliance, reason, thrift, education, tolerance, property, contract, and family. Government can undermine those values, but it cannot instill them.

When government taxes savings, we expect to see less thrift. When government abrogates contracts, we expect people to take their commitments less seriously. When government takes on the burden of caring for children and the elderly, we expect families to become less important. When government subsidizes uneconomic or environmentally destructive activities (building luxury condos on delicate barrier islands, for example), we expect more waste and environmental destruction. And only a truly crazy set of policies, as David Boaz points out, could induce millions of teenage girls to have children without any husbands in sight, tens of thousands of mothers to walk away from their babies, or hundreds of thousands of teenage boys to choose a life of crime. Still, in each case, while we work to change government policies, we should expect individual Americans to make responsible choices. Despite government disincentives, people should save for the future, live up to their contracts, start families only when they're prepared for them, and choose honest work over crime. Perhaps instead of the "Don't help a good boy go bad" ads that were ubiquitous a few years ago, we should have stuck with the traditional message, "Good boys don't steal cars."

One of the problems with the aggrandizement of government in the past generation is that government is no longer capable of playing its limited but essential role. While it slaps labels on record albums and teaches us how to have safe sex, government no longer protects us from violence. Every resident of a major city knows the futility of calling the police because of a mere automobile break-in, and in New York City police don't even identify a suspect in half the murders. Theft costs the American economy something more than $600 billion a year, much of it in industrial-strength locks, security guards, and home security systems that we purchase because government fails to protect us. Just possibly, if government stopped trying to fix the size of peaches and pick up the tab for every risk gone bad, it would be able to protect us from violent crime.

Disillusionment with the Status Quo

Crime, poverty, bad schools, expensive medical care, a faltering economy—the American people recognize those problems and are increasingly skeptical of government's ability to solve them. Since the 1960s their response has more and more been to tune out politics. Outside the South (where civil rights enforcement increased black voting), voter turnout is down 30 percent in three decades. In 1992 a heated three-way race featuring the country's leading anti-politician attracted a larger turnout, but it remains to be seen whether that increase will last. The long-term trend of declining turnout might indicate that the real mandate of the American people is for "none of the above" to run our lives. Young people between 18 and 24 voted at a rate of only 29 percent in 1988 and only 16 percent in the midterm elections of 1986 and 1990. According to elections analyst Curtis Gans, "Polling data shows that those who don't vote and are middle-aged or older tend to be angry and alienated by the conduct of politics while those who are younger tend to be indifferent to it." Gans points out that four presidential elections in a row "were won by leaders who campaigned against the concept of government." Yet the continuing failure of government "raises the question of whether government is capable of anticipating complex societal problems, whether it is responsive to basic citizen needs and whether the citizen's vote makes any difference." Gans concludes, "Who are the sane ones? Those who still troop loyally to the ballot box . . . ? Or, those who in increasing numbers eschew the system in protest?"[8]

Another loyal supporter of the political system, Theodore J. Lowi of Cornell University, writes, "One of the best-kept secrets in American politics is that the two-party system has long been brain dead—kept alive by support systems like state electoral laws that protect the established parties from rivals and by Federal subsidies and so-called campaign reform. The two-party system would collapse in an instant if the tubes were pulled and the IV's were cut."[9] The strong support for Ross Perot's outsider campaign is testimony to how Americans feel about the Democrats and the Republicans.

Gans argues, "None of the problems that have pushed voter turnout downward are insoluble." We beg to differ. Citizens increasingly recognize not just that politicians are indebted to special interests and will do anything to be reelected but that politics

[8]Curtis Gans, "Turnout Tribulations," *Journal of State Government*, January–March 1992, p. 13.

[9]Theodore J. Lowi, "The Party Crasher," *New York Times Magazine*, August 23, 1992, p. 28.

and government are becoming irrelevant to society's real needs. In our complex world, governments cause far more problems than they will ever solve; in fact, governments themselves cause most of the social problems they are then called on to solve. Since our experience with Jimmy Carter, Ronald Reagan, and George Bush teaches us that anti-government presidents don't really get government out of our lives, the next best thing is to try to ignore government and make the best lives possible for ourselves and our families. Thus we see a decline in voting and an increase in tax avoidance and evasion; private school attendance and even home schooling; private mail and other communications services; private police, security services, and courts; personal saving for retirement; and so on. Some of those developments reflect the lingering anti-establishment attitudes of the 1960s. The IRS, for instance, in a study of tax evasion, found that affluent young people have "a relatively high values-based predisposition to noncompliant behavior"—in other words, they don't like being told what to do.[10] Those citizens will not come back to the polls in response to charisma or vague calls for change. Only a real crisis in the functioning of society, or a candidate offering dramatic, believable changes, is likely to make a sustained difference in turnout rates.

The United States is not the only place where citizens are becoming disillusioned with political elites. When Canada's provincial governors and major parties submitted major constitutional amendments to a referendum, the voters delivered "a sweeping repudiation of all the country's national leadership," in the words of the *Washington Post*. Elites in Brussels drew up a treaty for a much more centralized European Community and presented it to the world as a fait accompli, the next step on the road to social progress and global community. The first voters to get a crack at it, in tiny Denmark, turned thumbs down on the idea. Under the European Community's rules, that ended the discussion because the treaty had to be adopted unanimously. But Europe's elites wouldn't take no for an answer; the Danish people may be given a chance to come to their senses in another referendum.

---

[10]"Tax Cheats Most Likely to Be Yuppies," (Madison, Wis.) *Capital Times*, August 16, 1985, p. 9.

The magnitude of the changes in the world and the irrelevance of politics have escaped most current political figures, especially in the United States, who continue to offer programs from a bygone era. Since the end of the fleeting Reagan Revolution, about the middle of 1981, conservatives have been floundering. Unwilling to admit that their decade in the White House has left the federal government bigger and more voracious than ever, they offer marginal changes—a capital gains tax cut, enterprise zones, and the like. In *The Conscience of a Conservative*, Barry Goldwater railed against a $100 billion federal budget and the Departments of Commerce and Labor. In 1980 Ronald Reagan promised to abolish the Departments of Energy and Education. A dozen years of Republican presidents saw no cabinet departments eliminated and one created, while federal spending rose from $678 billion to $1.5 trillion.

Meanwhile, other conservatives have decided that the real issue is not big government's impact on individual freedom but the need to use big government to impose conservative values on society. That approach seemed to peak at the Republican National Convention, where the Republicans gave evidence of relying on Henry Adams's advice: "Politics, as a practice, whatever its professions, has always been the systematic organization of hatreds."

Adams's insight has found a hearing on the other side of the political spectrum as well, with some Democrats deciding that "wealthy bankers," "people in elegant estates," and especially the nefarious Japanese would make fine political scapegoats. Rather than have America compete to be the best in a global economy, those politicians would blame the Japanese for their success, describe the sale of high-quality products to voluntary purchasers as "an economic Pearl Harbor," and build a wall of protection around uncompetitive industries.

Meanwhile, if the collapse of socialism has deprived the conservatives of an enemy, it has deprived anti-capitalist leftists of a theoretical argument for ever bigger government. Some have found their new justification in environmentalism. There are real environmental problems in the United States and the world, as Fred Smith and Kent Jeffreys argue in chapter 23, but some self-proclaimed "Greens" seem to view environmental problems primarily as a pretext for more state control of the economy. Socialist economist Robert Heilbroner, for instance, spent 50 years insisting that socialism works; finally, when Gorbachev threw in the towel, so did

15

Heilbroner. In two striking articles, he wrote, "Less than seventy-five years after it officially began, the contest between capitalism and socialism is over: capitalism has won. . . . Capitalism organizes the material affairs of humankind more satisfactorily than socialism." And again, "It turns out, of course, that Mises was right" about the impossibility of socialism.[11] He then proceeded immediately to insist that we will have to turn to socialism anyway because of our "ecologically imperilled society"—once again ignoring the empirical evidence of socialism's record.

As the world moves into the 21st century, rightwingers and leftwingers will continue to fight the battles of the 1950s. One valiant attempt to move beyond those retrograde positions has been made by David Osborne and Ted Gaebler in their important book *Reinventing Government: How the Entrepreneurial Spirit Is Transforming the Public Sector*. Osborne and Gaebler recognize that "the kinds of governments that developed during the industrial era, with their sluggish centralized bureaucracies, their preoccupation with rules and regulations, and their hierarchical chains of command, no longer work very well." Their arguments are reflected in Bill Clinton's call for a "revolution in government . . . to shift from top-down bureaucracy to entrepreneurial government that empowers citizens and communities." Osborne and Gaebler know all the things government should become: catalytic, community owned, competitive, mission driven, results oriented, customer driven, enterprising, anticipatory, decentralized, and market oriented. But we believe they dramatically underestimate the difficulty of getting coercive institutions to exhibit those characteristics. Osborne and Gaebler have done a heroic job of finding examples of government agencies that operate the right way: competitive service provision in Phoenix, results-oriented public housing in Louisville, an enterprising Olympics in Los Angeles. But every institution in the private sector of society operates according to those 10 attributes every minute of every day. Instead of undertaking the Herculean if not Sisyphean task of trying to get government agencies to be customer driven, market oriented, and so on, wouldn't it be better simply to rely on the voluntary sector for more

---

[11]Robert Heilbroner, "The Triumph of Capitalism," *New Yorker*, January 23, 1989; Robert Heilbroner, "After Communism," *New Yorker*, September 10, 1990.

of our needs? Osborne and Gaebler have set the right goals for 21st-century government; it only remains to discuss how we might best achieve them.

A Paradigm for the 21st Century

Market liberals offer an expansive, inclusive vision for society. We look forward to seeing men and women, in the words of the *Nation* in 1900, freed from the vexatious meddling of governments, once again able to devote themselves to their natural task, the bettering of their condition. Wherever we look in society, as the essays in this volume illustrate, we find social problems created by clumsy government intrusion into private relationships.

An unconstrained vision for society—a vision that sees women and men building a free, prosperous, and pluralistic society in every corner of the globe—requires a constrained vision of government. We need to restore in this country the Founders' understanding of government: a necessary evil, created for the sole purpose of securing our rights, with a few clearly specified powers. As Jefferson put it in his first inaugural address, "A wise and frugal government, which shall restrain men from injuring one another, which shall leave them otherwise free to regulate their own pursuits of industry and improvement, and shall not take from the mouth of labor the bread it has earned. This is the sum of good government."

That message—the liberation of individual creativity by the restraint of government power—is also needed in the rest of the world, especially in such places as China, Africa, and the Arab world, where people still suffer under brutally repressive governments. Fortunately, it appears that the world is slowly, grudgingly moving in that direction, as the benefits of liberal society become more apparent.

In his history of the 20th century, *Modern Times*, Paul Johnson wrote:

> Disillusionment with socialism and other forms of collectivism was only one aspect of a much wider loss of faith in the state as an agency of benevolence. The state was the great gainer of the twentieth century; and the central failure. . . . Whereas, at the time of the Versailles Treaty, most intelligent people believed that an enlarged state could increase the sum total of human happiness, by the 1980s the view was held by no one outside a small, diminishing

and dispirited band of zealots. The experiment had been tried in innumerable ways; and it had failed in nearly all of them. The state had proved itself an insatiable spender, an unrivalled waster. Indeed, in the twentieth century it had also proved itself the great killer of all time. . . .

What was not clear was whether the fall from grace of the state would likewise discredit its agents, the activist politicians, whose phenomenal rise in numbers and authority was the most important human development of modern times. As we have noted, by the turn of the century politics was replacing religion as the chief form of zealotry. To archetypes of the new class . . . politics—by which they meant the engineering of society for lofty purposes—was the one legitimate form of moral activity, the only sure means of improving humanity. . . . At the democratic end of the spectrum, the political zealot offered New Deals, Great Societies and Welfare States; at the totalitarian end, cultural revolutions; always and everywhere, Plans. . . . By the 1980s, the new ruling class was still, by and large, in charge; but no longer so confident. . . . Was it possible to hope that the "age of politics," like the "age of religion" before it, was now drawing to a close?[12]

By the end of the 1980s, confidence in politics and government had declined still further, and John Naisbitt and Patricia Aburdene could write in *Megatrends 2000* that "the great unifying theme at the end of the 20th century is the triumph of the individual."

As we approach the 21st century, there is a growing recognition by thinking people throughout the world that the old paradigm of structuring societal arrangements coercively through governmental mechanisms is crumbling. It is in the nature of human beings to be free, and increasingly we are coming to realize that freedom from bureaucratic institutions—in government and in the private sector—not only is consistent with human nature but is the source of human progress. Market liberalism provides a framework for a dynamic, pluralistic society that can yield a future of undreamed-of prosperity and human fulfillment. It seems to us that the time to unleash its potential is at hand.

[12]Paul Johnson, *Modern Times: The World from the Twenties to the Eighties* (New York: Harper & Row, 1983), pp. 729–30.

PART I

AN AMERICAN VISION

2. Freedom, Responsibility, and the Constitution: On Recovering Our Founding Principles

Roger Pilon

The quadrennial elections that give rise to volumes such as this afford an opportunity not simply to take stock and look ahead but to ask more searching questions having to do with what we stand for as a nation. After the monumental changes that have taken place around the world over the past four years, such questions would seem especially fitting. Yet the national debate during our recent elections hardly touched those deeper issues. Driven not by principle but by policy, not by visions of who we are but by visions of what we want, we seem near century's end to be stuck in the rut of the welfare state, part free, part controlled, unable to see beyond our immediate concerns. Nor should that surprise, since the mundane interests the welfare state has brought into opposition compel us to that war of all against all that the classical theorists so well understood. And we are all the poorer for it.

Indeed, our political life today is dominated by the view, held by politicians and citizens alike, that the purpose of government is to solve our private problems, from unemployment to health care, retirement security, economic competition, child care, education, and on and on. But having thus socialized our problems, our flight from individual responsibility does not end. For once we realize, however dimly, that social benefits require social costs—either taxes or regulations—we then seek to foist those costs upon the wealthy or the industrious. Yet that move has its limits—the rich and industrious can afford to leave, after all. So we try next to shift the costs of our appetites to our children in the form of the federal deficit. Tax and spend thus becomes borrow and spend as the flight from responsibility, and reality, continues.

To some extent, of course, the idea that the purpose of government is to solve the private problems of living has always been with us, but never have political and cultural conditions so encouraged it. In fact, recognizing that there would always be those who would be willing to relinquish responsibility for their lives to government authorities and institutions, and realizing the implications should that attitude ever command political respect, the founding generation tried to guard against that possibility by drafting a constitution for *limited* government. Over the years, however, the restraints set forth in that document have broken down, and with that breakdown has come the gradual demise of individual liberty and responsibility. If that trend is to be reversed, if we are to realize the potential that our founding principles permit, it is essential that we understand the forces that have been at work, the forces that have brought us from the vision of the founding generation to our current state of political conflict and paralysis.

The Original Design: From the Declaration to the Civil War Amendments

We are fortunate in America to have a philosophy, set forth in a series of documents, to which to repair to renew our first principles. That philosophy, stated succinctly in the Declaration of Independence, then more amply in the Constitution, the Bill of Rights, and the Civil War Amendments, can be seen as composed of two parts. First is the moral vision, the world of moral rights and obligations we all have prior to the creation of government, which we create government to secure. Second is the political and legal vision, the world of political and legal powers we authorize when we create government, which serve as the means of securing the moral vision.

Nowhere is that divide between the moral and the political more clearly seen than in the Declaration, whose seminal phrases have inspired countless millions around the world for more than two centuries. After placing us squarely in the natural law tradition—the "truths" that followed were held to be "self-evident," or truths of reason—the Founders set forth a premise of moral equality, which they defined with reference to our natural rights to life, liberty, and the pursuit of happiness. Only then did they turn to the second, the political or instrumental point—that to secure those rights, governments are instituted among men. And even then

22

they added a moral qualification—that to be just, government's powers must be grounded in consent—making it clear that political power, to be legitimate, must be derived from moral principle. Thus, the moral vision must be drawn first, the political and legal vision second, as a derivation from the former.

The Moral Vision

As just noted, the moral vision begins in the natural law tradition, with the individual, not with the group, and with the moral equality of all individuals, defined by our equal rights to life, liberty, and the pursuit of happiness. The importance of that starting point cannot be overstated. By placing us in the natural law tradition, the Founders were saying that there is a higher law of right and wrong, grounded in and discoverable by reason, against which to judge positive law, and from which to derive positive law. Without such a compass, positive law is mere will, the expression of the will of those in power. And mere will, whether of the king or of the majority, does not give law its legitimacy. Only principles of reason can do that.

Moral Rights. In that higher law tradition, then, we proceed from a premise of moral equality—defined by rights, not values—which means that no one has rights superior to those of anyone else. So far-reaching is that premise as to enable us to derive from it the whole of the world of rights. Call it freedom, call it live-and-let-live, call it, in the socialist planning context, the right to plan and live our own lives, the premise contains its own warrant and its own limitations. It implies the right to pursue whatever values we wish—provided only that in doing so we respect the same right of others. And it implies that we alone are responsible for ourselves, for making as much or as little of our lives as we wish and can. What else could it mean to be free?

The connection here between freedom and responsibility is especially important to notice. As the discussion throughout the founding period makes clear, freedom and responsibility were joined in the liberal mind in a thoroughly modern way. It was not, as an older way of looking at things had it (and as contemporary "communitarians" often imply), that we enjoy our rights as grants or "privileges," which we retain only as long as we exercise them "responsibly." No, we have our rights "by nature." Thus, we alone can alienate them—through contract, for example, or by committing torts or crimes. The mere "irresponsible" exercise of rights, short of violating the rights of others, is itself a right. What else could it mean to be responsible for oneself?

The discussion during the founding period also makes it clear that two rights serve as the foundation for all others—property and contract. Indeed, John Locke, whose thinking found its way to the heart of the Declaration, reduced all rights to property: "Lives, Liberties and Estates, which I call by the general Name, *Property.*" It should hardly surprise, upon reflection, that Locke and the American Founders would think that way. After all, to have rights to life, liberty, and the pursuit of happiness is to be "entitled" to those things, to hold "title" to them, and to be able to "claim" that others may not "take" them from us. As the very language of rights indicates, rights and property are inextricably connected: our property in our "lives, liberties, and estates" is what rights are all about. Thus, we discover what our natural rights are by spelling out the many forms the property we possess in ourselves and in the world can take, from life to liberty of action to freedom from trespass upon our person or property. Included among our natural rights, then, are both liberties (of action) and immunities (from the torts or crimes of others), both of which have property as their foundation. In general, whether in the area of expression or religion or commercial activity or privacy or whatever, we are free to enjoy what is ours except insofar as doing so prevents others from enjoying what is theirs.

Broadly understood, then, property is the foundation of all our natural rights. Exercising those rights, consistent with the rights of others, we may pursue happiness in any way we wish. One way to do that, of course, is through association with others. We come then to the second great font of rights, promise or contract. (The rights we create through contract are not natural rights—we do not have them "by nature"—but like natural rights they are a species of moral right.) Through voluntary agreements with others we create the complex web of associations that constitutes the better part of what we call civilization. Here, the rights and obligations created are as various as human imagination allows, whether they arise from spot transactions or from enduring agreements creating institutions ranging from families to churches, clubs, corporations, charitable organizations, and much else.

Legal Recognition. In outline, then, this is the moral world—described by our moral rights and obligations, both natural and contractual—that we created government to secure. In fact, when we look to the Constitution, the Bill of Rights, and the Civil War Amendments, we find explicit recognition of those rights. The Fifth Amendment's takings clause recognizes the right to private property, for example, as the Constitution itself recognizes the right to contract. In the Fifth and Fourteenth Amendments we find that no one may be deprived of life, liberty, or property without due process of law. (And by "law" the drafters could hardly have meant mere legislation or the guarantee would have been all but empty.) Similarly, the Thirteenth Amendment abolished at last the practice of slavery or involuntary servitude, making it plain that no one may own another, that each of us owns himself and himself alone.

The privileges and immunities clauses of both the Constitution and the Fourteenth Amendment hark back to our "natural liberties," as William Blackstone made clear in his *Commentaries on the Laws of England*. Likewise, the Seventh Amendment's reference to and, by implication, incorporation of the common law reminds us of Edward Corwin's observation, in *The "Higher Law" Background of American Constitutional Law*, that "the notion that the common law embodied right reason furnished from the fourteenth century its chief claim to be regarded as higher law." The First Amendment's guarantees regarding religion, speech, the press, assembly, and petition; the Second Amendment's recognition of the right to keep and bear arms; the several guarantees in the Constitution and the Bill of Rights regarding criminal investigations and prosecutions; and finally the Ninth Amendment's reminder that only certain of our rights are enumerated in the Constitution, the rest remaining unenumerated and retained, are among the many indications, ranging over nearly 100 years, of the kind of world earlier generations had in mind for government to secure.

That world, the moral vision the Founders first set forth, was one of private individuals standing in private relationships with one another, each with a right to make of himself as much as he wished and could, and each responsible for his choices and actions, good and bad alike. It was a world both static and dynamic. The minimal legal framework, designed to secure our rights and obligations, was static in the sense that it was derived from immutable principles of right and wrong, reflecting the human condition as such. Yet the Founders' world was fundamentally dynamic in that it allowed for—indeed, protected—the rich variety of human experience and experiment that we all know is possible under conditions of freedom. That dynamism was expected to come from individuals, however, not from government. In particular, it was not government's responsibility to promote prosperity. Rather, that was the business of individuals, alone or in private association with each other.

It is especially important to notice too that the world the Founders envisioned was largely a world of private law, which enabled people to prosper or fail, protecting them only from the depredations of others. It was not a world of public law, especially public redistributive law, which could only encourage people to look to government both for prosperity and for protection from failure. No, the purpose of government, as the Constitution states, is to promote the *general* welfare—that is, the welfare of all—by establishing justice, ensuring domestic tranquility, and securing the blessings of liberty. If government limited itself to those ends, individuals would be free, in their private capacities, to pursue their own welfare, for which they alone are responsible.

The Political and Legal Vision

To secure that moral vision, a vision of individual liberty and individual responsibility, governments were created and government powers were authorized. Here, two closely related problems arose, one moral, the other practical.

The Limits of Consent Theory. The moral problem, which had its practical aspect, stemmed from the Declaration's consent requirement (captured with respect to the states in the Constitution's ratification clause) that to be just or legitimate, power had to be derived from the consent of the governed. Plainly, if we begin with the right of the individual to be free and hence to rule himself, and himself alone, the consent requirement is necessary, for the individual may be bound by the will of others only if he has agreed to be bound. The difficulty in meeting that requirement, however, is substantial. To begin, although unanimity does produce legitimacy, it is all but impossible to achieve. But when we resort to rule by the majority, even by a large majority, we do not get legitimacy because the minority, by definition, has not consented. Yet there are problems even when we combine majoritarianism with prior unanimous consent to be bound thereafter by the majority—the classic social contract approach: the people who agreed to the original contract were few in number; even then we would still need unanimity; and the problem of binding subsequent generations, which subsequent elections do not really solve, remains. Finally, the argument from "tacit consent"—those who stay are bound by the will of the majority—has the majority putting the minority to a choice between coming under its will or leaving, which begs the very question that needs to be answered.

Those moral difficulties leave us with a pair of conclusions that were more or less understood by the founding generation. First, even democratic government has about it the character of a "necessary evil." Government is "necessary" to overcome the practical problems that surround the private enforcement of rights in its absence, problems that Locke and others had catalogued. But it is "evil" insofar as the consent requirement cannot be deeply satisfied. Thus, while majoritarian democracy may be preferable to other forms of rule in that it enables the ruled to participate in the decisionmaking process, in the end it is simply a process through which to decide, not a process that imparts legitimacy to the decisions that follow—as those in the minority are often the first to attest.

The second conclusion, or prescription, that follows from reflection on the moral difficulties that surround the creation of government stems from the realization that government, unlike a private organization, is a forced association. Given that character, it behooves us to do as little as possible through government and as much as possible in the private sector, the better to minimize the use of force. Thus, out of respect for the nature of government, at least, the founding generation sought to limit the power of this necessary evil, giving it only as much as would be necessary to accomplish its ends.

Limiting Power. Given those moral insights, the practical problem the Founders faced was to create a government that was at once strong enough to secure our rights yet not so strong as to violate those very rights in the process. Thus, they created a set of limited powers; but realizing that power tends to corrupt, they checked

27

and balanced those powers at every turn. One such check, of course, was the electoral process. Yet that process was itself checked by everything from representative government to the indirect election of senators and presidents to the lifetime appointment of judges. At the same time, power was divided between the federal and the state governments, with most reserved to the states, where presumably it could be more immediately controlled by the people. Meanwhile, at the federal level, power was separated among the three branches, each of which had checks upon the others. The final check was the power of the judiciary to review the acts of the political branches and the states and rule them unconstitutional.

But the most important restraint, especially given the power of judicial review, was meant to be found in the central strategy of the Constitution, which made it clear that ours was to be an extremely limited government. First, the Constitution was a document of enumerated powers, meaning that the federal government was to have only those powers that were strictly enumerated in the text. Second, the exercise of those powers was to be restrained by the necessary and proper clause, which authorized Congress to exercise its limited powers only through laws that were necessary and proper for doing so. And finally, a bill of rights was added to the Constitution, which together with the guarantees in the original document itself made it plain that the federal government was to be further restrained in the exercise of its enumerated powers by both enumerated and unenumerated rights.

Thus, while the federal government was given enough power to govern, the Founders' idea of governing was extremely limited, especially when contrasted with the governing done by European governments at the time and our own government today. Indeed, given the limits the Founders placed on government, it is difficult to understand how anyone could argue that the Constitution authorizes the kind of expansive government we have today. In fact, honest observers who are at the same time friends of the modern welfare state readily admit that to get to where we are we had to turn the document on its head. Others may wish to defend our present arrangements as constitutional. The concern here will be more constructive—to trace some of the forces that led to the breakdown of constitutional restraints on the growth of government, the better to understand what must be done to recover those restraints and the principles they secured.

The Demise of Principle, the Rise of Policy

In 1948 Richard M. Weaver wrote a book entitled *Ideas Have Consequences*, the title and text of which captured well the power of ideas in human history. In contrast, Karl Marx had pointed a century earlier to the importance of material forces. Marx was right to remind us of that, but as his own influence bears witness, he underestimated the far greater power of ideas—sound and unsound ideas alike. Indeed, the ultimate defeat of the Marxist vision is a tribute to the force of superior ideas, which triumphed in the face of brute material and military force.

Still, we do not have a clear picture, nor is it likely that we ever will, of just how ideas and events interact over time—whether it is by their intrinsic force that ideas prevail, or fail to prevail, or by the consequences that eventually result from adhering to one set of ideas rather than another, or by some combination of the two. We have an intuitive understanding, to be sure, that "the climate of ideas" matters. But just how it matters is, well, another matter—and rather less than a science.

The "Science" of Policy

The rise of science, however, has had more than a little to do with the demise of the Founders' vision, which is all the more ironic since those men, products all of the Age of Reason and the Enlightenment, were steeped in the science of their day and hardly of the view that later "science" might undermine their creation. Their science, however, had a healthier sense of its limits and of the balance between the rational and the empirical than later science would have. Indeed, the Founders' science of man, although buttressed by empirical observation, was essentially a rational undertaking in its normative aspects. Yet in time that moral vision—uncertainly grounded in reason, to be sure—would come under attack not simply from the skepticism that has been with us since antiquity but from skepticism armed with a new science of man. Reductionist (both theoretical and material) and empirical, this newer science would take as its task not the rational justification of principles of right and wrong but the empirical explanation of human behavior. Once we understood the forces of nature or nurture that made us behave as we did, the next step, of course, would be to devise social institutions to encourage desirable and discourage undesirable behavior. Could social planning—indeed, social engineering—be far off?

From Natural Law to Utilitarianism. But first, a frontal attack on natural law would prepare the way. Although not well appreciated until the German philosopher Immanuel Kant took note of it later in the century, the Scottish philosopher David Hume delivered perhaps the most telling blow to natural law in 1739 when he observed, almost in passing, that from descriptive propositions one could not derive normative conclusions, a shot that went to the heart of the relatively primitive epistemology of the natural law theorists. More direct and conclusory in his attack was Jeremy Bentham, the father of British utilitarianism, who in 1791 intoned that talk of natural rights was "simple nonsense: natural and imprescriptible rights, rhetorical nonsense,—nonsense upon stilts." Such attacks were not the stuff of the daily press, of course. Nevertheless, they slowly seeped into the climate of ideas, undermining in time the almost credulous faith that underpinned the Founders' vision and the institutions they created to secure it.

The central theme in the eventual breakdown of our structure of restraints, then, is the demise of the moral foundations of that structure and the rise of new rationales for political power. And what were those new rationales? As already noted, there was a growing faith during the 19th century and into the 20th in the ability of science to solve social problems. That faith was buttressed by the rise of utilitarianism in moral theory, which looked not backward to principles of right and wrong but forward to conditions of good and evil, reduced to intersubjectively verifiable and hence to empirically quantifiable reports of pleasure and pain. Policy and law came to be justified, in this approach, not by whether they secured rights but by whether they produced the greatest good for the greatest number. Respect for property and contract might yield that result. Then again it might not, depending on the circumstances. Policy, including legal policy, would have to adjust to changing circumstances and to the emerging theories of the new policy science.

Progress. Material changes were taking place as well, of course. The 19th century saw the dawn of the Industrial Revolution in America and with it the growth of urbanization. Poverty, endless work, child labor, and unhealthy living conditions had been tolerable, presumably, when dispersed throughout rural America. When concentrated in urban America, and when contrasted with the conditions of the emerging entrepreneurial class, they became "social" problems. Naturally, such problems played directly into, and reciprocally with, the themes of the emerging social sciences. At century's end, in fact, the *Encyclopedia of Social Reform* could state with confidence that "almost all social thinkers are now agreed that the social evils of the day arise in large part from social wrongs." Remedying such "wrongs" was clearly beyond the scope of private charity, administered by individuals who "suffered with" their recipients, making moral distinctions in the process. What was needed, rather, was public charity, administered by "professional" social workers, for "no person who is interested in social progress can long be content to raise here and there an individual," wrote Frank Dekker Watson, director of the Pennsylvania School for Social Service. Indeed, in *The Charity Organization Movement in the United States,* published in 1922, Watson commended the ongoing "crowding out" of private by public charity, for only thus would "public funds ever be wholly adequate for the legitimate demands made upon them."

Democracy and Good Government. Over the course of the 19th century, then, the climate of ideas gradually changed. In ethics, we moved from natural law to utilitarianism. In science, we moved from a conception of man as an autonomous being to one of man as determined by natural and environmental forces. Still, in a constitutional regime like ours, social workers armed with such theories and acting as "social engineers" could not simply impose "a divine order on earth as it is in heaven," as Owen Lovejoy, president of the National Conference of Social Work, envisioned in a 1920 article. Rather, in a government "of, by, and for the people," that new order would have to come in some way, at least, from the people. Thus conceived, however, democracy would prove no restraint. On the contrary, ignoring its individualist roots in *self*-rule, imbued with the collectivist overtones of "the people," and treated operationally as majoritarianism, democratic theory dovetailed quite nicely with the new policy science. After all, if policy and law were justified not with respect to rights but only insofar as they promoted

31

the greatest good for the greatest number, and if we could determine that they do that only empirically, then how better to do the utilitarian calculus than through the majoritarian process? By their votes the people will tell us which policies maximize their well-being.

Thus, by the Progressive Era, toward century's end, we had come to think of government not as a necessary evil, to be guarded against at every turn, but as a positive good—indeed, as an instrument of good, an instrument for doing good. Combining the force of law, viewed instrumentally, with the ambition of the new social sciences and the rationales of both utilitarianism and majoritarianism, government had come to be seen as an institution through which to solve our social problems. Plainly, that was a fundamental shift in our thinking. That shift, moreover, was not limited to social problems narrowly understood or to the political branches. When the common law courts began shifting in the middle of the 19th century from strict liability to a negligence standard in torts—to make the world safe for industry—and Congress in 1890 saw fit to pass the Sherman Antitrust Act—to restore effective competition to the market economy—those and countless other such measures were indications all of that fundamental shift: from government instituted to secure principle to government empowered to pursue policy. Just whose policy, and by what constitutional means, were questions that remained to be answered.

Instituting the Shift

It is one thing to have a shift in ideas—from a conception of limited government, instituted to secure rights, to a conception of expansive government, empowered to pursue policy—quite another to incorporate that shift through and in institutions that were designed precisely to restrain such a change. How, in short, can a limited government be turned into an expansive government when the constitution that authorizes the former not only contains no provision for the latter—save by amendment—but, to the contrary, contains provisions that explicitly restrict the creation of the latter?

For more than 200 years—albeit less frequently as the restraints have broken down—that question has confronted every person and every movement that has sought to expand the federal government.

And for nearly three-quarters of that time, up until the New Deal, the constitutional restraints did largely hold. But as noted above, inroads on the original design were being made all along. The change in the climate of ideas was gradually taking its toll, first on the most political branch of government, the Congress, then on the second of the political branches, the executive, and finally on the branch that in principle is nonpolitical, the judiciary.

It is important to stress, however, how slow that change was in coming. Today, it seems almost quaint to recall that, for the better part of the 19th century, Congress actually debated about whether it had constitutional authority to do what some of its members wanted from time to time to do. And when Congress did act along lines of dubious authority, presidents often vetoed those acts as unconstitutional. Finally, those measures that did make it through both of the political branches had to withstand Supreme Court scrutiny, which was by no means assured. In short, unlike today, when the political branches all but assume their authority to expand government, which the courts have acquiesced in and now restrain only in limited domains (and sometimes themselves affirmatively assist), earlier officials in all branches took seriously their oaths to support the Constitution.

In the Political Branches. In the 19th century, in fact, the constitutional debate often never reached the rights side of the question— the side that dominates modern discussions—because the focus was largely on whether Congress (or the executive) had the power to undertake a given activity. An early example was a 1794 statute appropriating $15,000 for relief of French refugees who had fled to Baltimore and Philadelphia from a Negro insurrection in San Domingo. As the principal author of the Constitution, Virginia's James Madison remarked that he could not "undertake to lay his finger on that article of the Federal Constitution which granted a right to Congress of expending on objects of benevolence the money of their constituents." In fact, so dubious was the authority for this act of charity that it was rewritten, still dubiously, to be part payment of loans earlier obtained from the French Republic. Two years later, in 1796, a similar bill, for relief of Savannah fire victims, was defeated decisively, a majority in Congress finding that the general welfare clause afforded no authority for so particular an appropriation. As Virginia's William B. Giles observed, "The House should not attend to what generosity and humanity required but what the Constitution and their duty required."

The 19th century saw growing pressure on Congress to engage in a wide range of "general welfare" spending, the constitutional ramifications of which have been well documented in Charles Warren's *Congress as Santa Claus*, written on the eve of the New Deal. Almost as intense, however, was the opposition, from constitutional principle, to having such projects undertaken or even funded by the federal government. Thus, in 1817 President Madison vetoed a bill authorizing Congress not to *undertake* a public works project—for there was clearly no enumerated power to that end in the Constitution—but simply to *appropriate money for* that purpose under the general welfare clause. Madison could find not even this limited a power, for as he had earlier written, "Money cannot be applied to the General Welfare, otherwise than by an application of it to some *particular* measure conducive to the General Welfare," and that particular measure must be "within the enumerated authority vested in Congress."

Nevertheless, the view that Alexander Hamilton had advanced, that Congress had a general welfare power to fund at least "national" projects, eventually triumphed when President Monroe endorsed it in 1822 as part of a veto message. Still, efforts to have the federal government take the next step and actually conduct such projects were resisted by Presidents Jackson and Van Buren. Indeed, throughout the 19th century we find presidents ranging from Tyler, Polk, Pierce, and Buchanan, before the Civil War, to Grant, Arthur, and Cleveland, after the war, standing athwart such efforts by Congress to expand its powers. Nor should it be thought that their vetoes were merely "political" and not principled. In 1854, for example, President Pierce was faced with a bill, championed by a luminary of the day, Dorothea Dix, that would have given as a gift to the states 10 million acres of federal lands for the benefit of the indigent insane. Faced with a distinction between donating land and donating general tax revenues (which would be the next target of public avarice), and with such congressional pleas as "Our forefathers left the hands of the Government unfettered to spend what it might choose for their benefit," Pierce stood his ground on both counts—and on principle as well.

> I cannot find any authority in the Constitution for making the Federal Government the great almoner of public charity

throughout the United States. To do so would, in my judge-
ment, be contrary to the letter and the spirit of the Constitution and subversive of the whole theory upon which the
Union of these States is founded.

Thirty-three years and many vetoes later, in 1887, President
Cleveland would take a similar stand against a bill that would
have appropriated $10,000 from general revenues to buy seeds for
distribution to Texas farmers suffering from a drought.

I can find no warrant for such an appropriation in the Constitution, and I do not believe that the power and duty of the
General Government ought to be extended to the relief of
individual suffering which is in no manner properly related
to the public service or benefit. A prevalent tendency to
disregard the limited mission of this power and duty should,
I think, be steadfastly resisted, to the end that the lesson
should be constantly enforced that though the people support the Government, the Government should not support
the people.

It should not be thought, however, that Congress over the course
of the 19th century simply rolled over to special interests, although
that trend was gaining. In fact, throughout the century we see in
Congress not simply the political but the constitutional debate as
well. Thus, as late as 1887 we find Republican Sen. John J. Ingalls
of Kansas decrying a measure to distribute moneys from the Treasury to the states to establish agricultural experiment stations.

It illustrates the tendency of this class of agitators to demand
the continual interposition of the National Government in
State and local and domestic affairs, with the result, as
I believe, of absolutely destroying the independence and
freedom of individual conduct and subverting the theory
on which the Government is based and in the conduct of
which hitherto it has reached such great results. . . . It is
not desirable that there should be uniformity of methods
and results in the different . . . States. It is the conflict of
the contrariety of opinions in this country upon these subjects that results in the greatest good to the greatest number.
It is the collision and contest between opposing ideas or
views of contending localities that enable us to reach the
highest results in the departments of activity and government.

35

Notice how the language of utilitarianism had crept into the debate. More generally, notice how Ingalls's rationale, although in part constitutional, is grounded rather more in policy than in principle. Not only is "the greatest good to the greatest number" his criterion, but "great results" and "highest results" are his focus rather more than the inherent wrong of "continual interposition" in state, local, and domestic affairs.

As federal "interposition" increased, that shift from principle to policy would increase as well, not least because principle was being abandoned. Thus, we find South Dakota Sen. Thomas Sterling objecting in 1914 that a proposal appropriating $4.5 million annually for states to give instruction in farm work and home economics "costs too much, and the nation itself will, in the end, feel the enervating influence of such a policy." In the same consequentialist vein, moreover, there was growing recognition, however faint, that federal programs were indeed moving us in the direction of the classic war of all against all. Thus, senators from California and Connecticut inquired of this bill, perhaps rhetorically, "Why should we expend the public money for educating the farmers of this country any more than the mechanics?" As if to meet that challenge and raise the stakes, Congress three years later appropriated $7 million annually to pay states for the training of teachers in agriculture, home economics, industrial subjects, and trade. The answer to an objection based on unfair consequences, apparently, was not to return to principle—for there was no longer any principle to return to—but to expand the program to include some of those left out. That expansion, of course, never ends.

In the Courts. Thus it went for some 150 years, with discussion of principle gradually yielding to discussion of policy. But again, it is important to note how much of the discussion took place in the political branches. Not that the Supreme Court played no part at all; rather, its part was smaller than we might imagine today, largely because things less frequently got to the Court. The ambitions of Congress grew only slowly, and were often checked in that branch. Then when bills did get out of Congress, the executive branch was there to check them. What part the early Court did play, especially under Chief Justice Marshall, was largely one of securing its jurisdiction and ensuring the authority of the federal government over that of the states—although again, in a rather limited way by today's standards.

At the same time, it needs to be said that when the 19th-century Court was presented with claims not simply about powers but about rights as well, it was not always solicitous of the individual confronted by an assertion of public power. Just after the Civil War, for example, the Court considered a challenge brought by a number of New Orleans butchers to a Louisiana statute chartering a private slaughterhouse corporation as a monopoly within an 1,150-square-mile area. The complaining butchers claimed that the effect of the statute was to prevent them from practicing their trade in the district and hence, among other things, to deny them their privileges and immunities contrary to the guarantees of the recently passed Fourteenth Amendment: "No state shall make or enforce any law which shall abridge the privileges or immunities of citizens of the United States." As noted earlier, the debate surrounding the adoption of the Fourteenth Amendment had made it clear that the right to pursue one's livelihood unfettered by such interference as the Louisiana statute interposed was at the core of those privileges and immunities that Blackstone had located in our "natural liberties." Nevertheless, by a vote of 5 to 4, a sharply divided Court found for the state, effectively removing the clause from the Constitution.

As a harbinger of the Court's future jurisprudence, however, one line in the majority opinion in *Slaughterhouse* stands out: "Such a construction [as plaintiffs urge] . . . would constitute this court a perpetual censor upon all legislation of the States, on the civil rights of their own citizens, with authority to nullify such as it did not approve as consistent with those rights." Indeed, such a role, at least with respect to the federal government (prior to the Civil War Amendments), is precisely what Madison had in mind when he characterized the Court as the "bulwark of our liberties." Its job is to stand astride the political branches, ensuring that their acts both proceed from authority granted them and are consistent with rights restraining them, failing either of which those acts must be found unconstitutional. If the Court cannot or will not be a "perpetual censor," it has no business engaging in judicial review because it has no business existing.

That single sentence, however, speaks volumes about the majority's misunderstanding of the Court's function, a misunderstanding that would emerge full-blown from the New Deal Court. The choice of the deprecating word "censor," for example, suggests a failure to appreciate how limited, yet crucial, the Court's power is. To be sure, it has the power to negate—to give the censor's "no." But the power to "nullify" is not the power to "(dis)approve" insofar as "approve" suggests a power to make value judgments. Rather, as the sentence continues, it is a power to decide merely whether the legislation is or is not "consistent" with the civil rights of citizens. To do that, however, the Court must know what those civil rights are. And here, the ambiguity of the majority's formulation comes to the fore. For either the legislation is "on" the civil rights of the citizens, declaring in positive law just what those rights are, in which case it could never be inconsistent with "those rights" (unless the positive law were internally inconsistent). Or else the legislation is declaratory of the citizens' rights, but the rights it declares have some *independent* basis such that the legislation might "get it wrong" in its declarations, in which case "those rights" might indeed be inconsistent with the rights declared by the legislature.

Clearly, it was the latter scenario that the Founders, and the authors of the Fourteenth Amendment, had in mind when they derived our positive law from higher law—and especially when they spoke in the Ninth Amendment of retained rights. Subsequent legislators (or even courts) might get it wrong when they set about declaring the law: they might declare that a right existed when in fact, by higher law standards, it did not; or they might authorize a power, as here, the effect of which was to extinguish a right that, by higher law standards, did exist. To determine those kinds of questions, however, the Court would have to know and understand the higher law. And that, precisely, is what the *Slaughterhouse* majority refused to undertake, despite the impassioned yet reasoned example of the minority, arguing from "the natural and inalienable rights which belong to all citizens."

During the early years of the Republic, courts had not been nearly as reluctant as the *Slaughterhouse* majority was to proceed from first principles. Writing in the *University of Chicago Law Review* in 1987, Suzanna Sherry documented a number of cases during the first 30 years of the nation in which we find courts turning to both written and higher law to reach their decisions. After that, however, the decline of natural law and the rise of alternative rationales undoubtedly took their toll on the judiciary, the only branch that must justify its decisions in written opinions that are subject to the scrutiny of the world. As time went on, those opinions were grounded increasingly within the "four corners" of the written text, making little if any reference to the higher law that stands behind that text. The advantage of doing things that way, of course, is a certain intellectual security and objectivity: the Court can always point to the explicit language on which it grounds its opinion. That advantage can be deceptive, however, particularly if what emerges is a less than complete and hence misleading reading of the text, especially in its broad passages. In fact, the result too often is a narrow, clause-bound jurisprudence, reflecting nothing so much as the lack of an overarching, integrated theory of rights that gives content and order to the Constitution's broad language. Lacking such a theory, it is no surprise that the *Slaughterhouse* majority could find in the text no right of the plaintiffs to ply their trade free from the monopoly restriction the state had created.

Notwithstanding the shortcomings of the *Slaughterhouse* majority's narrow constitutional positivism, that approach has dominated our Supreme Court jurisprudence ever since, with selective exceptions during two periods—in the early decades of the 20th century and during the Warren and Burger Courts more recently. To understand how this jurisprudence and these jurisprudential shifts have affected the growth of government, it is useful to distinguish two constitutional avenues along which that growth has progressed. On one hand, an accelerating accretion of government programs instituted under a "general welfare" rationale—although usually not proceeding explicitly under that constitutional provision—has resulted in what today are massive transfers from taxpayers to individual recipients, as discussed above. On the other hand, countless programs today attempt to accomplish the same welfare ends not by redistributing funds through the Treasury but by enacting regulations aimed at compelling private individuals and organizations to act in ways that are thought to be beneficial to other private individuals and organizations. The power of Congress to regulate commerce under the commerce clause of the Constitution is usually the rationale for this second set of programs, which today are ubiquitous. The question arises, however: how could either of those two kinds of programs have been found to be constitutional under a Constitution that was designed to limit government to securing individual liberty?

The General Welfare Clause. As discussed earlier, wealth transfers that involve redistribution through the Treasury arose slowly, in the face of political opposition grounded in constitutional principle, and, in the end, without clear constitutional authority. Although the general welfare clause was the implicit, and sometimes the explicit, rationale for such programs, it was often not invoked by proponents who felt themselves constrained to some extent by Madison's interpretation of the clause: after all, why would powers have been enumerated if Congress could, under the general welfare clause, spend on virtually any project it deemed to be for the general welfare? Thus, congressional spending during the 19th century often began under an enumerated power but then expanded to be, in effect, a general welfare expenditure. Sales of land under the territorial power clause, for example, evolved into gifts of land for agricultural colleges, then into gifts of proceeds from the sale of land, and finally into gifts from the Treasury generally. Similarly, with two early and small exceptions, not until 1867 were gifts of money to private citizens made, and these were justified chiefly under the war powers. In 1874, however, gifts to flood sufferers were given under a theory of general welfare, a precedent that was repeated seven times over the next 30 years.

Thus, by small steps Congress moved from clear, to less clear, to no authority, creating limited programs that served later as precedents for more expansive programs. Background developments were not irrelevant to this evolution. Indeed, our changing conception of government only encouraged the process. Thus, as precedents accumulated, not only were constitutional questions replaced by policy questions but the idea of government as the engine of progress took on a life of its own.

What was especially distressing for constitutionalists, however, was the absence of any secure ground on which to raise a challenge, particularly after the Supreme Court decided in 1923 that neither citizens nor states had standing to sue to enjoin the secretary of the Treasury from making such expenditures. Echoing the *Slaughterhouse* majority, the Court in that case, *Frothingham v. Mellon,* refused "to assume a position of authority over the governmental acts of another and co-equal department," leading Attorney General William D. Mitchell to observe in a 1931 speech to the American Bar Association that "no one has yet been able to devise a method" by which the constitutional validity of appropriations of the national funds may be presented for judicial decisions.

Nevertheless, in 1937, in *Halvering v. Davis*, a challenge based on the general welfare clause was presented against the New Deal's Social Security Act. In that case, however, not only did the Court's majority follow a decision handed down a year earlier that had rejected Madison's understanding of the clause, but in repeating its recent finding that the clause did serve as an independent source of power for Congress to tax and spend—thereby gutting the doctrine of enumerated powers—the majority went on to say that the Court would not itself get into the question of whether a given exercise of that power was for the general or for a particular welfare. Shades again of *Slaughterhouse*, with the Court deferring to the political branches. And with that, the Progressive Era's stream of welfare programs, especially under Presidents Roosevelt and Wilson, became a New Deal river.

The Commerce Clause. If attempts to restrain the growth of welfare transfers failed, attempts to restrain the growth of regulatory transfers fared no better. Here, however, the opportunity to litigate was greater since these transfers took place not through the power of Congress to tax but through its power to regulate. The regulations that today bestow benefits on some by regulating others—in areas ranging from transportation to manufacturing, employment, housing, discrimination, and on and on—constitute restrictions on the liberties of those others. Because they do, they can be challenged in the courts.

Once again, however, we have to determine first the source of whatever power Congress may have, then examine the implications for individual rights. Unlike the welfare programs, these schemes are based on an independent source of power. The commerce clause, unlike the general welfare clause, sets forth one of the enumerated powers of Congress, giving that branch the power "to regulate Commerce . . . among the several States." On its face, the power would appear to be plenary, save for its limitation to "commerce," not other activities, and to commerce "among" the states, not within them. Unfortunately, both those limits are gone today, and the power is indeed all but plenary. Accordingly, we need to begin at the beginning, by placing the power in its historical setting.

There can be little doubt about the principal purpose of the commerce clause. Under the Articles of Confederation, state legislatures had become dens of special-interest legislation aimed at protecting local manufacturers and sellers from out-of-state competitors. The result was a tangle of state-by-state tariffs and regulations that impeded the free flow of commerce among the states, to the detriment of all. Only a national government could break the logjam. Indeed, the need to do so was one of the principal reasons behind the call for a new constitution.

The commerce clause was aimed, then, at giving *Congress*, rather than the states, the power to regulate commerce among the states. Its purpose was thus not so much to convey a power "to regulate"—in the affirmative sense in which we use that term today—as a power "to make regular" the commerce that might take place among the states. And in fact the so-called negative or dormant commerce power, which restricts states from intruding on federal authority over interstate commerce even when there has been no federal legislation in a given area, operates largely in that way.

At bottom, then, the commerce clause was intended to enable Congress to break down state barriers, to prevent states from restricting the free flow of commerce among themselves. What has happened in litigation over the years, however, is not unlike what has happened with the Tenth Amendment. There, the principal purpose was to make clear that ours was a government of enumerated powers, the balance of power being "reserved to the states . . . or to the people." Ignoring those final four words, the discussion, not unlike that over the commerce clause, has focused not on the substantive question—how freedom might be secured—but on the jurisdictional question—who should control, the federal or the state government. The assumption that one or the other government must control commerce goes all but unchallenged.

Yet once we think of the commerce clause as conferring not only a negative but an affirmative power to regulate, questions about how to limit the power come immediately to the fore. And noting that the power to regulate interstate commerce is one of Congress's enumerated powers only highlights the problem. For if that power becomes all but boundless, as it has, the doctrine of enumerated powers becomes an empty promise.

To see how that has happened, and how regulatory programs have grown over the years, we need to consider the issues in the abstract for a moment. More precisely, we need to analyze the relation between the purpose of the commerce power and its terms. Again, those terms limit Congress to regulating "commerce," not other activities, and commerce "among" the states, not within them. When Congress is further restrained by the original purpose of the clause, a four-part test emerges: to be justified under the commerce clause, a regulation must (1) facilitate the free flow of (2) interstate (3) commerce (4) without violating the rights of any party. Conditions 2 and 3 are those of the clause, of course. Conditions 1 and 4 stem from the purpose of the clause: when interstate commerce is free from governmentally imposed restraint, private parties are at liberty to make whatever agreements they wish, limited only by the common law. Thus, any regulation that facilitates the "free" flow of interstate commerce by restricting the rights of some in order to give benefits to others would not pass the test. That is not free but managed trade—trade managed for some other end.

Limited then to its original negative purpose, the commerce power is largely unproblematic because it functions only to prohibit state regulations that restrict the free flow of interstate commerce. To be sure, there could be too much federal prohibition. But the test would be whether the state regulation prohibited by the federal power does in fact restrict the free flow of interstate commerce. Similarly, an affirmative commerce power that executed certain police power functions would be unproblematic if it met the four-part test. Thus, a regulation that clarified rights in uncertain contexts or another that controlled the interstate shipment of dangerous goods would present no problems—provided, of course, that the police power specifications of such regulations were consistent with the underlying theory of rights.

What happens, however, if conditions 1 and 4 are eliminated? What happens, that is, if the commerce power is no longer restrained by its original purpose but by its two limiting terms alone? Can those terms bear the entire burden? Worse still, what happens if purposes other than the original purpose start driving the interpretation of the clause? Suppose, for example, that we stop thinking of the clause as intended to facilitate the free flow of interstate commerce by ensuring economic liberty and start thinking of it instead as an instrument through which to pursue various social goals? That would open up a whole new set of possibilities for men and women of public vision, against whom parchment barriers alone, especially in the hands of a clause-bound Court, would provide little resistance.

Indeed, consider very briefly the expansion of the commerce power over railroads. Like so many other areas, the railroad cases are complicated by early government subsidies that encouraged patterns of development that probably never would have arisen from market forces alone. Thus arose local railroad monopolies, which encouraged farmers and other shippers to demand and get state regulation of railroad rates. Such regulation reaches far beyond a state's police power, of course, and should have been actionable as such; but it is hard to gainsay such controls where government subsidies created the monopoly in the first place (again demonstrating how one intrusion in the market leads to still others). When different states imposed inconsistent rates on the same interstate carriers, however, suit was brought. In 1886, in *Wabash, St. Louis & Pacific Railway v. Illinois*, the Supreme Court held that only the federal government could regulate interstate railroad rates. The following year the Interstate Commerce Act was passed and so the federal government was now in the rate-making business—a quantum leap beyond making commerce "regular" among the states by removing state barriers.

The Supreme Court never questioned this rate-making function, of course, or tried to square it with the original purpose of the commerce clause. Its concern rather was jurisdictional—whether Congress or the states should set rates. Clearly, rate-making was within the *terms* of the commerce clause: it was "commerce" that was being regulated, not other activity, and commerce "among" the states, not within them. But just as clearly, this was an expansion of the commerce power well beyond its original purpose.

The expansion did not end there—and that is the lesson to be learned from the railroad cases, so difficult to gainsay in themselves—for once in the rate-making business, the Interstate Commerce Commission found reason to extend its reach. Thus, the line between interstate and intrastate regulation was breached in 1914 in the Shreveport rate case when the Court found that Congress could extend "its control over the interstate carrier in all matters having . . . a close and substantial relation to interstate commerce"—this to prevent discriminatory interstate/intrastate rates, yet another displacement of the original purpose of the commerce clause. And eight years later, in *Wisconsin Railroad Commission v. Chicago, Burlington & Quincy Railroad*, the Court upheld the Transportation Act of 1920, which replaced specific with comprehensive railroad regulation, helping to cartelize the industry by imposing comprehensive rate-of-return regulation. Thus, a constitutional clause aimed at facilitating the competition that arises from the free flow of commerce ended up being used to suppress competition. The new attitude was perhaps best captured by the 1922 Court: "Congress in its control of its [sic] interstate commerce system is seeking . . . to make the system adequate to the needs of the country by securing for it a reasonable compensatory return for all the work it does." Thus did "our" system become socialized. In effect, railroads were no longer private businesses but instruments of public policy.

But if the reach of the commerce power was expanding, so too, of course, were the rights of individuals receding. Thus, the Sherman Antitrust Act of 1890, also passed under the commerce power, prohibited private parties from entering into contracts in restraint of trade. Shortly thereafter, the United States brought suit against a combination of most, but not all, of the railroads that operated between Chicago and the Atlantic coast, charging that those companies had entered into a cooperative agreement with each other that was aimed at shutting out competition. No longer having a privileges and immunities clause on which to rely—for the *Slaughterhouse* Court's narrow reading of the clause (against the states) might now be used in reading the version that was in the Constitution itself—the defendants invoked their Fifth Amendment right to freedom of contract, but to no avail. For in 1898 the Court found in *U.S. v. Joint Traffic Association* that Congress had the power to pursue a policy of promoting economic competition. And failing to distinguish between private and public arrangements, it held that a private agreement did in fact prevent competition. It is no small irony that 24 years later, when it upheld the Transportation Act of 1920, the Court would approve a public arrangement that truly did prevent competition in the railroad industry—by force of law.

The Decline of the Court. Notwithstanding its 1898 opinion, the late 19th-century Court was in the beginning of its "Lochner" era, so called for the Court's 1905 decision in *Lochner v. New York* upholding the challenge of a New York baker, on freedom of contract grounds, to a New York State statute limiting the hours that bakers might contract to work. Over a series of cases, the Progressive Era Court withstood a number of efforts to gut the Constitution's economic guarantees in the name of public policy. But the cases were uneven and never deeply grounded. It is as if the Court were searching for its place in a world that was moving inexorably toward public policy on all matters previously thought to be private.

The crisis came during the Depression, of course, when the political branches, driven by the mandates of 1932 and, especially, 1936, undertook the reordering of our political arrangements not by amending the Constitution but by ignoring it. President Roosevelt's July 1935 letter to the House Ways and Means Committee speaks volumes: "I hope your committee will not permit doubts as to constitutionality, however reasonable, to block the suggested legislation." When for a while the Court resisted the legislative avalanche, Roosevelt early in his second term tried to pack its ranks with six additional members. The ploy backfired on the surface, but the Court got the message, stepped aside, and let the modern era begin. With the Court's decision in *Carolene Products* in 1938, the foundations for our modern jurisprudence were laid. Thereafter the Court would essentially defer to the political branches in all matters pertaining to economic transfers and regulation. Only when "fundamental" rights were at stake would the Court's scrutiny be heightened.

Thus freed from constitutional restraints, the political branches began to respond to all manner of interests, both general and special. Not surprisingly, the interests those interests pursued through public channels grew increasingly short term, and increasingly in conflict with one another. Government, after all, is a zero-sum game (after administrative costs, the sum is negative); one man's gain is another man's loss. But the powers that prosper by the game have grown skilled at packaging it otherwise, at telling us that we can accomplish great things through government. And so, measure by measure, the war of all against all has expanded until the battles can no longer be ignored. Our flight from individual responsibility is by now well advanced. Yet we are powerless to change the reality that makes the flight so futile. Government will

46

not, because it cannot, solve our problems. Our biggest problem today is our reluctance to recognize that.

Recovering Our Principles

This brief review of the forces that have brought us from the vision of the founding generation to where we are today concludes with the jurisprudence of the New Deal because with that, quite simply, the constitutional game was over. Building slowly since the Civil War, the core idea of the new policy sciences, that government could and should be responsible for a wide range of "social" problems, came to the fore in the Progressive Era. Those used to thinking of liberalism and progressivism as one may find it sobering to reflect that in 1900, as the Progressive Era was getting under way, the editors of the *Nation* could observe in a piece lamenting "the eclipse of liberalism" that "the Declaration of Independence no longer arouses enthusiasm; it is an embarrassing instrument that requires to be explained away." With so fundamental a change in the climate of ideas, it remained only to institutionalize that change. After episodic resistance, the New Deal Court accomplished that at last— with alacrity on the part of some of its members, with reservations from others, who felt, rightly or wrongly, that they could no longer resist the political juggernaut. And so in 1938 the revolution was completed, by the Court, the Constitution itself having changed by not a word.

Constitutional Jurisprudence Today

There has followed a jurisprudence that is all but inscrutable to the average American. Never mind that the *Carolene Products* case from which it flows involved a piece of blatant special-interest legislation, the Court read the case as standing for pure democracy of a kind that it saw no need to review. So it took itself largely out of the reviewing business, thus making the nation safe for democracy, which of course is majoritarianism, which of course is special-interest logrolling (for those willing to notice it). Indeed, the reviewing function the Court reserved for itself would be concentrated thereafter not on ensuring freedom but on enhancing the democratic process: viewing the political arena as the essence of our republic, the Court would limit itself largely to ensuring the participation of all in that process. Thus, voting and speech cases would find a receptive ear at the Court. Cases complaining that

47

the political process was restricting economic well-being would not. And all who searched for the roots of this bifurcated jurisprudence in the text of the Constitution would be disappointed, for it was a product, pure and simple, of the vision of the Progressive Era, brought to fruition through the politics of the New Deal.

As time has passed, we have seen this jurisprudence solidify: first, by the accumulation of a massive body of transfer and regulatory programs and, second, by the unwillingness of opponents of those programs to challenge them on constitutional grounds. Today, both liberals and conservatives are in essential agreement with the New Deal shift; their differences relate largely to the decisions that came from the Warren and Burger Courts in the 1960s and 1970s. During that period of "judicial activism," a "liberal" Court enlarged on the *Carolene Products* formula when it started resisting those outcomes of the political process that conflicted with "fundamental" rights the Court was finding in the "penumbras" of the Constitution—consulting not the classic theory of rights in this, as America's early courts had done, but "evolving social values." Conservatives complained that it was curious that those values just happened to coincide with the values of America's emerging liberal elite. Still, the differences between the two camps were confined largely to this relatively limited area of the Court's jurisdiction—liberals wanting the Court to frustrate majoritarian preferences in such areas as abortion, school prayer, the death penalty, and the rights of criminal suspects; conservatives wanting the Court to step aside and let majorities rule. In neither case has there been a serious challenge to the fundamental finding of the New Deal Court, that the political branches have far-reaching powers to regulate our lives, especially in the economic arena.

Yet for all that, the nagging doubt that the New Deal Court got it seriously wrong remains—indeed, grows as the scope of government expands. Consider, for example, the expansion of government's control over property owners, who today are all but unable to move without official permission. The rights of property owners should not be difficult to determine: after all, the Fifth Amendment states plainly that private property shall not be taken for public use without just compensation. In a given case, all a court has to determine is (1) whether a government action takes property for public use (by implication, there is no power to take for private use); (2) if so, whether the act is justified under the police power, which enables government to prevent people from using their property in ways that injure others; and (3) if not, whether just compensation has been paid. Government is not prohibited by the takings clause from taking private property; it simply has to pay for the property it takes rather than leave the costs of public policy to be borne by the individual property owner.

Naturally, the compensation requirement puts a crimp on the expansion of public policy: that, together with a concern for justice, is why the Founders put it in the Constitution. Not surprisingly, therefore, governments anxious to expand their power at no cost to the public have sought both to narrow the definition of "property" and to expand the scope of the police power—and over time the courts have acquiesced. Thus, in 1921, in *Block v. Hirsh*, the Supreme Court was faced with a challenge to a wartime rent-control statute—a classic regulatory transfer, which keeps rents low for tenants by taking the rights of owners to charge market rates for their rental units. Finding that "public exigency" outweighed any such property right, the Court ruled the controls constitutional.

After seventy-one years and countless regulations, covering everything from zoning to historic landmark preservation to comprehensive land-use planning, the Court revisited the takings issue in its last term in *Lucas v. South Carolina Coastal Council*. The facts of the case were simple: the South Carolina legislature had passed a statute, aimed at providing a set of public goods ranging from scenic preservation to tourism to wildlife habitat, the effect of which was to deny Mr. Lucas his right to develop his property. For a court willing to return to first principles, the case should have been easy. Since the uses denied Mr. Lucas in no way threatened others, the statute could not be justified under the police power; thus, as a taking requiring compensation, it remained only to determine the difference in the values of the land before and after the statute was enacted and to order the difference paid to Mr. Lucas.

Unfortunately, the Court was unprepared to reach so principled a solution. Instead, Justice Antonin Scalia, writing for the Court's majority, took note of the Court's "70-odd years" of regulatory takings jurisprudence in which "we have generally eschewed any 'set formula,'. . . preferring to 'engage in essentially ad hoc, factual inquiries.'" Rather than jettison that jurisprudence, which Justice

49

John Paul Stevens once called "open-ended and standardless," Scalia tried instead to draw upon it. Thus, he distinguished cases in which regulations deny "all economically beneficial or productive use of land" from cases in which regulations leave some uses to the owner, noting that plaintiffs in the latter kinds of cases would not necessarily, even ordinarily, get relief. Since Mr. Lucas's loss was nearly total, he should get relief on remand, Scalia concluded. As for the millions of other Americans who suffer less than total losses at the hands of federal, state, and local regulators, "takings law is full of these 'all-or-nothing' situations." Indeed, failing completely to distinguish takings of rights from diminutions of value, Scalia stretched for the Progressive Era rationale that "government hardly could go on if to some extent values incident to property could not be diminished without paying for every such change in the general law."

Ideas Have Consequences

Deference to government is thus by now deeply entrenched in a body of precedents—by no means economic precedents alone—that the Court appears quite unwilling to revisit, however constitutionally unwarranted they may be. In fact, then-judge Scalia said as much in 1984 in a Cato Institute debate with Richard Epstein on the subject of judicial protection for economic liberty, although he grounded his unwillingness not simply on his view that "the position the Supreme Court has arrived at [in rejecting substantive due process in the economic field] is good"—about which he said nothing further as a matter of constitutional law—but primarily on misgivings about whether "activist" courts would do their job well. On one hand courts might extend their activism beyond the economic arena, which deeply concerns Scalia; on the other hand they might find economic "rights" that are quite without foundation. Those are not idle concerns, to be sure, but as Epstein observed in response, constitutional responsibility aside, they are no reason to defer to the political branches, where the risks of failure are at least as great.

Judge Scalia went deeper in that debate, however, to observe that "a guarantee may appear in the words of the Constitution, but when the society ceases to possess an abiding belief in it, it has no living effect. . . . Even *Brown v. Board of Education*," he continued, "was only an elaboration of the consequences of the nation's deep belief in the equality of all persons before the law." Because he could detect no "national commitment to most of the economic liberties generally discussed that would enable even an activist court to constitutionalize them," Scalia concluded that to seek to develop that sentiment "by enshrining the unacceptable principles in the Constitution is to place the cart before the horse." Thus, "the first step" is to recall society to that belief in the importance in economic liberty that the Founders shared—to create "a constitutional ethos of economic liberty."

Setting aside Justice Scalia's larger point for the moment, "the economic liberties generally discussed" do not have to be "constitutionalized"—much less by an "activist" Court. They are *already in* the Constitution. They need simply to be recognized and enforced by a "responsible" Court—a Court responsible to the Constitution its members swear to uphold. That is not judicial activism. It is judicial responsibility. Moreover, it requires no "national commitment" for the Court to uphold the Constitution. Indeed, it took federal troops to enforce *Brown v. Board of Education.* And more recently, when the Court decided in *U.S. v. Eichman* that flag-burning was constitutional—a decision in which Justice Scalia himself concurred—there was hardly a national commitment behind that decision. No, the point of having a Court, as Madison said, is to have an institution that can serve as "the bulwark of our liberties." To be such a bulwark, however, the Court must have both convictions and the courage of those convictions. Today, both are lacking. The climate of ideas has sapped the convictions that give life to the bare text of the Constitution. And when those convictions fail, courage goes with them.

Justice Scalia's larger point, then, that there is a deep connection between the climate of ideas and the capacity of the Court, cannot be ignored. The Court must do its job, to be sure, but it does not work in an intellectual vacuum. For too long, the climate of ideas in America has been molded by people and institutions that in many respects are profoundly out of step with our founding principles, principles that today are taking root in many other parts of the world. Perhaps it is because those others have known personally the tragedy that befalls a people when it follows the path of public policy to its end that wisdom has at last set in. One would hope that in America we will not have to learn that lesson from experience alone.

And in this, we can take comfort from the fact that our Constitution is still intact, despite the damage we have done to its meaning. And the English language is still essentially what it was when the document was written. What has changed is our confidence in the ideas that stand behind that document and those words. And that is unnecessary and unwarranted. Indeed, much has been done in recent years to give force and foundation, to say nothing of clarity, to the belief of the founding generation in natural law. But even absent that, what else is there but natural law? Only force. Yet to resort to force is to give up all pretense to legitimacy. That is not what either our political leaders or our people do. They all pretend to legitimacy. The job, then, is to get to the real foundations of legitimacy, and those can be found only in a higher law of natural rights.

It is the clarification of these ideas, then, that is the principal business ahead of us. That means showing, for example, that the business of government is doing right, not good, between which there is all the difference in the world. Few would doubt the sincerity of at least many of those who today call for government to do good. What is needed is repeated demonstration of how doing good for some by doing wrong to others is wrong. Yet it is just that wrong that constitutes the stuff of so much of our government today.

And these lessons must be raised in every public forum. Who cannot but be impressed by the *constitutional* arguments that characterized the debates in Congress in the last century? The courts are not the only forum for constitutional debate. Indeed, those arguments deserve to be heard everywhere because they are the arguments that define us as a people. Today, we are out of sympathy with our founding principles. Is it any wonder, when we are out of sympathy with our deepest selves, that there is trouble in the land? The time has come to recover those principles and to take personal responsibility for our lives. Nothing less will do, for nothing less will free us as a people.

3. Reclaiming the Political Process

Edward H. Crane

Politics in America has slowly evolved into a rigid, closed system. It is a system designed not just to protect incumbents, but to protect the status quo. Our democracy is in danger because elections have become the closest thing to being rigged: they are, for the most part, lifeless, ideologically hollow show elections with gerrymandered districts, voter indifference, and absurdly high reelection rates. Election night celebrations, dutifully reported on television, would feature empty halls absent the politicians' enormous staffs, the grinning special interests, their families, and assorted hangers-on.

If American industry is being choked by excessive taxation and layer upon layer of regulations, the American political process is nearly comatose. Ironically, the bipartisan efforts of incumbents to protect themselves from competition have perhaps been too successful. The deafening silence from the American people at election time, from the statehouse to Congress—as evidenced by low voter turnout and even lower enthusiasm for the candidates— has increasingly drawn the attention of the media and various self-appointed public-interest groups.

From Common Cause to the television networks there is a steady drumbeat to do something about the political malaise—not apparently to change the policies that the current system is generating, but to enlist a little popular support for those programs. Invariably, however, the solutions proffered by establishment institutions would further rigidify the political system by funding campaigns with taxpayer dollars and limiting campaign expenditures. But government involvement in the political process is the primary source of the problems we face. To restore vibrancy to American politics we need to look elsewhere. We need to look to the term limitation movement and to a *removal* of campaign contribution limits.

Term Limits

The nationwide movement to limit the number of terms state legislators and members of Congress may serve received a tremendous boost in the November elections when 14 of 14 states, including California, Michigan, and Florida, approved term limit initiatives. Most of those initiatives limited the respective states' congressional delegates to three terms in the House and two terms in the Senate. If term limitation passes constitutional muster, one-third of Congress will be term limited. Supporters of the concept hope that will constitute a large enough contingent to force the issue to the floor of Congress for debate (something that heretofore has been systematically blocked). Once a constitutional amendment is proposed, the theory goes, there will be intense pressure to vote yes, with 75 percent of the constituents back home favoring term limits.

Opponents of term limits put forth four basic reasons for rejecting the idea. First, they argue, term limitation is a restriction on democracy—we should be able to vote for whomever we please. But the electoral process already restricts access to the ballot. State election laws require a minimum number of signatures for minor party candidates to get on the ballot. The Constitution itself precludes us from electing as president anyone who is not born in the United States or who is under the age of 35. That said, the reality is that term limits will *enhance* the democratic process. Open seats are always more hotly contested than are seats held by incumbents seeking reelection. Under term limits, at least a third of the House seats would be open in every election, and even those that were not open would invite spirited competition from opponents seeking name recognition in hopes of gaining the soon-to-be-open seat. Popular interest in elections would be increased and the democratic process enhanced as a result of term limits.

A second reason put forth by opponents is that term limits would deny us experienced legislators. To which proponents might justifiably respond, "Let's hope so." In fact, it was the experienced legislators who gave us the savings-and-loan crisis by expanding federal deposit insurance, thereby guaranteeing that the newly deregulated thrifts would speculate with deposits from investors utterly uninterested in the integrity of the financial institution with which they were dealing. It was the experienced legislators who gave us the 1990 budget deal that actually placed the federal government on a faster spending track over the following five years than it had been on during the previous five years. The greatest tax increase in American history was instituted without eliminating a single one of the 4,000 domestic federal programs or, indeed, sacking a single federal employee. Such is the record of America's experienced legislators.

Third, it is argued that lobbyists, federal bureaucrats, and congressional staffs will run amuck without senior members of Congress to hold them in check. But a recent Gallup Poll of just those three groups showed that nearly 60 percent of them *opposed* term limits. Except for politicians themselves, those three groups are the strongest opponents of term limits to be found anywhere. The lobbyists have invested years in cultivating the specific members of Congress who take care of their interests. They hardly want to "retrain" new people every four or six years. (Indeed, an added benefit of term limitation is that it would reduce the incentives for political action committees and other special interests to invest in politicians.) Federal bureaucrats are generally on much better terms with senior members of Congress who have made their accommodation with the bureaucracy than they are with freshmen legislators who often take an adversarial stance with bureaucrats on behalf of their constituents. As for congressional staff, they quite obviously gain personal power as their member gains seniority and power. Of all the groups in the Gallup Poll, they were the most overwhelmingly opposed to term limits.

Finally, it is said that term limitation, if implemented on a state-by-state basis as it now is, will reduce the "clout" of those states with limits relative to those states without them. That argument is credited with having defeated the Washington State term limit initiative in 1991. The truth is that there is no positive correlation between the seniority of state congressional delegations and the federal pork handed out to the states. But let's assume there is. Would that be a good thing? Is that what the Framers had in mind for Congress—a giant free-for-all in which each state competed to get more per capita federal largesse than the next? Presumably not. In any case, the impact Congress has on us as individuals is much greater in terms of national legislation than it is in terms of state-specific pork. We should seek members of Congress who have sensible approaches to national policy rather than an aptitude for logrolling.

Opposed to these weak reeds of opposition to term limits, there are two powerfully compelling arguments in favor of the concept. First, it overcomes what is clearly an adverse preselection process in existence today. The American Founders believed that for democracy to work, it must be representative. Yet today we have a Congress that is 92 percent male, and 46 percent of the members have law degrees. Why? Because those who are successful in the private sector—whether they are entrepreneurs, teachers, computer programmers, or farmers—consider the prospect of running for Congress and realize they'd have to be there 10, 15, or even 20 years to have any real influence under the current regime. They may be perfectly willing to spend some time in Congress as a public service, but not if their time has no impact. They like what they do for a living in the private sector and are disinclined to spend a significant portion of their lives as politicians. Yet those are precisely the kinds of men and women who should be in Congress.

In contrast, there are those like former California state assemblyman Mike Roos, who complained that the term limit movement was out to take his career away from him. In a debate over the 1990 California Proposition 140 term limit initiative (which eventually passed, prompting Roos to retire), he argued that he had wanted to be a legislator all of his life. He had studied political science in college, gotten a masters degree in public administration, taken a job with a state assemblyman, and then run for and won his current seat some 13 years ago. One would guess that Mike Roos might also have been blackboard monitor (or crossing guard—whatever political post was available) in the fourth grade. The problem, of course, is that Roos's profile is all too common in state legislatures and especially in Congress.

None of which is to suggest that the Mike Rooses of the world are bad people, or have nefarious aims to undermine the Republic. Quite the contrary. They undoubtedly embark upon their career paths with the best of intentions. The point is simply that they are not *representative*—in fact they are quite unrepresentative—of the public they seek to represent. Members of Congress are supposed to represent the private sector. If they are career politicians, they are part of the public sector. They end up not telling government what the people want, but instead lobbying the people to support more government.

A strict, three-term limit for members of Congress would bring a much more diverse—and representative—population onto the ballot. Indeed, that has already proven to be the case in California's state legislative races. *People serving in Congress should view their time there as a leave of absence from their real jobs.* Terms limits would represent a major step away from professional politicians and toward a true citizen legislature.

The second major reason to support term limits is that even assuming we had a truly representative Congress, over time even the best people can lose their perspective in the "culture of ruling" that exists in the state capitals and inside the Beltway in Washington, D.C. Common sense is the victim in an environment in which one is constantly surrounded by other people—at work or socializing at a Redskins game—whose job it is to spend other people's money and regulate other people's lives.

The power, perks, and privileges of being a member of Congress are slowly corrupting, not necessarily in the direct sense of the House banking scandal, although that is a case in point, but in the sense of losing one's humility and sense of proportion. There is something unnatural about having people shove microphones in your face day in and day out, seeking your opinion on everything under the sun. Pretty soon, it's easy to overestimate the importance of your opinion and think that perhaps you should codify it whenever possible. In fact, groups like the National Taxpayers Union have documented that the longer people are in Congress, the more expansive (and expensive) their legislative initiatives become— whether they are conservatives or liberals.

It is important to recognize that the term limit movement is not an aberration in American politics. The concept of rotation in office has its roots deep in our colonial history and was, in fact, included in the original Articles of Confederation. That it was not subsequently included in the Constitution probably reflects the fact that the tradition of serving in Congress and returning to one's real job was so ingrained in our society at the time that it was deemed superfluous to include it. On the other hand, there are those who maintain that by the time the Constitution was debated there were enough Americans who had tasted political power (something virtually absent from the colonial period) that the omission may have been conscious.

Regardless, the idea of term limits is time-honored. Evidence of that abounds, but one of the most perceptive statements on the subject was penned by two Englishmen, John Trenchard and Thomas Gordon, in *Cato's Letters* (after which, it should be noted, the Cato Institute is named).

> Men, when they first enter into magistracy, have often their former condition before their eyes: They remember what they themselves suffered with their fellow subjects from the abuse of power, and how much they blamed it; so their first purposes are to be humble, modest and just; and probably, for some time, they continue so. But the possession of power soon alters and vitiates their hearts, which are at the same time sure to have leavened and puffed up to an unnatural size, by the deceitful incense of false friends and by the prostrate submission of parasites. First they grow indifferent to all their good designs, then drop them. Next, they lose their moderation. Afterwards, they renounce all measures with their old acquaintance and old principles, and seeing themselves in magnifying glasses, grow in conceit, a different species from their fellow subjects. And so, by too sudden degrees become insolent, rapacious and tyrannical, ready to catch all means, often the vilest and most oppressive, to raise their fortunes as high as their imaginary greatness. So that the only way to put them in mind of their former condition, and consequently of the condition of other people, is often to reduce them to it, and to let others of equal capacities share the power in their turn. This also is the only way to qualify men, and make them equally fit for domination and subjection. A rotation therefore, in power and magistracy, is essentially necessary to a free government.

That argument is as sound today as it was when it was written 250 years ago. By reducing exposure to the culture of ruling and increasing the diversity of people seeking office, term limits will restore respect for the institution of Congress. The common sense and integrity of the American people will be more accurately reflected in a term-limited Congress, and that is something that is essential to the preservation of a vigorous democracy.

End Contribution Limitations

In 1974 Congress passed one of the few laws of recent decades that has achieved its true intent. The Federal Election Campaign Act, as a review of the debate that took place in Congress will confirm, was designed to shore up support for the two-party system in the wake of the Watergate scandal and growing disenchantment with politics in general. Ironically, one of the leading proponents of the bill on the House floor was John Anderson, an Illinois Republican who subsequently challenged the two-party system with an underfunded (thanks in large measure to the FECA) independent presidential campaign. Anderson explicitly warned his colleagues that without the radical campaign reform law, they faced the prospect of viable third parties and the kind of multiparty system that is prevalent in other Western democracies.

The FECA as originally passed would have strictly limited expenditures on and contributions to federal campaigns while providing federal funding for such campaigns and for the presidential nominating conventions of the two major parties. In January 1976 the U.S. Supreme Court, in a decision of contorted logic remarkable even for that incoherent institution, ruled that limits on campaign expenditures offended the intent of the First Amendment, but limits on campaign contributions did not. Federal funding of congressional campaigns was struck down, but federal funding of presidential campaigns and party conventions was not.

In his excellent dissent from the broader Supreme Court ruling on the FECA, Chief Justice Warren Burger pointed out that "limiting contributions, as a practical matter, will limit expenditures and will put an effective ceiling on the amount of political activity and debate the Government will permit to take place." To Burger, "contributions and expenditures are two sides of the same First Amendment coin."

Former senator Eugene McCarthy, one of the appellants challenging the law, agreed, stating: "I think there are two areas of our life which ought to be really somehow exempted from government support, and therefore government influence. One is religion, and the other is politics."

Senator McCarthy's own experience in presidential politics is a pointed example of why unlimited campaign contributions are—contrary to the conventional wisdom—essential to the preservation of a free society. In 1968 opposition to the war in Vietnam was growing dramatically—not just among leftist hippies and fellow travelers, as the leading politicians of both parties claimed, but among the American middle class. The tension created by the effective disenfranchisement of tens of millions of Americans was palpable and our society was in danger of having its social fabric ripped apart by pent-up frustration.

Onto that scene strode the lanky senator from Minnesota, a maverick liberal, former baseball player, and hardly a threat to the American way of life. Yet he had no national political base. His campaign—the only national effort based primarily on opposition to the Vietnam War—was able to get off the ground because of the support of a handful of wealthy liberals, Stewart Mott among them, who made large, six-figure contributions to the McCarthy effort. The energy thereby released by the McCarthy candidacy was so powerful that it forced an incumbent president, Lyndon Johnson, to shut down his reelection campaign. Eugene McCarthy, to this day, states unequivocally that had the FECA been in place in 1968, his campaign would have drawn little or no attention.

American history would have been rewritten if the FECA had existed eight years earlier. We have no way of knowing how the natural development of American society has been distorted in the years following its enactment. We do know that it is not the proper role of government to regulate elections in such a manner as to distort their outcome.

The case against campaign contribution limits is not an easy one to make. There is something intuitively "fair," at first blush, about limiting the influence wealthy people might have on elections. But a closer look at the issue reveals a different perspective, at least if we have faith in the idea of democracy. While incumbent officeholders and "public interest" groups tell us that limits are a way for government to protect us from manipulation by the wealthy, the truth is, as the McCarthy candidacy affirms, precisely the opposite. The truth is that the tens of thousands of individuals in America with the financial wherewithal to bring political issues to our attention represent a potentially effective check on manipulation by government.

One of the contortions of the Supreme Court ruling on the FECA was that candidates for federal office could spend as much of their own money on their campaigns as they wished, because you can't "contribute" money to yourself. Hence, individual candidates are making *expenditures*, rather than contributions, when they give to their own campaigns. Thus, Ross Perot has legal privileges as a candidate that we mere voters do not.

But there is nothing wrong with candidates' spending all they want on their own campaigns. Indeed, that "loophole" that the Court carved in the FECA underscores the dangers of contribution limits. Without that loophole, how could the American people have made such a dramatic statement about their dissatisfaction with the choices being offered by the two major parties? The problem lies not in Ross Perot's ability to spend significant sums of money on his own campaign, but in the illegality of his spending similar sums on other candidates. In fact, if he could have contributed large sums to someone else, one could argue that he would have been hard pressed to justify his own candidacy. Would not, say, Paul Tsongas have been a more viable candidate to tackle the deficit issue than a Ross Perot with all the negative baggage his campaign had to carry?

Those with a kind of Common Cause, patronizing attitude toward the average American assume as a matter of faith that money is the root of all political evil—that unrestricted contributions would thoroughly corrupt our political process. Yet with contribution limits in place, we've seen more corruption in the two political branches of government than at any time in our history. At least part of that corruption is a direct result of the noncompetitive electoral process generated by the vast array of incumbent-protection legislation, contribution limits included. Even with Ross Perot factored in, the 1992 presidential campaign spent only about $3 per voter. The average congressional contest spends a little over $1 per voter. It can be argued that we are spending far too little on campaigns, given the enormous impact their outcomes have on our lives.

Besides, there is substantial evidence that, with full disclosure, voters can decide for themselves whether large contributions should or should not be a factor in voting for a candidate. The list of failed multimillionaire candidacies is substantial, going back to John Connally's $10 million, one-person delegation to the 1980 Republican National Convention. More recently we've seen voters

61

reject department store heir Mark Dayton's $7 million campaign for the U.S. Senate in Minnesota, perfume heir Ron Lauder spend over $13 million on his futile effort to become governor of New York, and Clayton Williams do little other than become a source of ridicule with his $8 million contribution to his campaign for governor of Texas.

To be certain, wealthy candidates often do prevail. Jay Rockefeller's $10 million loan to himself for his victorious 1984 U.S. Senate campaign in West Virginia is an example. But the important point is that voters can, and often do, reject such candidates. There is nothing wrong, in any case, with a candidate's forsaking large contributions as a matter of principle, or at least as a campaign strategy. Lawton Chiles did just that in his 1990 race for governor of Florida; he accepted no contributions in excess of $100 and won a convincing victory. Of course, he was a former U.S. senator from Florida and had the advantage of name recognition, lack of which might preclude another candidate's adopting such a strategy.

Contribution limitations for political campaigns greatly favor the two major parties and the well-recognized names within those parties—typically the targets of the term limit movement: career politicians. For Democrats and Republicans to pass such a law is analogous to Walmart's getting a law passed that allows anyone to compete against it in the retail business, but only up to $1,000 in advertising. New companies, new ideas, new candidates all need large amounts of seed capital to have a chance to challenge the status quo. We should not have to depend on the candidates themselves to have the wealth to make that challenge.

One of the many advantages of capitalism over state monopolies is that entrepreneurs have thousands of sources of capital. A person with a great new product need find only one person willing to put up the funds to give the product a market test. Everyone can say no to the venture capital project except one person, and our whole nation of consumers benefits, if the product is, in fact, worthwhile. Were entrepreneurs required to get their funding from a Federal Entrepreneurs Commission, it's a good bet the commission would go along with the majority of "experts" and deny the request.

Americans have a right to expect as dynamic a political system as they do an economic system. Contribution limitations have been passed into law for the same self-serving reasons that corporations lobby for protectionist bills of their own, complete with all the "public interest" rhetoric. But instead of ensuring an open, dynamic election process, the FECA has had a chilling, rigidifying impact on the choices available to Americans each November.

(The fact that so-called independent expenditures may be made by individuals in unlimited amounts should not be taken as a serious rebuttal to the case against contribution limitations. The law is complicated and intimidating—only a handful of people make independent expenditures each election. Even then they are not allowed to communicate with the candidate or his campaign, much less try to induce someone to run on the basis of forthcoming support.)

A major benefit of "outsider" campaigns funded by large contributions—quite aside from ousting unpopular presidents, as in the case of Eugene McCarthy—is that they can raise issues that the establishment, career politicians who dominate the election scene will not. The Cato Institute is not alone, for instance, in suggesting that the Social Security system is a looming financial disaster for America if something is not done soon. Yet no politician running for federal office under the current system is willing to say anything suggesting there might be a serious problem with Social Security. That Ross Perot at least raised the issue, albeit tentatively, is indicative of the potential a more dynamic political system holds.

Finally, and quite aside from the practical benefits specifically related to the electoral process, the elimination of campaign contribution limits represents something else. For it is, at bottom, consistent with the nature of the kind of free society the United States of America is all about. As Senator McCarthy put it, "The signers of the Declaration of Independence did not write 'We mutually pledge to each other our lives, our fortunes *up to $1,000* and our sacred honor.' " There are indeed risks associated with living in a free society, but they pale in comparison with the risks involved with turning over to government responsibility for decisions we as independent citizens should properly make ourselves. In his dissent on the constitutionality of the Federal Election Campaign Act, Chief Justice Burger wisely wrote, "There are many prices we pay for freedoms secured by the First Amendment; the risk of undue influence is one of them, confirming what we have long known: freedom is hazardous, but some restraints are worse."

The First Amendment protects the right of millionaires who own newspapers, such as Katharine Graham of the *Washington Post*, to spend tens of millions of dollars editorializing in favor of certain candidates, or shaping news coverage to reflect a given philosophical perspective. Millionaire cartoonist Garry Trudeau, whose work appears in hundreds of papers across the country, gave Bill Clinton millions of dollars' worth of promotion by devoting most of his strips to bashing President Bush and Ross Perot during the last two months of the campaign. Conservative radio talk show personality Rush Limbaugh did the same for George Bush. Would anyone seriously deny those wealthy people the right to do those things? Is it not obvious that the political debate is more vigorous thanks to their efforts? But why should they have the opportunity to be important figures in political debate while others are denied it simply because they chose a career other than the media?

As so much of mankind throughout the world seems to be grasping the benefits of limiting government primarily to protecting individual liberty, it is tragic that here in the United States, where the seeds of the worldwide market-liberal revolution were created, we seem to be headed for a more closed system, one controlled by professional politicians whose interventionist ambitions would appear to have no limits. The entrenched political status quo must be challenged if we are to preserve our heritage as a free, open, and pluralistic society. The two proposals suggested in this chapter—one popular at the moment, and one not—would work well together to reinvigorate our stagnant democracy.

PART II

ECONOMIC POLICY

4. Balance the Budget by Reducing Spending

William A. Niskanen and Stephen Moore

Most American families, firms, and state and local governments have recently reduced their spending in response to a lower-than-expected growth of income. Most, that is, other than the federal government. Real federal domestic spending during the Bush administration increased at a higher rate than during any administration since that of Kennedy. The combination of a rapid growth of federal spending and a slow growth of tax revenues increased the federal deficit from $153 billion in fiscal year 1989 to an estimated $331 billion in FY93.

The long-term projections are even more discouraging. The Congressional Budget Office, assuming no increase in real discretionary spending and no intervening recession, forecasts a federal deficit of $400 billion in fiscal year 2000 and over $500 billion in fiscal year 2002. In the absence of major changes in federal fiscal policy or an increase in economic growth, the future federal deficit will probably be even higher than forecast. The huge federal deficit will have to be financed at a time when U.S. private savings are expected to remain low and net borrowing by other nations is expected to increase.

One might have hoped that the deficit would be addressed in the 1992 campaign, but it was not. Both President Bush and Governor Clinton promised to finance their new proposals by offsetting changes in spending and taxes, but neither offered any substantial proposals to reduce the baseline deficit. Only Ross Perot made a major issue of the federal deficit, but he did not defend the specific proposals of the plan that had been prepared for him. Several new citizen groups pressed candidates for Congress to commit to reducing the deficit. And only a few more votes are needed in Congress to approve a balanced budget–tax limitation amendment for subsequent ratification by the states.

We should have learned the following lessons from the economic and fiscal record of the past decade.

- A federal deficit does not lead to a corresponding increase in private savings. Instead, a federal deficit leads to some combination of reduced domestic investment and increased U.S. borrowing from other nations. In effect, we are increasing the tax burden on future generations, who had no role in authorizing the present debt. Incurring such debt may be appropriate to finance a war or a temporary increase in public investment, but it is not a viable long-term fiscal policy.
- Economic growth will not be sufficient to reduce the federal deficit without a major change in current fiscal policies, but economic growth is a necessary condition.
- An increase in federal taxes is likely to be counterproductive because it will reduce economic growth and invite an increase in federal spending.
- Major reductions in the main federal spending programs are necessary to reduce the growth of total federal spending. Although there is plenty of "pork" and other waste in the federal budget, reducing that waste would not reduce spending sufficiently, nor would it be easy to do. (Most wasteful expenditures are made because someone in authority wants them.)

The primary implication of those lessons is that we cannot long avoid a major reduction and restructuring of the major federal spending programs. Many state governments have already made the hard choices reduced spending entails. Making those choices will not be much fun for our federal politicians, but if they are not willing to do so, they are part of the problem and should be replaced.

The federal budget *can* and *should* be balanced before the end of the decade by reductions in spending, *not* tax increases. Herein we describe the program changes and the magnitude of the spending reductions that should be considered to achieve that goal. Our proposed changes, of course, are not the only ones possible; other combinations of reductions would also work. The specific spending reductions we propose are based on the following general criteria.

- Maintain mandatory spending. The only types of spending that we regard as fixed obligations of the federal government are interest payments on the federal debt, payments for other goods and services previously supplied, expenditures for deposit insurance, and the real pension benefits of retired federal employees and *current* recipients of Social Security.

- Respond to changed conditions. The most important changed condition, of course, is the end of the Cold War. That has primary implications for the appropriate size of the defense budget.
- Correct unsustainable conditions. For some years, spending for medical care has increased at roughly twice the rate of the gross domestic product. That increase cannot be sustained, and it is better to correct the condition early.
- Reduce high-income benefits. A significant part of federal spending generates benefits for high-income people. Those benefits should be reduced.
- Eliminate low-priority programs. Hundreds of unnecessary domestic programs should be abolished or financed by state and local governments.

We suggest that any serious proposal to reduce the deficit should address the implications of each of those criteria.

The case for balancing the budget by spending reductions, rather than tax increases, is based on a judgment that the federal government has grown too large and that most people do not get their money's worth from government spending. The popular vote for the presidential and gubernatorial candidates of the incumbent party, for example, generally declines in response to an increase in real per capita spending and taxes since the prior election. Similarly, net migration among the states is generally from high-tax to low-tax states. Those two patterns are inconsistent with a belief that increased government spending is broadly popular. Total government spending is now about $20,000 per household; we doubt that most Americans find that the benefits of government spending are worth the cost. Moreover, each additional dollar of tax revenue collected now reduces the output available for private use by over $1.50; we doubt that there are more than a few federal programs for which the value of the last dollar spent is worth that additional cost. Ask yourself: should the budget be balanced by reducing government spending or by increasing your taxes? We doubt that many Americans value most federal programs enough to support higher taxes. For that reason, we outline a plan to balance the budget by scaling down federal spending to a level that would be broadly supported.

The Federal Budget Outlook

Table 4.1 summarizes the (August 1992) Congressional Budget Office estimate of the FY93 budget and their forecast of the budget through FY98. First, it is important to recognize that the CBO forecast probably *underestimates* future outlays; total real outlays subject to annual appropriations are assumed to be reduced by about 10 percent through FY95 and to be constant in subsequent years. Table 4.1, however, is sufficient to convey the magnitude of the spending reductions necessary to balance the budget. Assuming, as a first approximation, that changes in federal spending do not affect economic growth, inflation, and interest rates, total outlays in FY98 must be reduced by $311 billion to balance the budget by the end of that year. Total program outlays need not be reduced

Table 4.1
THE FEDERAL BUDGET OUTLOOK (BILLIONS OF DOLLARS)

	Fiscal Year					
	93	94	95	96	97	98
Outlays						
Defense	297	284	284	287	290	293
Social Security	302	318	336	354	374	394
Medical	226	251	280	314	349	389
Other	482	487	491	507	520	565
Total	1,307	1,340	1,391	1,462	1,533	1,641
Deposit insurance	49	17	5	−7	−16	−20
Offsetting receipts	−67	−69	−72	−74	−76	−79
Net interest	204	223	244	263	284	303
Total	1,493	1,511	1,567	1,644	1,745	1,845
Revenue	1,162	1,242	1,323	1,390	1,455	1,534
Deficit	331	268	244	254	290	311
Debt	3,326	3,597	3,847	4,167	4,403	4,720

Source: CBO, August 1992.

quite that much, because early reduction of outlays would also reduce the growth of net interest payments.

Table 4.1 also makes it clear that a substantial reduction of the major federal programs is necessary to balance the budget by spending restraint; as of FY98, for example, three programs—defense, Social Security, and medical care—are expected to account for about two-thirds of total program outlays. In the absence of a substantial reduction in spending on those programs, real spending for all other activities of the federal government would have to be reduced by more than 50 percent to balance the budget. And finally, Table 4.1 illustrates that current levels of spending for several federal budget items are not sustainable. Medical care, net interest payments, and total federal debt held by the public are each expected to increase as a percentage of total national output. A "politics as usual" approach to the federal budget would only defer the necessary hard choices, increasing the fiscal problems of the next administration.

The Path to a Balanced Budget

To balance the budget, we propose a five-step approach based on the criteria summarized at the beginning of this chapter.

1. Reduce the defense budget in response to the end of the Cold War.
2. Reduce the rate of increase of real Social Security benefits for future retirees.
3. Sequester 4 percent of the outlays for all other domestic programs in the second half of FY93 and freeze total real outlays for those programs from FY94 through FY98.
4. Reduce the rate of increase of spending on medical programs consistent with the sequester and freeze.
5. Reduce outlays for other domestic programs consistent with the sequester and freeze.

The following subsections make the case for each of those steps and present rough estimates of the consequent budget savings.

National Defense

The Cold War is over. We won. And the Soviet Union has collapsed. We do not now face any significant military threat to our vital national interests except that of a missile attack on the United

States, against which we have no defense. No more dramatic change in conditions could be imagined, but the Department of Defense has been busy fantasizing new missions rather than reducing forces to a level consistent with the new realities. Moreover, the level of real defense spending proposed by President Bush is about the same as it was during the peak of the Cold War in the early 1960s. And Congress has resisted the cancellation of some contracts and the closing of some bases because of concern about local employment. One of the primary reasons for a commitment to balance the budget is to overcome the bureaucratic and political resistance to reducing programs and budgets even when there is a substantial decline in the demand for them.

For over 40 years U.S. military forces have been designed to deter or simultaneously counter one major adversary (the Warsaw Pact) plus one or two minor adversaries in other regions, often referred to as 1½ or 2½ war strategy. There is reason to question whether U.S. and allied forces ever had that capability, but fortunately that question is now moot. The basis for U.S. force planning should now be changed in response to both the collapse of our major adversary and the substantial increase in the military capabilities of our allies.

Several responsible groups of defense analysts have recently developed proposed U.S. defense programs that would reduce the real defense budget to about one-half the FY92 level by the end of this decade. Those programs differ in some details but share the following general characteristics.

Strategic Forces

- Eliminate land-based multiple-warhead missiles.
- Limit the B-1B to carrying cruise missiles.
- Limit purchase of B-2s to the 20 now authorized.
- Deploy 17 Tridents, only 9 with D-5 missiles.
- Reorient Strategic Defense Initiative research and development to large-area defense against small attacks.

General Purpose Forces

- Reduce active ground forces to 6 Army divisions and 2 Marine divisions.

- Reduce active tactical air forces to 12 Air Force wings, 6 carriers, and 2 (double) Marine air wings.
- Phase out all combat units in other countries.
- Substantially reduce the rate of force modernization.
- Increase relative reliance on Reserve and Guard forces.

Research and Development. Maintain active R&D to assure technological leadership and ability to deploy new weapons in response to increased threats.

Budget and Active Military Personnel

- Reduce Department of Defense budget authority to $183 billion by FY98.
- Reduce active military personnel to 1.1 million by FY98.

The proposed force structure would be adequate to maintain a survivable strategic nuclear force, sufficient active forces to meet the types of minor threats that might arise with short warning, and a sufficient mobilization base to respond to a major threat that could only develop over a period of years. The proposed force would *not* be enough to maintain a global military presence and deploy a force the size of the one used in Operation Desert Shield, but there are strong reasons to question whether either of those capabilities is now worth the large cost. American weapons would continue to be the best in the world. And the proposed defense budget would be higher than that of any other nation and much higher (adjusted for inflation) than in any peacetime year before the Cold War. The dramatic change in global military conditions since 1989 should make the defense budget a major source of the savings necessary to balance the budget. The changes described above would reduce total outlays for defense (including small outlays by other agencies) to about $100 billion below the level now projected for FY98.

Social Security

Social Security has been interpreted as a political contract between the working-age population and people who are now retired. We accept that implicit contract and do not propose to reduce the real pension benefits of those who are now retired. That eliminates the possibility of any substantial saving in Social Security outlays in the near term, but it should not cause us to defer dealing with the long-term problems of the system.

The new administration should consider two major reforms to put Social Security on a sustainable basis. First, the increase in the retirement age that is already scheduled should be accelerated. Beginning in 1993 the retirement age (and early retirement age) should be permanently increased by two months per year for the next 30 years. That would mean that the age at which one would receive full retirement benefits would be 66 in 1999, 67 in 2005, 68 in 2011, and so on. Incrementally increasing the age for receiving full benefits would be a substantial step toward cushioning the impact of the demographic time bomb that will explode in the next 20 years when the baby-boom generation begins to retire. Without a change in retirement age, the ratio of workers to retirees is expected to fall to less than 2 to 1 by the year 2030. Such a dependency ratio would place considerable strain on the economy and a larger burden on today's children—the next generation of workers. If the retirement age had risen at the same pace as life expectancy since the inception of Social Security in the mid-1930s, the retirement age would be 76 today.

The second recommended change to Social Security is to index the growth in future benefits (technically called the bend points and the earnings history) to the consumer price index rather than to wages. The benefit formula determines the starting cash benefit level of each Social Security recipient. If that formula were indexed to inflation, future retirees would still receive increasing real benefits over time, but at a slower rate than currently projected. Real benefits under the formula would double rather than triple over the next 70 years. That change would gradually transform Social Security benefits from a floor on relative benefits to a floor on real benefits, protecting the poor but increasing the incentive of others to save so as to have a higher level of retirement income.

Together, the two reforms would yield only minor savings of $5 billion to $10 billion by the year 2000. But the resulting savings would be hundreds of billions of dollars by the third decade of the next century. Both reforms are essential to avoiding the rapid increase in Social Security tax rates that would otherwise be necessary to finance the system over the next 40 years. Implementing the reforms early would give current workers a long time to adjust to the changes.

At some time, it would also be valuable to undertake a more fundamental reform of Social Security. The next generation of workers will earn a very low rate of return from Social Security, with or without the proposed reforms. Allowing workers to opt out of the Social Security system in favor of a private pension plan or an expanded IRA would increase both the return on their savings and the private savings rate. This proposal, however, would require some general revenue money to finance Social Security benefits, and the case for this reform depends on the amount by which the additional savings would increase economic growth.

A Sequester and Freeze

The federal domestic budget has increased rapidly during the past four years. Notwithstanding the rhetoric about savage Republican budget cuts, the real rate of growth of the domestic budget since 1989 has been more than 7 percent per year—the fastest 4-year expansion of the budget in 30 years. Some areas, such as health care and social welfare spending, grew faster than others, but every domestic program except agriculture shared in the domestic spending build-up.

Clearly, the 1990 budget deal failed to restrain domestic expenditures. One reason for the failure is that all the spending reductions were to occur in 1993, 1994, and 1995. Yet Congress is already shying away from making those modest reductions. There is a good chance that without a new budget strategy for the next four years, Congress will choose to evade the budget ceilings of the 1990 budget deal for 1994 and 1995 or shift savings from the military portion of the budget to the domestic portion.

Domestic programs can and should be cut substantially in the next four years, and reductions in domestic spending should take effect soon. We believe that the most realistic way to achieve long-term spending restraint is for the new administration to adopt the following strategy.

First, within the first 100 days, the new president should call for an immediate 4 percent across-the-board spending reduction, or sequester, effective in the second half of FY93. The sequester should cover all programs in the domestic budget except Social Security. The benefit levels of formula-payment programs would have to be reduced by 4 percent. For discretionary programs the sequester would be carried out in much the same manner as the 1986 Gramm-Rudman sequester. The following benefits would be produced by a sequester in the first 100 days of the new administration.

- The sequester would reduce domestic expenditures by $14 billion in FY93.
- The sequester would *permanently* lower the baseline spending levels for every domestic program other than Social Security. Hence, the savings would multiply in every future year, thus setting a solid foundation for balancing the budget by 1998.
- The sequester would signal to the public, the Congress, and the financial markets that the new president is serious about reducing deficit spending during his administration.

Second, a ceiling on all domestic outlays (other than Social Security) should be established at the projected inflation rate of 3.4 percent per year from FY94 through FY98. Congress would have discretion in allocating funds among programs under the cap. For the overall ceiling to be enforced, any excess spending in one year would require a reduction of equal magnitude the next year. That approach would have several benefits. First, since overall spending would be allowed to increase at the rate of inflation, the package might be politically viable. Second, the overall cap would force programs to compete with each other for funding. Congress would be forced to curtail the growth of medical care and other formula-payment programs because, if those programs were allowed to grow unimpeded, they would crowd out other domestic spending. During the Gramm-Rudman era of 1986–89, when a similar cap on expenditures existed, funding for formula-payment programs increased at only 1 percent above inflation.

Many changes in current programs, of course, would be necessary to stay within the limits of the proposed freeze on real domestic outlays. The remainder of this section describes the types of changes to the medical programs and other domestic programs that would be sufficient to implement a freeze.

Medical Care

For many years, the government has stimulated the demand and restricted the supply of medical care. The consequence has been rapid growth of both medical care prices and expenditures. In 1991, for example, the relative price of medical care increased 5.8 percent,

76

and real per capita expenditures for medical care increased 5.2 percent. The cost of health insurance is the most rapidly increasing component of private payrolls. And payments for public medical programs are the most rapidly growing component of government budgets. The CBO forecasts that real federal expenditures for Medicare and Medicaid will increase at a 7.8 percent annual rate for some years.

Our political system, however, appears ready to *increase* the problem by broadening health insurance to the roughly 35 million Americans who are now uninsured. President Bush endorsed a combination of new tax credits and deductions for private health insurance. Governor Clinton endorsed a proposal by congressional Democrats for a "play or pay" system that would require all employers to either provide health insurance or pay an additional 7 percent payroll tax to finance a public plan. Either of those plans would increase the demand for medical care, thereby augmenting current pressures for an increase in medical care prices and expenditures. Neither candidate proposed a credible plan to reduce the rapid increase in medical prices and expenditures.

The current American system of financing and supplying medical care cannot be sustained. Total expenditures for medical care have increased from about 5 percent to 13 percent of GDP over the past 30 years. The primary reason for that increase is that the share of health care costs paid directly by the patient has declined from about 50 percent to about 20 percent during that period. Moreover, the rapid increase in medical expenditures does not appear to have had any significant effect on average health status and life expectancy. There are strong reasons to believe that the additional medical services patients receive are not worth the additional costs. Something must give. Given the dominance of third-party payments, neither patients nor physicians have an adequate incentive to control the costs of medical care. No claim on GDP can increase indefinitely. And it is better to correct such unsustainable conditions sooner rather than later.

The demand for medical care will continue to increase in response to an increase in real incomes and the relative size of the elderly population. The primary focus of public policy should be on reducing the growth of demand attributable to tax-subsidized private and public health insurance. Any measure to broaden health insurance coverage to include those who would otherwise be uninsured should be part of a more comprehensive plan to reduce the average amount of tax-subsidized insurance and change the nature of that insurance.

A substantial part of tax-subsidized health insurance accrues to higher income people. Higher income people are more likely to be privately insured, and the value of the tax deduction increases with their marginal tax rate. Similarly, the people on Medicare who have the highest incomes are likely to live the longest, and the value of Medicare increases with their marginal tax rate. Clearly, the amount of tax-subsidized health insurance could be substantially reduced without much change in the insurance available to the poor.

It should be noted that the term "health insurance" is a double misnomer. The event that is insured against is not some adverse change in health status but the use of some type of medical care. Moreover, most plans are not accurately described as insurance. The basic concept of insurance is to reduce the variance of costs among those with the same prior risks. Most plans, however, include people with very different prior risks in the same premium pool. Such plans are best described as medical prepayment plans rather than health insurance. In effect, those plans redistribute income from people who use few medical services to people who use more medical services, regardless of the prior risks or income of either group.

In summary, a reduction in tax-subsidized medical prepayment plans is necessary to reduce the growth of demand for medical care. That subsidy should be reduced primarily for higher income people to ensure that they bear part of the burden of balancing the budget. Tax-subsidized medical plans should be restructured as indemnity insurance, like auto insurance. Patients would be paid a fixed amount (above some deductible) per illness or accident but would bear the full cost of any elective medical care. One or more of the following measures should be considered as a way of achieving those objectives.

- Maintain the tax deduction only for "Medisave" types of indemnity insurance. A full deduction for that type of insurance should also be extended to purchasers of individual plans.
- Limit or eliminate the tax deduction. A limit could be set at some rate, such as $150 a month, that would be sufficient only for a

high income-tested deductible. In either case, reduce the payroll tax by a corresponding amount; elimination of the tax deduction, for example, would permit a 2.2-percentage-point reduction in the payroll tax for all workers but have no net effect on federal revenues.

- Establish an income-tested deductible for the sum of payments under Part A and Part B of Medicare. That deductible could, for example, first be set at 1.5 percent of adjusted gross income (AGI) in the prior year and then increased 1.5 percentage points each year for four years. Thus, beginning in the fifth year, the deductible would be 7.5 percent of the prior year's AGI, the same rate that is now in the individual income tax code. Payments above the deductible, in most cases, would be fixed payments to the patient per illness or accident. The plan should probably be augmented to pay for one visit to a physician a year to encourage preventive care.
- Establish a similar plan with a high income-tested deductible for all Americans, including those who would otherwise be uninsured. That comprehensive catastrophic health insurance plan would replace the current tax deduction for private insurance and the outlays for Medicare and Medicaid. The plan should probably be augmented to pay for several visits to physicians each year by pregnant women and infants.

In all cases, firms and individuals would be allowed to buy any other amount and type of health insurance they desired, but only with after-tax income.

Each of those measures would reduce the growth of the demand for medical care, the relative inflation of the price of medical services, and total private and public expenditures for medical care. The measures are listed in the order of increasing budget savings. We have not estimated the specific budget savings attributable to each measure, but even a Medisave plan would generate substantial budget savings, without changing the federal insurance programs, by reducing the relative increase in the price of medical care.

Any of the suggested measures would reduce the growth of outlays for medical care by at least 1 percentage point a year, so a $50 billion annual savings by FY98 could reasonably be expected. Each of the measures would also reduce the pressure on state

Medicaid budgets that has been caused by the rapid increase in the relative price of medical care. Even with such savings, outlays for medical care would increase at a steeper rate than those for any other major federal program. More fundamental reforms will someday prove necessary to stabilize total expenditures for medical care as a share of GDP.

Other Programs

Once a cap on federal expenditures is in place, the president will need to set priorities for spending. There are hundreds of programs in the federal budget that serve no general public interest and ought to be terminated. Yet in the last four years, not a single program was eliminated. Only a small handful of programs has been closed down since 1980, despite a growing bipartisan consensus that tens of billions of dollars in savings could be generated by such measures.

What follows is a detailed list of 50 program terminations and reforms that would yield the savings needed to produce a balanced budget by 1998. We have chosen these budget reductions not only because they are all advisable on policy grounds, but because we believe that they may be politically achievable. For instance, most of the budget changes we list have been recommended in full or in part by House Budget Committee Chairman Leon Panetta. Others have been suggested by nonpartisan groups, such as the Congressional Budget Office and the General Accounting Office. Table 4.2, which appears at the end of this section, is our proposed list of discretionary budget changes. It notes which of those budget cuts have been recommended by the CBO or the House Budget Committee. Each recommendation would save at least $1 billion by 1998.

1. End additional U.S. financial support for the International Monetary Fund (IMF) and the World Bank. The mission of the IMF and the World Bank is to promote development of less developed countries. After tens of billions of dollars of U.S. investment in those multilateral organizations, there is no evidence that they have had any success in promoting growth in the countries they supposedly are assisting with their lending programs. Often, they give countries precisely the wrong advice, as when they urge tax increases to balance the budget or provide funding for government public works projects.

2. End U.S. foreign aid to Israel and Egypt. Israel and Egypt each receive more than $1 billion in U.S. taxpayer support each year. Considering the huge military budgets of those two nations and the elimination of the Soviet threat in the Middle East, the case for massive U.S. assistance has been substantially reduced. The United States can and should assist the economies of those countries through free-trade arrangements with both.

3. Eliminate U.S. funding of the Agency for International Development (AID) and the Export-Import Bank. Development economist Peter T. Bauer of the London School of Economics has written that the major impact of U.S. international aid programs has been to reward wasteful and irresponsible economic policies in less developed countries. Bauer has found that AID funds do not regularly encourage free enterprise, free markets, and local entrepreneurship. But those three things are the essential keys to development. Since there is no evidence that AID promotes development, it should be closed down. Similarly, the Export-Import Bank subsidizes exports of major U.S. firms, including Boeing Co., General Electric Co., and Westinghouse Electric Co. A report by the Federal Reserve Bank of Minneapolis concludes that the bank's subsidy program "does not offset other nations' [trade] distortions; it adds to them."

4. Cancel the super collider and the space station. The super collider is quickly becoming one of the most expensive public works projects in U.S. history. Increasingly, the scientific community is questioning the collider's scientific importance, and its supporters cannot justify its multi-billion-dollar price tag. Every year the cost estimates for the project have risen—from an original estimate of $6 billion in 1987 to $11 billion today. Similarly, the scientific benefits of the space station's manned missions to the moon and Mars are not expected to come close to matching its $10-billion-plus five-year price tag. The space station has come under criticism from the CBO, the National Research Institute, the Office of Technology Assessment, and many private research groups. It should be scuttled.

5. End Bureau of Reclamation water projects. The Bureau of Reclamation was formed in 1902 to promote the economic development of the arid West. After 90 years that mission has been accomplished—all too often to the detriment of the environment. There are very few free-flowing rivers left in the West, thanks to the bureau's agricultural irrigation projects. John Baden of the Foundation for Research on the Environment and the Economy says that the government's below-market pricing of bureau water fostered huge inefficiencies in the use of scarce water resources in California and other states.

6. *End any net federal land acquisition.* The federal government owns more than one-quarter of all the land in the United States. Yet each year the Department of the Interior's National Park Service and Bureau of Land and Mineral Management and the Department of Agriculture (Forest Service and other agencies) spend roughly $1 billion buying tens of thousands of additional acres. Well over half of the government's land holdings have no environmental or recreational significance. Massive government land holdings are inconsistent with a nation founded on the premises of free enterprise and respect for private property. The new president should place an immediate moratorium on any net increases in government land holdings and require an orderly auctioning of federally owned land that does not serve any national interest.

7. *End all U.S. Department of Agriculture conservation programs.* U.S. farmers are far and away the most productive and enterprising in the world. They do not need the federal government's encouragement or subsidies to safeguard the value of their most important asset: their land and soil. Yet each year the federal government spends roughly $1.5 billion to pay farmers to remove erodible land from production. Cato Institute adjunct scholar James Bovard has found that in some cases the taxpayer reimburses farmers as much as three times the rental value of their land if they participate in government conservation programs. The real agenda of those programs is to provide yet another subsidy to farmers, not to promote sound resource management.

8. *Terminate all federal wastewater treatment subsidies.* For the past 20 years the federal government has provided grants and loans to local governments to build wastewater treatment facilities to comply with federal clean water statutes. The provision of federal moneys has had two perverse effects. First, the CBO reports that federal

support has often kept cities from building such facilities on their own, because they prefer to wait for federal money, even while their wastewater is violating clean water standards. Second, the program has shifted the burden of paying for water cleanup from local polluters to federal taxpayers. Such subsidies thus encourage more pollution, not less.

9. Phase out all agriculture crop subsidies over five years. In the 1980s farm subsidies were the fastest growth area in the entire budget—they grew at an even faster pace than Reagan's defense build-up. The U.S. Department of Agriculture budget ballooned from $4 billion in 1980 to $21 billion in 1989. Those funds subsidize production of a whole range of commodities: cotton, wheat, wool, and corn. Most Americans continue to believe the popular folklore that crop subsidies benefit struggling family farmers. In fact, most of the money subsidizes huge million-dollar-plus agribusinesses. The USDA concedes that two-thirds of the payments are made to the richest 15 percent of U.S. farmers. Moreover, the net worth of the average farmer today is twice as great as that of the average U.S. family, and the farmer's income is, on average, 25 percent higher. Federal supports are such a vital element of farm incomes today that it has become a truism that many farmers now produce for the government, not the market. All major crop subsidy programs should be reduced by 20 percent per year through 1998 and then permanently canceled.

10. End federal dairy subsidies. Since 1980 dairy subsidies—which artificially raise the price of milk, cheese, butter, and other products—have cost U.S. consumers an estimated $40 billion. Meanwhile, the federal government has spent $17 billion purchasing excess dairy products—many of which eventually rot in massive government warehouses. The Office of Technology Assessment estimates that because of new technologies and increased productivity, by the end of the century there could be as few as 5,000 commercial dairy farmers left in the United States. If the current program is not ended, taxpayers will soon be providing over $200,000 in support for each dairy producer in order to pay higher prices for dairy products at the store.

11. End the Export Enhancement Program, the Market Promotion Program, the Agriculture Extension Service, and other obsolete USDA programs. Both the Export Enhancement Program and the Market Promotion Program are intended to increase U.S. agricultural exports. In practice they are simply a taxpayer subsidy to foreign purchasers of U.S. agricultural products. Moreover, most of the U.S. companies that have benefited from those programs are in no need of federal support. They include McDonald's, Pillsbury, Sunkist, and the Ernest and Julio Gallo Winery. Rep. Charles Schumer calls those programs "corporate welfare." The Agricultural Extension Service was formed in 1914 to provide technical farming assistance at a time when more than a third of all Americans lived on farms. Today only 2 percent of Americans are farmers, yet few of the AES's 3,000 field offices have been closed. The agency now provides courses in such vital fields as home economics, urban gardening, sewing, and gourmet cooking.

12. Reform Farmers Home Administration (FmHA) lending policies. The FmHA administers an array of direct and guaranteed loan programs for housing low-income families in rural areas. It has a woefully poor lending record, even for a government agency, with accumulated losses estimated at $60 billion by the GAO. The delinquency rates on several FmHA loan programs are over 40 percent. Meanwhile, the program continues to encourage further home building in rural areas even though the problem in most rural areas is a surplus, not a shortage, of housing. All FmHA housing lending should be immediately terminated. The FmHA's fast-growing inventory of defaulted properties should be sold. Very poor rural residents in need of housing assistance should be served through a housing voucher program.

13. End all Rural Electrification Administration (REA) lending and subsidies. The REA is the federal government's ultimate anachronism. It was created in 1935 to bring electricity and telephone service to rural America, and its mission has been accomplished. More than 98 percent of all rural homes now have access to electrical and phone service. Yet the agency continues to loan over $2 billion at subsidized rates to rural electric co-ops each year. The Treasury is now owed over $8 billion in those low-cost loans. This costly subsidy continues only because of the political clout of the rural electric cooperatives.

14. Terminate Community Development Block Grants (CDBGs), the Economic Development Administration (EDA), and the Appalachian Regional Commission (ARC). After 25 years, federal community development grants and loans have had little success in promoting urban renewal. Gary, Indiana, for example, has received more than $1,000 per resident in federal aid to build a convention center and other new municipal facilities, yet the area continues to lose people and businesses. CDBGs and the EDA were supposed to help only distressed areas, but both have been criticized by the CBO for increasingly funneling money to wealthier and more politically powerful areas. The ARC has spent almost $6 billion and built some 2,500 miles of new roads, yet high poverty rates still persist in Appalachia. The federal government should get out of the business of providing funding for local programs. With few exceptions, the cost of local government activities should be borne entirely by local taxpayers.

15. End Social Security Block Grants (SSBGs), Community Service Block Grants (CSBGs), and Title X Family Planning Grants. The CSBG and SSBG programs are offshoots of President Lyndon Johnson's War on Poverty. They fund a wide range of job-training, employment, health, energy, and child-care services, virtually all of which are local and state responsibilities and should be funded by those entities, if at all. The primary beneficiary of the funds has been a huge and politically influential human services industry. It not only lobbies for additional funding, it also helps create regulatory barriers, such as licensing or certification requirements for day care and many forms of anti-poverty assistance, that lock out much less costly alternatives for human service delivery. After 20 years, several studies have shown that Title X family planning grants have had no success in reducing unintended pregnancies. An estimated $50 million of those grants goes to a handful of groups, including the National Family Planning and Reproductive Health Association and Planned Parenthood of America, which could certainly raise the funds they need privately.

16. Eliminate the Small Business Administration. The best way for the federal government to help U.S. small businesses is to cut wasteful spending and the excessive taxes that pay for it. The SBA loan programs assist less than 0.5 percent of all small businesses.

To qualify for an SBA loan a business must have been turned down for a loan by at least two banks. Not surprisingly, the SBA has a terrible record in selecting businesses to support—as many as 20 percent of its loans go sour in any given year. The SBA does not, of course, create an additional pool of capital for small businesses; rather, it redirects capital from enterprises that are likely to succeed to enterprises that are likely to fail.

17. Terminate all earmarked highway demonstration projects. The 1991 highway bill contained $5 billion for "highway demonstration projects"—or almost one pork-barrel project for every congressional district. The sole purpose of those projects is to get members of Congress reelected. Recent projects include a parking garage in Chicago to "demonstrate" that parking facilities reduce on-street parking problems, a new road in rural West Virginia to reduce congestion, and a highway access ramp to an amusement park in Toledo, Ohio. Those projects violate an 80-year-old congressional rule that highway bills should never fund any specific road. Decisions about road building are supposed to be made by the individual states. The new Congress should wipe the slate clean by defunding every one of those costly and indefensible projects.

18. End subsidies for urban mass transit. Since 1965 the federal government has spent nearly $50 billion on urban mass transit, yet ridership has actually declined since then. The 1990 census revealed that in virtually every city that built an expensive new rail project in the 1980s with federal support, mass transit had a declining share of the commuter market. Two prominent examples of costly failures are Miami's Metrorail, which cost federal taxpayers more than $1 billion to build but carries only 15 percent of the projected ridership and is losing over $100 million a year, and Detroit's People Mover, which received $200 million in construction funding from Washington and yet is almost bankrupt today because of low ridership. In the mid-1980s then-senator William Proxmire gave urban transit subsidies his Golden Fleece Award because, as he said, they had proven to be a "spectacular flop" and served no purpose other than "playing Santa Claus to America's cities." The program is no better today.

19. Terminate federal airport grants. The federal government should not be subsidizing airline travel. More than 3,000 airports receive federal assistance each year. That assistance comes primarily from the airline ticket tax. Most of the assisted airports are in small cities, and the major beneficiaries are owners of small private planes— hardly a financially stressed class of citizens. The grants should cease, and airports that cannot survive without taxpayer subsidies should be closed or privatized.

20. Reduce Amtrak subsidies by 20 percent per year and privatize the railroad in 1998. The federal government should not be in the business of running a railroad. Federal subsidies to Amtrak average roughly $25 per passenger. Train travel is 20 to 100 times more heavily subsidized on a per-passenger-mile basis than is travel by automobile, bus, or air. When bankrupt passenger lines were taken over by the federal government in 1972, the newly created Amtrak was supposed to receive a temporary infusion of federal funds and then be moved back to private ownership. Now 20 years later it is not only still federally subsidized, it is requesting a multi-billion-dollar infusion of additional federal money to cover capital expenses. That request for funds should be declined, and Amtrak should be given five years to reduce its costs—by renegotiating outmoded labor rules, shedding money-losing routes, improving marketing plans, and raising ticket prices. Then the railroad should be auctioned off in full or in part.

21. Reform the student loan program to minimize taxpayer losses. The federal student loan program has quickly mushroomed into one of the federal government's largest middle- and upper-income subsidy programs. College loans are now available to virtually all students. That explains the program's broad base of support. Today students can receive loans for going to bartending school or for learning hairdressing and cosmetology. The program is taxpayer subsidized because the federal government offers below-market interest rates and does not fully charge for the risks of nonpayment. Default rates on student loans are typically 10 to 15 percent, and the current portfolio of bad loans exceeds $11.5 billion and is mounting. Those losses can be minimized in the future by (1) charging market interest rates on student loans once the student leaves or finishes school, (2) reducing federal payments to lenders by one-quarter of a percentage point, and (3) refusing high school dropouts student loans. To reduce future demand for the program and place financing responsibilities back on the shoulders of families, a new tax-free college savings account should be established by the federal government.

22. Cut elementary and secondary education funding by 50 percent. The problem with America's schools is not that they are underfunded. In constant 1990 dollars, the schools spent roughly $1,500 per student in 1950, $3,000 per student in 1970, and $6,000 per student in 1990. Moreover, the federal share of elementary and secondary school funding is much larger today than it was in 1950 when the schools were much better. Schools have had to subject themselves to more federal guidelines and regulations while sacrificing local autonomy. Federal funding for elementary and secondary education should be cut in half, and the remaining funds should be rechanneled to low-income parents in the form of vouchers. School choice is the reform that offers the most hope for innovation and increased productivity in the schools. Federal aid currently inhibits rather than encourages change.

23. End funding for the National Endowment for the Humanities (NEH), the National Endowment for the Arts (NEA), and the Corporation for Public Broadcasting (CPB). Art and culture play an important role in society, but that is not an argument for government financing of such activities. Most programs of the type funded by the NEH, the NEA, and the CPB should and would be financed entirely with private money. The clientele for each of those programs tends to be the affluent, who can afford to pay for the art and culture they want. The highly controversial nature of much of the programming and the projects that receive funding, such as the Mapplethorpe exhibit financed by the NEA, is a further argument for withdrawing taxpayer money.

24. Terminate Impact Aid Part B. Impact Aid compensates local governments for the ostensible cost of educating the children of military employees. Impact Aid Part B is a payment to local districts for the 1.5 million children of parents who work on military bases but do not live there. Those families already pay state and local taxes; hence Impact Aid is not needed. Impact Aid is based on the erroneous premise that military bases are a cost for local communities. Yet the current fierce resistance to closures of even highly obsolete bases demonstrates the value of those bases to local communities. When Hurricane Andrew wiped out Homestead Air Force Base in Florida that was supposed to be closed, the community lobbied successfully to have it rebuilt. Given the benefits local communities derive from the jobs and infusion of funds associated with military bases, there is no reason to provide additional dollars through Impact Aid.

25. *Reduce National Institute of Health (NIH) subsidies for overhead expenses.* Reports by both the GAO and the CBO have faulted the NIH for reimbursing universities, hospitals, and other outside institutions for excessive overhead expenditures. More than 30 percent of NIH grants pay for costs not directly associated with the research being funded. The recent Defense Department contract scandals at Stanford University have brought to the public's attention the problem of universities' overcharging for indirect expenses. Now over 250 schools are under investigation by the NIH. Cutting indirect cost reimbursement by 20 percent would not sacrifice valuable biomedical research, but it would give institutions a greater incentive to control costs.

26. *Reform the Federal Housing Administration (FHA) mortgage guarantee program.* Next to Social Security, the FHA, which insures mortgages on single-family and multifamily homes, is perhaps the largest middle-income subsidy program in the federal budget. The FHA now controls roughly 55 percent of the mortgage insurance business, because of its attractive subsidies to home buyers. In recent years those subsidies have forced federal taxpayers to swallow billions of dollars in losses on defaulted mortgages. During the Depression, the FHA was the only available mortgage insurer. Today there are many private mortgage insurance alternatives to the FHA. To reduce its future losses and to pave the way to a gradual exit from the market, the FHA should (1) require a 10 percent down payment on all loans and (2) discontinue insurance of refinanced loans, purchases of second homes, and investment properties.

27. *Eliminate the Job Corps, the Job Training Partnership Act (JTPA), and Trade Adjustment Assistance (TAA).* Federal job-training programs for youth and retraining programs for adults have a long history of failure. For example, it costs the Job Corps about $30,000

per client, or roughly what it would cost to send those youngsters to Harvard. The JTPA has a very poor record of successfully training and placing its clients in good-paying jobs. Years of experience indicate that the best job training is on-the-job training. The Job Corps and JTPA often delay workers' entry or reentry into the labor force. The TAA gives workers displaced from their jobs because of foreign competition up to 78 weeks of paid benefits. Yet there is no reason why workers who lose their jobs as a result of foreign competition should be entitled to a longer period of government assistance than workers displaced for other reasons. The TAA should be abolished and replaced by the normal unemployment insurance program.

28. Repeal the Davis-Bacon Act. The 1931 Davis-Bacon Act requires construction contractors to pay their workers at least the "prevailing wage" on all federal construction contracts. In practice the prevailing wage has become the union wage. It inflates the cost of all the tens of billions of dollars of federal construction contracts by an estimated 30 percent. Moreover, the purpose of the act was to keep blacks and immigrants from competing with white unionized workers on federal construction contracts. Today it continues to have that effect. Hence, the law is discriminatory not only in intent but in practice. The CBO, the GAO, the Grace Commission, and many other independent groups have called for the repeal of Davis-Bacon. Repealing it would save at least $2 billion per year.

29. Repeal the Service Contract Act, all minority set-aside programs, and Buy America provisions that raise the cost of federal contracts. The Service Contract Act is the counterpart of Davis-Bacon for all federal service contracts. Its prevailing wage requirements, which limit competition from low-cost contractors, inflate the cost of federal contracts by roughly $1 billion per year. Minority contract set-asides are a form of affirmative action for federal contractors. Set-asides discriminate against nonminorities and add about 10 percent to the costs of federal contracts. Buy America provisions require contractors to use U.S.-made parts on selected contracts, even when lower cost, higher quality imports are available. That form of protectionism does not serve the interests of U.S. taxpayers, just as protectionism generally ill-serves U.S. consumers.

30. Cut all agency overhead by 2 percent. The federal workforce grew by 100,000 workers between 1984 and 1992. The federal budget grew by 30 percent in real terms from 1989 to 1992. A 2 percent across-the-board reduction in overhead costs should be easily achievable without sacrificing government services. Most businesses and households cut their budgets by at least that amount during the 1990–91 recession.

31. Cut federal pay by 10 percent. A 1988 Office of Personnel Management report found that the voluntary quit rate in the federal government was lower than it was in the private sector during the Great Depression. Moreover, there is a huge queue of qualified workers waiting to become federal employees. In recent years the wages of federal blue-collar employees have been rising faster than those of private-sector employees. Those statistics suggest that the federal government could significantly reduce wages without sacrificing service quality or productivity.

32. Auction off the electromagnetic spectrum. The Federal Communications Commission has the authority to license and regulate unassigned frequencies on the electromagnetic spectrum. Currently, those frequencies are assigned through a lottery system. That confers a huge windfall on the winning applicant, who often turns around and sells the frequency rights for a large profit. An auctioning system would be more economically efficient and would reduce the national debt by about $3.5 billion.

33. Lease the Arctic National Wildlife Refuge (ANWR). According to U.S. geologists, ANWR probably contains more oil than any remaining onshore area of the United States. In 1987 the U.S. Department of the Interior estimated that the net benefit to the U.S. economy of developing ANWR could approach $80 billion. Extreme environmentalists have prevented its exploitation, even though the area that would be developed would be only a tiny fraction of that vast uninhabited wilderness. If a portion of the revenues raised from ANWR's development were used to create a national wildlife trust fund, the environmental objections to drilling could be surmounted.

34. End all Power Marketing Administration subsidies. The federal government generates electric power at 127 federal dams under the authority of five Power Marketing Administrations (PMAs). The PMAs charge below-market rates for electricity. The subsidies cost the federal government roughly $1.5 billion annually. Under-priced federal electricity powers affluent neighborhoods and even gambling casinos in Las Vegas. Ideally, the PMAs should simply be privatized and operated as for-profit businesses. If Congress will not allow that, it should at least end the inefficient and costly subsidies to the PMAs.

35. Cut congressional and White House staff and expenses by 33 percent. George Bush suggested this reform in the 1992 presidential cam-paign. Since the early 1960s the overall size of the congressional staff has roughly tripled. Committee staffing has grown even faster. In real dollars, the cost of running Congress today ($2.8 billion) is 2.5 times what it was in the mid-1960s. Members of Congress make $130,000 salaries, and more than 350 staffers make at least $100,000. White House salaries often run even higher. Belt tightening in the legislative and executive branches would result in better and less intrusive government.

36. Reduce the U.S. Department of Commerce budget by 50 percent. Other than the functions of the U.S. Census Bureau, almost none of the activities of the Department of Commerce serve any overriding national interest. Many of its activities revolve around trade promo-tion, regulation of trade, and economic development. Not only are those inappropriate activities for government, but the Commerce Department has not proven effective in carrying them out. The new president should undertake a comprehensive review of all the agencies of the Commerce Department and terminate those that are not inherently governmental in nature.

37. Eliminate the U.S. Department of Energy. The U.S. Department of Energy was created by Jimmy Carter in 1977 during the height of the oil crisis. Over the years, the price controls and subsidies of the DOE have cost U.S. taxpayers, consumers, and industry tens of billions of dollars. The length and severity of the oil crisis of the 1970s were directly attributable to the regulatory apparatus of DOE—namely, oil price controls. Other projects, such as the Synfuels Corporation, were multi-billion-dollar flops that never produced a kilowatt of electricity. The lesson of the 1970s and 1980s is that energy markets serve consumers and industry best when the free market is permitted to operate. Finally, about half of the

DOE's budget is dedicated to nuclear weapons testing and experimentation. The end of the Cold War has reduced the urgency of such programs. Those that are still vital to national security should be shifted to the Defense Department.

38. End Veterans' Administration health care benefits for non-service-related injuries and illnesses. The original purpose of veterans' medical benefits was to treat combat-related injuries and other illnesses sustained during the time of service. That is an appropriate government compact with the men and women who served in the military. But those health benefits have been expanded to cover impoverished and sick veterans, whose afflictions have no connection with their military service. The CBO reports that in 1987 almost 80 percent of Veterans' Administration health care, including 1.3 million hospital stays and 19 million doctor visits, went for non-service-related medical problems. Those veterans should be covered by other public programs or by private health insurance.

39. Cut regulatory agency budgets by 25 percent. Federal regulations grew at a rapid pace in the period 1989–93, reversing the anti-regulation policies of Ronald Reagan. At the same time, the budgets of all regulatory agencies grew at twice the inflation rate. That period proved that more money and more regulators lead to more stifling regulation. A 25 percent reduction in the total budgets of regulatory agencies would help eliminate unnecessary and capricious regulation and force agency personnel to concentrate their resources on their highest priorities. That would unshackle business from frivolous regulatory burdens that have contributed directly to the current very sluggish economic growth.

Reducing Federal Entitlement Spending

It is virtually impossible to balance the budget without significantly curtailing spending on what have become known as entitlement programs. Entitlement programs automatically provide cash or benefits to individuals who meet the eligibility criteria. The major categories of entitlements are retirement benefits, health care, and welfare. From 1989 to 1992 real entitlement spending increased by $115 billion to $600 billion—a 23 percent increase over inflation. In addition to the health care and Social Security reforms mentioned above, we propose the following spending reductions.

40. *Require the states to pay a minimum of 50 percent of the costs of Food Stamps, Aid to Families with Dependent Children (AFDC), and Medicaid.* States are beginning to aggressively experiment with cost-reduction reforms in welfare and health care. The most ambitious of those experiments, designed to get people off welfare in a hurry, have been adopted in Wisconsin under Gov. Tommy Thompson. Unfortunately, cost cutting is often discouraged by the current federal reimbursement scheme, because any welfare or Medicaid expense reduction means smaller checks from the federal government. One method of spurring innovation in welfare and government health care insurance is to force all states to pay at least half the cost of the Food Stamps, AFDC, and Medicaid programs. That measure should be combined with a substantial reduction in the federal mandates so as to allow state governments increased flexibility to structure the supply of welfare services. Eventually, all government low-income programs should be financed by the states and localities.

41. *End military cost-of-living adjustments for veterans retiring before age 62.* Neither Social Security nor most private pension programs offer retirement benefits before the age of 62. Yet it is not unusual for members of the armed forces to retire in their 50s. Simply ending cost-of-living adjustments to the pensions of military personnel who retire before the age of 62 would save at least $2.5 billion per year.

42. *End the lump-sum Civil Service Retirement System (CSRS) option and require federal workers to cover a larger share of the cost of the CSRS system.* The unfunded liability of the CSRS has already exceeded $1 trillion, and the amount is growing larger each year. Because many civil servants are also eligible for Social Security, it is not uncommon for a federal retiree to receive two government pensions worth more than $75,000 per year. The excessive benefits offered under the CSRS program should be curtailed by (1) eliminating the lump-sum retirement option, which allows retirees to withdraw lump-sum payments from CSRS equal to the total of their own contributions to the system; (2) increasing the federal retirement age from 55 to 65; and (3) applying a means test to those retirees who are eligible for both CSRS and Social Security.

43. *Replace AFDC, Food Stamps, public housing assistance, the earned income tax credit (EITC), and other welfare programs with a cash assistance*

program requiring work. The federal government, along with the states and cities, spends an estimated $180 billion per year on anti-poverty programs. That is almost two and a half times the $75 billion that would be needed to lift every family now below the poverty level to above the poverty level. But the poverty rate in the United States is still extremely high. One reason is that a large portion of anti-poverty spending is captured by welfare bureaucracies and service providers. Milwaukee, Wisconsin, for example, has more than 70 separate welfare assistance programs. America's current fragmented system of welfare delivery serves no one but a large and growing welfare industry. AFDC, public housing, Food Stamps, the EITC, and other welfare programs should be merged into a single welfare cash assistance program. The program should have a spending ceiling of 70 percent of the current welfare programs folded into it. All employable recipients should be required to work in exchange for their monthly checks.

44. Eliminate Food Stamps, public housing, and other welfare benefits for all able-bodied adults. Many states, including Michigan and Massachusetts, have begun to eliminate public assistance for employable adults—a category they have tended to define as those without disabilities or young children at home. Yet many federal programs, including, most prominently, the Food Stamp program, offer benefits to low-income Americans even if they are fully capable of working. Today, for example, roughly 24 million people—or 1 of every 10 Americans—receives Food Stamps. The vast majority of those recipients are able to work. This category of federal public assistance should be ended.

45. Sharply reduce unemployment insurance benefits and delay benefits for one month. Studies have shown that roughly one-third of all unemployment in the United States is a result of the federal government's perverse unemployment insurance system. It rewards those who become unemployed for staying unemployed. Yet in the past two years Congress has made the unemployment insurance system far more rewarding by extending benefits from 26 weeks to 52 weeks or more. Almost all unemployment insurance claimants are able-bodied employable adults. Benefits should be delayed for one month upon layoff or firing and reduced by 5 percent per week for 20 weeks.

46. End all federal child-care subsidies. Only in the past few years has anyone thought of child care, which was once called baby sitting, as a federal responsibility. Yet today the federal government spends roughly $3 billion annually on payments to government child-care centers and subsidies to parents who place their children in private child-care facilities. That means that families with two parents working and a child in day care receive a federal subsidy paid for in part by parents who make the financial sacrifice of having only one parent work and the other take care of the child at home. Financing child care, regardless of the type families choose, is the proper responsibility of parents, not taxpayers.

47. Reduce Head Start funding by 50 percent. The budget for Head Start has climbed by two-thirds since 1989—after adjusting for inflation. Although Head Start is one of Washington bureaucrats' most popular programs, the evidence of its success is mixed, at best. Several studies document that Head Start does offer children a head start, but that their lead over non–Head Start children dissipates after several years in school. The most negative impact of Head Start is that it has created a huge and expanding preschool bureaucracy.

48. End all new construction of public housing. Even many advocates of public housing now concede that the huge public housing projects built in the 1960s and 1970s were an expensive mistake. Public housing projects became unlivable centers of crime, drugs, teen pregnancy, juvenile delinquency, and a vicious cycle of poverty. Yet under George Bush from 1989 to 1992, new public housing starts accelerated. In almost all areas of the country today, the low-income housing problem is one of lack of affordability, not lack of availability. And the short supply of low-income housing in some cities is a result of counterproductive government housing policies, such as rent control, building code regulations, and exclusionary zoning. Rather than build more public housing units, the federal government should combat policies that reduce the housing opportunities of the poor.

49. Target all children's nutrition subsidies to families with incomes below the poverty level. The federal government spends $800 million each year on school lunches, breakfasts, and other nutrition subsidies for children of families that are middle class, not poor. In 1988 subsidized meals at home day-care centers cost $250 million a year—and 70 percent of the children come from families with incomes over $30,000. A strong case could be made for abolishing the feeding subsidies entirely; if they continue, they should provide assistance only to children from families under the poverty line.

50. End low-income home energy assistance. The low-income home energy assistance program was created in the 1970s during the energy crisis to provide subsidies for home heating to low-income families. The energy crisis ended a decade ago. Home heating costs are now at about their pre-OPEC levels. Since the crisis has ended, so should the subsidies.

Table 4.2 summarizes the proposed program changes and the estimated savings specific to each measure. The sum of the proposed spending cuts would reduce total spending by about $120 billion relative to the level now projected for FY98.

A final note: We do not necessarily endorse any federal program by its omission from this list. The current federal budget share of GDP is about 10 times what it was in 1929, and many of the new programs added since then merit reconsideration. Our budget plan would reduce federal outlays from 25 percent of GDP in 1992 to about 19 percent by 1997. We invite readers to identify their own least favorite programs to add to our list.

Table 4.2
RECOMMENDED DOMESTIC BUDGET CUTS
(BILLIONS OF DOLLARS)

	1994	1998	Panetta	CBO
Discretionary programs				
End participation in IMF and World Bank	0.5	1.0		
End aid to Israel and Egypt	0.2	1.5	x	
Cancel super collider and space station	1.5	3.5	x	x
End Bureau of Recla- mation water projects	1.3	2.0		

(Continued on next page)

Table 4.2—Continued
RECOMMENDED DOMESTIC BUDGET CUTS
(BILLIONS OF DOLLARS)

	1994	1998	Panetta	CBO
End all federal land acquisition	1.0	1.0		x
End agricultural conservation programs	0.2	1.0		
End wastewater treatment subsidies	0.1	2.0	x	x
Phase out crop subsidies	3.0	6.5		x
End dairy subsidies	0.5	1.0		
End miscellaneous agricultural programs	1.0	1.0		x
Terminate SBA	0.2	2.0	x	
Cancel highway demonstrations	0.6	1.5	x	
End transit subsidies	1.3	2.0	x	x
Terminate airport grants	0.3	2.0	x	x
Terminate community development grants	0.8	1.0		
Phase out all Amtrak subsidies	0.1	1.0	x	
Reform FmHA lending	0.6	1.5	x	x
Reform student loan program	1.0	2.0		x
Cut elementary and secondary education funding	3.5	5.0		
End NEA/NEH/CPB	1.0	1.0		
Cut NIH subsidies for overhead	1.2	1.5	x	x
End SSBG/CSBG	0.4	2.0		
Repeal Davis-Bacon	1.0	2.5	x	

Table 4.2—Continued
RECOMMENDED DOMESTIC BUDGET CUTS
(BILLIONS OF DOLLARS)

	1994	1998	Panetta	CBO
Repeal Service Contract Act	1.0	2.0		
End Impact Aid	0.4	1.0	x	
Cut agency overhead 2%	0.6	6.0	x	
Cut AID and Export-Import				
Bank	0.3	2.0	x	
Auction spectrum	0.0	1.0	x	x
Eliminate Department				
of Energy	1.5	6.5		
Reform veterans'				
health care	0.5	2.5		x
Lease ANWR	0.1	1.5		
Reform FHA				
lending policies	1.0	1.0		
Cut federal pay 10%	1.0	1.0		
Reform REA	0.1	1.0		x
Cut Job Corps/JTPA/				
TAA 50%	0.2	1.5		
End power marketing				
subsidies	0.1	1.0		x
Cut congressional/				
White House budgets	0.2	1.0		
Cut Dept. of Commerce				
budget 50%	0.2	1.5		
Cut regulatory agency				
budgets	0.2	1.5		
Total	28.5	79.0		
Entitlement reforms				
Require states to pay				
50% match	0.6	4.0	x	x
End miliary COLAs at				
age 62	0.3	2.5	x	x
Reduce CSRS				
benefits	0.3	4.5	x	x

(Continued on next page)

Table 4.2—Continued
RECOMMENDED DOMESTIC BUDGET CUTS
(BILLIONS OF DOLLARS)

	1994	1998	Panetta	CBO
Consolidate welfare programs	1.5	10.0		
End welfare benefits for able-bodied	1.5	6.0		
Reduce unemployment insurance benefits	1.5	5.0		
End day-care subsidies	0.2	3.0	x	
Reduce Head Start funding	0.5	2.0		
End new public housing construction	1.5	3.5	x	
Target children's nutrition	0.3	1.0	x	x
End low-income home energy assistance	0.2	1.0		x
Total	8.4	42.5		

Total Savings and the Budget

The sum of the measures described above would be sufficient to balance the budget by FY98 with no increase in taxes. Table 4.3 summarizes those savings by major category.

The defense budget would bear the largest proportional cuts. The many domestic programs other than Social Security and medical insurance would bear the largest absolute cuts.

Table 4.3
PROPOSED BUDGET SAVINGS (BILLIONS OF DOLLARS)

	Fiscal Year					
	93	94	95	96	97	98
Defense	0	16	41	61	81	101
Social Security	0	0	1	2	3	4
Medical	0	1	7	18	30	50
Other	14	35	41	58	72	118
Net interest	0	2	8	16	30	49
Total	14	54	98	155	216	322

Table 4.4
THE PATH TO A BALANCED BUDGET (BILLIONS OF DOLLARS)

	\multicolumn{6}{Fiscal Year}					
	93	94	95	96	97	98
Outlays						
Defense	297	268	243	226	209	192
Social Security	302	318	335	352	371	390
Medical	226	250	273	296	319	339
Other	468	452	450	449	448	447
Total	1,293	1,288	1,301	1,323	1,347	1,368
Deposit insurance	49	17	5	−7	−16	−20
Offsetting receipts	−67	−69	−72	−74	−76	−79
Net interest	204	221	236	247	254	254
Total	1,479	1,457	1,470	1,489	1,509	1,523
Revenue	1,162	1,242	1,323	1,390	1,455	1,534
Deficit	317	215	147	99	54	−11
Debt	3,317	3,532	3,679	3,778	3,832	3,821

NOTE: CBO projections (Table 4.1) less the amounts saved by implementing the authors' recommendations.

Many beneficiaries of current federal programs, of course, will regard the proposed cuts as draconian. So be it. After the cuts are made, however, the federal budget would still finance the largest defense budget in the world, maintain the real pension benefits of Social Security recipients, finance a continued substantial increase in expenditures for medical care, and maintain most other domestic programs. Total outlays in FY98 would be 18.8 percent of GDP, a higher share of national output than in any peacetime year prior to the 1970s. And total outlays for domestic programs would be 14.5 percent of GDP, a higher share of national output than in any year prior to the 1980s.

Finally, Table 4.4 summarizes the path to a balanced budget. The combination of measures described above would yield a small surplus in FY98 and a rough balance in the several subsequent years. Further changes in federal medical programs would still be necessary to put those programs on a sustainable basis. For the first time in 30 years, however, we would be financing total federal outlays without increasing the tax burden on either current workers or their children. It is not very important to achieve a balanced federal budget every single year, but it is very important to try. That is the only way to force a sorting out of our fiscal priorities and to constrain total federal spending to a level that is broadly supported.

5. Reduce Federal Regulation

William A. Niskanen

Federal regulation has become a major burden to the U.S. economy. The gross annual cost of federal regulation is now about $500 billion and is expected to increase, under current trends and recently enacted legislation, to about $600 billion by the year 2000 (both estimates in 1990 dollars).[1] Moreover, the new Congress is expected to address several bills that would further increase those costs—including mandated family leave, mandated health insurance, extending the Medicare compensation rates to all private payers, and the first federal regulation of the insurance industry. The cost of regulation is often a special burden on small firms and has contributed to increased foreign sourcing by large firms.

The Record of Economic Deregulation

The record of economic deregulation, initiated by Presidents Ford and Carter and sustained by President Reagan, is now quite clear. Since 1976 the older forms of price and entry regulations have been successively reduced or eliminated for domestic aviation, railroads, trucking, banks, oil, intercity buses, long-distance telephone service, ocean shipping, cable television, and natural gas production. In every case, deregulation led to an increase in services and (except for cable TV) a reduction in real prices to consumers. The annual net benefits of deregulation are now about $50 billion. Deregulation also led to some restructuring within each of the affected industries and some pressure for reregulation—especially of airlines, railroads, banking, and cable TV. The effects of the partial deregulation of banks were especially misunderstood, and the savings-and-loan crisis led to some new regulation of bank capital standards and the asset portfolios of the S&Ls. And the increase in cable TV rates led

[1]Thomas D. Hopkins, "The Costs of Federal Regulation," *Journal of Regulation and Social Costs*, March 1992, p. 25.

to some recent reregulation of that industry. For the most part, however, there appears to be a political consensus to maintain the deregulation of most of those industries. One wonders why the lessons from recent experience have not led to further deregulation of the partially deregulated industries and to deregulation of other industries.

The Regulatory Record of President Bush

For three years, in the name of a kinder and gentler America, the Bush administration encouraged or allowed a rapid increase in regulation. President Bush nominated aggressive regulators to head the Environmental Protection Agency, the Food and Drug Administration, and the Securities and Exchange Commission. More important, the administration endorsed a series of new regulatory laws that will impose substantial continuing costs on the economy, including

- a higher minimum wage,
- a complex new compensation schedule for physicians' services financed by Medicare,
- the Americans with Disabilities Act,
- the Clean Air Act amendments of 1990, and
- the Civil Rights Act of 1991.

Moreover, the administration allowed the White House regulatory review process to be weakened by the absence of a confirmed nominee to head the Office of Information and Regulatory Affairs (OIRA) and by allowing Congress to circumscribe the effectiveness of that office.

The Bush administration, to its credit, made several proposals to reduce the older forms of economic regulation. One proposal would have eliminated the restrictions on interstate banking and on the range of financial services offered by banks, but Congress, maybe correctly, deferred approval of that proposal until the deposit insurance issue is resolved. A proposal to reduce the regulation of public utility holding companies was approved in late 1992. In response to pressure from the White House Council on Competitiveness, the Food and Drug Administration implemented several measures to reduce the time required for approving new drugs. And Bush appointees at the Federal Communications Commission and the Federal Energy Regulatory Commission also initiated several valuable deregulatory measures.

The net increase in the cost of federal regulation during the Bush administration has not been estimated (the Clear Air Act amendments alone will cost about $30 billion a year when the new rules are fully implemented), but the indirect indexes of the magnitude of federal regulation are most disturbing. The number of employees in federal regulatory agencies increased from 106,000 in 1989 to 122,400 in 1992. The number of pages added to the *Federal Register* each year increased from 55,000 to 70,000 in the first two years of the Bush administration.

In the fall of 1991 President Bush—who, as vice president, had served as chairman of both the Task Force on Regulatory Relief and a special task force on financial reform—apparently had a change of heart. Concern about the sputtering economy and long-term economic growth led the Bush administration to change course on yet another dimension of its economic policy. In his January 1992 State of the Union address, President Bush announced a 90-day moratorium on new federal regulations that would reduce economic growth. Bush later extended the moratorium for another 120 days and committed the administration to estimating and announcing the expected benefits and costs of future regulatory bills considered by Congress. The administration released a (disputed) estimate that the initial 90-day moratorium reduced the long-term costs to consumers and workers by $15 billion to $20 billion.[2]

Most of the proposed new rules, however, were written by men and women that Bush had appointed under laws that he had endorsed, inherently limiting the potential effect of the 1992 moratorium. Bush was not initially ready to replace any of the key regulatory officials or to criticize any of the basic regulatory legislation. After considerable controversy within the administration, however, Bush resisted any major new commitments at the 1992 Earth Summit. And during the presidential campaign, Bush raised questions about some of the basic environmental legislation and vetoed bills to mandate family leave and reregulate cable TV.

[2]Office of Management and Budget, *Mid-Session Review of the Federal Budget*, July 1992, p. 395.

Those actions raised the question of which was the real Bush, the "environmental president" of the 1988 campaign or the "people first" president of the 1992 campaign? The most likely answer is both. Bush had a genuine concern both about the environment and about regulations that cost too much in lost output and jobs. In that sense, the Bush position did not differ much from that of Democratic candidate Arkansas governor William Clinton, but it did differ sharply from the quasi-religious "earth first" environmentalism of Clinton's running mate Al Gore.

The regulatory record of the Bush administration is probably best explained by a combination of economic and fiscal conditions. Good times produce new political demands, and the long Reagan recovery should have been expected, with a lag, to increase the demand for environmental benefits, aid to the disabled, and the like. The federal fiscal condition, however, increased the incentive to meet those demands by regulation rather than by additional spending or tax preferences. The weak economy of the past several years, in turn, has deferred demands for new regulation and increased concern on the part of both the administration and Congress about the effects of regulation on output and employment. For those who are concerned about the prospect of a continued increase in regulation, the current challenge is to shape the perspective on the appropriate limited role of regulation before an economic recovery revives proposals for new regulation.

A Deregulatory Agenda for the New Administration

A regulatory reformer faces the same type of challenge as a budget reformer: eliminate those regulations that never did or no longer do serve the general interest, revise the remaining regulations to increase their efficiency and responsiveness to changing conditions, and promote a set of principles and a review process that will lead to better decisions on proposed new regulations. That is a massive task and will not be completed in the course of one administration or, probably, one lifetime. Nevertheless, it is worthwhile to consider a regulatory reform agenda for each new administration. A president of either major party will want to maintain an effective White House regulatory review process. Regulation is now too large a burden on the American economy to treat casually without a guiding set of principles.

Economic Regulation

Most types of economic regulation, whatever their public rationale, have *increased* the average price of goods and services sold by the regulated industry, thus protecting existing firms against potential new domestic and foreign competitors at the expense of American consumers. Many of those regulations have also led to an artificial structure of the regulated industries, reducing productivity and the range of goods and services offered for sale. As a consequence, the selective reduction of federal price and entry controls, which began in the late 1970s, has generally led to lower prices, higher productivity, and an increased range of goods and services. The only exception to that pattern was the deregulation of cable TV rates without allowing additional firms to enter each local market. Recent experience should lead the new administration to consider the following steps to reduce economic regulations.

Agriculture

- Eliminate those marketing orders that restrict the sale or size of fresh produce.
- Eliminate the milk marketing system and the ban on reprocessing powdered milk for human consumption.
- Eliminate the import quotas on dairy products, meat, peanuts, and sugar.

Communications

- Allow the regional telephone companies to manufacture equipment and offer cable TV and information services.
- Establish property rights in the electronic frequency spectrum and allow market exchanges of those rights.
- Require government users of the frequency spectrum to pay user fees.
- Eliminate the Intelsat monopoly on international satellite communications.
- Consider federal preemption of state regulation of local telephone service where cellular telephone is a viable competitor.

Energy

- Repeal the Public Utility Holding Company Act.[3]
- Allow free entry in electric generation.

---

[3]*Regulation*, Winter 1992, includes a set of articles on the regulation of electric utilities.

- Eliminate rate controls on electric transmission grids and gas pipelines that are user owned.
- Repeal the several types of mandated energy conservation regulations.
- Consider substituting regional for state regulation of local electric and natural gas distribution companies.

Finance

- Eliminate the restrictions on interstate banking.[4]
- Eliminate the restrictions on the services supplied by bank holding companies, in combination with a major reform of the regulation of insured depository institutions.
- Eliminate the restrictions on the types of assets that may be owned by commercial and savings banks.
- Consider establishing a federal charter for insurance companies; those firms electing a federal charter would be subject to federal solvency regulation but would be free of state rate regulation.
- Consider changing those federal securities regulations that penalize insider trading and restrict takeover bids.

Trade

- Approve the North American Free-Trade Agreement.[5]
- Complete and approve the Uruguay round of multilateral trade negotiations.
- Repeal the anti-dumping provisions of U.S. trade law.
- Consider establishing a free-trade agreement with any country that is prepared to grant the United States equal treatment.

Transportation

- Repeal the remaining rate controls on trucking, railroads, and ocean shipping.[6]
- Allow increased access by foreign airlines to the U.S. market in exchange for similar access by U.S. carriers to the markets of the foreign airlines' home countries.

---

[4]*Regulation*, Spring 1991 and Spring 1992, includes a set of articles on banking and insurance regulation.

[5]*Regulation*, Winter 1993, includes a set of articles on current trade issues. Brink Lindsey makes the case for a more ambitious unilateral free-trade agenda in chapter 13 of this book.

[6]*Regulation*, Summer 1991, includes a set of articles on transportation regulation.

- Allow foreign shipping lines to carry traffic between U.S. ports.
- Eliminate the Postal Service monopoly on first class mail.
- Consider federal preemption of state rate controls on intrastate traffic.

That is a substantial agenda but far from complete; for example, some parts of U.S. antitrust and labor law should also be reviewed. Implementing any substantial part of the proposed agenda, however, would generate meaningful benefits for the U.S. economy. Those measures would also generate some budget savings, because they would permit the elimination of the Interstate Commerce Commission and the Federal Maritime Commission and a substantial reduction in the staff and budgets of the Federal Communications Commission, the Federal Energy Regulatory Commission, the International Trade Commission, and the Securities and Exchange Commission. To facilitate implementation of any part of the agenda outlined above, the president should make a case for continued economic deregulation as part of a general strategy to increase productivity, appoint committed deregulators to the relevant commissions, and enlist the support of those private interests and state governments that would be best served by the proposed measures.

Social Regulation

Most of the increases in the costs of federal regulation are attributable to broader and tighter regulation of health, safety, and the environment. From 1977 to 1990, for example, the cost of federal economic regulation declined about $45 billion, but the cost of social regulation increased about $67 billion (both in 1990 dollars).[7] Moreover, most of the projected increase in the cost of regulation is attributable to new social regulations approved in the part several years.

There is reason to presume, and considerable evidence, that most economic regulations are counterproductive. The issues touched by social regulation are much more complex. Most health, safety, and environmental concerns could be addressed by some combination of information, contract or tort law, insurance, fiscal measures, and regulation. The relevant question is whether regulation is the

[7]Hopkins, p. 25.

most efficient instrument to address those concerns, and the answer, in many cases, is no.

Safety and Health. The record of the Occupational Safety and Health Administration (OSHA) illustrates that point.[8] OSHA sets workplace safety standards, inspects about 1 percent of workplaces each year, typically finds a few violations per inspection, and levies small fines. In 1982, for example, OSHA assessed about $6 million in fines at a time when firms paid about $10 billion in premiums for workers compensation and about $69 billion in compensating wage differentials in the less safe workplaces; OSHA's fines are trivial in comparison with other financial incentives to reduce workplace risk. In addition, occupational safety is a function of both workplace conditions and employee behavior; a safer workplace may induce less careful employee behavior and thus have little net effect on accident rates. One should not be surprised that there is no evidence that OSHA has significantly increased occupational safety and health. For similar reasons, there is no evidence that the Consumer Product Safety Commission (CPSC)[9] or the National Highway Traffic Safety Administration (NHTSA) has significantly increased product or traffic safety. In commercial relations, in both the labor market and the markets for goods and services, there should be a strong presumption to rely primarily on information, contract law, and insurance—not on regulation—to achieve a mutually acceptable level of health and safety. The direct and indirect costs of OSHA, CPSC, and NHTSA are substantial, yet their activities have no significant effects on health and safety. Those agencies may best be eliminated or restricted to a research, information, and advisory role. One wonders how our occupational and product safety were protected before the creation of those agencies about 25 years ago; the answer is, "Quite well, thank you." Death rates from accidents of all types declined steadily for many decades before those agencies were created.

The Food and Drug Administration (FDA) seems to assume that drug companies are irresponsible, physicians are incompetent, and all patients are children. Extraordinarily demanding tests of both

[8]Thomas Knieser and John Leeth, "Improving Workplace Safety," *Regulation*, Fall 1991, pp. 64–70.

[9]Paul Rubin, "Why Regulate Consumer Safety?" *Regulation*, Fall 1991, pp. 58–63.

the safety and the effectiveness of new drugs have substantially delayed the approval of new drugs, reduced the number of new drugs introduced, increased the price of all drugs, and restricted the subsequent use of approved drugs.[10] The average time required to approve a new drug in the United States is about twice that required in Europe. The average cost to the drug companies per new drug approved is now about $250 million. FDA regulations on advertising and labeling have reduced the flow of information to physicians and consumers. Under pressure from AIDS activists, the FDA has allowed some drugs to be used before complete testing for effectiveness but only on an exceptional basis. Under pressure from the White House, the FDA has recently implemented several measures to reduce the time required to approve new drugs. Those recent changes indicate that the FDA has substantial flexibility under current law. The primary lesson here is that the new administration should appoint a sensible FDA administrator and maintain pressure on the FDA as part of a more general strategy to reduce the rapid inflation of the price medical care.

The Environment. The 800-pound gorilla in the mountain of social regulation, of course, is the Environmental Protection Agency (EPA). The total cost of environmental regulation is now about 3 percent of gross domestic product.[11] More important, the benefits of most recent environmental regulations appear to be substantially less than the costs. Most of the problems of environmental regulation are attributable to the major environmental laws and could not be substantially reduced without changing those laws. Congress, with the endorsement of most presidents from Nixon through Bush, has set progressively broader and tighter environmental standards and, in many cases, has prescribed the means of achieving those standards. The EPA has some discretion and should make use of better scientific information and risk assessment procedures, but the cost of environmental regulations will continue to increase unless the major laws are changed.

Some amount and type of regulation is the most efficient means of addressing many, maybe most, environmental concerns. In the

[10]Michael Ward, "The Overregulation of Legal Drugs," *Regulation*, Fall 1992.

[11]Dale Jorgenson and Peter Wilcoxen, "Environmental Regulation and U.S. Economic Growth," *RAND Journal of Economics*, Summer 1990, pp. 314–40.

absence of extensive property rights in air, water, migratory animals, and the like, most people treat those resources as a common pool. And, given the dispersion of both polluters and the population affected, tort law is not sufficient to address those concerns. A major reform of environmental laws, not a mindless proliferation of new laws and regulations based on insufficient scientific information and inadequate economic analysis, should be the goal of the new administration. That may be politically easier for a Democratic administration with a clear commitment to broadly shared environmental concerns. The major principles that should guide the reform, I suggest, are the following:

- Broaden property rights in the common-pool resources as much as possible. That is most likely to be effective when there is a small number of identifiable polluters and the effects are quite localized. In those cases, tort law can be an adequate means of social control.
- Do not set national standards to meet unusual local or regional concerns. Such standards are likely to be too high for most regions and too low for some regions.
- Do not set a standard if the scientific evidence is not clear. It is easier to set a standard later than to repeal a mistaken standard. That is most important for potentially very expensive measures, such as those to reduce global warming.
- Set standards at a level such that the expected *marginal* benefits equal the *marginal* costs, given the authorized means to meet the standard.
- In general, strengthen the scientific and economic bases for estimating risks and setting standards.

Public support for environmental measures will increase if citizens have a better sense that existing measures are effective and generate net benefits. For that reason, the new administration should appoint a credible environmental reformer, not an ideologue or an imperialist, as EPA administrator and make the case for a major reform of most existing environmental laws.

One set of environmental programs (not administered by the EPA) presents a special problem: endangered species,[12] wetlands,

[12]Robert J. Smith, "The Endangered Species Act: Saving Species or Stopping Growth?" *Regulation*, Winter 1992, pp. 83–87.

and historic properties. The benefits of those programs are diffused, but the costs are concentrated on the specific property owners whose rights of use have been expropriated by a regulatory taking. The costs of those programs should be paid from the general tax base, rather than by the current owners of the affected property. Moreover, our political system would make much better decisions on what species, wetlands, and properties to protect if the costs of acquiring the relevant easements were on the budget than if they are acquired by an uncompensated regulatory taking. And the current owners would have better incentives to maintain those characteristics of their property that are of general value to others if they faced potential compensation rather than expropriation. Those three programs have caused intense outrage among those who bear their costs, may be unconstitutional, and probably cannot be sustained. Those programs should also be candidates for careful review and substantial reform.

Reform of the Regulatory Process

For several years, Congress has weakened the White House regulatory review process. That partisan action was clearly shortsighted: a Democratic president would also want an effective and comprehensive review of new regulatory legislation and proposed new rules. Among the first actions of the new administration should be to appoint an able political official to head OIRA and to strengthen that office.

More recently, several proposals for reforming the regulatory information and review process have been considered. One proposal would create a regulatory budget similar to the fiscal budget. My judgment is that periodic estimates of the costs of regulation, rather like the estimates of tax expenditures, provide useful information, but that those estimates are too imprecise for a regulatory budget to be an effective instrument of cost control.

More promising is a proposal, considered by the Bush administration in 1992, to issue an executive order on risk assessment procedures. The current procedures for estimating the risks of potential carcinogens, for example, involve an extrapolation from the effects on rodents of very high doses to an estimate of the effects on humans of very low doses; there is reason to believe that current procedure overestimates risks by several orders of magnitude, and few of the estimated risks have been confirmed by epidemiological evidence.[13] A more accurate process of risk assessment could substantially reduce the number of toxins subject to regulation without any change in the legislated standards.

And third, a broad bipartisan coalition in Congress has recently endorsed a proposal to require an analysis of the economic impact of all new proposed regulatory legislation and proposed rules, authorizing any member of Congress to enforce the requirement by a point of order or any citizen to do so by a legal challenge.[14] That measure would probably slow the growth of new regulations, but it risks creating a paper mill. The major limitation of that approach is that it does not force a similar periodic analysis of the huge body of existing regulatory laws and regulations.

More promising than any identifiable change in the regulatory process would be a revival of the constitutional doctrines limiting restraints on interstate commerce, restrictions on private contracts, the uncompensated taking of property rights, and the undue delegation of policy decisions to regulatory agencies. Unfortunately, discussion of those more important and more complex issues must be postponed until another day.

[13]Richard B. Belzer, "The Peril and Promise of Risk Assessment," *Regulation*, Fall 1991, pp. 40–49.

[14]The Fiscal Accountability and Impact Reform (FAIR) Act, introduced in July 1992 by Rep. James P. Moran (D-Va.).

6. Government Regulation: The Real Crisis in Financial Services

Bert Ely

The savings-and-loan crisis has garnered enormous attention in recent years, as have problems in the banking and state-regulated insurance industries. Less attention has been focused on government regulation, which is common to and underlies the problems of those industries. Government regulation is the real crisis in financial services. An inherently flawed regulatory mechanism caused the S&L crisis and then magnified that crisis once it erupted. That same mode of regulation, which also has caused serious problems in banking and insurance, increasingly distorts the financial services marketplace.

This chapter will first discuss the increasingly evident and irreparable shortcomings of government regulation of financial services, notably safety-and-soundness regulation that seeks to prevent the failure of individual financial institutions. It will identify the many costs defective government regulation imposes on the economy and then present the standards that any sound regulatory mechanism for financial services must meet. The chapter will close by summarizing the 100 percent cross-guarantee concept for privatizing deposit insurance in a manner that meets those regulatory standards. The cross-guarantee concept is embodied in legislation Rep. Tom Petri (R-Wis.) introduced on September 30, 1992.

The S&L Crisis—Regulation Gone Amuck

The S&L crisis is the purest example of government regulation gone amuck. The roots of this crisis reach back to the 1930s, when federal deposit insurance was enacted. Federal policies of that era also encouraged S&Ls to begin funding their long-term, fixed-interest-rate home mortgages with short-term deposits. That "maturity mismatching" transformed S&Ls into very unsound financial institutions. Numerous regulatory strictures imposed on S&Ls during the postwar years made them more unsound. The most notorious of those impositions occurred in 1966 when the Federal Reserve's deposit interest rate controls were extended to S&Ls. By the late 1970s the S&L industry was a disaster waiting to happen.

Disaster struck in 1979 when the Fed, no longer able to keep the lid on interest rates, let them skyrocket. Overnight, Paul Volcker became a convert to monetarism. S&Ls collectively lost $9 billion in 1981 and 1982. High interest rates trimmed the value of S&L mortgage portfolios, driving the industry at least $100 billion under water. Unfortunately, in addition to bungling deregulation and failing to reform deposit insurance, the Reagan administration avoided addressing the S&L crisis.[1] It was not tackled until the beginning of the Bush administration.[2] By then, however, the groundwork had been laid for a legislative and regulatory overreaction to the S&L crisis that has proved the old adage that regulation is like a broken clock—it is almost always wrong. The only question is by how much.

Government Regulation Is the Underlying Problem

To date, the political process has tried to put the regulatory Humpty Dumpty back together by attempting to make regulation work better, primarily by giving regulators more power to micromanage banking and insurance firms. Regulatory micromanagement, however, will simply continue to burden America with a risky and inefficient financial services industry that increasingly resembles the totally discredited central planning practiced in the former Soviet Union and Eastern Europe. The time has come to bring perestroika to America's financial services industry.

Attempts to make established regulatory philosophies work more effectively will not succeed because the political process focuses on the consequences of faulty regulation rather than the real causes of problems in banking and insurance. Most public policy analysts

---

[1] Joe Stilwell, "The Savings and Loan Industry: Averting Collapse," Cato Institute Policy Analysis no. 7, February 15, 1982, provided one of the first warnings about the looming S&L crisis. Congress and the administration ignored that warning, as they did many others.

[2] Bert Ely and Vicki Vanderhoff, "Lessons Learned from the S&L Debacle: The Price of Failed Public Policy," Institute for Policy Innovation, February 1991, describes 16 different public policy failures that contributed to the S&L crisis. Nine of them predate 1979.

today are about as skilled in detecting the *causes* of problems that attract political attention as 18th-century physicians were in detecting the causes of diseases.

In sum, the underlying crisis, common to all financial institutions, is the predictable failure of the political micromanagement of marketplace activities. Sadly, that failure has not been recognized, even as its consequences are routinely decried. Instead, the political process, fearful of losing power over the marketplace, proceeds further and further up the blind alley of government regulation.

Why Financial Services Regulation Has Become Obsolete

Financial services regulation does not work as well as it once seemed to because electronic technology, specifically computers and modern telecommunications, has destroyed the efficacy of this form of regulation. Efficacious regulatory schemes work tolerably well only if three conditions are met.[3]

First, the technology and other external factors affecting a regulated industry must change very slowly because the political process that enacted the regulatory scheme adapts very slowly to change, primarily because change harms the status quo, which heavily influences the political process. The future, unfortunately, does not have its own political action committee. Electronic technology, of course, is rapidly altering the economics of providing financial services and threatening the existence of many types of firms, such as stock brokers, insurance agents, S&Ls, and real estate agents.

Second, the regulated industry must be easily isolated from the rest of the economy in order to avoid confusion about who shall be among the regulated. Technology, however, has permitted the unbundling of financial services transactions, such as home mortgages, so that various pieces of those transactions can just as easily be performed by an unregulated firm as by a regulated firm. In effect, unbundling has fuzzed the lines of demarcation between the highly regulated and the unregulated. The highly regulated, such as banks, S&Ls, and insurance companies, quickly lose market share to unregulated firms that skim off the more desirable pieces of the business, such as lending to low-risk borrowers.

---

[3] Bert Ely, "Technology, Regulation and the Financial Services Industry in the Year 2000," *Issues in Bank Regulation* 9, no. 3 (Fall 1988): 13–19.

Third, all firms operating under a particular regulatory regime must be relatively homogenous so that all can reasonably expect to make an acceptable rate of return on their equity capital. As a result, firms in a regulated industry tend to have similar operating styles because all participants must adapt to the same regulatory scheme. But because homogeneous operating styles do not serve all segments of a market equally well, unregulated firms differentiate themselves in order to compete successfully against regulated firms. Regulated firms respond by trying to act as much like unregulated firms as they can, specifically by attempting to match the specialization and differentiation of their unregulated counterparts. Regulatory strictures, though, chafe badly in this environment, and one size no longer fits all, or even a few.

Regulatory invasions also set off regulatory turf wars. For example, the Securities and Exchange Commission (SEC) and the bank regulatory agencies have battled recently over mark-to-market (MTM) accounting. The SEC favors MTM for publicly held banks and thrifts. All four bank and thrift regulatory agencies, however, vigorously oppose MTM, as much because they are aggressively fighting the SEC's attempt to intrude onto their long-held regulatory turf as for substantive reasons. Of course, the existence of four bank and thrift regulatory agencies, when one agency would do, further impairs the efficiency and therefore the competitiveness of banks and thrifts.

Regulatory turf battles, as well as parallel turf battles among regulated industries, reflect the underlying war—the titanic struggle between the political process and the marketplace for control over the financial services industry and the flow of capital in the economy. The amount at stake is significant: at the end of 1991 the nation's private-sector financial institutions held almost $13 trillion in assets,[4] more than twice the nation's annual gross domestic product (GDP). Contrary to trends elsewhere in the world, particularly in the former communist countries and the Third World, the political process in the United States is steadily gaining power over the financial services industry at the expense of the marketplace.

[4] "Balance Sheets for the U.S. Economy, 1960–91," Board of Governors of the Federal Reserve System, September 28, 1992, p. 35.

Government Regulation Is Very Expensive for the Economy

Federal and state regulation of financial services, specifically banking and insurance, has been very expensive for the American economy for five reasons. These reasons go beyond the $200 billion cost to taxpayers (on a present-value basis) of the S&L crisis. They include the cost of failures of financial institutions, the cost of distorting the financial market's allocation of credit, regulatory protections for obsolete firms, regulatory arbitrage that promotes less efficient funds intermediation, and unintended and difficult-to-measure consequences for the entire economy caused by regulatory micromanagement of some financial service providers.

First, the total cost of failures of financial institutions since 1981, when the S&L crisis really kicked off, approaches $300 billion. That amount includes not only the taxpayer cost of the S&L crisis, but also the cost of insolvency losses to surviving banks and thrifts (which they have paid for through higher deposit insurance assessments) and the capital of failed banks and thrifts wiped out by losses prior to the failure of those institutions. The $300 billion sum equals about 5 percent of current GDP. It also equals the nation's net investment in fixed assets for 1990 and 1991 combined.[5]

Second, government regulation of financial institutions has greatly distorted the credit allocation process. The regulatory process causes suboptimal investing funded partially (or in some cases entirely) by loans made by banks, thrifts, and insurance companies. Consequently, the nation's inadequate savings are not being put to their most productive use. The Congressional Budget Office has estimated that the S&L crisis caused $500 billion in lost GDP, measured in 1990 dollars.[6] "The chief impact of the [S&L] crisis was to waste or misallocate billions of dollars of savings that would otherwise have been invested in [more productive] assets."[7] The overbuilding of commercial real estate in recent years is the best visual evidence of that waste.

[5] Net investment equals gross fixed investment in those years in residential and nonresidential structures and producers' durable equipment minus consumption of fixed capital, as estimated by the Bureau of Economic Analysis, U.S. Department of Commerce.

[6] "The Economic Effects of the Savings and Loan Crisis," Congressional Budget Office, January 1992, p. 35.

[7] Ibid., pp. 30–31.

Government Regulation Causes Underpriced Credit

For the following reasons, the interaction of the first two reasons causes credit to be underpriced, which not only leads to credit misallocations, but in extreme cases helps inflate speculative asset bubbles that inevitably burst.

Federal deposit insurance protects depositors in banks and thrifts while state guaranty funds protect those insured by insurance companies. Losses incurred in protecting depositors and insureds are assessed against surviving firms on a nonactuarial basis years after the actions that caused the losses were undertaken. Consequently, under the present insurance and guaranty schemes, *potential* losses from bad lending and investing decisions are not charged against the persons who make bad decisions at the time they make them. The future cost of bad decisions is therefore *not* incorporated in the interest rate charged for those loans or in the yield sought from those investments. The same analysis holds true for the protection given to customers of securities broker-dealers by a government-chartered corporation, the Securities Investor Protection Corporation.

In effect, credit offered by banks, thrifts, and insurers often is underpriced, sometimes significantly so, because it does not incorporate the cost of the option depositors and insureds have on the capital of others should their bank, thrift, or insurer fail. Regulatory micromanagement, such as limits on loans to any one borrower or prohibitions on certain types of investments, attempt to minimize such losses. But the events of the 1980s demonstrate that regulatory micromanagement cannot prevent them.

Underpriced credit inflates speculative bubbles because potential returns on the speculation, such as in the stock market or real estate, look very promising relative to the price of the borrowing used to help fund the speculative investment. Eventually, though, some event bursts the bubble. Bursting bubbles cause severe asset deflations that dramatically increase the failure rate of highly leveraged lenders, such as banks, thrifts, and life insurers. Asset deflations also increase the leverage ratio of the owners of those assets, often at a time when the cash flow they need to service their debts is shrinking.

In a deflationary environment, many economic actors quickly become focused on reducing their debts in order to get their balance sheets and debt service burdens back to normal. During the adjustment process, which can take several years, those businesses and individuals curtail their demand for goods and services, especially durable goods and investments largely funded by new debt. A prolonged recession, such as America is now experiencing, is the unavoidable consequence.[8] Government regulation clearly is a primary cause of the current recession.

Regulation Impedes Financial Services Productivity

Using the regulatory process to protect entrenched and often obsolete businesses is the third reason the regulatory process has become costly for this country. Often, the political-regulatory process has been used to bar or distort technologies, usually to prevent the melding of different types of financial services activities that technology has made economically feasible. For example, there is no defensible reason why many forms of life, property, and casualty insurance cannot be sold to consumers by banks and thrifts, yet present law substantially restricts such integrated marketing. Industry turf wars, over things such as the extent to which banks and thrifts can engage in insurance or real estate brokerage, employ scores of high-priced lawyers and consultants. Those turf wars parallel the ones constantly being waged by the regulatory agencies.

The regulatory process also encourages substantial regulatory arbitrage that further impairs the efficiency of financial intermediation. That is the fourth way in which financial services regulation has become very expensive for America.

Regulatory arbitrage occurs when the marketplace shifts funds intermediation from highly taxed and regulated intermediaries, such as depository institutions, to less taxed and regulated channels of intermediation, such as money market funds, the commercial paper market, asset securitization, government-sponsored enterprises, and the like. In effect, regulatory arbitrage distorts the intermediation process in the same way that tax shelters distorted real estate investing prior to the 1986 Tax Act.

---

[8]The purest and most easily documented example of a speculative bubble, and its deflationary aftermath, is the American farm crisis of the early 1980s. Bert Ely and Vicki Vanderhoff, "The Farm Credit System: Reckless Lender to Rural America," Ely & Company, Inc., November 1990, presents one analysis of that crisis.

In many cases the less taxed and less regulated channels of inter-mediation are less efficient (in terms of real resource consumption) than the more heavily taxed and regulated channels of intermediation. Depository intermediation is more efficient in most cases because the process of shifting the funding of financial assets from depository institutions to less taxed and regulated channels of inter-mediation involves a second round of underwriting and administrative costs.[9]

Some data reinforce that point. The percentage of the total U.S. workforce employed in banking, finance, and insurance has doubled since the end of World War II. The percentage of GDP needed to finance and insure the tangible assets of the economy (reproducible assets plus privately owned land) also has doubled since the end of that war.[10]

Finally, other unintended consequences of the increased regulatory micromanagement of the banking and insurance industries harm the economy in ways that are hard to quantify. Because credit flows lubricate the entire economy, the importance of those two industries is far greater than their direct contribution to GDP. In particular, regulation drives away good management; after all, why would a talented manager want to work in an industry in which the regulatory process increasingly constrains managerial discretion, often irrationally? Hence, a very important sector of the economy is steadily losing good judgment, at great cost to the overall economy and to the American people.

Why Such Harmful Regulation Exists

Why regulate financial services firms if the outcomes are so bad? Historically, proponents have suggested several reasons.

First, governments learned long before Willie Sutton was born that banks are where the money is. Consequently, governments have long used banks as a means to finance government debt, both by forcing banks to buy government bonds and by using banks to sell government debt to the general public. For example, the British

---

[9] Bert Ely, "Commercial Banks Are Not Obsolete—And the Federal Government Should Stop Trying to Make Them So," Paper presented at the 28th Annual Conference on Bank Structure and Competition, Federal Reserve Bank of Chicago, May 7, 1992. To be published in the proceedings of the conference.

[10] Ibid.

government initially gave the Bank of England a banking monopoly in exchange for the bank's owning and underwriting government debt to help finance the Crown's periodic wars.[11]

Second, governments have used regulation to protect favored interests. Restricting entry to regulated lines of business is a key way in which regulation protects established firms from new competitors. The protected usually reciprocate with substantial political contributions to legislators whose votes support the protection.

Third, there is broad public support for preventing banks, thrifts, and insurers from failing in order to protect depositors and insureds from losses arising from such failures.

Fourth, government regulation provides a tool for manipulating the economy, specifically for controlling the money supply and allocating credit to borrowers perceived by the political process as "socially desirable."

Is Any Regulation Necessary?

Some will argue that all forms of financial services regulation are unnecessary; therefore, the present regulatory structures should simply be blown away. That is an enticing thought as the American economy continues to suffer from a regulatory overreaction induced by the federal government's failed regulation of the S&L industry. Clearly, many aspects of financial services regulation serve no legitimate purpose and should be abolished. However, some forms of regulation have proven socially desirable and economically justifiable over time. For example, one can defend a system of honest weights and measures and fair and full disclosure, such as truth-in-lending and truth-in-savings regulations, if reasonably applied.

More contention arises over the question of the extent to which, if at all, the political process should attempt to protect the principal and accrued interest of depositors and the prepaid premiums, cash values, and policy claims of insureds. Some argue for "depositor discipline"—that individual depositors and insureds should assess the financial condition of their banks, thrifts, and insurance companies and suffer the consequences if they place funds in an institution that later goes belly up.

---

[11]Bert Ely, "Repeal of Glass-Steagall and Ending the Separation of Banking and Commerce," Testimony before the Subcommittee on Technology and Finance of the House Committee on Energy and Commerce, July 10, 1991, p. 9.

Depositor discipline is not desirable, though, for two reasons. First, relying primarily on depositor discipline will not permit depository institutions to strike an optimal balance between balance sheet leverage (the ratio of an institution's assets to its capital) and stability within the financial system. Increased leverage permits all types of financial intermediaries, not just banks and thrifts, to pass funds from sources to uses at less cost. However, higher leverage increases the likelihood that depositors and others with incomplete information will incorrectly assess the financial condition of the institution. Incorrect assessments, or "false negatives," will lead to financial instability, specifically runs on solvent banks and thrifts. Bank runs are costly because they destroy marketplace franchises in which depository institutions have invested lots of money. That destruction represents real economic waste.

Second, the political process will quickly short-circuit depositor discipline if that discipline leads to costly financial instability. Political intervention to stabilize a financial system is sound economically even though the regulatory structure that creates the need for such intervention is indefensible. To not intervene once a crisis erupts would be tantamount to destroying the economy in order to save it. Fortunately, that notion died in Vietnam. Consequently, the implicit federal policy assumption that big banks and thrifts and other types of large financial firms are "too big to fail" (TBTF) is defensible on economic grounds.[12]

The problem with TBTF is that the existing, highly politicized regulatory process too easily lets individual firms reach the point where taxpayer funds must be used to protect depositors or insureds from a loss in order to maintain financial stability. Successful firms usually are the first parties taxed to provide that protection; in an extreme case, such as the S&L crisis, the general taxpayer is tapped to provide protection. The cross-guarantee system discussed below will eliminate the need for crisis-driven political interventions because financial instability triggering such intervention will never occur.

[12]Bert Ely, "Abandoning Too-Big-to-Fail: The Impossible Dream," Testimony to the Subcommittee on Economic Stabilization of the House Committee on Banking, Finance and Urban Affairs, May 9, 1991.

Standards for Justifiable Regulation

Hence, the big question: how to regulate in an economically sound manner? Simply prescribing more of the same, that is, more intense regulatory micromanagement, clearly is not the answer.

The appropriate regulatory mechanism for any type of financial services provider should focus only on legitimate public policy objectives. Economic manipulation or the protection or enrichment of favored interests are not legitimate objectives for a regulatory process armed with the might of the law. By contrast, the following are legitimate public policy objectives for the financial system.

- A stable financial system that works smoothly, efficiently, and without disruption by protecting depositors and insureds against losses arising out of the failure of individual financial firms.
- A safe financial system in which insolvent firms can be disposed of without triggering a financial crisis.
- Private capital voluntarily placed at risk bears all losses incurred in protecting the depositors and insureds of failed financial firms.
- Honest delivery of financial services.

Privatizing Deposit Insurance through 100 Percent Cross-Guarantees

The public policy challenge for several centuries has been to develop a *market-driven* alternative to heavy-handed government regulation of financial institutions that will meet the above objectives. The 100 percent cross-guarantee concept meets all four objectives while freeing the financial system, or at least banks and thrifts, from increasingly politicized regulatory micromanagement. The cross-guarantee concept is based on the notion that less regulation of the right kind is far better for society than more regulation of the wrong kind.

The cross-guarantee concept, as applied to banks and thrifts, is incorporated in legislation Rep. Tom Petri introduced on September 30, 1992.[13] That bill, the Taxpayer Protection, Deposit Insurance Reform, and Regulatory Relief Act of 1992 (H.R. 6069), meets the

---

[13]The legislation is summarized in Thomas E. Petri and Bert Ely, "Real Taxpayer Protection: Sound Deposit Insurance through Cross-Guarantees," Heritage Foundation *Policy Review*, Spring 1992, pp. 25–29.

objectives cited above by creating a marketplace that will protect depositors more efficiently than can government regulation.

The Petri bill will create a marketplace in which each bank and thrift will have to seek a cross-guarantee contract that will protect *all* of its deposits and most of its other liabilities and commitments against any loss or failure to perform should the institution become insolvent. Qualified parties will voluntarily provide the guarantees called for in those contracts in exchange for a risk-based premium. The guarantors can be other banks and thrifts, general business corporations, insurers, endowment and pension funds, and even very wealthy individuals.

Each bank and thrift will recruit a syndicate of guarantors from a large pool of guarantors that meet certain statutory requirements. The terms of each cross-guarantee contract will be negotiated solely by the guaranteed institution and its guarantors. Key terms of contracts will include the formula according to which the risk-based premium will be calculated and the safety-and-soundness standards that will be applicable to the bank or thrift. Market-driven premiums, based on leading indicators of banking risk, will deter unwise lending that feeds speculative bubbles that inevitably burst.

No longer will depository institutions be subject to one-size-must-fit-all government regulation; instead, the marketplace will tailor safety-and-soundness requirements to the operating style of individual institutions. The tailoring process will permit banks and thrifts to specialize and thereby compete more effectively against firms that currently are less regulated.

The Petri bill creates a regulatory mechanism for the cross-guarantee marketplace, but the mechanism focuses on the ends or objectives of the process, not on how those ends are met. Specifically, the bill establishes certain requirements for each cross-guarantee contract and further requires that each contract be approved by a federal agency before it takes effect. Key statutory requirements each contract must meet include protecting all deposits and most other liabilities of the guaranteed institution, mandating certain "stop loss" limits that will spread large or catastrophic losses widely but thinly over the capital of many guarantors, requiring that each guarantor who is not a guaranteed bank or thrift have a net worth of at least $100 million, and establishing specific risk-dispersion requirements for each contract and each guarantor. In addition, no cross-guarantee can be canceled or allowed to expire unless a replacement contract has been obtained.

The Petri bill bars the government from objecting to any contract provision dealing with the pricing of cross-guarantees, safety-and-soundness requirements imposed by guarantors, or the conditions under which a bank's or thrift's cross-guarantee syndicate can assume control of the institution. In other words, the government's say over contract terms will not extend beyond what is specifically required by statute.

The cross-guarantee concept, and especially its stop-loss feature, eliminates all taxpayer risk from deposit insurance. However, because depositors have come to rely on federal deposit insurance, the Petri bill retains the federal government as a backup insurer for deposits up to the present limit of $100,000. The cross-guarantee system, though, will be so strong that any economic catastrophe that bankrupted the system would already have caused our increasingly indebted federal government to default on its obligations.

Two other features of the Petri bill warrant special mention. First, the bill is a "narrow bill" in that it reforms only deposit insurance. It does not address other aspects of banking regulation that restrict competition or impose unwarranted inefficiencies on banking, such as branching restrictions and the separation of investment from commercial banking. Those issues can be dealt with more easily once deposit insurance has been privatized.

Second, while the Petri bill addresses only federal deposit insurance for banks and thrifts, the cross-guarantee concept is applicable to any type of financial intermediary operating in any market economy in which contracts are readily enforceable. Hence, it will be relatively easy to extend the cross-guarantee concept to the securities and insurance industries as well as to the financial systems of other countries.

Conclusion

Government regulation of banks and thrifts has caused great harm to the American economy, most recently by fostering several speculative bubbles whose bursting has saddled our economy with painful asset deflation and a sluggish recovery. Increased regulatory micromanagement only makes matters worse by employing an increasing number of bureaucrats to override the marketplace.

Congress must make a dramatic U-turn by enacting 100 percent cross-guarantees to privatize deposit insurance and all of the regulatory apparatus than now encrusts the nation's banking system. Only then will America begin to enjoy a safe, efficient, and stable financial system.

7. Telecommunications: Starting the Next Century Early

Thomas W. Hazlett

Every candidate endorses apple pie and the American flag. But just suppose one party also worked quietly to organize a flag cartel, making flags far too expensive for average patriotic Americans, and another had arranged to impose production quotas on apples, seriously restricting the U.S. consumer's ability to enjoy a Golden Delicious—fresh, baked, or sauced. Would you be shocked? Not you, you sophisticated yet streetwise analyst of the Pennsylvania Avenue power corridor.

As coincidence would have it, every candidate is solidly in favor of improving America's telecommunications infrastructure. It's apple pie with a little flag stuck in the middle. Atari Democrats cheer high-tech solutions to America's problems of jobs, education, health care, and the environment; Republicans rally to endorse the promise of private-sector dynamism, the wave of economic development that a new generation of capitalist research and development will deliver. But established interests have displayed an aptitude for driving America's telecommunications future in a quietly reckless way, blocking traffic and impeding tremendous new sources of consumer-pleasing innovation. The new administration can strike a delightful blow for consumer sovereignty by peeling away the anti-competitive restrictions that have been so artfully placed in the way of consumers' dialing around the telecommunications marketplace.

If there is any sector of the U.S. economy that should give progressive thinkers hope for the future, it is assuredly telecommunications—a broad infrastructure industry dominated by breathtaking advances in computing technology, globally propelled by innovative American firms. There is much ground for optimism. Moreover, the divestiture of the world's largest private company, American Telephone & Telegraph, in the dramatic 1984 federal consent decree settling *U.S. v. Western Electric,* has proven that regulators can, in fact, ambitiously create workably competitive market structures to replace creaky (and leaky) monopolistic ones.

The success of the U.S. telecom sector in leading the world into new services and greater efficiency should burn a nice little warm spot into the hearts of pro-consumer regulators everywhere. Indeed, the recent results of the McKinsey Global Institute's worldwide study on comparative economic productivity revealed two facts that startled even the research group's own team: (1) The U.S. economy leads Germany and Japan by about 20 percent each in productivity per worker per hour. (2) That lead is primarily accounted for by American superiority in important service industries such as retailing and telecommunications.[1]

The importance of telecommunications in the global competitiveness race is beyond doubt. While protection of old-line manufacturing industries is a favorite project of the populists, the results of the McKinsey research indicate precisely the opposite course to be America's appropriate national economic strategy. America's productivity lead over Germany actually widened in the 1980s, that study finds, because of great advances stimulated by the deregulation of key U.S. sectors—in particular, telecommunications. The more competitive U.S. telephone industry, for instance, achieves double the productivity per worker of the German telephone monopoly. What prompts even greater enthusiasm for the success of American regulatory liberalization is that the service sector in general and the telecommunications sector in particular are, by every estimate, becoming more central to the overall functioning of all market economies. Advances in telecom productivity, new services for U.S. business and consumers, and progressively falling rates will stimulate greater efficiencies not only in consumer communications services but in retailing, basic research, education, health care and, yes, even manufacturing.

Relying on central planning to pick economic winners is fraught with danger, as every serious student understands. What is fundamental to the challenges posed in the telecom sector, however, is

---

[1]See Sylvia Nasar, "U.S. Rate of Output Called Best," *New York Times,* October 13, 1992, p. D1.

that the growth of American entrepreneurship is absolutely dependent on increases in the ability of the economy to respond quickly and accurately to new information. Telecommunications is the highway upon which such information travels. Despite notable American successes in allowing new drivers to scale the on-ramp to this highway, many large obstacles remain if the economy is to travel at cruising speed. Those potholes on the telecommunications roadway may be technically removed with great ease; it is the political forces favoring the status quo that block our highway crews. Overcoming such inertia is the definition of leadership.

Blurry Vision

There are, by formal mathematical proof, an unlimited number of detailed, compelling, even internally consistent "visions for America's telecommunications future." All of those plans appear splendid prior to implementation. And they have one extra special feature: by the time they make a historical splat, the system designers will have long since moved on to public fame and political fortune.

My advice to America's telecommunications planners is to measure history carefully. The evidence underlines the inescapable limitations of deducing future consumer demands or technical breakthroughs from the foggy confines of the present. Vision? Only through a very blurry window.

Fortunately, the rough edges of history more sharply detail where the policy infrastructure can be laid to induce market innovation. Attendant to economic progress are a set of basic rules to order and motivate socially desirable behavior, namely lively marketplace competition and consumer-appetizing technical change. Our present institutions have great difficulty in settling on those fundamental preconditions for economic success, not only because they are fuzzy about achieving them in their own right, but also because our regulatory system is preoccupied with old questions about how special considerations are dispensed. That is the familiar bias of pork-barrel politics.

What a shame. By every account, the U.S. economy now floats upon the first ripples of a huge wave of telecommunications inventiveness. Thanks to the astoundingly rapid decline in the cost of computational intelligence, technical advances in high-speed, high-quality, digital transmission are swamping the old constraints on electronic communications. American firms, in particular, are pioneering airwave and wireline compression techniques that stand to revolutionize the way we use the telephone, cellular telephone, television, and radio networks of today.

Personal communications services (PCS) technology alone promises to compete with cellular phones in the immediate future (2 to 5 years), driving down wireless phone talk-time charges and driving penetration up 5- to 10-fold, and to challenge even our ubiquitous wireline telephone network (supplied primarily by local exchange companies) in the medium to long run (10 to 25 years). The possibilities for PCS suppliers to compete in paging, messaging, and data transmission (with both wireless modems and wireless faxes) are vast.

The delightful new service applications—from medical devices that could monitor an outpatient's heart functions with a wireless link to a local hospital computer, to anti-theft devices that might track your car-jacked automobile—are limited only by the human imagination.

And good ol' American technologists will create and build the systems, attachments, and software that control such gizmos. They will reduce the cost of wireless telecommunications, rationalize telephone network messaging, provide tremendous consumer benefits, and slash the business operations expenses of U.S. corporations. There are currently over 100 American companies experimenting with PCS on temporary licenses granted by the Federal Communications Commission. They are chomping at the bit to employ some famous Yankee ingenuity to work a little creative destruction in the telecom sector.

But here's the rub: not a net nickel's worth of consumer satisfaction nor a penny's of U.S. business efficiency drops from the PCS technology unless the federal government allows entrepreneurs access to the full-fledged spectrum rights necessary to deliver wireless services. And it looks like the administrative task—the easy, no-brain part of the digital communications revolution—will take years and years. The granting of new licenses will be "process intense," as incumbent suppliers resist challenges to the status quo and rival interest groups squabble over how new entry rights are to be divvied up.

What becomes painfully apparent, as telecommunications policy speeds towards the 21st century, is that traditional structures of

19th-century public utility regulation and early 20th-century broadcast spectrum licensing are increasingly ill-suited for our public purposes. There has been widespread recognition of that historical dilemma, not only within the academic literature. The entire theory of the federal government's 1974 antitrust suit against AT&T, and of the 1984 modified final judgment, which it eventually became, was that the contours separating regulated monopoly from regulated competition from unregulated competition were in the midst of glacial shift. In pulling one part of the old Ma Bell (long-distance service) out of the franchised monopoly into semiregulated competition, and yanking another part (telephone equipment) all the way over to, virtually, laissez faire, the government left only one part (local telephone service) that resembled a traditional public utility. The government graphically demonstrated the declining importance of textbook regulatory structures in today's world.[2]

Elsewhere, we have been neither so focused nor so observant. Particularly in our management of the electromagnetic communications spectrum—where a 1920s licensing program still reigns supreme—we have pointedly failed to move with the times. Take, for instance, current U.S. policy toward high-definition television (HDTV).

In 1992 the FCC sought to establish its long-range vision of what it hopes and assumes will be the next generation of television transmission technology. The commission established a 16-year change-out of our old TV sets and broadcasting facilities, the ones we now use to send and receive TV signals, and upgrade to a new HDTV standard with much higher resolution (and hence picture clarity). The first step on that ambitious road to enhanced home viewing is for the FCC to select one HDTV standard from the several now being considered by a federal advisory commission. That is scheduled to happen sometime in 1993. The plan then calls for U.S. very high frequency (VHF) and ultra high frequency (UHF)

---

[2] I do not mean to imply that the modified final judgment ended the discussion about where appropriate lines should be drawn between competition and monopoly, regulation and deregulation. I mean only that the government's position in *U.S. v. Western Electric et al.* underlined the common inapplicability of old-style rate-of-return regulation. (This point was soon seconded by the FCC, which began introducing price caps in place of rate of return.) On problems associated with the divestiture and its regulatory aftermath, see Gerald Faulhauber, *Telecommunications in Turmoil* (Cambridge, Mass.: MIT Press, 1987).

TV broadcasters to receive an additional 6-MHz bandwidth (duplicating their current allocation) in which to simulcast their present broadcasts in high definition. (It is presumed that an old TV set will be unable to receive the new HDTV signals, although converters will probably be available.) Broadcasters will be required to phase in their HDTV programming schedule, between 1996 and 2003, or risk losing their licenses altogether. Dual broadcasts will be required, so as to not abandon viewers who have old TV sets, until the year 2008. At that time, the change-out should have been completed, and broadcasters will be required to give back the TV signals they currently use.

Sounds a little risky. Here's why. First, no one knows what the consumer demand for HDTV will be. The consensus view is that a high-definition picture looks superb—crystal clear, bright and lively—but only on relatively large screens, say four feet by six feet. On conventionally sized television receivers, the picture improvement is minor. Essentially, the HDTV leap forward necessitates a major consumer investment in complementary inputs: a wall unit sufficiently large to display HDTV's superior picture quality *and* a viewing room sufficiently spacious to comfortably accommodate such a screen. A household that prefers to watch small- to medium-sized monitors in small- to medium-sized rooms is not likely to demonstrate a pronounced demand for the new service. Given that the price of a large-screen HDTV receiver may well be 10 times that of a 25-inch set (we don't know what the price premium will be for HDTV wall units because they are not currently in mass production), many, most, or even the great majority of U.S. households may reap no daily viewing benefits from this new investment.

Second, the opportunity cost to millions of consumers who refuse to make expensive new complementary capital investments is significant, even if placed in the shadows by the regulatory process: broadcasting HDTV signals effectively blocks out scores of alternative viewing choices. The U.S. high-definition standard will ironically be an excellent one; because the United States was unable to match the aggressive approach taken by the Japanese, who got out in front of the competition with an early standard, the American HDTV signal is likely to be digital, not analog. Digital transmission affords great advantages, the foremost of which is the possibility of easily manipulating data to more efficiently use any given bandwidth. Engineers now estimate that perhaps 10 to 20 current channels could be broadcast over a single 6-MHz band using digital compression techniques. The 1993 HDTV signal, in contrast, will almost certainly hog the entire 6 MHz for a single channel of programming. The tradeoff arises: would consumers rather get one super-duper picture on their wall units or 10 to 20 channels of existing-quality broadcasts to enhance their video selection and drive down cable TV subscription prices?[3]

The FCC's current policy regime presumes it can answer that question today, and pretty much cover all contingencies through the year 2008. Nancy Reagan's astrologer would be impressed. The initiative does include some steps to evaluate trends and change policy accordingly, but the regulations themselves have the practical political effect of making it unlikely that any midcourse corrections will be made. Most pointedly, the rules essentially *mandate* that television licensees use a particular broadcast technology. Not only will the producers of that technology have a vested interest in the mandate proceeding, regulators will come to identify enforcement of the rules with the public interest (and loosening of the rules as a capitulation to corporate interests—which it would be, in that the only interests with sufficient information and incentive to lobby for change are firms with a financial stake in the outcome).

In any event, the FCC gods must be crazy. The escape valve that reliably adjusts to changing conditions and the arrival of new information is market competition. Here, that avenue of adjustment is blocked off. The federal government, so often condemned for its short-sightedness, is certainly looking to the very long run, laying out a 16-year transition to a new technology at a time when virtually all the information that is important for determining whether such a plan is in the public interest is unknown. Just how

---

[3]George Gilder makes a convincing argument that the HDTV format is already being made obsolete by rapid advances in television interactivity. To Gilder, the TV set of tomorrow will be a fast-moving two-way street, which HDTV (with its very large information requirements) will only slow down. He argues that receiving prettier pictures will be very low on the consumer's list of priorities. He may be right, for all the FCC knows. If so, U.S. consumers would be leapfrogged by technology, chained to an outmoded infrastructure by government policy. See George Gilder, *Life after Television* (New York: Norton, 1992).

unknown is mind-boggling. Think about the time frame: 16 years. And invert it.

It was in 1976—16 years *ago*—that the glue was drying on the first Apple computer in Steve Jobs's garage. Within the space of 16 years the personal computer was invented and produced, spread into every nook and cranny of the modern economy, and grew into the megaindustry that it is today. Innovation, it seems, moves at the computational rate of a 486 chip. PCs were word processors, learning devices, video games, and business tools—and suddenly, when linked with one another, they became high-capacity networks substituting for the mainframes of just . . . 16 years ago. How could that winding pathway of creativity, trial, error, invention, acceptance, dominance, and displacement have possibly been predicted?

Question: what if, in 1976, the foresight of FCC planners had been put to the task of mapping out the 16-year change-out from mainframe to PC? And yes, it is cheating to type your answer on a Toshiba notebook!

As the world advances, so should our communications standards. Ossified government regulation, nestling so comfortably into yesteryear's standards, is a drag on social momentum. The marketplace, when rules are well defined and investments well protected, harbors no such sentimental attachment to the status quo. TV broadcasters are far more likely to cater to consumer preferences if the government allows them flexibility about which broadcast standard to select than if they are tied to the government's best guess of some 16 years earlier.

One would think that the debacles of past FCC plans would serve as neon warning lights. The 1952 FCC television allocation table included room for a vast amount of UHF television transmission: channels 14–82. That 420-MHz tract, which served only trivial viewing shares over the following decades, ate up a Texas-sized swath of the radio dial. And it was in a burst of futuristic zeal in the early 1980s that the commission set aside a healthy band for the provision of direct broadcast satellite; that advertised competitive challenge to cable television's multichannel video monopoly has yet to emerge, but it has succeeded in depriving other proven technologies, such as wireless cable, of critical channel capacity. Such gargantuan gambles with the public's telecommunications interests are likely to be bad bets. Still, the political interests love to spin that wheel.

What to Do

If the essential problem of regulation is that it is an inflexible tool that affixes leg weights to a dynamic society, the best telecom reform would be to unleash private players to compete without asking permission. The very process of permitting, of directing all new entrants to request a special license to compete, creates a haven for incumbent protectionism and sounds the death knell for Schumpeterian competition. The burden of proof should be shifted from those who dare to risk their capital on the untried to those who enjoy the status quo. The movement of federal regulation away from monopoly protection in wireline telecommunications toward open network architecture is an attempt to do just that. The most important step now awaiting us is to free access to the electromagnetic spectrum—our vital "invisible resource."[4]

That crucial mandate can best be pursued via license flexibility. When the FCC grants a license to a private user, be it an AM radio broadcaster, a point-to-point microwave service, a cellular telephone company, or whatnot, that license is very specific about what frequency space the user is able to occupy. Such licensing rules are fundamental to the orderly functioning of the telecommunications sector.[5] While policymakers at the FCC and the National Telecommunications and Information Administration are well informed about the critical nature of a regime of noninterfering property rights, they are also aware that the extreme additional

[4]This term was coined by the late Harvey Levin in *The Invisible Resource* (Washington: Resources for the Future, 1971).

[5]It is not necessary that license assignments be made through comparative hearings or lotteries, as is current FCC practice. The essential point is that exclusive rights must be established to resources, competing uses of which are mutually exclusive. Else, a "tragedy of the commons" ensues. Rights could be assigned in ways other than "public interest" licensing. For instance, Coase details how the most straightforward means of assigning property rights would be by auctions. Ronald Coase, "The Federal Communications Commission," *Journal of Law & Economics* 2 (October 1959): 1–40. The author has shown that broadcast spectrum rights were first awarded in the United States via homesteading rules of common law, or "priority in use." Thomas W. Hazlett, "The Rationality of U.S. Regulation of the Broadcast Spectrum," *Journal of Law & Economics* 33 (April 1990): 133–75.

regulatory constraints attached to licensees inhibit the realization of all but a tiny fraction of the social benefits of the invisible resource. The FCC manages the spectrum by performing two broad functions. First, it engages in a zoning process that separates various bands along the dial, determining what types of services can be provided over a particular frequency range. That is commonly referred to as the *allocation* process. Once parcels have been zoned for distinct types of service, the commission must then award them to the licensees who will actually use the spectrum. That is called *assignment*.[6]

It is curious that both economists and the popular press have been critical of FCC policy with regard to assignment and almost wholly silent on allocation. For instance, the federal giveaway of free cellular telephone licenses by lottery has received some comment in newspapers and magazines, although considering the dollar amounts involved, the publicity seems quite modest.[7] Economists have focused very narrowly on auctions, however, concentrating much theoretical discussion on how the government may obtain the highest payments for spectrum rights.[8]

Both quarters have missed the fundamental flaw in spectrum allocation. Far more important to consumers and U.S. competitiveness than how the government squanders spectrum license revenues is the ability of upstart entrepreneurs with innovative technologies to gain access to the telecommunications market in the first

[6]For a thorough description of the technicalities of FCC spectrum regulation, see John O. Robinson, "Spectrum Management Policy in the United States: An Historical Account," FCC, Office of Plans and Policy, Working Paper no. 15, April 1985.

[7]In 1991 the NTIA placed the sales value of urban cellular licenses at $79.9 billion. National Telecommunications and Information Administration, "U.S. Spectrum Management Policy: Agenda for the Future," U.S. Department of Commerce, NTIA Special Publication 91–23, February 1991, p. D-5. Those licenses grant broadcast coverage of about 80 percent of the U.S. population. Instead of selling licenses, however, Congress constrained the FCC (which had been denied its request to auction licenses) to dispensing those assets via comparative hearings or lotteries. The commission chose the latter and conducted lotteries for all but 30 of the 733 markets licensed between 1984 and 1989. License values increased dramatically after the FCC issued the licenses, however, so it is not likely that the federal government would have reaped the entire $80 billion to $100 billion (including rural areas) implied by the above estimates. A very conservative estimate of the aggregate license values would assume $20 per capita, or $5 billion nationally. Thomas W. Hazlett and Robert J. Michaels, "The Cost of Rent-Seeking: Evidence from Cellular Telephone License Lotteries," *Southern Economic Journal*, January 1993.

[8]A very good analysis of this issue is found in Congressional Budget Office, "Auctioning Radio Spectrum Licenses," March 1992.

place. The spectrum bottleneck created by the FCC's Soviet-style command and control licensing methods severely constrains the realm within which America's leading high-tech providers can use their talent and ingenuity to experiment and grow. The rigid limitations on licenses implanted during the allocation process, wherein government planners dictate exactly what services can be provided via which technology using what standards, strangle new, marginal players who have an abundance of ideas but a paucity of spectrum space.

The main goal of spectrum management should be, not to protect incumbent telecom providers, but to protect customers—who are best served, not by stable markets that resist change, but by markets freely accessible to creative risk-takers building better mousetraps. Squeezing more revenue out of licensees through auctions is fine, as long as the spectrum is made available quickly and flexibly to those who can provide new and better service to the public.[9] From an efficiency point of view, the issue is not revenue maximization during the licensing process; it is promoting competition and innovation in the telecommunications markets. Auctions can lower the transactions costs associated with the assignment process, and so conserve economic resources. But the key issue is getting the spectrum out into the market and, in the final analysis, driving the price of spectrum down.

Cheap spectrum should be the goal of telecommunications policy. It is remarkable that so many regulators believe just the opposite: that the spectrum is a very valuable social resource and should be made even more valuable by government policy. (That view quickly turns into the protectionist view: we have to be careful about another "disruption of the marketplace" when so many billions have been invested in spectrum rights.) Radio waves are an economic *input*; the output consists of services delivered to consumers. The more abundant and lower priced

---

[9]Under certain circumstances the government may attempt to restrict the number of licenses issued in order to raise revenues (i.e., it may price the spectrum as a monopolist would). That is not in the interest of even the U.S. Treasury, however, because licenses withheld from the public will lower overall economic activity and reduce tax receipts, and it is assuredly not in the interest of the U.S. taxpayer, who is also a consumer of telecommunications services. Thomas W. Hazlett, "Revenues and Efficiency in Spectrum Auctions," FCC, March 1992.

that crucial input, the more service delivered to customers, the more efficiency created for U.S. business, and the better the living standards created for American citizens. Put any patriotic tag on it that you will: federal policy should aim to reduce the scarcity value of the spectrum.

You will hear it said that there is simply no room on the dial to do that, that the airwaves are already jammed with a multitude of users, that our spectrum is too crowded to squeeze in any more licensees. While competition would be great, there are overwhelming *technical* reasons why it is impossible.

Indeed, this appears to be true: If you were to invent a wonderful new wireless communications service today, you would be told by a smart Washington lawyer that it is very, very tough to find any place to put your new service. The airwaves are very crowded.

But tremendously underutilized. The spectrum is like a 12-lane superhighway on which traffic is regulated by urban planning graduates gone mad. Certain lanes are reserved for cars of a certain color, others are open only to cars bearing special license plates. Others are reserved for use some time in the next century, while still others are open only to vehicles with rotary engines. There is hardly any traffic on this highway, although long lines of cars wait at the on-ramps (because once or twice a decade the policeman signals a waiting car to drive on). So yes, the on-ramp is very congested, but there is nothing technical about the tie-up.

All the FCC must do to give wireless telecommunications a chance for high-speed travel is to give it the green light, to allow licensees flexibility to devise new ways of speeding down old corridors, delivering new services, and employing advanced technology. The federal government can enforce the boundaries between the lanes, as it is theoretically supposed to do in its role as traffic cop of the airwaves. But it should not tell motorists what cars to buy, how to drive, or what goodies to deliver. The zoning rules—which now inhibit any service or technology that is too creative to have been drawn on a spectrum map by a government engineer or too threatening to a respected telecom supplier—are the "technical reasons" that make the electromagnetic spectrum appear to be so jam packed.

The loss in social value that zoning restrictions on the spectrum place on the American economy is enormous, yet hidden from public view. The new industries that do not develop, the new technologies that never emerge, the new competition that never materializes are very difficult to quantify. Moreover, there is no interest group with a direct stake in this issue: the key information transmitted to the marketplace is that spectrum rights are extremely expensive (albeit because of the FCC's creation of artificial scarcity) and that researching innovative ways to employ wireless telecommunications is therefore a financially dubious proposition.

But I slightly overstate the case. Some estimates of the value lost to excessive regulation are now being made because of two things: First, the ripplings of progressive reform are now coming from the FCC itself. Second, we are confronted by technological advances so overwhelming that private interests are pressing their case to be given the right to "buy out" incumbent users of the spectrum so as to bring their products to market. The plan to introduce flexibility into the zoning process has been dubbed "voluntary reallocation." It would merely give present licensees the right to modify their service menu within their specified frequency band. In practice, it takes the form of a trade: an existing radio spectrum user agrees to vacate a desirable band to make room for a newcomer— for a negotiated price. (The seller will either relocate to another frequency, generally a higher band that is less intensely used and somewhat more expensive to transmit on, or abandon service.) That is, a market develops. Noninterfering lanes along the spectrum are dealt to their most highly valued use, as determined by consumer demand.

Of course the FCC has been reallocating the spectrum for decades. When the commission allocated a band for cellular telephone service in 1968, it grabbed the top 13 channels (78 MHz) of UHF television (channels 70–82). But the process is slow and over-lawyered. A pioneering study just released by the FCC's Office of Plans and Policy shows how market transactions could improve social welfare in practice. Analyzing the specific question of what would be the net benefit to society from voluntary reallocation of one UHF television station in Los Angeles to cellular telephone service, the authors (one an economist, the other an engineer) find that as of the late 1980s a Los Angeles UHF signal was at least *10 times* more valuable to consumers if converted to cellular telephone service.[10]

The basic allocation dilemma is clear: why force an old regulatory pattern on a changing world? The 1952 TV allotment was made before a single movie mogul had dialed up anybody's "girl" from a car phone to "do lunch," before even the first UHF television audience had been assembled. How could those planners have known to what use a particular 6-MHz swath of Los Angeles's frequency space might best be put in 1992? Is a city teeming with television stations, cable systems, video cassettes, and the like really going to value the least-watched UHF signal more highly than additional access for rush-hour mobile phone users, customers who today have trouble getting a dial tone? Offhand, I don't know the answer, and I suspect that those regulators who set out the TV band allocation in 1952 didn't either.

The logic underlying the Kwerel and Williams policy approach is sound: don't *mandate* that a UHF-TV station switch to cellular telephone service—simply don't interfere with its doing so. Granting license flexibility will force broadcast spectrum users to make their own self-interested evaluations of where consumer demand lies and of the cost at which it may realistically be met. It is always possible to construct arcane theories of market failure, or to stipulate that certain values unimportant to consumers should be observed and subsidized by holding consumers hostage in the quarters of some telecommunications monopolist. Yet the stories of government failure aren't in the least arcane; they are simply out of electoral harm's way.

The new administration can strike a blow for real leadership by exposing the cost of license inflexibility, inviting in daring new

[10]Evan Kwerel and John Williams, "Changing Channels: Voluntary Re-allocation of UHF Television Spectrum," FCC, Office of Plans and Policy Working Paper no. 27, November 1992. The estimates of the relatively high value of cellular frequencies have been reduced in recent months as a result of the assumption that a new wireless telecom service, PCS, will erode cellular's prices and market power. That empirical effect actually buffers—on a theoretical basis—the study's conclusion supporting voluntary reallocation. The fact is that PCS will be precluded from entering the wireless market unless voluntary reallocation makes spectrum available for *its* use.

telecom entrepreneurs, and allowing the American public to reap the bountiful rewards of the information age.

Legalizing the Telecommunications Revolution

You want specifics? I'll give you specifics. The most important spectrum issue before the FCC right now is rulemaking on personal communications services (PCS) and personal communications networks (PCN). That marvelous new technology will look very much like cellular, only better. Using a microcell architecture, digital transmissions, and ubiquitously portable pocket phones, PCS appears to be the communications system of the future. It seems destined to introduce a cornucopia of individual and business services to dramatically upgrade the social benefits of modern telecommunications.

That assessment could be right, or it could be wrong. We'll only find out if we get out of the way of the scores of firms anxious to risk billions of dollars to prove it correct. But we should be careful to step aside in a manner that serves the consumer-taxpayer's best interests. What are they and how can they be served? Let me take a stab.

- *Make abundant spectrum available for PCS.* If 220 MHz are realistically (politically speaking) available, allocate the entire band, not half of it as the FCC has indicated a willingness to do. Why be parsimonious? The argument that the commission should keep a so-called spectrum reserve is technically inaccurate in that the entire spectrum is a reserve—future uses of the spectrum are not precluded by sending communications signals through it today. There is no technical reason to store up a nondepletable resource, and doing so makes no economic sense. Any spectrum that fails to deliver consumer services is gone, wasted. Not a good way to build for the future. Finally, it sets a bad policy rule: new users must come to the government and ask for permission to deliver new wireless services. Better to get lots of competitive private users experimenting with numerous innovations and thereby speed the introduction of new uses.
- *Use voluntary reallocation.* No spectrum? This is how we create an economic resource: we take it out of less valued employment. (In the real economy nothing is created or destroyed, just switched to more highly valued uses.) Incumbent users of the

spectrum should be grandfathered on current assignments and then given the right to wheel and deal with newcomers. Protests from incumbents about technical problems and public interest considerations are most likely just the protectionist squeals of special interests trying to cut a fatter deal. Let them negotiate in good faith in private market transactions, not as terrorists who would hold up social progress.

- *Maximize license flexibility.* PCS will be a broad family of new telephone services, some of which will look much like the old, some of which will be quite distinct. We think. No one really knows. There is no reason to limit newly licensed PCS competitors to just those services that sound good to FCC planners today. Above all, do not narrowly tailor licenses in an attempt to either (1) assure success of the newly licensed PCS firms or (2) protect the revenues of existing wireline and wireless telephone companies. Ensuring the success of new firms means licensing comfortably noncompetitive companies whose high prices will easily cover costs. Protecting incumbents means more high prices for consumers. Let PCS be an innovative battleground with lots of dueling technologists discovering what services can be sent via the magic of digital wireless. Standards are difficult to set in such an industry. Let the industry do it here, much as has been done in the personal computer and video cassette recorder industries.
- *Permit nationwide licenses.* The cellular telephone licensing scheme—two per market in 733 markets—was very funny. But seriously, folks, for the past decade the marketplace has been trying to put Humpty Dumpty back together again. Cellular One (McCaw and Southwestern Bell) is trying to patch a nationwide network together; all the other major players are working on a rival. Brokerage fees alone easily amount to over $1 billion, but the real social cost of partitioning markets so finely is that consumers have to wait years to get decent roaming service and rates. Since the idea of a mobile phone is that one can move around, it is apparent that nationwide licenses should not be artificially precluded.
- *License a sufficient number of competitors.* Because an FCC license will form an airtight barrier to entry (loosening license inflexibility elsewhere would help to alleviate the problem, though), the licensing process should be seen as an antidote. In assigning

licenses to particular private suppliers and by preventing post-assignment mergers (common FCC policy), the agency engages in a sort of poor man's antitrust regime. It is simple, structural, and does not involve the endless litigation of antitrust policy in the unlicensed economy. Here the policy should not be onerous in its deconcentration requirements; it should allow each competitor to easily achieve necessary economies of scale with respect to spectrum size. But the monopoly profits and high prices attendant to the cellular duopoly markets should convince us that two are not enough.[11]

- *Auction licenses.* The billions of dollars' worth of licenses that will have to be awarded will provoke billions of dollars in pure rent-seeking expense if lotteries are employed. That may even prove somewhat embarrassing to the administration, as "application mills" advertise lottery applications as get-rich-quick schemes via federal giveaways.[12] The approach of traditional regulators has been to toughen requirements for entry into the lotteries so as to limit them to applicants that are genuinely interested in being PCS providers. Well, that's been tried. America found out that there were about 400,000 "real" cellular telephone applicants when, in setting up those lotteries, entrants had to "prove" that they had the capability and capital to actually be cellular operators. If lotteries are to be conducted, instead of stiffening entry requirements (and predictably encouraging even more talent to be wasted on dressing up investors to look like real telecommunications players), the qualifying criteria should be *lowered* to proof of U.S. citizenship. Indeed, a random drawing by Social Security number for a large number of good-sized PCS licenses would be the ideal allocation scheme: by allowing instant license resale, a competitive market would be produced with a minimum of wasted resources.

---

[11]The NTIA's 1991 analysis put urban cellular systems at a market value of about $80 billion, while physical capital was valued at only $6.7 billion. That is strong evidence of the existence of market power.

[12]The essential problem is that the fly-by-nighters were economically correct: there was easy money in the cellular lotteries. Michaels and I estimated, for instance, that there was an expected return of over five to one in the 1988–89 rural license lotteries. Hazlett and Michaels.

- *Do it fast.* Speed turns out to be very important. Every month the American economy goes without the tremendous new PCS industry is a month wasted by federal policymakers. This valuable new service helps the macroeconomy and virtually every microsector you can name (health, manufacturing, education, communications, transportation, and personal security are just a few of the easy ones). But history should alarm us. Although the cellular telephone licenses were issued between 1982 and 1989 (with a couple dozen rural licenses still in dispute), cellular telephone technology was actually developed . . . in 1946. Even being very generous about the causes of delay, the uncontestable costs associated with the regulatory lag are astounding. In a 1991 study by the National Economic Research Associates, which conservatively assumes a 10-year delay, FCC policy indecision cost the U.S. economy over $86 billion.[13] Delay a year here, a year there . . . and pretty soon it gets to be real dead-weight loss.

---

[13]National Economic Research Associates, "Estimate of the Loss to the United States Caused by the FCC's Delay in Licensing Cellular Telecommunications," November 8, 1991. Mines describes the regulation-induced delay in some detail and implies that it consumed far more than a single decade. Christopher W. Mines, "Regulation and the Re-Invention of Cellular Telephone Service in the United States and Great Britain," Kennedy School of Government, Program on Information Resources Policy, February 9, 1992.

PART III

DOMESTIC POLICY

8. Social Security's Uncertain Future

A. Haeworth Robertson

Social Security is a program of promises—two separate and distinct kinds of promises. One is the promise that specified benefits will be paid to the retired segment of the population; the other is that specified taxes will be collected from the working segment of the population. Benefit promises are made to one generation and taxation promises to that generation's children.

Those promises are equally important, but, unfortunately, we have tended to place more emphasis on our promises to the retired population than to the working population. We have placed more emphasis on the benefit promises than on the taxation promises.

Under a pay-as-you-go system of benefits based on social adequacy instead of individual equity, there is virtually no relationship between the benefit promises and the taxation promises made to an individual or to a group.

Some would argue that there is a connection between benefits and taxes because the system is partially funded in advance. That is false; the system is not, in reality, advance funded at all. The government collects more Social Security taxes than are needed to pay current benefits; it spends the "excess" taxes on other government programs; and it issues an IOU (Treasury bond) to the Social Security trust funds, which simply means that the government intends to collect general revenue in the future to redeem the bonds, plus interest thereon, when Social Security needs the money to pay benefits.

In other words, part of our Social Security taxes will be used to pay for other government programs during the trust fund's "build-up"; and an equivalent amount of general revenue (enhanced by interest) will be used to pay Social Security benefits during the trust fund's "liquidation" period.

It takes a fantastic imagination to believe that that process will strengthen the security of future benefits or that it will reduce the future tax burden (taking into account both general revenue and payroll taxes). The present trust funds, and probably the future trust funds, are mere window dressing that has no economic reality. There clearly is no advance funding, government rhetoric to the contrary notwithstanding.

Some would argue that during its working years a particular generation pays taxes that are equivalent to the benefits it will receive; that a generation buys and pays for its own benefits. That is false. Social Security, by its very nature, does not provide an individual or an entire generation with benefits equivalent to taxes paid.

Benefit promises and taxation promises are separate and distinct promises made to different groups of people, among which there is a certain amount of overlapping. Therein lies the crux of the Social Security problem.

Benefit Promises vs. Taxation Promises

What promises have we made, and can we keep them? The latest reports of the trustees of the Social Security system contain the projected costs of our benefit promises that are to be financed primarily by the Social Security payroll tax: the Old-Age, Survivors, Disability, and Hospital Insurance programs.

The cost is projected to rise from its current level of 14 percent of covered, taxable payroll to between 26 and 44 percent of that payroll by the middle of the next century, depending on whether you accept the "intermediate" or the "pessimistic" projections (see Figure 8.1). No credence whatsoever should be given to the "optimistic" projections. The pessimistic projections are the appropriate ones to use in assessing whether or not we can fulfill our benefit promises.

What level of taxes have we promised future generations they must pay to finance those benefits? We have promised the indefinite continuation of current payroll tax rates—7.65 percent for employees and 7.65 percent for employers. In addition, general revenue equivalent to approximately 1 percent of payroll will be generated (principally from taxation of Social Security benefits). Those tax revenues will be sufficient to finance only 50 to 70 percent (based on the pessimistic and intermediate projections, respectively) of the benefit promises we have made to the baby-boom generation.

Some analysts who want to create a false sense of security about the future of Social Security try to ignore Medicare, an important

Figure 8.1
PROJECTED COST OF SOCIAL SECURITY AS A PERCENTAGE OF
TAXABLE PAYROLL

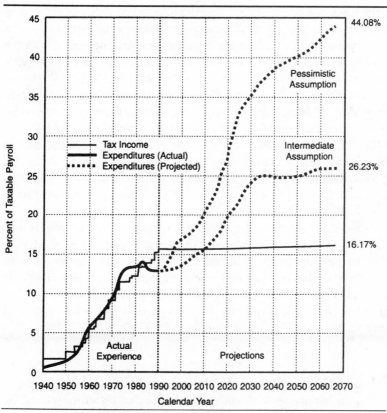

NOTE: Tax income includes Old-Age, Survivors, Disability, and Hospital
Insurance taxes and revenues.

component of Social Security's rising future cost. In 1989 the average cash annuity paid to a retired worker and spouse was $922 per month. The average monthly value of the "medical care annuity" provided such a couple was $304 for Hospital Insurance benefits and $200 for Supplementary Medical Insurance benefits. Thus, the value of the Medicare portion of Social Security was 55 percent of the value of the cash annuity portion.

It is misleading to state that Social Security will be financially sound well into the future and thus imply that Social Security's currently scheduled taxes will be adequate in the future. That is clearly not true since an important component of Social Security taxes is used to finance the Hospital Insurance part of Medicare.

In assessing the adequacy and the financial viability of retirement benefits to be provided by Social Security to the baby-boom generation, we should consider the medical care annuity as well as the cash annuity. Even if Medicare is someday separated from what we now call Social Security, the question of its viability will remain.

In addition, of course, there is the promise to provide Supplementary Medical Insurance benefits—medical services not covered by Medicare's Hospital Insurance. The taxation promise for SMI is a little murky. At present approximately 25 percent of the cost of SMI is covered by "premiums" paid by persons eligible for benefit protection, and the remaining 75 percent is drawn from general revenue. Under present law the portion financed by general revenue will increase over time.

It would seem that the taxation promise is that taxpayers will have to pay whatever amount of general revenue is needed in the future to provide SMI benefits, but taxpayers have not been informed of that obligation. (In fact, the SMI trustees' reports show projected future costs for only the next 10 years, but we can project that the cost of SMI will rise from its current level of 2 percent of payroll to some 8 to 11 percent by mid–21st century.)

Which Promises Will Be Broken?

It is indisputable that some of Social Security's promises will be broken. The questions are, Which promises, when, how, and for what group of the population?

From Social Security's financial standpoint, there is little need to break either benefit promises or taxation promises during the next 10 to 15 years. Social Security's income and outgo will approximately balance during that period.

But beginning in the year 2006, when the first baby boomer reaches age 60, we shall have to renege. We can reduce benefits for the baby boomers, or we can increase taxes for the boomers still working as well as for all of the boomers' children. I submit that the choices we make will be much more significant and far-reaching than we now envision.

Break the Taxation Promises

We could break the taxation promises and keep the benefit promises. People could continue to retire in their early 60s.

One of the consequences would be very high Social Security taxes. There are several well-publicized reasons for the high projected cost of Social Security: the baby boom followed by a baby bust, longer life expectancies, extraordinary increases in medical care costs, and the assumption of a continued pattern of retirement between ages 60 and 65.

In 1930 the remaining life expectancy for a 65-year-old male was 11.8 years; for a female it was 12.9 years. In 2030 the remaining life expectancy at age 65 is projected to be 16.8 years for a male and 20.8 years for a female.

In 1950 there were 16 Social Security taxpayers for every benefit recipient; today the ratio is about 3.3 to 1, and in 2030 it will probably be less than 2 to 1 if present retirement patterns continue. All of those factors have obvious implications for a pay-as-you-go Social Security system (see Figure 8.2).

Although higher taxes may be a feasible solution, their assessment would have a marked effect on the standard of living of both the working and the retired segments of the population. Workers would obviously have less discretionary income; there would also be fewer resources available for improved education, a cleaner environment, improved health care, a better maintained infrastructure of roads and bridges, and so forth.

In the future, it is unlikely that a workforce consisting primarily of people under 65 will be large enough to produce all the goods and services needed to support the entire population. If those workers were able to do so, they would retain such a small proportion of what they produced, and there would be such a massive redistribution of income, that the nation would have moved a long way—if not all the way—toward a socialist economy.

All of those consequences would flow, not from deliberate decisions about how to allocate resources, but from

- having adopted a social insurance system in the 1930s that effectively divides the population into workers and nonworkers,
- misrepresenting the nature of the system in order to gain public acceptance, and thus

153

Figure 8.2

RATIOS OF RETIRED WORKERS AND OTHER SOCIAL SECURITY BENEFICIARIES TO WORKERS PAYING SOCIAL SECURITY TAXES

48 Million
1 Million
2 Million
1950
133 Million
15 Million
25 Million
1990
150 Million
Intermediate Assumption
20 Million
57 Million
138 Million
Pessimistic Assumption
21 Million
60 Million
2030
Workers Paying Taxes
Retired Workers
Other Beneficiaries

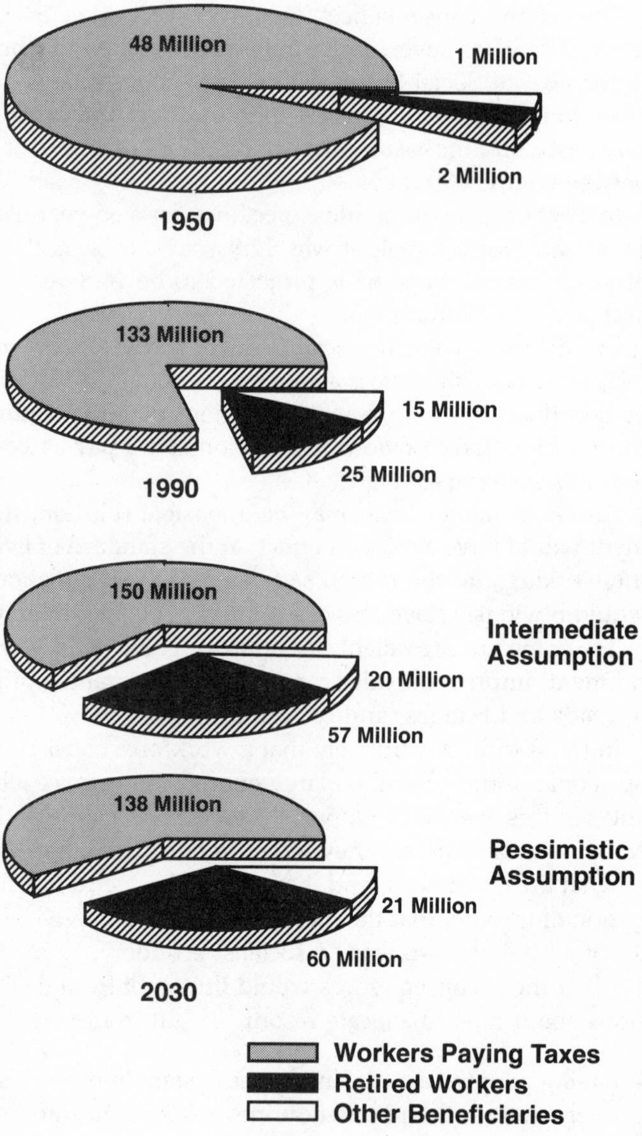

- causing the public to consider the system inviolable and not subject to change to adjust for conditions unforeseen in the 1930s: a baby boom followed by a baby bust, improved but more costly medical care, and longer life spans.

Break the Benefit Promises

We could break the benefit promises and keep the taxation promises. Benefits to baby boomers might have to be cut by as much as 50 percent. Obviously, people would not be able to retire as early as they had hoped and planned.

Because of the nature of Social Security's promises, the consequences of breaking them should not be underestimated. The Social Security program promises a certain level of retirement benefits in exchange for the payment of taxes during one's working years. Moreover, the Social Security Administration emphasizes that Social Security retirement benefits are not sufficient to fully replace the earnings lost through retirement and encourages workers to participate in private pension plans and to save and invest on their own in order to have a total retirement income that will be sufficient for their needs. If, after several decades of playing by those rules, workers are abruptly notified that Congress has chosen to reduce Social Security retirement benefits, they may well be unable to adjust their own savings and pensions to compensate for the lower Social Security benefits. Workers may then face the difficult choice of delaying their retirement (if possible) or adjusting to a lower standard of living than planned.

In addition to the immediate impact on the retirement plans of workers and their families, and the loss of public confidence in the Social Security program, such broken promises could have another serious ramification—complete loss of confidence in the government itself. Social Security is probably the last major government program in which the public still has any significant degree of confidence.

Without the confidence and support of the public, the institution of orderly government cannot long survive. If a major default occurs in the Social Security benefit promises, anarchy may not be far behind.

Is There a Better Choice?

Is there a better choice than anarchy or socialism? We will probably have a little of each, because we have already waited too long to be honest with the public. We have misrepresented the nature of Social Security and its long-range cost and implications for so long now that we cannot completely avoid the consequences. We can, however, minimize the adversity of those consequences with timely and well-chosen action.

There is no single best solution; the preferred solution depends on one's objectives and philosophy. But whatever the solution may be, in order to minimize future turmoil it must have three characteristics:

1. It must be decided on and communicated to the public very soon (i.e., within the next five years so that the baby boomers will have time to adjust their retirement plans).
2. It must generally be considered fair, or at least to call for an "equal sacrifice" by the various segments of the population.
3. It must result in a more complete utilization of the nation's human resources over each person's life.

The nation should provide an environment in which the capabilities of each individual can be utilized effectively, an environment that fosters meaningful activity, not empty idleness. Both the incentive and the opportunity should exist to enable all individuals to work and produce throughout their lifetimes in a series of endeavors compatible with their changing physical and mental abilities. Government policies should be directed toward those goals, not toward removal from the active workforce of able-bodied persons—persons who must then be supported by the remaining active workers.

It will not be easy for the nation to move in the direction of full utilization of its human resources. The alternative will be continued high unemployment and underemployment, an ever-increasing pool of idle "disabled" and "aged" persons, and a total cost to society that will become increasingly unbearable and will eventually become destructive.

But before we can start developing solutions, more people must be aware that we have problems. And they must understand the nature and magnitude of the problems. A better understanding of Social Security is essential if it is to evolve into a system that will appropriately meet the needs of the baby-boom generation, as well as ensuing generations, at a price that future taxpayers will be willing and able to pay.

9. The Learning Revolution

Lewis J. Perelman

The collapse of the Soviet empire is just one of the most dramatic symptoms of the dawn of the new knowledge-age economy. One of the most critical of the many profound impacts of the technological revolution is the global obsolescence of traditional education and training institutions. Prosperity in the new economy depends on a complete replacement of worn-out public policies that are intended to subsidize and "save" those institutions. The new policy paradigm must focus on (1) abolishing the wasteful paper chase for academic credentials and (2) commercializing (not just privatizing) the economy of academia, the biggest and probably the last great socialist empire on earth.

The New Economy

In the new economy being formed by explosive advances in information technologies, knowledge has become the crucial factor of production. Contrary to much of the conventional (and backward-looking) wisdom driving most recently proposed economic strategies, software has displaced manufacturing as the key to national economic strength, and learning has become the crucial form of work required for self-reliance and prosperity.

With learning now the indispensable focus of work, entertainment, and home life, the attempt to keep learning confined in the box of the government-controlled empire of school and college classrooms threatens to be as counterproductive as were political efforts at the beginning of the 20th century to protect the vast horse industry against the threat of the automobile.

National economic leadership, security, and prosperity at the beginning of this century depended on the swift, wholesale *replacement* of the horse-based transportation system by an all-new system based on the automobile (and shortly thereafter, the airplane). In the same way, economic progress in the 21st century will depend

159

on the rapid replacement of schools and colleges—a $445-billion-a-year industry in the United States alone—by a new commercial industry based on the technology I call hyperlearning (HL).

Henry Ford's Model T was not an invention so much as the integration of a set of technical advances in power plants, rubber tires, electrical systems, and other components as well as fuel refining, production engineering, employment policies, and marketing strategies—a total system that changed not just transportation but the entire fabric of Western society. Similarly, HL represents the integration of skyrocketing advances in the so-called artificial intelligence of computers and robotics, broadband multimedia communications, "hyper" software needed to cope with the resulting information explosion, and even "brain technology" that is expanding our understanding of how human and artificial brains work.

"Hypermated" learning loops increasingly form the core of just about every kind of economically productive activity. The London Stock Exchange has replaced legions of shouting floor traders with an automated telecomputing network, following the lead of America's NASDAQ. The most prosperous farmers today spend more time working with computers than combines. Political rhetoric notwithstanding, factory "jobs" are not coming back: they are bound to become as productive, and hence as scarce and knowledge demanding, as farm jobs. General Electric's state-of-the-art light bulb factory in Virginia employs one-third the number of workers employed by the factory it replaced—and none ever touches a light bulb. Each of the few workers employed in Corning Glass's most modern plants is trained to be able to run every operation in the factory, not to do a "job." The work is primarily troubleshooting and managing the software of the automated systems that do the actual manufacturing.

The HL revolution cannot be brought about by any "reform" or "restructuring" of schools and colleges, any more than the horse could be retrained or even genetically rebred to become a car. "Break-the-mold" schools can't and won't.

Education: A Barrier to Progress

A critical feature of the new world order marked by the collapse of socialism is that education, once widely viewed as an engine of prosperity, has become the major *barrier* to global economic progress.

The *overeducation* of the workforce is one of the major causes of the economic slump that has plagued the U.S. and other modern national economies for some three years. Roughly three-quarters of the thousands of employees being eliminated by major employers such as IBM, General Motors, and TRW are managerial, professional, and technical workers with extensive college and postgraduate education. In the present recession, corporate middle managers have been 2.5 times more likely to become unemployed than the average worker. In past recessions, laid-off factory workers were rehired when sales recovered, but the recent rapid growth of white-collar unemployment represents the permanent elimination of jobs. In the recession of the early 1980s, white-collar employment kept on growing, and 90 percent of white-collar employees who lost their jobs were rehired within a few months. In the latest recession, white-collar employment has declined, and fewer than 25 percent of the displaced white-collar workers have been able to find new jobs.

Recent political campaign proposals called for more "investment" in the U.S. workforce in the form of expanded spending on traditional education and training programs. The rhetoric masked the reality that the United States currently has the most highly schooled workforce in its history: from 1970 to 1989, workers with four years of high school increased from 31 to nearly 39 percent of the workforce, and the proportion of the U.S. workforce with at least four years of college nearly doubled from less than 11 to over 21 percent. Fewer than 23 percent, and probably no more than 15 percent, of U.S. jobs will call for college degrees in the 1990s. With over a quarter of the workforce planning to earn college diplomas, it is likely that 10 percent of U.S. college graduates will be unemployed by the end of the decade, and between a quarter and a half of the graduates will be underemployed in jobs that do not really require their degrees.

The ongoing deflation of academic credentials will only be accelerated by the end of the Cold War. In the wake of the "brain glut" unleashed by the collapse of the Soviet Union, U.S. companies such as AT&T, Corning, and Sun Microsystems have been hiring top Russian scientists and engineers, among the best educated and most skilled workers in the world, to work in Russia for salaries on the order of *$60 a month*. And some 2 million of America's own most technically schooled and skilled workers are destined to become unemployed over the next two years as a result of defense spending cuts and force reductions.

A prime flaw in the whole educational system is that it was designed in the midst of the Industrial Revolution of the 19th century to prepare people for industrial-era jobs. But the kinds of skills required to work productively in the knowledge age are almost the opposite of the skills demanded for academic success. And the message buried in the statistics is that "jobs" for both the over-schooled and the unschooled are fast disappearing. Entrepreneurial skills are the ones most needed in the new economy, where the majority of the "workforce" will be made up of contractors, consultants, free agents, and traditional business creators and owners. Yet the competencies needed for successful entrepreneurship are almost totally ignored by the existing educational and training system.

Even as the services of the scholastic sector become increasingly irrelevant to the economic aspirations of the great majority of Americans, the cost of the obsolete academic bureaucracy continues to soar. Add the $50-billion-plus that employers spend to educate employees to the $450-billion annual school and college budget, and throw in at least another $100 billion a year spent on "hidden" forms of education (such as conferences and conventions), and the education sector is virtually tied with the health care sector as the biggest industry in the U.S. economy.

The upward spiral of costs has been almost as explosive in education as in health care. Real spending per student in U.S. K-12 schools (discounting inflation) has grown some five times since the 1950s. In the 1980s real U.S. spending on K-12 schools grew by nearly a third; spending on colleges grew even more, by about a half.

Productivity, the key issue that has been neglected by education and training policies, needs to be the focal point of the new policy paradigm. Growth in productivity—increasing the amount of wealth produced by each hour of labor—is the essential measure of a nation's standard of living and relative "competitiveness." Weak growth in productivity has been the central symptom of America's economic malaise for some two decades.

Poor and declining productivity is the main reason the education sector has become a barrier and a threat to economic progress in the modern world. Education as an industry is nearly twice as labor intensive as is the average U.S. business, and its relative labor costs are more than twice those of high-tech industries such as telecommunications. Moreover, while the productivity of other information-based industries has been advancing smartly, even explosively, the soaring costs and stagnant output of the education sector have spelled a steady decline in productivity at least since the 1950s.

The sheer size of the education sector, America's first or second biggest industry, thus has been dragging down average growth in productivity. And education is undermining the national standard of living even more because, in addition to being a very large business, it is one that is strategically critical to the growth of a knowledge-age economy. With the learning enterprise playing the central economic role in the knowledge age that steel making played in the industrial age, a weak and declining learning sector is undercutting the development of nearly every other modern business.

The productivity-focused goals of the new paradigm of national learning policy that should replace intrusive and irrelevant "national education goals" can be summarized in four simple words: More, Better, Faster, and Cheaper. That is, policy needs to ensure the rapid development of HL systems that enable citizens of all ages to learn more about everything; to learn better, especially those things that are relevant to productive work; to learn faster, with less waste of time; and to do all that at lower and steadily declining cost.

HL technology already exists and is achieving those productivity goals in the segments of the national learning enterprise that are compelled by competitive forces to seek more and better learning in less time at lower cost—notably, in corporate and military organizations. For instance, U.S. corporate and military educators spend about 300 times more of their instructional budgets than public schools do on systems based on increasingly advanced computer and multimedia technology. The reason is that, in the competitive environments of the marketplace and the battlefield, learning objectives are focused on competency rather than credentials, and there are powerful rewards for productivity and thus for innovation.

The Action Plan

The national action plan needed to replace the worn-out and outdated education establishment with a 21st-century HL industry has four key strategies.

Decredentialize

First, America needs to eliminate the economic value of academic credentials. Credentialism has been the key barrier that has thwarted a half century of attempts at educational reform and restructuring. As long as the public has reason to believe that elite academic credentials—based on attendance at the "right" institutions—are the essential passports to lucrative employment and other economic opportunities, the public will continue to resist any reform that gives learning and competency priority over testing and sorting. As long as public policy continues to presume that the cognitive needs of the "work-bound" population warrant categorically different, and hence inferior, treatment than those of the "college-bound" population, expenditures on education will continue to undermine rather than strengthen economic progress.

The economically productive alternative to credentialism is certification of competency. In short, people's opportunity to participate in employment or entrepreneurship should be based only on what they know and what they can do. There is simply no job or enterprise in this economy that truly requires an academic diploma or degree for successful performance. As Chief Justice Warren Burger wrote in the landmark civil rights case of *Griggs v. Duke Power*, "History is filled with examples of men and women who rendered highly effective performance without the conventional badges of accomplishment in terms of certificates, diplomas or degrees."

A broad, even universal, commitment on the part of U.S. employers, as well as financing and other institutions, to eliminate the currency of diplomas would lead necessarily to a huge demand for effective tools to assess the know-how of applicants for jobs, small-business loans, and so forth. Sophisticated assessment tools already exist and are being used by leading employers such as the U.S. Army, Corning, Allstate, and Toyota. Making competency-based employment (and other economic access) a universal practice would spawn the rapid growth of a high-tech, profitable, cost-effective assessment industry. Funding for that new industry would come from some of the hundreds of billions of dollars that would be saved when tax and tuition payers were freed from paying tribute to the diploma mills.

There are several steps the new president should take to help achieve the goal of a diplomaless economy.

Federal Employment and Contracting. As the nation's biggest employer, the federal government should demonstrate its commit- ment to decredentialization by reforming its own employment and contracting practices to eliminate all requirements for and refer- ences to scholastic diplomas and degrees. Military and other federal agencies already are more advanced than many other employers in relying on competency-based employment and training proce- dures, so the scope of this reform is not likely to be drastic. Much of it probably can be achieved by executive order, although some new legislation may be required to reconcile competency testing with civil rights law.

"SCANS II." The Secretary's Commission on Achieving Neces- sary Skills (SCANS), which was convened by Secretary of Labor Elizabeth Dole and included representatives of a range of American industries, worked productively from 1990 to 1991 to define a set of competencies needed for employment in the modern economy, as well as criteria for assessing those skills. The new administration should help move the SCANS work from theory to practice by inviting U.S. employers, either through trade associations or indi- vidually, to join a coalition pledged to implement the kind of compe- tency-based employment practices suggested by SCANS within a reasonable period of time—say, by January 1, 1995. The coalition could establish an oversight committee or council to monitor prog- ress and to target regulatory or legal barriers that the government needs to reduce. The president also might establish, either through an executive agency or the employer coalition, something like the Baldrige Award (for quality management) to acknowledge leaders in competency-based employment.

Civil Rights. The new president should order the Justice Depart- ment to review existing civil rights laws and regulations to deter- mine to what extent employment discrimination based on academic diplomas may be in violation of the law.

Assessment Research and Development. Through executive directive and whatever enabling legislation may be necessary, the new president should establish a new federal program of research and development on human performance assessment, aimed at advancing the cost-effectiveness of the technology needed to measure what people know and can do in the context of real work requirements. The program might best be centered in the National Institute of Standards and Technology (Commerce Department)—with active collaboration of the Defense Department (e.g., the Defense Advanced Research Projects Agency, the Office of Naval Research, and the Army Research Institute) and the National Science Foundation—or in the new Department of Knowledge Resources suggested below.

Entrepreneurship. The new president should order that, in all the above initiatives and others, preparation for and competency at entrepreneurship should be given priority at least equal to or greater than that given to employment.

Commercialize

In recent years many politicians, business leaders, and families have begun to appreciate the essential importance of breaking up the socialist monopoly of the government-controlled education system. "Privatization" of public education is much needed and should be a national goal of the new president. But "school choice" is an inadequate strategy for achieving the benefits of a market economy in the learning sector or for unleashing the growth of the strategically crucial HL industry.

In a long list of problems, the primary flaws in the school choice (including college choice) strategy are *vouchers* and *nonprofit organizations*. Because classroom teaching is technologically and economically obsolete in the HL era, choice in the form of vouchers for tuition at present-day schools is as irrelevant to hyperlearning as the choice of horses is to modern transportation. Because the commercial profit motive is absolutely indispensable to drive the rapid technological innovation the HL era demands, choice programs that merely redistribute public moneys among nonprofit schools—whether government owned, private, or church affiliated—are bound to be irrelevant and ineffectual.

Instead, the new administration should be committed to *commercial* privatization of the entire education sector, based on a strategy of *microchoice* using the financing mechanism of *microvouchers.*

To illustrate the idea of microchoice: If our choice of television channels worked the way school choice is proposed to, changing channels from HBO to CNN would require unplugging the TV set, taking it back to the store, exchanging it for a different model, and moving to a new neighborhood. In reality, of course, choosing among dozens or hundreds of video options requires no effort more strenuous than pushing a button. Similarly, modern HL technology can offer the individual even more choices of "teachers" and "schools" than of cable TV channels. HL's broadband, intelligent, multimedia systems permit anyone to learn anything, anywhere, anytime with grade-A results by matching learning resources precisely with personal needs and learning styles.

Microvouchers that use modern electronic card-account technology can enable individual families or students to choose specific learning products and services, not just once a year or once a semester, but by the week, day, hour, or even second by second. Unlike vouchers for school or college tuition, microvouchers will create a true, wide-open, location-free, competitive market for learning that has the elasticity to efficiently and quickly match supply and demand.

Over 90 percent of funding for U.S. public education is supplied by state and local governments, which also have the major policy-making role. Nevertheless, there are several steps the new president can take to commercialize the government-controlled education sector and to promote the development of the American HL industry that must replace it.

Federal Microvouchers. The new president should seek legislation to merge 90 percent of the existing student loan, Pell grant, Job Training Partnership Act, Trade Adjustment and Assistance Act, Job Opportunities and Basic Skills program, Chapters I and II of the Education Consolidation and Improvement Act, and other federal education and training funds into a single, means-tested microvoucher program that eligible families or individuals could draw on to meet the learning and development needs of people of all ages. Funds should be allocated directly to households, in proportion to individual or family need, to be used for the purchase of any service or product that is demonstrably relevant to learning and development needs. The instrument of expenditure would not be paper stamps or vouchers but electronic account cards similar to credit or bank cards. The HL microvoucher program should leave families free to decide how best to distribute the account resources between adults and children and generally among the members of the household. That provision would recognize that the needs of disadvantaged children in many (perhaps even most) cases may be served best by immediately improving the economic opportunities and status of the parents, as well as by developing their parenting skills.

Family Learning Account. As a complement to the means-tested microvoucher program, the new administration should consider adding a tax-exempt saving program. Individuals should be permitted to make contributions to Family Learning Accounts (FLAs). Those contributions, which would be similar to contributions to Individual Retirement Accounts (IRAs), would be deductible from taxable income, up to some reasonable level, during the year the contributions were made. Unlike withdrawals from IRAs, withdrawals from FLAs would be exempt from both penalty and tax as long as they were expended through the microvoucher program. And such microvoucher expenditures could be repaid to FLAs (with interest) without being counted against the annual contribution limit. Beyond some age limit, provision may be made for FLA funds to be transferred to estates or pension accounts, with appropriate treatment of deferred taxes. Another difference from IRAs would be that FLAs would be designed to serve family rather than just individual needs. The general concept of the FLA is to encourage households to gradually replace the direct government grant funds in microvoucher accounts with tax-favored savings contributions.

Leveraging. Federal funds for education and training represent only about one-tenth of total public expenditure on those areas. A federal-only microvoucher program would, therefore, provide significant benefits only to the most disadvantaged portion of the U.S. population, although it would give the poor more of the freedom of choice and access to learning tools that the well-off already enjoy.

Although most of the economic problem caused by an obsolete, overfunded public education bureaucracy lies in the domain of state and local authorities, the president can use the power of the federal government to influence the direction of state policy. Specifically, the new president should consider making part or full eligibility for the consolidated federal microvoucher-FLA program dependent on state and local participation. The precedent for such a policy exists in a variety of federal transportation, welfare, health, and other programs. For instance, federal law required states to raise the legal drinking age to 21 to be eligible for federal highway funding. The new administration should determine whether such a policy may be necessary, in addition to the oft-cited "bully pulpit," to induce states to reconstruct their education budgets and bureaucracies along the lines recommended here.

Capitalize

The nearly total absence of investment in research, development, and implementation of new technology may be the main reason the education sector is a barrier to the growth of the HL industry and a brake on our whole economy. While the average U.S. business spends 2 percent of its annual revenues on R&D, and leading high-tech companies plow 7 to 20 percent or more of their annual sales receipts into R&D, the education industry invests less than 0.1 percent of its revenues in the research and development of new, improved technology.

The health care sector, which is essentially tied with education as America's biggest industry, spends about $18 billion annually on R&D; roughly half of that amount comes from government, and the other half comes from companies. In contrast, only about $300 million is spent annually in the United States on research and development of advanced learning technology, and virtually all of that amount is spent by the Defense Department. Another $2 billion a year for the development and acquisition of associated training systems may be hidden in DOD weapons budgets. Defense cutbacks threaten to whither that critical national technology asset, and currently there is no plan to preserve, much less expand, it.

Equally dismal is the education sector's record on capital investment—money that pays for the acquisition and application of technology to improve the quality of products and the productivity of operations. The average American business invests about $50,000 in capital for each job. In high-tech industries, such as computers or telecommunications, from $100,000 to $1 million needs to be invested for each worker. In the education sector, total capital investment per employee is less than $50.

The funding needed to close the yawning technology gap is on the order of $8 billion to $20 billion a year and should come entirely from the reallocation of some of the $445 billion now being wasted annually on the nation's obsolete and bloated education system.

Again, the federal government accounts for only a small fraction of the total funds spent on public education and training in the United States. If the technology gap is to be closed by reallocation from existing expenditures, it follows that most of that money will have to come from state and local rather than federal sources. This is an area in which the new president can and should use federal influence to leverage state policies.

National Institutes of Learning. Part of the 10 percent of existing federal education and training program funds not applied to the microchoice program discussed above should be used for challenge grants to reward states that agree to set aside at least 2 percent of their total current state (and local) education and training budgets for HL research and development. The challenge grants might represent a federal supplement of 10 percent or more to state R&D allocations. The R&D funds should be administered by state Institutes of Learning.

As the states implement the new policy, the state institutes should form a consortium, which could be called the National Institutes of Learning, perhaps with the federal government acting as coordinator. Although government organizations cannot and should not duplicate the product-development role of commercial business, the mission of the National Institutes of Learning should be, from the outset, to realize the ultimate goal of commercialization of advanced learning (that is, HL) technology.

Commercialization necessarily implies effective cooperation between government R&D programs and private industry. The U.S. agricultural research system and the federal Small Business Innovation Research program are two rather successful models that might be productively adapted to this new endeavor.

Learning Redevelopment Banks. The remainder of the 10 percent reserved from current federal education and training funds should be used for another matching grant program to induce states to set aside at least another 3 percent of their total current state (and local) education and training program budgets to help finance the reconstruction of the education sector's socialist economy. Education needs the same kind of major capital investment that other ex-socialist economies need to replace obsolete technology and retrain managers and workers who have little experience with or understanding of market operations. Those funds should be administered by redevelopment banks that, like the World Bank or the European Bank for Reconstruction and Development, will provide loans and grants to help replace government-controlled institutions with private, competitive, profit-seeking enterprises. Those funds and financial institutions need not and probably should not be permanent—a "sunset" provision that would shut them down after no more than 10 years should be included in their charters. But they should be given adequate funding and a long enough lifetime to speed the commercial privatization of the education sector.

Bypass

The huge, century-old Bell Telephone monopoly was forced to break up a decade ago largely because it was bypassed by new technologies that enabled consumers to get superior products and services from other suppliers. Today, "distance learning" technology—using telecommunications and other media to deliver instructional services and resources from anyone, anywhere to anyone, anywhere—is well enough established in America to start to topple the public education monopoly in a similar way. Along with the variety of private school options, the expansion of distance learning will increase the ability of learning consumers to bypass the control of the public school and college bureaucracy, thereby shrinking the government system's client base and reducing its ability to resist the kinds of policies called for above.

In general, the new administration should pursue a strategy of expanding the ability of learning consumers—both families and businesses—to bypass and abandon the established education system in favor of budding HL alternatives. That strategy requires acting swiftly to redistribute consumers, finances, and political influence from the scholastic institutions of the past to the HL enterprises of the future.

171

Break the Telecommunications Logjam. There is an intimate connection between the creation of the broadband, digital so-called "information superhighways" needed to form the strategic infrastructure of the knowledge-age economy, on the one hand, and replacement of the medieval scholastic establishment by a high-tech HL industry, on the other: The more rapidly high-capacity, multimedia networks are expanded nationally, the sooner they will bypass and replace academia. And the commercial privatization of the education sector represents a multi-hundred-billion-dollar market opportunity for private investment to reap the rewards of the information superhighway system.

Thwarting both developments is an ongoing stalemate among telephone, cable TV, broadcast, newspaper, and other media interests that have been vying for control of the new communications infrastructure. The new president should act aggressively to end that gridlock by convening a national "summit" meeting of the interested parties and pressing them to forge an effective consensus that can be enacted in federal legislation.

End Direct Institutional Aid. Pending the broad restructuring of federal program funds into the microchoice program described above, the new president should take whatever actions may be necessary to end the allocation of federal funds directly to schools and colleges for instruction-related purposes (as opposed to research grants). The tax exemption of supposedly not-for-profit institutions also should be ended. The idea is to direct funds to the greatest extent possible into the hands of consumers rather than to school and college bureaucracies and to eliminate the tax subsidies that favor would-be nonprofit over commercial suppliers.

Federal Reorganization. Finally, the new president should use his authority to reorganize the executive branch to reflect the technological and economic opportunities of the future rather than the special interests of a fading era. Specifically, the president should create a new Department of Knowledge Resources by merging the Education and Labor departments, the National Science Foundation, the Federal Communications Commission, the National Aeronautics and Space Administration, and part or most of the Department of Energy's national laboratories. The administration also should consider including other relevant research- and knowledge-oriented organizations, such as the Commerce Department's

National Institute of Standards and Technology, National Oceanic and Atmospheric Administration, and Census Bureau. The president also should encourage Congress to revise its committee structures along similar lines.

Conclusion

America was founded by people who had the vision and audacity to overthrow tradition and to establish an unprecedented political community, grounded in the radical principles of human liberty and equality. We have now entered a new era when the fabric of whole societies is being rewoven around the world. From Berlin to Vladivostok and from Capetown to Buenos Aires, every major social structure is subject to reappraisal, redesign, and replacement.

Inevitably, the challenges of the dawning knowledge age will demand that the most conservative social glue, education, be reinvented as well. The same HL technology that is driving the overthrow of arthritic bureaucracies holds the key to achieving social reformation swiftly and productively. America's political legacy, her technological vitality, and her responsibility as the world's greatest power all demand that she lead the hyperlearning revolution that promises a new birth of freedom, prosperity, and peace.

10. Returning Medicine to the Marketplace

Michael Tanner

Americans are increasingly coming to believe that there is something seriously wrong with our health care system. Costs are skyrocketing. Twenty years ago health care was a $42-billion-per-year industry. Today total U.S. health care spending tops $662 billion, more than 14 percent of our gross domestic product. Soaring costs are putting enormous financial pressures on American businesses, forcing thousands of small businesses to reduce or drop benefits for their employees. Moreover, health care costs are an increasing burden to already strained family budgets. And nearly 35 million Americans lack health insurance.

With the upset victory of Harris Wofford in Pennsylvania's special Senate election in 1991, health care leaped to the forefront of America's political agenda. Few issues have sparked as much discussion and debate. In 1992 alone, Congress considered more than 100 bills on health care. They ranged from 2 pages long to more than 200 pages. The Bush administration released a 94-page outline of its health care reform program. Bill Clinton countered with a health care plan of his own. And nearly every think tank with a word processor contributed a proposal.

Despite all the noise, there has been little constructive action in Washington. Some think the answer is to force all Americans into a socialized, government-run, tax-funded health care bureaucracy, but only solutions that build on a free market in health care will ultimately be successful in controlling costs and increasing access to care. Government involvement in health care has been steadily increasing for 30 years, with disastrous results. It is time to seek solutions in a different direction, time to look to the power of the free market.

The idea that America has a free-market health care system is little more than a myth. America does have a health care system that is largely privately owned, but government intervention has removed market mechanisms from the health care equation. Myriad federal and state regulations, largely designed to protect powerful special interests, restrict both the provision and the purchase of health care services. Those regulations are a significant factor in driving up health care costs and reducing access to health care, and they may even be harming the quality of care.

In addition, government tax policies have worked to remove the consumer from health care decisionmaking. By encouraging employer-provided coverage to the detriment of individually purchased coverage or out-of-pocket payment, or both, our tax policy increases the trend toward divorcing the health care consumer from the payor of health care costs. As a result, most health care consumers no longer pay for their health care. On average, for every dollar of health care services purchased, 76 cents is paid by someone other than the consumer who purchased it. That means that consumers have little incentive to question costs and every incentive to demand more services. Government itself has also increasingly become a source of health care payment, with predictable increases in both the demand for and the price of services.

Despite the record of government failure, too many politicians think the answer to our health care problems is to force all Americans into a socialized, government-run, tax-funded health care bureaucracy. While Europe and Canada are searching for ways to restore market mechanisms to their national health care systems, America is in serious danger of adopting a health care system that will limit patient choice and ration the availability of care but do nothing to hold down health care costs.

Such a system would come at enormous cost to American taxpayers. Even supporters of national health care admit that such a system would require $60 billion in new taxes. However, most economists put the cost much higher, possibly as high as $339 billion in additional taxes. Let me give you an idea of what that would mean to you as taxpayers. Raising an additional $339 billion would require one of three things: a 15 percent payroll tax on all businesses, a 10 percent national sales tax, or a 14-percentage-point increase in income tax rates.[1]

---

[1]Aldona Robbins and Gary Robbins, *What a Canadian-Style Health Care System Would Cost U.S. Employers and Employees* (Dallas: National Center for Policy Analysis, February 1990).

For all the new tax money, we would buy surprisingly little health care. The one common characteristic of all national health care systems is a shortage of health care services. For example, in Great Britain, a country with a population of only 55 million, more than 800,000 people are waiting for surgery. In New Zealand, a country with a population of just 3 million, the number waiting now exceeds 50,000. In Canada the wait for hip replacement surgery is nearly 10 months; for a mammogram, 2.5 months; for a pap smear, 5 months. Surgeons in Canada report that heart surgery patients are in greater danger of dying on the waiting list than on the operating table.[2] According to Alice Baumgart, president of the Canadian Nurses Association, emergency rooms are so overcrowded that patients awaiting treatment frequently line the corridors.

Let's put things in human terms with a short story that illustrates what this country could be facing. Joel Bondy was a two-year-old child with a serious congenital heart defect that urgently needed surgery. It was a serious operation, but one that was performed many times each day in hospitals across the United States. Unfortunately, Joel did not live in this country. He lived in Canada, where the country's national health care system has resulted in a severe shortage of cardiac care facilities. Canada has only 11 open-heart surgery facilities to serve the entire country. The United States has 793.

Joel's operation was repeatedly postponed as more critical cases preempted the available facilities. Alarmed at their son's deteriorating condition, Joel's parents arranged for him to be operated on in Detroit. Embarrassed by the media coverage of Joel's situation, Canadian authorities told the Bondys that, if they would stay in Canada, Joel would be moved to the top of the list and could have his surgery immediately. Joel was taken on a four-hour ambulance ride to a hospital equipped for the procedure, but there was no bed available. The family had to spend the night in a hotel. Joel Bondy died the next day.

National health care systems do not control the rising cost of health care. Proponents of national health care make much of reported differences in the proportion of GDP spent on health care

[2]John Goodman and Gerald Musgrave, *20 Myths about National Health Insurance* (Dallas: National Center for Policy Analysis, 1992).

by Canada and the United States. It is true that Canada spends only about 9 percent of GDP on health care, while U.S. costs have skyrocketed to more than 14 percent of GDP. However, such comparisons are seriously misleading.

Between 1967 and 1987, the Canadian GDP grew at nearly double the rate at which the GDP of the United States grew. Therefore, any comparison of health spending should be adjusted to compensate for the differing rates of economic growth. Additional adjustments should be made for such factors as population growth; general inflation; currency exchange rates; the larger U.S. elderly population (the elderly require more, and more expensive, health care); higher U.S. rates of violent crime, poverty, AIDS, and teen pregnancy; and greater U.S. investment in research and development. When all such factors are taken into account, Canadian health spending is virtually identical to that of the United States and has actually been rising faster over the last several years.[3]

National health care is not particularly efficient. Certainly, there are many inefficiencies in the American health care system, such as too much waste and too much paperwork, but socialized medicine has its own inefficiencies. For example, Canadian health care has a tremendous bias in favor of hospitalization. In this country outpatient procedures now outnumber inpatient ones. In Canada patients still go into the hospital for procedures that are done on an outpatient basis in the United States. The average Canadian who goes into the hospital is less sick than the average American hospital patient but stays in the hospital almost twice as long.

Canadian hospitals are increasingly being used as glorified nursing homes. There are several reasons for that. One is that Canada has never developed a good system of home care. Another is that from a hospital administrator's point of view it makes sense to fill the hospital with patients who are essentially using the hospital's hotel functions, who need little more than meals and to have their beds changed. After all, a Canadian hospital administrator's number-one concern is staying under his budget cap, and nursing-home patients are a lot cheaper to care for than are people in intensive care. The result is that at a time when people are dying for lack of

[3]Ibid.

178

a hospital bed, 25 percent of all the hospital beds in Ontario are being used for nursing-home care.

If socialized medicine will not solve our health care problems, what will? Logic, economics, and history show that the only reforms likely to have a significant impact on America's health care problems are those that draw on the strength of the free market.

Deregulate the Health Care Industry

There should be a thorough examination of the extent to which government policies are responsible for rising health care costs and the unavailability of health care services. We can help lower health care costs and expand health care access by taking immediate steps to deregulate the health care industry, including eliminating mandated benefits, repealing certificate-of-need programs, and expanding the scope of practice for nonphysician health professionals.

For example, having decided that people are not smart enough to choose their own health insurance benefits, all states have laws that mandate that all health insurance contracts in the state provide coverage of specific disabilities or diseases and specific health care services. Those mandates add significantly to the cost of health insurance.

Most people without health insurance are employed or are dependents of employees. Nearly two-thirds of those people work for businesses with fewer than 100 employees, and nearly half work for businesses with fewer than 25 employees. Surveys of small businesses have repeatedly shown that the cost of health insurance is the primary reason those businesses do not offer health benefits. By making insurance more expensive, mandated benefits contribute directly to the number of uninsured.

In addition, the majority of states continues to maintain regulatory restrictions on health care services, such as certificate-of-need requirements, that act as a barrier to competition. CON regulations say that if you want to build a new hospital, or buy a new piece of medical equipment, or offer a new type of medical service, you must first get permission from the government.

Certificates of need are based on the bizarre economic theory that greater supply and increased competition will lead to higher prices. However, studies have repeatedly demonstrated that CON programs not only fail to contain costs; they may actually lead to increased costs, while limiting the availability of medical services, particularly in rural areas. The Federal Trade Commission has concluded that, nationally, "hospital costs would decline by $1.3 billion per year if states would deregulate their CON programs."[4]

We also need to rethink our medical licensing laws. Studies have repeatedly shown that qualified midlevel nonphysician practitioners can perform many medical services traditionally performed by physicians. Yet the medical profession has consistently used licensure and other regulatory restrictions to limit competition. The result has almost inevitably been higher prices for consumers. For example, 37 states continue to outlaw the practice of midwifery. In most states nurse practitioners cannot treat a patient without direct physician supervision. Chiropractors cannot order blood tests or CAT scans. Nurses, psychologists, pharmacists, and other practitioners cannot prescribe even the most basic medications.

Recently, in Georgia, the legislature accidentally almost outlawed most of the practice of nursing. In the final moments of the 1992 session, the legislators were debating a proposal to prohibit the practice of dentistry without a license, a bill designed to keep dental hygienists from cleaning teeth. At the request of ophthalmologists who were attempting to prohibit laser eye surgery by optometrists, the bill was amended to prohibit anyone except licensed physicians, veterinarians, podiatrists, and dentists from performing "any surgery, operation, or invasive procedure in which human or animal tissue is cut, pierced or otherwise altered."[5] Since routine injections pierce the skin, nurses would have been prohibited from giving injections, drawing blood, or starting intravenous fluids. Medical care in Georgia was nearly brought to a halt. Fortunately, a judge has issued an injunction against enforcement of the law until it can be amended.

The problem, however, goes far beyond one misguided piece of legislation. The blame lies with a process whereby, as the *Atlanta*

---

[4]D. Sherman, *The Effect of State Certificate-of-Need Laws on Hospital Costs: An Economic Policy Analysis*, Federal Trade Commission, January 1988.

[5]"Nurses Protest Aid Curb," *Gwinnett* (Ga.) *Daily News*, May 28, 1992.

Constitution noted, "medical care professionals are constantly turning to the legislature to protect their economic interests, usually from the incursions of other health care professionals."[6]

Medicare and Medicaid reimbursement regulations are also a significant factor in driving up hospital costs. For example, Medicare rules require hospitals to provide 24-hour nursing service, furnished or supervised by a registered nurse in each department or unit of the facility. Medicare also requires hospitals to use only licensed laboratory and radiological technicians. Medicare even requires hospitals to have a full-time director of food and dietary services. Alternatives to hospitals, such as rural health clinics and community health centers, must also meet stringent administrative and staffing requirements under Medicare and Medicaid rules.

Sometimes it appears that the government simply can't tolerate success. For example, one very positive trend in health care has been the move toward outpatient surgery. The proportion of operations performed on an outpatient basis has been increasing at a remarkable rate since 1980. And in 1990, for the first time, the number of outpatient surgical procedures constituted a majority of all surgeries. It is estimated that by the end of the century, 65 to 70 percent of all surgery will be performed on an outpatient basis.[7] That should be good news. Outpatient treatment is far less costly than hospitalization. Therefore, a move toward outpatient surgery will help reduce overall health care costs. In addition, because an increasing number of surgical procedures are being performed at nonhospital surgical clinics, there may be an important opportunity to expand access in areas—such as rural communities—that do not have full-blown hospitals. But Congress appears to be ready to kill the golden goose, by requiring extensive new licensing, accreditation, training, and reimbursement regulations that will certainly slow, if not reverse, that trend.

Further, federal and state tax laws prohibit health care facilities from participating in cooperatives and other arrangements to provide less expensive cost-management, laundry, and housekeeping services. Other regulations that increase health care costs include

[6]"General Assembly's Bad Medicine," *Atlanta Constitution*, May 30, 1992.

[7]"Outpatient Surgery on the Rise: Regulation Doesn't Keep Pace," *New York Times*, July 1, 1992.

recent rules by the Occupational Safety and Health Administration and the Health Care Financing Administration governing procedures for clinical laboratories. The costs of the paperwork burden of and compliance with those new regulations, which cover such critical issues as where a doctor may hang a lab coat, are estimated to be as high as $40,000 annually for each laboratory. It is expected that as many as 4,000 small independent laboratories will be put out of business and the cost of lab tests significantly increased.

Abolish the Food and Drug Administration

One of the most destructive of all federal government agencies is the Food and Drug Administration (FDA). The mission of the FDA is ostensibly to protect the public from unsafe or ineffective medications (and foods, of course). However, in reality, the FDA has provided little additional public protection but has driven up health care costs and deprived millions of the health care treatment they need.

It now costs more than $231 million to bring a new drug through discovery, clinical testing, development, and FDA approval, an increase of 327 percent since 1976. It also takes approximately 12 years for a new drug to reach the market.[8] A substantial portion of that time and money is the result of the FDA approval process.

Some studies have indicated that the FDA approval process doubles the cost of developing a new drug.[9] That cost, of course, is passed along in the form of higher prices to consumers. In addition, the high cost of the approval process acts as a barrier to entry, benefiting large pharmaceutical companies by preventing competition from smaller firms that have limited capital resources.

Even more tragic is the loss of human life that results from delays caused by the FDA approval process. For example, during the 10-year delay in allowing propranolol (the first widely used beta-blocker for treatment of angina and hypertension) to be marketed in the United States, approximately 100,000 people died because

[8]Pharmaceutical Manufacturers Association, *Good Medicine: A Report on the Status of Pharmaceutical Research* (Washington: PMA, 1992), pp. 8–10, citing figures by Joseph DiMasi, Tufts University, 1990.

[9]Samuel Kazman, "Deadly Overcaution: The FDA's Approval Process," *Journal of Regulation and Social Costs*, September 1990.

the drug was unavailable. And, according to George Hitchings, co-winner of the 1988 Nobel Prize in medicine, the FDA delay in approving the anti-bacterial drug Sepra cost more than 80,000 lives.[10]

In addition, the FDA places restrictions and qualifications on the advertising of pharmaceutical products; those restrictions have the effect of preventing consumers from having all the information necessary to make fully informed medical decisions. For example, the FDA has forbidden aspirin manufacturers to advertise its benefits in preventing heart attacks.

Now, the FDA is attempting to expand its reach, seeking to extend its authority to cover such items as vitamins and herbal remedies. The agency is also seeking broader subpoena, seizure, and surveillance powers to enforce existing regulations.

The FDA is clearly an unnecessary burden to the American health care system. There is no evidence that the agency offers the American people any real protection. Ideally, the FDA should be eliminated. That may be politically unachievable, but certainly the size and power of that dangerous agency should be restricted, not expanded. Several alternatives exist. For instance, the FDA's veto power over drugs could be changed to a system of certification. The agency would continue to review the safety and efficacy of drugs, but unapproved drugs—clearly labeled as such—would be available to individuals who chose to use them. Even better would be the rise of a private-sector organization to provide certification, much as the Underwriters Laboratory certifies electrical appliances, which would eliminate the government's role altogether. If the FDA were not entirely eliminated, it could return to its pre-1962 mission of evaluating only the safety of new drugs. Issues of efficacy could be left to the marketplace. Lesser steps would include accelerating the approval process, as proposed by the Bush administration; allowing the use of overseas safety data; and privatizing the new-drug application review process.

Restructure Tax Policy

If we are serious about expanding access to health care for uninsured Americans, one of the most important reforms is to change tax

[10]Arthur D. Little, Inc., *Cost-Effectiveness of Pharmaceutical #7: Beta-Blocker Reduction of Mortality and Reinfarction Rate in Survivors of Myocardial Infarction: A Cost-Benefit Study,* 1984.

laws that discriminate against people who do not have employer-provided health insurance. In addition to expanding health care access, such tax changes would (1) establish a basic fairness in government policy—giving the same tax break to the waitress who has to buy her own health insurance that we are currently giving to the well-paid executives of wealthy corporations—and (2) hold down overall health care costs by increasing consumer involvement in the health care marketplace.

Current federal and state tax laws exclude from taxable wages the cost of health insurance provided by an employer. Therefore, a vast majority of Americans, those who receive health insurance through their employers, do not pay federal, state, or Social Security taxes on the value of their policies. Moreover, employers can deduct the full premium cost as a business expense. Employers do not even pay Social Security payroll taxes on those benefits. In short, the entire cost of employer-provided insurance is paid for with *before-tax* dollars.

However, those Americans not fortunate enough to receive employer-provided health insurance face entirely different tax laws. For example, self-employed individuals and their families may deduct only 25 percent of the cost of health insurance. In addition, self-employed individuals must pay Social Security taxes on money used to purchase health insurance. Part-time workers, students, the unemployed, and everyone else not receiving employer-provided health insurance—including most employees of small businesses—are unable to deduct *any* of the cost of health insurance.

That difference in tax treatment creates a disparity that effectively doubles the cost of health insurance for people who must purchase their own. For example, the family of a self-employed person—who earns $35,000 per year, has to pay federal and state taxes with only a 25 percent deduction, and has to pay Social Security taxes—must earn $7,075 to pay for a $4,000 health insurance policy. A person working for a small business that offers no health insurance would have to earn $8,214 to pay for a $4,000 policy.

The results of that inequity can be clearly seen. Those workers who must use after-tax dollars to purchase health insurance are 24 times more likely to be uninsured than are those who are eligible for tax-free employer-provided coverage. Significantly, the poor and minorities, who are less likely to have employer-provided insurance, are the most likely to be left without access to health insurance Thus, the perverse impact of our tax policies is to subsidize the purchase of health insurance by the most affluent and to penalize those less well off.

Our tax policies also have an adverse impact on health care prices. By encouraging employer-provided coverage to the detriment of individually purchased coverage or out-of-pocket payment, our tax policy increases the trend toward divorcing the health care consumer from payment of health care costs.

Establishing tax equity would encourage health care consumers to become more involved in the health care system. Individuals who purchase their own insurance are more likely to shop around for the best deal. And individuals who purchase health care out-of-pocket are much more likely to make cost-conscious health care decisions.

It would take only a relatively simple reform to solve the problem. We should enact legislation making the purchase of individual health insurance and out-of-pocket expenditures for health care fully tax deductible.

Establish Individual Medical Accounts

Another proposal to return consumers to the center of the health care equation is individual medical accounts (IMAs), also known as Medical IRAs or Medi-Saver Accounts. Individuals would be exempted from taxes on money deposited in Medical IRAs, in the same way they currently pay no taxes on deposits to IRAs. Money could be withdrawn without penalty to pay medical expenses.

With such a program in place, employers could be expected to change the way they provide insurance. Rather than continuing to provide high-cost insurance benefits, with low deductibles and extensive benefits, employers would provide each employee with an annual allowance of perhaps $2,000, which the employee could deposit in an IMA. For medical expenses in excess of the $2,000, the employer would continue to provide health insurance, but such catastrophic coverage would be relatively inexpensive.

The individual would be responsible for paying his own health care expenses under $2,000, using funds from his IMA. (It should be noted that less than 12.5 percent of all insured individuals have

185

annual claims in excess of $2,000.)[11] Unspent money in the account would accumulate and belong to the account holder. Before age 65, there would be a penalty applied to withdrawals for other than health care expenditures.

IMAs would have six major advantages. First, they would be particularly beneficial to low-income employees. Most current health insurance policies have low deductibles, often $100, which can cause hardships for those with little discretionary income. Deductibles offer a perverse incentive for low-income workers. They are often forced to forgo preventive care or early intervention because they can't afford the deductible. Yet once the deductible is met, there is no incentive not to incur additional, perhaps unnecessary, expenses. With an IMA, the incentive is to spend wisely throughout the year, rather than to punish the first expenditure of the year.

Second, IMAs would be completely portable. One of the most serious problems of our current health care system is that insurance is so closely linked with employment. That means that an individual who loses his job or changes jobs is in danger of losing his insurance. Half of the 35 million Americans estimated to be without health insurance at any given time are uninsured for four months or less, and only 15 percent are uninsured for more than two years.[12] With an IMA, those individuals would continue to have funds available to pay for health care during changes or temporary interruptions in employment.

Self-employed individuals would also benefit. Currently, lack of health insurance is 10 times greater among the self-employed than it is among those who work for others.[13] A medical IRA would allow the self-employed to receive a substantial tax break for saving for their health care.

[11]Based on claims experience in Chicago, one of the nation's highest cost areas. In more typical areas, only about 9 percent of claims exceed $2,000. From claims distribution analyses by Tilinghast Corporation.

[12]Katherine Swartz and Timothy McBride, *Spells without Health Insurance: Distributions of Durations and Their Link to Point-in-Time Estimates of the Uninsured* (Washington: Blue Cross and Blue Shield, 1990).

[13]Health Care Solutions for America, *Federal Tax Policy and the Uninsured: How U.S. Tax Laws Deny 10 Million Americans Access to Health Insurance* (Washington: HCSA, 1992).

Third, IMAs would give individuals greater flexibility in the types of health care they could purchase. Such items as prescription drugs, dental care, and eyeglasses are frequently not covered by traditional employer-provided health benefit plans. Likewise, most employer plans do not cover nontraditional health care professionals such as chiropractors and naturopaths. But an individual could use his IMA to pay for such services.

Fourth, there would be no administrative overhead costs for expenses paid out of IMAs. That would reduce both the overall cost of health care and the paperwork burden on doctors. The administrative costs for private insurance average 11 to 12 percent of premiums. It has been estimated that payment of medical bills with funds from IMAs could reduce administrative costs to 1 to 2 percent.[14]

Fifth, IMAs would increase America's savings rate and thus have a positive overall effect on the economy, and finally and most important, IMAs would establish an incentive for consumers to act responsibly in making health care decisions.

Privatize Medicaid and Medicare

The current Medicaid and Medicare systems have clearly failed. Costs are skyrocketing. Medicare costs have increased to the point where the systems are in serious jeopardy. Medicare Part A, which primarily pays for hospital care and services, is projected to be unable to meet its financial requirements by the year 2005. It is estimated that to restore the fund's financial stability will require increasing the Medicare payroll tax from 2.9 percent to at least 6.5 percent. Medicare Part B, which pays for physicians' services, is in no better financial shape. General revenue contributions to Medicare Part B may increase 300 percent by the end of the century. And the premium contribution by the elderly may increase by a similar percentage.[15] Medicaid is in much the same situation. The state share of the joint federal-state program is growing twice as fast as overall state spending. Some estimates indicate that state spending on Medicaid could increase a phenomenal 480 percent

---

[14]Mackinac Center for Public Policy, "Health Care: Solving the Administrative Cost Question," June 8, 1992.

[15]*1988 Annual Report of the Board of Trustees of the Federal Old-Age and Survivors Insurance and Disability Insurance Trust Funds*, May 1, 1988, appendix F.

by the year 2000. The federal share of the program is growing even faster.

Furthermore, patients are receiving second-rate care. Studies have shown that Medicare and Medicaid recipients have higher mortality rates than patients with private insurance. And providers are being shortchanged. Both Medicare and Medicaid reimburse providers at a rate well below the actual cost of procedures. As a result, fewer and fewer providers are willing to participate in the programs. Those who do pass along their costs to patients with private health insurance, a practice known as cost shifting.

The time is ripe for drastic reform. The federal government should begin to restructure the system to give Medicaid and Medicare recipients more flexibility to obtain private health insurance that meets their individual needs. As much as possible, responsibility for care of the poor and the elderly should be moved from the public to the private sector.[16]

Conclusion

It has long been noted that the Chinese character for "crisis" is the same as the character for "opportunity." Clearly, America's health care system is in crisis. But we also have a unique window of opportunity to reform our health care system in a way that will guarantee that American health care will continue to be the best in the world.

The only reforms that are likely to have a significant impact on America's health care problems are those that draw on the strength of the free market. By developing a market-oriented strategy that draws on the strengths of competition and consumer choice, we will reduce health care costs and extend access to care.

Only a comprehensive market-based program will take America's health care system off the critical list. However, we must act quickly. If we do not seize this opportunity to establish free-market health care reforms, those who favor increased government intervention will surely fill the vacuum. That would be disastrous for the future of health care in America.

---

[16]For a discussion of options for privatizing Medicare and Medicaid, see John C. Goodman and Gerald L. Musgrave, *Patient Power: Solving America's Health Care Crisis* (Washington: Cato Institute, 1992). See also Michael Tanner, "Medicaid Reform: Giving Georgia's Poor a Choice," Georgia Public Policy Foundation, February 1992.

11. Reviving the Inner City
David Boaz

America's most difficult problem in the 1990s is not a military threat, nor the overhyped environmental problem, nor the deficit, nor even two decades of slow economic growth. It is the interrelated ills of race, poverty, crime, and the underclass. It is millions of Americans afraid to leave their homes at night; millions of Americans (some of them the same people) who feel permanently shut out of the mainstream of society; racial tensions and even racial hatreds on the rise at a time when they should be disappearing.

The *New Yorker* had it right in its May 11, 1992, "Talk of the Town":

> Either we can start to seriously confront the plight of our inner cities, and treat it as the national emergency we all know that it has become . . . [or] we can ignore the problem, and continue to humiliate and dehumanize the residents of our inner cities, and try to contain their rage by relying more and more heavily on police intervention and on the prison system.

None of us can fail to be moved by the searing images of the inner city: the pregnant children, the fatherless boys, the squalid tenements, the police sirens, the law-abiding folk cowering in fear, the desolation, the resentment, the despair.

To seriously confront that emergency, we must first understand the nature of the problem: Is the root issue racism, or poverty, or welfare, or the collapse of moral and family values? Or all of the above? Whatever our decision, it is clear that we can no longer ignore the issue. The Los Angeles riots sent a wake-up call to Americans: something is dreadfully wrong in our inner cities, and we will not have a peaceful or just society until we deal with this tangled web of problems.

As usual in our political debates, the right and the left are talking past each other with increasingly irrelevant arguments. On the left, we constantly hear the demand for more money. "The poor have been abandoned, we need a Marshall Plan for the cities, the rich get richer and the poor get poorer." But if government money could solve the problems of the urban poor, surely the poor would be drinking champagne toasts by now. From 1980 to 1990 per capita spending in cities with populations over 1 million rose from $1,748 to $2,283 (in constant 1990 dollars)—a real increase of 31 percent. For cities of 500,000 to 1 million, spending rose from $1,225 to $1,498—a 22 percent real increase. Spending on poverty reached $226 billion in 1990, or five times the real amount in 1964, when the War on Poverty got under way—yet the poverty rate, which was falling dramatically before the War on Poverty, has changed little in the past 25 years. Money is not the root of America's poverty problem.

Those on the left also tell us that racism is the biggest problem facing black Americans. Racism exists, of course, but can it really be more widespread today than it was 30 years ago? Public places are far more integrated than they were before the civil rights revolution; two-income black families have made dramatic income gains over the past two decades; the two highest paid entertainers in America are black; immigrants of all colors (including those from Africa) still find America a land of opportunity; schools, colleges, and businesses practice affirmative action; a black governor has been elected in the capital of the Confederacy, and a black woman has been elected to the Senate from America's most representative large state, which is 78 percent white. No society in the world has eliminated racial prejudice, but it stretches credulity to blame the problems of the black poor in America on racism.

There are mirror images of those errors on the right. Conservatives say that poverty isn't a problem any more because, after all, the poor get lots of government benefits. Now, there *is* a serious point to be made here: There is virtually no grinding material poverty in the United States. In 1990 the real per capita expenditures of the one-fifth of the U.S. population with the lowest incomes exceeded the per capita income of the average American household in 1960. The average American poor person (as defined by the Census Bureau's annual report on poverty) has twice as much living space as the average Japanese citizen and more than the average West European. Most poor households own a car, and almost half have air conditioning.[1] But the conservative argument ignores the basic point. To be dependent on government handouts, to live in government housing, to be subjected to the indignities of the social services industry *is* poverty. The problem is not that people are starving, it is that for whatever reason millions of Americans do not participate in the economy, do not achieve the satisfaction of providing for themselves and their families. It is callous and disingenuous to dismiss their plight as "not really poverty."

Conservatives rightly reject the notion that racism is the source of blacks' problems in America. But they go too far when they respond: "We've outlawed discrimination, instituted affirmative action, and spent $2.5 trillion on poverty. Why can't blacks make it in America?" They ignore the very real crimes that white America—or at least the U.S. government—has committed against blacks. First, the government ignored its own principles to hold blacks in chattel slavery. Then, it passed Jim Crow laws to prevent blacks from succeeding in the post–Civil War marketplace. Then, when it finally repealed the Jim Crow laws, it created a welfare state that ensnared many blacks, trapping them in neighborhoods with lousy government schools and terrifying crime rates. One hundred twenty-five years after the Thirteenth Amendment, millions of blacks are still on a plantation—given money by a white master and subject to his rules.

Understanding the Problem

So if liberals and conservatives are both wrong, how should we understand the roots of our urban problems? First, we should acknowledge that educated, affluent whites have created most of the conditions we now deplore, albeit often with the best of intentions. Second, we should understand just *how* white elites have gone astray.

Over the past 70 years or so, white elites—notably legislators and judges—have shown a declining respect for the rules of property and contract. Legislators have taken more and more of our

[1] Robert Rector, "America's Poverty Myth," *Wall Street Journal*, September 3, 1992; Robert Rector, "Perplexities of the Poverty Data," *Washington Times*, September 8, 1992.

income in taxes and circumscribed property rights through regulations aimed at securing everything from low-cost housing to panoramic views. Judges have not only upheld those legislative decisions, ignoring provisions of the U.S. Constitution that protect property rights; they have also voided contracts that they thought reflected "unequal bargaining power" or that otherwise were not in "the public interest."

With property and contract getting less respect at the top of society, is it any wonder that such attitudes trickle down through society? In courses on "values clarification," schools teach children that honesty is an interesting idea, not a moral standard; résumé fraud seems to be rampant; 2 percent of the merchandise in American stores is stolen; and newspapers report an increase in the number of people who buy expensive clothes, wear them once to a party, and then return them to the store. Smokers blame cigarette companies for their tobacco-induced illnesses, while high school students who cheat on the SAT blame a materialistic society. We can and should deplore the irresponsibility and dishonesty of individuals, but we should recognize that they are reflecting a message that comes from the highest authorities.

The essence of that message is that it is appropriate to transfer goods from the person who earned them to another person who did not, and that people need not live up to the contracts they make. The elites who began that shift in traditional values may have thought it could be contained—that it would be carried out carefully by thoughtful judges and legislators—but it seems likely that the decline in respect for property and contract, the growing irresponsibility and dishonesty, is partly responsible for the burglaries, car-jackings, and murders that now terrify urban residents. The perpetrators of many of those crimes may unconsciously believe—and some looters in the Los Angeles riots came close to saying explicitly—that what they are doing is just taking redistribution into their own hands.

The Welfare State

In another way, the policy elites bear an even more direct responsibility for the problems of the urban poor, for they created the welfare state and its corollaries that trap people in ghettos. The sound and fury over family values, single motherhood, and Murphy Brown obscured the real point: We don't have to condemn the single mother to acknowledge that *of course* it is better to be reared in a two-parent family. Children living in fatherless homes are five times more likely to be poor. And beyond the problem of poverty, it is increasingly clear that mothers alone have great difficulty controlling—civilizing—teenage boys. That problem is worse for black single mothers than for white, because white single mothers tend to live in communities dominated by two-parent families. But in some inner-city black neighborhoods, 80 percent of the families are female headed. There are hardly any role models from whom young boys can learn how to be responsible men.

There will always be some unwed mothers and some divorced or widowed mothers. But a society that offers pregnant teenagers enough money to get an apartment of their own should not be surprised that teenage pregnancy and motherhood are on the rise. When people pay for the consequences of their actions, they still make mistakes—but they make fewer than when government absolves them of responsibility.

The stark truth is that as long as the welfare state makes it possible for young women to have children without a husband and to survive without a job, the inner city will continue to be marked by poverty, crime, and despair. What, then, can we do about America's most difficult problem? Many solutions have been offered, most of them promising more of the same or niggling reforms. After the Los Angeles riots, many people blamed "the Reagan-Bush cutbacks" and demanded that we spend more money on the cities and the poor. Most of those people had a clear self-interest: they were social-services providers, mayors, urban congressmen. But the Old Paradigm flag was proudly waved even by such a distinguished scholar as Anthony Downs of the Brookings Institution: "The conclusion that social programs don't work is dead wrong. Throwing money at poverty works beautifully. The problem is, we haven't thrown enough money at it, and not in the most effective ways."[2]

One has to wonder, though, with anti-poverty spending five times higher in real terms than in 1964, just how much more money the Old Paradigmers think might work. Many of them are throwing in the towel. One prominent liberal Democratic social-policy analyst

___

[2]*Los Angeles Times,* June 6, 1992.

told me recently that he thought well-designed and well-funded government programs could improve the urban-poverty situation by maybe 5 percent. If that's the argument for doing more, it seems time to do something different.

The latest "something different" is requiring that welfare recipients either work or enter job training. Such plans are now being tried in several states, by both Democratic and Republican governors, but

> a review of workfare programs with strong job-search components conducted by the Manpower Demonstration Research Corporation found employment gains among welfare participants generally no better than 10 percent. Even the administrators of Massachusetts' celebrated ET-Choices program could claim a net drop in the welfare rolls of only 4.5 percent from 1983 to 1986, a time of vigorous statewide economic growth. Similarly in New York, another state with extensive and highly touted job training and employment programs, the welfare caseload has fallen by a mere 4.5 percent over the same period.[3]

Aside from the general problem of inefficiency in government bureaucracies, we might note the incentive problems in such an effort: What happens to social workers if they get all their clients off welfare? How many people will work hard to eliminate their own jobs? Yet another problem is that we flinch at enforcing such rules: If a welfare recipient doesn't find—or doesn't take—a job, do we cut her off, leaving her children to go hungry next week? If we are not ready to summon the will to do that, then workfare is doomed to fail. Widespread support for workfare and similar programs probably reflects a somewhat surly and paternalistic attitude on the part of taxpayers—"If they're going to take our money, let's at least make 'em work"—rather than a concern for the well-being of those trapped in the welfare net or a real conviction that workfare would actually move people into the productive economy.

In any case, now that dissatisfaction with the existing welfare system is widespread, and faith in "enough money" is dying, we are probably doomed to a decade of piecemeal reform, with another

---

[3]Kevin R. Hopkins, "A New Deal for America's Poor," *Policy Review*, Summer 1988, p. 70.

generation of children coming of age in a system much like today's. Charles Murray, a long-time evaluator of social programs who has become the most trenchant critic of welfare, was asked a few years ago to point out one or two programs that had actually worked. His reply was, "I cannot think of a single large program, state or federal, that I consider to be a meaningful success."[4]

A bold president or governor would reject the Gorbachev-like attempt to make our homegrown socialism work and move forthwith to the Yeltsin era: recognize that socialism *doesn't* work and be done with it. Such an executive would recognize that no one has come up with a compelling program better than the "thought experiment" Charles Murray proposed at the end of *Losing Ground*.

> We have available to us a program that would convert a large proportion of the younger generation of hardcore unemployed into steady workers making a living wage. The same program would drastically reduce births to single teenage girls. It would reverse the trendline in the breakup of poor families. It would measurably increase the upward socioeconomic mobility of poor families. These improvements would affect some millions of persons.
>
> All these are results that have eluded the efforts of the social programs installed since 1965, yet, from everything we know, there is no real question about whether they would occur under the program I propose. . . .
>
> The proposed program, our final and most ambitious thought experiment, consists of scrapping the entire federal welfare and income-support structure for working-aged persons, including [Aid to Families with Dependent Children], Medicaid, Food Stamps, Unemployment Insurance, Worker's Compensation, subsidized housing, disability insurance, and the rest. It would leave the working-aged person with no recourse whatsoever except the job market, family members, friends, and public or private locally funded services. It is the Alexandrian solution: cut the knot, for there is no way to untie it. . . .
>
> The prospective advantages are real and extremely plausible. In fact, if a government program of the traditional sort (one that would "do" something rather than simply get out of the way) could *as plausibly* promise these advantages, its

---

[4]Charles Murray, "Aw, Never Mind," *Washington Monthly*, June 1988, p. 40.

passage would be a foregone conclusion. Congress, yearning for programs that are not retreads of failures, would be prepared to spend billions.[5]

Murray's program is more than bold. It is in many ways harsh. Real people would suffer from the abolition of welfare. Perhaps those who would be hurt the most are those—like divorced or widowed women—who use welfare the way it was intended, as a temporary support while they work out a new way of supporting themselves. Without welfare, they would have to find other arrangements. But the very fact that they remain on AFDC only temporarily means that they are capable of finding jobs, new marriages, or other means of support.

Those who stay on welfare for years at a time would have a more difficult adjustment, but there are high costs associated with the attempt to absolve people of the consequences of their actions. When we offer pregnant teenagers their choice of a subsidized abortion or a subsidized apartment, we will get more pregnant teenagers. And the long-term consequences of that—for the teenagers, for their fatherless children, and for the rest of us—have become appalling. If we can change the incentive structure in the inner city, we have some hope of giving people there a decent living. Clearly, the welfare state will never do so.

Education: The Blocked Way Out of Poverty

As long as the welfare state exists, the inner city will remain a morass of bad incentives, fatherless families, and broken lives. But the welfare state is not solely responsible for that condition. A second contributor is the public school system. The statistics on American education as a whole are bleak enough: Test scores are significantly lower than they were 30 years ago, even while real expenditures per pupil have tripled. The average Japanese student outscores the top 5 percent of American students on math tests.[6] Inner-city schools are far worse than average. They have a dropout rate of around 50 percent. But poor education may take a

[5]Charles Murray, *Losing Ground: American Social Policy, 1950–1980* (New York: Basic Books, 1984), pp. 227–29.

[6]See David Boaz, ed., *Liberating Schools: Education in the Inner City* (Washington: Cato Institute, 1991), esp. pp. 2–4.

back seat to violence as a problem in inner-city schools. The *Evening Sun* reveals that 20 or more students were arrested in 23 Baltimore schools during the spring 1992 semester. Washington is considering installing metal detectors in high schools. New York City has announced a $28 million program to put weapons scanners and police officers in the schools, reflecting the fact that in or near New York City's public schools during the 1991–92 school year, 16 students were shot and 6 were killed; 5 teachers were shot and 1 was killed. It's no surprise that 30 percent of the public school teachers in Los Angeles send their own children to private schools, as do 46 percent of teachers in Chicago and more than 50 percent in Milwaukee.[7]

The public schools are monopoly bureaucratic institutions, politically controlled in districts so large as to be virtually immune from political pressure, certainly pressure from uneducated and unorganized parents. Inner-city parents have no choice about where to send their children and little hope of their getting a decent education in the schools to which they are assigned. Thus, it's no surprise that half of inner-city students drop out before high school graduation and that many of those who stay for 12 years graduate uneducated and unprepared to enter the mainstream economy. Wisconsin State Rep. Polly Williams, author of Milwaukee's school voucher program, declares that the Milwaukee public schools have a 90 percent failure rate—60 percent of the kids drop out, and only 10 percent of the ninth graders eventually graduate able to read. In today's complex economy, students who don't get a good basic education are going to be left behind after they leave school. Once again, the inner-city poor are the victims of a system designed by upper-middle-class elites.

In every sector of the economy, competition produces better results than bureaucracy and monopoly. (Not just the economy, in fact: liberalism involves competition in political and intellectual life as well as economic life.) That's why the public schools don't work very well. They offer about as much scope for flexibility, innovation, consumer responsiveness, and experimentation as did Soviet factories. Private schools work better, because they have to provide a service that parents will pay for and also because they

[7]Ibid., pp. 8–9.

can tailor their programs to the needs of different students and parents. Unfortunately, many families can't afford private schools.

Poor parents need to be given the same opportunity to choose decent schools that wealthier parents have. Each state should implement an education scholarship plan to give students a choice between public and private schools. Each child should receive a scholarship, worth, say, 50 percent of the amount the state or city spends per child, that could be taken to any public or private school in the state. Schools would then be reimbursed by the state for the total amount of scholarship vouchers they collected from students.

An educational choice plan would bring competition to our schools. Schools that couldn't attract customers would go out of business. Those that served children and parents best would expand and be copied by other schools. We recognize the benefits of free enterprise and competition in other markets; we should apply those lessons to education, our last and greatest monopoly.

Educational choice would do wonders for education in every neighborhood. But its greatest effect would be in the inner city, where the public schools are worst and from which parents are unable to escape. Parents generally know that inner-city schools are atrocious; they just lack the means to escape them, either by moving to more expensive neighborhoods or by paying private school tuition. If every inner-city parent had a voucher worth, say, $3,000 per child, we would see a flourishing variety of schools spring up in the inner city—Catholic, fundamentalist, Afrocentrist, traditional, even for-profit schools like those promised by Chris Whittle's Edison Project. Children might be born into poverty, but they would have a better chance at getting a good education, which has always been the ticket out of poverty.

Choice would have one more benefit for the inner city that is not widely noted. Today, middle-class families move to suburban districts because the schools are better, even though they might prefer to stay in the city because of its diversity, its nightlife, or its convenience to work. By separating the choice of where to live from the choice of where their children will attend school, an educational scholarship plan might bring some middle-class families of all races back to the city.[8]

[8]I am indebted to William Niskanen for this point.

War and Peace in the Inner City

The War on Drugs is another policy implemented by elites that has devastating effects on the inner city. First, of course, one can hardly ignore the fact that though drug users are overwhelmingly white, almost half the people arrested for drug violations are black. While many blacks call for a stronger police effort against drugs in their neighborhoods, others understandably see the disproportionate arrest figures as a sign of a white conspiracy against the black community. Second, the War on Drugs has brought an unprecedented level of crime to inner cities. By now it should be clear: Drugs don't cause crime, drug laws cause crime. Drug laws drive prices and profits in the drug trade to astronomical levels and force drug sales into the black market. Like alcohol prohibition in the 1920s, drug prohibition in the 1990s means not that drugs are unavailable but that they are available only from criminals. Half the crime in major cities is committed by addicts trying to pay for a habit that would be easily affordable if it were legal. The more visible and frightening crimes—the record murder rates in cities from New York to Richmond—result from the fact that black-market buyers, sellers, and competitors have no way to settle disputes peacefully. That is why young black men in Watts or the South Side of Chicago are more likely to be killed than were American soldiers in Vietnam. The violent crime arrest rate for juveniles has tripled since 1965; it's five times as high for black juveniles as for whites and 19 times as high as for "other races."[9] Much of the violent crime among teenagers is a result of the black market in drugs.

Thanks in large measure to the drug laws, people in the inner city feel under assault from criminals, or drug enforcers, or both. But beyond those effects, drug prohibition has created a world turned upside down in the inner city, a world in which criminals are role models, mothers ask their teenage sons for the rent money, and young men see three alternatives open to them: welfare, "chump change" at a low-skilled job, or big money dealing drugs. Drug laws make a mockery of the work ethic, undermine the family,

[9]Federal Bureau of Investigation study reported in "The Young and the Violent," *Wall Street Journal*, September 23, 1992.

and destroy the natural order of the community. In so doing they also destroy the possibility of legitimate economic development.

Thus, the third crucial reform for the inner-city poor is to end the War on Drugs—to make the use and sale of drugs by adults legal. The level of crime created by drug prohibition should be intolerable to civilized people, and it would be if that crime came to the neighborhoods of the white elite. In Washington, 482 people were murdered in 1991, the fifth straight annual record. Only a handful of those people were white. One wonders whether, had it been 100 white people murdered, the public policy status quo would have prevailed.

Besides eliminating the crime associated with the black-market drug trade, legalization would free 30,000 state and local law enforcement officials to work on violent crime. A recent study of the drug war in Illinois found that increasing the focus on drug crimes has had the effect of diverting resources from other crime-prevention efforts.[10]

The federal government should repeal its drug prohibitions and leave it to the states to set their own drug policies, as was done with alcohol policy after the repeal of Prohibition. Some states would doubtless maintain prohibition, but others would quickly recognize the benefits of legalization. Drug legalization would not solve all of America's drug problems, but it would dramatically bring down the crime rate, make drug use safer, relieve our clogged courts and prisons, and make honest work more attractive to talented and ambitious inner-city youth. It would allow churches, families, and community organizations to treat drug abuse as an ethical and medical problem rather than asking the police to try to enforce futile laws.

Conclusion

This is the world white elites have given inner-city blacks: a welfare plantation, schools that fall somewhere between baby sitting and prison, and a community under siege from violence.

Rapper Sister Souljah's interview with the *Washington Post* achieved notoriety for its racist elements, but it also included some insights such as this one:

[10]Bruce Benson and David Rasmussen, "Illinois' War on Drugs: Some Unintended Consequences," Heartland Institute Policy Study no. 48, April 21, 1992.

Usually this system is successful in crushing the spirit, the mind and the hearts of young people. Because I've been able to grow up in the welfare system, and go through the public housing system, and go through all these government programs, and come out still in control of my own mind and thoughts, it's unusual.[11]

Those who escape that crushing system deserve our admiration; those who remain trapped deserve a better chance.

The three reforms suggested here are by no means the only policy changes that would help the urban poor. Other beneficial reforms would include repeal of minimum-wage and licensing laws, which prevent low-skilled people from getting jobs; repeal of rent-control and zoning laws that destroy housing and increase homelessness; tax reduction for businesses and self-employed people in the inner city to encourage business formation; and reduced regulation. Cities don't need Marshall plans and central planners; they need to give freedom, voluntarism, and markets a chance to work.

Today, despite civil rights laws, affirmative action, and the clear evidence of black economic progress, racial relations in America seem more acrimonious than ever. College students scrawl racial epithets on black and Asian students' doors, black entertainers find a wide audience for racist and anti-Semitic lyrics, resentments fester—even though polls indicate that blacks and whites earnestly *want* to get along. Both black and white Americans find that when they talk to each other, they feel like ambassadors from their race, carefully measuring their words to maintain the proper diplomatic balance.

The weak economy is partly responsible for the tension; people look for scapegoats in bad times. But the economy can't explain the whole picture. I suggest that the welfare state and affirmative action—policies adopted often with the best of intentions—have had sweeping unintended consequences. The welfare state and the War on Drugs have combined to create a horrifying amount of violence in the inner city, leading ghetto residents to suspect a conspiracy to destroy them, and middle-class whites to fear black crime. The coercive, government-mandated form of affirmative

[11]David Mills, "Sister Souljah's Rebellion Rap," *Washington Post*, May 13, 1992, p. B4.

action (along with such corollaries as race-norming and contract set-asides) reflects the worst aspects of welfare liberalism: white guilt combined with an unspoken belief that blacks can't make it in a competitive society without such help and a preference for group identification over ability. Affirmative action has done little or nothing for poor and uneducated blacks while causing resentment among white males, who fear that they are losing college and job opportunities that they deserve. Note that, as Thomas Sowell points out, we are not seeing a "return" to racism on college campuses; we didn't have racial slurs scrawled on college campuses in the 1950s. Maybe what white students resent is the appearance that minority students aren't being held to the same standards that they are. (Political correctness is also probably responsible for some of the racist outbursts on campus; students today know that they can't shock the dean by showing a pornographic film, but they can throw the whole campus into turmoil by saying something racist or sexist.)

Another problem is the continuing growth of government. As government controls more of society, who controls government becomes more important. If the American government takes half of our income, runs our schools, regulates our businesses, sets quotas for jobs and college admissions, subsidizes art and literature, and interferes in our personal lives, then it becomes vitally important to make sure that "we" control the government. That political struggle plays a role in creating cultural wars in America and real wars in Ireland, South Africa, Yugoslavia, and other multiethnic states with centralized governments. We can reduce racial tensions by removing more aspects of life from the political process, letting people work together—or apart—peacefully in the market process.

One response to crime, poverty, and racial tension is to harden our positions. Sister Souljah urges that we have "a week to kill white people," while Pat Buchanan calls for "taking our country back, block by block." Even more moderate people despair of getting along. Poor blacks become convinced that the system is stacked against them. Charles Murray warned several years ago that the continuing problems of the underclass would lead white liberals to throw up their hands in despair and support a policy of "custodial democracy"—maintaining the welfare-state programs but confining the underclass to a carefully circumscribed geographic area, like an Indian reservation.[12]

Instead, we must renew our effort to build a society based on the virtues of choice, self-respect, and responsibility. As Murray has pointed out in two provocative books, when we try to enhance the self-esteem of the poor by assuring them that they are not responsible for their condition, we deny them the self-respect that can only come from achievement. Distinguishing self-esteem from self-respect, Murray puts it this way: "The threshold condition for self-respect is accepting responsibility for one's own life, for which the inescapable behavioral manifestation is earning one's own way in the world."[13] We need to give the poor as much opportunity for choice—in schools, housing, neighborhoods, and so on—as we can, and then grant them the dignity of holding them responsible for the consequences of their actions, as we (still usually) hold responsible those we consider our peers. A healthy, vibrant culture in the cities has been ruptured by social engineers and patronizing politicians who have destroyed jobs, wrecked schools, and shifted community functions to City Hall or even Washington.

There is a better answer, one that we will eventually arrive at. We can only hope it will be sooner rather than later. That answer is to recognize the failure of the welfare state, and to extend political and economic freedom to the inner city.

[12]Charles Murray, "The Coming of Custodial Democracy," *Commentary*, September 1988.

[13]Charles Murray, *In Pursuit: Of Happiness and Good Government* (New York: Simon & Schuster, 1988), p. 122.

12. Privatizing Essential Services

Robert W. Poole, Jr.

One of the most widely used tools for reordering government priorities is privatization. First used in the United States by Peter F. Drucker in 1969,[1] the term refers to a number of different techniques for shifting functions from government to the private sector. The four major techniques of privatization are as follows:

- Divestiture: government sells, leases, or gives away an asset or enterprise to private parties who are thenceforth responsible for its operations.
- Long-term franchise: instead of developing a new infrastructure project itself, government issues a long-term (25- to 50-year) franchise to private enterprise to design, finance, build, and operate the facility.
- Contracting out: instead of delivering services using government employees, government obtains service providers, via competitive bidding, for relatively short-term (one- to five-year) contracts.
- Vouchers: government issues a class of service users certificates that they can spend on the provider of their choice; the government reimburses the provider for the amount of the voucher.

The federal government has a long-standing policy (OMB Circular A-76) that supposedly mandates contracting out services whenever it can be shown that doing so is less costly than in-house provision. To get the best value for the taxpayers' dollars, that policy should be rigorously enforced. And vouchers can stimulate competition among the providers and empower the users of many social and educational services, discussed in other chapters.

This chapter will focus on the first two forms of privatization: divestiture and franchises. The federal government is a major

[1]Peter F. Drucker, *The Age of Discontinuity* (New York: Harper & Row, 1968).

funder or provider, or both, of infrastructure, and it is the owner and operator of many large-scale business operations, most of which are run very poorly: investment decisions are made for pork-barrel reasons, rather than return-on-investment criteria; services are priced in irrational ways that promote waste and misuse; and government fails to be a good steward of its valuable properties, be they forestlands or the air traffic control system. In short, government is bad at running businesses.

The Worldwide Privatization Revolution

The past decade has seen an unprecedented rethinking and downsizing of government around the world. By the end of 1991, some $260 billion in state-owned enterprises had been sold to private investors, and some $100 billion in franchised infrastructure projects were under way worldwide.[2]

This trend knows no geographical or ideological boundaries. It has been pioneered in advanced industrial countries (Britain, Japan) and the rapidly growing Asian nations (South Korea, Hong Kong, Malaysia). It is revitalizing the economies of developing countries in Latin America (Argentina, Mexico) and figures strongly in the plans of much poorer countries (Ghana, Pakistan, Sri Lanka). And privatization is the cornerstone of the historic transitions under way in the former communist countries of the ex–Soviet Union and Eastern Europe.

Although many associate privatization with conservative leaders such as Britain's Margaret Thatcher, privatization has been embraced enthusiastically by leaders of many ideologies, including Spain's Socialist Felipe Gonzalez, New Zealand's Laborite Roger Douglas, and Argentina's Peronist Carlos Saul Menem.

Governments divest state-owned assets and enterprises for several reasons: to improve the management and productivity of the enterprise by freeing it from state constraints, to give the firm access to private capital markets, to broaden share-ownership among the populace. But the most common underlying reason is financial. Selling a state-owned enterprise typically has three major financial impacts on government: (1) its sale price is a one-time windfall, (2)

[2]Lynn Scarlett and David Haarmeyer, eds., *Privatization 1992* (Los Angeles: Reason Foundation, 1992).

it ends a budgetary drain in the form of subsidies, and (3) it puts the enterprise on the tax rolls as an ongoing source of corporate and property tax revenues.

Likewise, governments use the private sector to finance, develop, and operate new infrastructure for both performance and financial reasons.[3] Forcing a highway, airport, or water system to meet a market test helps to sort out poor projects from sound ones. The private sector's use of market pricing helps to get optimum use of the project's capacity; market pricing gives users tangible incentives to conserve on their use of the resource, especially at peak periods. And providing the project with a built-in source of revenue ensures proper ongoing maintenance. Financially strapped governments in dozens of countries are finding that private capital can supplement limited government resources in meeting pressing needs for improved infrastructure.

The United States today is strangely out of step with worldwide trends. Although the federal government—like most of the governments that have embarked on large-scale privatization—runs huge annual deficits and builds up enormous debt, it has only privatized a single enterprise (Conrail in 1987). A handful of state and local governments have experimented with infrastructure franchises, but such projects have been hindered by federal grant regulations and the federal tax code.

The new administration can embark on a much bolder course, crafting a privatization agenda that builds on a decade of experience around the globe. Doing so will shrink the budget deficit and improve productivity by stimulating new investment in vitally needed infrastructure improvements.

Selling Federal Assets and Enterprises

With its endless stream of budget deficits and soaring national debt, the United States is long overdue for a sustained, long-term program of downsizing government. Our major industrial competitors—including Britain, Germany, Italy, Japan—are all engaged in large-scale national programs of privatizing state-owned assets and enterprises. Although federal assets and enterprises account for a

---

[3]Robert W. Poole, Jr., "Incentives for Mobility: Using Market Mechanisms to Rebuild America's Transportation Infrastructure," Reason Foundation Issue Paper no. 116, August 1989.

smaller share of GDP in this country than in most countries in Europe, a privatization program would make a significant contribution to a long-term deficit-reduction effort that included basic reform of entitlement programs.

The groundwork for such a privatization program was laid in the late 1980s. The President's Commission on Privatization outlined and justified an initial privatization agenda.[4] And that agenda was followed by a more sweeping set of recommendations from the ad hoc Privatization Task Force representing a number of public policy think tanks.[5]

Those efforts identified over $300 billion in salable federal assets and enterprises. The Privatization Task Force estimated that selling those entities and using the proceeds to pay down federal debt would produce annual interest savings of $29 billion, eliminate over $6 billion per year in operating subsidies, and generate $1.5 billion per year in new federal corporate tax revenue.[6] The following paragraphs discuss some of the major assets that could be sold.

Air Traffic Control System

The air traffic control system is owned and operated by the Federal Aviation Administration, the agency responsible for regulating airlines and airports for safety and for licensing pilots, mechanics, and air traffic controllers. The ATC system is a vital high-tech organization that must operate reliably 24 hours a day, 365 days a year—as must the telephone system and oil and gas pipelines (virtually all of which are privately owned and operated).

The aviation community is painfully aware that the ATC system is failing to keep pace with the needs of commercial aviation. Airline traffic has increased by two-thirds since deregulation, but the controller workforce is one-third smaller in relation to traffic levels than before the 1981 controllers' strike. Because of civil service constraints, the FAA cannot attract and keep enough experienced controllers in the busiest, most stressful locations. ATC computers,

[4]David F. Linowes, *Privatization: Toward More Effective Government* (Washington: President's Commission on Privatization, March 1988).

[5]Robert W. Poole, Jr., ed., *Federal Privatization: Toward Resolving the Deficit Crisis, Report of the Privatization Task Force* (Santa Monica: Reason Foundation, June 1988).

[6]Philip E. Fixler, Jr., Robert W. Poole, Jr., and Lynn Scarlett, *Privatization 1989* (Santa Monica: Reason Foundation, 1989).

radars, and other equipment are often outdated and unreliable; indeed, it is literally the case that the FAA is the country's largest user of vacuum tubes!

One result of those problems is flight delays. Because of the ATC system's limited capacity to handle flights safely, it uses a process called "flow control" to hold aircraft on the ground. A recent study by the Aviation Consumer Action Project found that half of all airline delays were due to ATC problems (in contrast to the FAA's claim that weather causes most of the delays).[7] The Department of Transportation has estimated that delays cost airlines and travelers some $5 billion per year.

Another problem is decreased safety. Although the trend lines for aviation accidents continue downward, ATC deficiencies have contributed to a number of recent fatal crashes, including ground collisions at Detroit Metro and Los Angeles International airports. Both of those accidents resulted from the lack of a functioning ground radar system.

The fundamental problem is that the ATC organization is crippled by being a government agency. Civil service rules and federal procurement regulations are incompatible with efficient management of a demanding, high-tech service business. Federal budget constraints and congressional oversight also hamstring the ATC system. And operating the ATC system gives the FAA a built-in conflict of interest. Like the former Atomic Energy Commission (which was charged with both promoting nuclear power and regulating its safety), the FAA is supposed to promote the economic health of aviation and regulate its safety. Spinning off ATC would put that system at arms length from FAA safety regulators, as are the airports, aircraft producers, and airlines.

Spinning off ATC has been recommended by several think tanks, the Air Transport Association, and the Aviation Consumer Action Project. Several other countries have done or are in the process of doing just that. Five years ago New Zealand corporatized its ATC system by setting up a 100 percent user-funded Airways Corporation of New Zealand. The company is profitable and has completed a major upgrade of the ATC system. It is on the list of state-owned

---

[7]James Ott, "Consumers Urge U.S. to End FAA Control of ATC Services," *Aviation Week & Space Technology*, July 20, 1992.

firms to be privatized. In 1988 the Swiss congress spun off its ATC system as SwissControl. Though the Swiss government holds 71 percent of the shares, the remaining shares are owned by airlines, airports, and user groups.

Other countries are moving in the same direction. The German parliament enacted constitutional amendments that will merge civilian and military ATC and spin it off as a user-funded company in 1993. The South African government took similar action in 1992, to take effect in mid-1993. The Air Transport Association of Canada has proposed that the Canadian government do likewise, given the successful model of Airways Corporation of New Zealand. And the Association of European Airlines is promoting the unification of European ATC as a user-funded corporation.

Privatizing our ATC system would free it from bureaucratic constraints, provide access to private capital, and accelerate its badly needed modernization.[8]

Amtrak

The National Railroad Passenger Corporation (Amtrak) was created in 1971 to take over passenger service from the major railroads. Amtrak was intended to become a profitable corporation, and a minority of its shares are privately owned. But for 20 years Amtrak has operated at a loss. Its subsidy peaked at $881 million in 1981 and has declined steadily since then. In 1981 fares covered only 48 percent of operating costs; in 1992 they are expected to cover 84 percent.

Although Amtrak gets half its passengers from the Northeast Corridor (NEC), its costs there are extremely high, in part because there alone it owns and must maintain the track. Amtrak is also hobbled by numerous federal laws and regulations, some of which were relaxed for Conrail to facilitate its successful privatization in 1987.

Overseas, privatization of passenger railroads began several years ago with the reorganization of Japan National Railways. In 1987 JNR, which had run up debts of $264 billion, was split into six passenger rail companies, a freight railroad, and several ancillary firms (including a property disposal firm to sell real estate for debt

[8]Robert W. Poole, Jr., "Building a Safer and More Effective Air Traffic Control System," Reason Foundation Policy Study no. 126, February 1991.

reduction). By 1991 all six passenger railroads were in the black, and several may be privatized in 1992 or 1993.

Elsewhere, both Argentina and New Zealand plan to privatize their national railways by 1993. Sweden and Britain are taking a different approach, setting up a track corporation to manage the infrastructure and opening access to competing rail service firms. Sweden's first private rail firm, BK-Train, has cut fares in half and increased ridership by 40 percent.

Amtrak's improved performance during the past decade has led some rail advocates to support its privatization. For example, Andrew Selden and others have suggested that reform of NEC operations, slimmed-down management, development of traffic hubs, and regulatory reform would permit Amtrak to become profitable.[9] In particular, Amtrak employees should be shifted from Railroad Retirement to Social Security and from the Federal Employee Liability Act to ordinary workers' compensation.

Rather than grant Amtrak new, permanent subsidies (it is now requesting entitlement to a portion of federal gasoline taxes), Congress should give it, say, a four-year restructuring period, capped federal assistance, and immediate regulatory relief, after which all subsidies would be terminated and the government's shares would be sold.

U.S. Postal Service

As a business, the U.S. Postal Service is inefficient and user unfriendly. In those areas where competition is legal, it has steadily lost market share: it retains only 5 percent of the parcel business and 11 percent of overnight express delivery. Despite investing billions in automation, it remains extremely labor intensive, hobbled with cost-increasing work rules. (For example, while competitor United Parcel Service uses 40 percent part-timers and Federal Express 30 percent, the Postal Service has fewer than 20 percent part-timers.) Postal wages are about 25 percent higher than market levels.

Competition would force the Postal Service to streamline, but under its present bureaucratic style of management (and oversight

[9]Andrew C. Selden, Statement presented to the Transportation Subcommittee on Amtrak Privatization of the House Energy and Commerce Committee, April 9, 1987.

by Congress), the Postal Service would be at a disadvantage. Hence, privatization should by accompanied by deregulation, freeing the Postal Service to enter any related business (e.g., electronic mail) and to tap the private capital markets. Douglas Adie has proposed breaking up the huge Postal Service into several regional companies that would be sold via public stock offerings.[10] Blocks of shares would be set aside for postal employees, giving them a stake in the success of the new firms.

Several other countries are moving toward privatization of postal services. New Zealand has deregulated and corporatized its postal service and Australia is studying privatization. Malaysia's parliament has passed legislation to privatize Pos Malaysia; Singapore plans to do likewise. Denmark has decided to corporatize its postal service and sell 25 percent of the shares to investors. Sweden's new government includes postal service among its privatization targets. Canada plans to sell shares in Canada Post to its postal workers. Most recently, the British government announced a major review of the future of the British Post Office, which will include consideration of a buyout by management and workers.

A state-owned postal monopoly is becoming an anachronism. Adie's analysis indicates that the government could net over $11 billion by selling the Postal Service. A competitive mail delivery industry would be a boon to businesses and individuals alike.

Electric Utilities

The federal government is the largest single producer and marketer of electricity in the United States. The Tennessee Valley Authority is the nation's largest utility firm, and five federal power-marketing administrations (PMAs) supply 6 percent of all U.S. wholesale electric power.

All over the world, governments are divesting themselves of such enterprises. Britain broke up its massive Central Electricity Generating Board into two generating companies and 12 transmission firms, valued at over $19 billion, all of which were sold to investors in 1990 and 1991. Argentina is selling SEGBA, the state electric utility in Buenos Aires. In Canada the provincial utility Nova Scotia Power has been sold off this year. Other countries

---

[10]Douglas K. Adie, *Monopoly Mail: Privatizing the U.S. Postal Service* (New Brunswick, N.J.: Transaction Books, 1989).

selling electric utilities include Austria, Chile, Finland, Nigeria, the Philippines, and South Korea.

Douglas Houston has proposed that the TVA be split into several generating companies and a transmission company, which would be sold separately for about $12 billion.[11] The five PMAs may be worth as much as $14 billion; their sale would also eliminate nearly $2 billion a year in federal subsidy. Putting all of those enterprises on the market, with generation separated from transmission, would foster the emerging trend toward a more competitive national electricity market. The elimination of federal subsidies and market pricing of electricity, reflecting the true cost of the resources used in producing the energy, would motivate conservation.

The production and distribution of electricity are being privatized around the world. We are far behind in applying to our remaining government-owned utilities the lessons the rest of the world has learned.

Electromagnetic Frequencies

The past decade has seen the development of exciting new communications technologies, including direct broadcast satellites, cellular mobile phones, and personal communications networks. A major factor constraining the growth of such technologies is the misallocation of the frequency spectrum. Under the historic doctrine that treats the spectrum as a commons, a government agency—the Federal Communications Commission—is charged with making decisions to allocate portions of the electromagnetic frequency spectrum to competing uses.

Nearly all other scarce resources are allocated by market forces, and market forces are equally applicable to the frequency spectrum. What's needed is to define and auction property rights to specific frequency bands and to permit market exchange among the various owners.

In 1989 New Zealand became the first country to implement that approach.[12] It switched to auctions as the method for allocating the spectrum, and it defined long-term, tradable property rights for AM

[11]Douglas Houston, "Privatization of the Tennessee Valley Authority," Reason Foundation Issue Paper no. 106, October 1988.

[12]Milton Mueller, "Reform of Spectrum Management: Lessons from New Zealand," Reason Foundation Policy Study no. 135, November 1991.

and FM radio, UHF television, cellular frequencies, and microwave bands. Auctions were held for all of those segments in 1989 and 1990.

A proposal by Milton Mueller for the U.S. frequency spectrum would create permanent property rights for AM, FM, VHF, and UHF broadcast frequencies. Incumbent broadcasters would pay a one-time fee to acquire their property right, after which they would be free to buy or sell as they chose. The plan would raise an estimated $8.6 billion.[13] Mueller proposed that $2.5 billion of that sum be used as an endowment for public broadcasting, to free it from the need for ongoing subsidy.

Privatization would permit frequencies to go to their highest and best use, thereby responding to changing consumer needs. It would also eliminate federal licensing and content regulation, a threat to First Amendment freedoms.

Surplus Military Bases

The end of the Cold War has greatly increased the potential number of surplus military bases in this country. Only 300 of some 1,300 such bases have been defined by the Defense Department as "essential" to national security—and that was during the height of the Cold War.

Much of the local opposition to base closings is unfounded. A 1986 Pentagon study of 100 base closings found that 138,000 new jobs were created to replace the 93,000 military-related jobs that were lost. That's hardly surprising, since most such bases can be readily recycled into industrial parks, schools, or airports. Most come well equipped with an infrastructure of roads, water, sewers, and electricity, even if their buildings are not usable.

Unfortunately, present federal law on base closings is rigged against the taxpayers. The order of procedure stresses giveaways, not sales: first, other federal agencies are asked if they want the base; if they don't, then state and county governments can ask for it, for free. Only if all else fails does the Defense Department try to sell the property to investors.

---

[13]Milton Mueller, "Property Rights in Radio Communications: The Key to the Reform of Telecommunications," Cato Institute Policy Analysis no. 11, June 3, 1982; and Milton Mueller, "Privatization of the Airwaves," Reason Foundation Policy Study no. 105, April 1988.

That order of priority should be reversed. The first alternative should be to put the property on the market, for sale to the highest bidder. Many of the nonessential bases are premium properties: the Presidio in San Francisco; Ft. Sheridan on the shore of Lake Michigan north of Chicago; Camp Pendleton in booming Orange County, California; Ft. DeRussy on the beach at Waikiki. Selling 200 bases valued at an average of $50 million would yield $10 billion. That would be a handsome addition to the savings in operating costs to be realized from downsizing the military.

Naval Petroleum Reserves

Despite having spent over a billion dollars creating the Strategic Petroleum Reserve during the 1980s, the government still retains ownership of two commercial oil fields. The Naval Petroleum Reserves consist of the oil fields at Elk Hills, California, and Teapot Dome, Wyoming.

The President's Commission on Privatization found that those reserves no longer play a key role in Defense Department planning for an energy emergency and recommended that they be sold. The commission cited studies estimating the value at between $3.6 billion and $4.2 billion. Their finding is equally valid today.

Commodity Lands

The federal government is by far the largest landowner in the United States. Including national forests, grazing lands, wilderness areas, national parks, defense installations, and other categories of property, the government owns some 2.2 billion acres. Of that total, 273 million acres (about 12 percent) are commercial forest and grazing lands.

Although those lands are operated by the Forest Service and the Bureau of Land Management as commodity-producing, ostensibly commercial undertakings, the two federal agencies manage to lose about $1.3 billion per year. The Forest Service spends a fortune building logging roads to areas whose timber value cannot begin to justify the road-building costs. And the BLM charges grazing fees that are less than half the going rate on comparable private land.

Economist Terry Anderson has reviewed the potential value of those commodity lands. Assuming that the lands in the lower 48 states would bring an average of $500 per acre at auction, and

215

those in Alaska half that amount, the total proceeds would be $160 billion.[14]

Anderson suggests several provisions to mitigate opposition. Existing lease obligations could be written into future land contracts, so that purchasers would have to honor them. The government could donate parcels with low commodity value but high amenity value to environmental land trusts before any auctions. And user fees for recreation programs should be implemented throughout the federal lands, so that having to pay for access becomes routine, rather than something encountered only on privately owned lands.

Land sales of that magnitude should not take place all at once, for there would be a serious risk of swamping the market and depressing price levels. Anderson suggests a 10-year cycle of auctions, with the proceeds dedicated to debt payoff. He cites a precedent from America's early history: between 1789 and 1840 land sales were used to fully retire our original national debt.

Table 12.1 provides a summary of potential federal asset sales and their resulting budgetary impacts.

Empowering State and Local Governments

Like the federal government, state and municipal governments in the United States own and operate far more commercial enterprises than most people imagine. State and municipal socialism is alive and well in the land of free enterprise. Yet as dozens of other countries are realizing, government has no comparative advantage in operating utilities and infrastructure enterprises that lend themselves to direct user charges. Selling or leasing those enterprises can improve their performance while helping cities and states out of their current fiscal crises.

What do cities and states have to sell? Table 12.2 itemizes selected infrastructure enterprises that are considered potential candidates for sale. The table includes only those facilities that could be fully self-supporting from user payments, independent of government support or contracts. Thus, it excludes public housing, jails and prisons, public schools, and other types of infrastructure that would

[14]Terry Anderson, "Rekindling the Privatization Fires: Political Lands Revisited," Reason Foundation Issue Paper no. 108, July 1989.

Table 12.1
FISCAL IMPACTS OF FEDERAL PRIVATIZATION
(BILLIONS OF DOLLARS)

Asset to be Sold	One-Time Sales Revenue	Interest Savings[a]	Annual Fiscal Impact		
			Federal Subsidy Eliminated	Corporate Tax[b]	Local Property Tax[c]
Commodity lands	160	11.2	1.3	–	2.40
Loan assets	95	6.6	–	–	–
PMAs	14	1.0	1.8	0.5	0.20
TVA	12	0.8	–	0.4	0.20
U.S. Postal Service	11	0.8	0.2	0.4	0.20
Surplus military bases	10	0.7	1.0	–	0.15
Airwaves	9	0.6	0.4	–	–
Naval Petroleum Reserves	4	0.3	–	–	0.10
D.C. airports	2	0.1	–	0.1	0.03
Air traffic control	1	0.1	1.2	–	–
Amtrak	1	0.1	0.5	–	0.02
Total	$319	$22.3	$6.4	$1.4	$3.30

[a]Interest savings assuming an average interest rate of 7 percent (note that the 1988 Privatization Task Force used 9 percent, reflecting the higher rates then prevailing).
[b]Corporate tax rate of 34 percent on revenues equal to a 10 percent return on investment.
[c]Property tax based on 1.5 percent of asset value.

Table 12.2
SALABLE STATE AND MUNICIPAL ENTERPRISES

Enterprise Type	Estimated Number	Estimated Market Value ($ Billions)
Airports (commercial)	87	29.0
Electric utilities	2,010	16.7
Gas utilities	800	2.0
Highways and bridges	n/a	95.0
Parking structures	37,500	6.6
Ports	45	11.4
Turnpikes	8	7.4
Water systems	34,461	23.9
Wastewater facilities	15,300	30.8
Waste-to-energy plants	77	4.0
Total		$226.8

depend on government contracts. As can be seen, those *salable* enterprises have an estimated value of $227 billion.[15]

Although most of those enterprises are traditionally public-sector activities in the United States, the worldwide trend is toward privatization of all of them. Some two dozen countries (including Britain, Canada, Denmark, Germany, and Greece) are now actively involved in airport privatization, either selling existing airports or franchising the private sector to produce new airports or terminals. Some 36 governments worldwide (among them are those of Britain, Hong Kong, Malaysia, Singapore, and Venezuela) are considering privatizing their seaports or are already doing so. Water supply and wastewater treatment are 70 percent privatized in France and 100 percent privatized in Britain. Municipal electric and gas utilities and parking structures are the exception to the general U.S. practice of investor ownership of those types of facilities; there would be a ready market if they were put up for sale.

In fiscal year 1992 Congress and the president each made an important start on giving state and local governments the power

---

[15]Robert W. Poole, Jr., David Haarmeyer, and Lynn Scarlett, "Mining the Government Balance Sheet: What Cities and States Have to Sell," Reason Foundation Issue Paper no. 139, April 1992.

to privatize. Congress included far-reaching privatization provisions in the Intermodal Surface Transportation Efficiency Act of 1991 (ISTEA). And President George Bush issued Executive Order 12803 on Infrastructure Privatization on April 30, 1992. The new administration must see to it that full advantage is taken of those promising initiatives.

Privatizing Highways

ISTEA reversed the federal government's historic opposition to direct user payments for highways. Although it is still not legal to add tolls to most Interstate highways, ISTEA does permit states to convert all other federally aided highways, bridges, and tunnels to toll facilities. It also allows states to sell or lease existing highways and bridges to the private sector and grant long-term franchises to finance, build, and operate new ones. Those changes could have a major impact on this country's deteriorating highway and bridge infrastructure.

The Federal Highway Administration's latest report on the condition of our highway system calculated that simply to maintain our highways' present mediocre physical condition would require spending $13 billion more each year than we spend at present (and to restore the level of quality of 20 years ago would take a $42 billion annual increase). One recent analysis estimated that the privatization provisions of ISTEA could attract some $19 billion per year in net new private investment to rebuild and expand existing highways and bridges and to add selected new capacity.[16] That would represent a 50 percent increase in current investment levels.

Another major increase in investment could be brought about by repealing various federal mandates on highway construction. Repealing the Davis-Bacon Act would cut highway project costs by up to 30 percent, the equivalent of a 30 percent increase in available investment funds. Minority set-aside and "Buy American" provisions add another 15 percent. Thus, removal of federal mandates could bring about another 45 percent increase in net investment.

---

[16]Robert W. Poole, Jr., "Private Tollways: How States Can Leverage Federal Highway Funds," Reason Foundation Issue Paper no. 136, February 1992.

The Federal Highway Administration has begun a project to encourage state transportation departments to make use of privatization provisions. The new administration should accelerate those efforts, perhaps by creating demonstration projects in a number of states. And it should encourage Congress to remove the remaining ban on including Interstate highways in the privatization program. Some of the highways most in need of upgrading are Interstate facilities. And urban Interstates would especially benefit from the shift to direct user payment, with higher charges at rush hours to control traffic congestion.

A growing number of other countries are using the private sector to finance, build, and operate highways under long-term franchise agreements. In Europe, Italy, France, and Spain have developed much of their intercity superhighway network by that method over the past 30 years. In the last few years, Britain and Greece have launched their first privatized highway and bridge projects, and now Hungary, Czechoslovakia, and other East European countries are following suit. The Channel Tunnel is currently the world's largest private infrastructure project, at some $14 billion. Private tollways are also spreading to Latin America (Argentina, Mexico, Venezuela) and the Pacific Rim (Australia, China, Hong Kong, Malaysia, Thailand).

Before passage of ISTEA, five states and Puerto Rico had enacted legislation to permit private tollway projects. As of 1992 the first such project (a toll bridge in San Juan) was under way, and two toll roads (one in California and another in Virginia) had been designed and capital for their construction was being raised.

Selling State and Local Enterprises

Executive Order 12803 on Infrastructure Privatization was designed to do for other types of state and municipal infrastructure assets what ISTEA did for highways and bridges: permit and encourage the sale or lease of existing facilities and encourage the private sector to add needed new capacity. The order directs federal agencies that have made grants to assist with any type of infrastructure (e.g., airports, highways, housing, schools, prisons, ports, water systems, waste disposal systems) to approve requests by states or cities to sell or lease those facilities. It sets forth clear rules on repayment of federal investment and on use of the proceeds by the state or city that sells the asset.

Although the executive order has received little publicity, a number of cities and states have begun exploring the sale or lease of infrastructure. Maryland, Michigan, and New York have state-level commissions or task forces identifying candidates for privatization; Dallas and Philadelphia are among the cities that are doing so. Los Angeles is looking into privatizing or corporatizing its major airport.

The principal motivation for those efforts is financial. States and cities are fiscally stressed, as is the federal government. But states and cities generally have balanced-budget requirements. Privatization of infrastructure enterprises offers them a way of converting physical assets into financial assets—what some have termed "mining the government balance sheet." In addition to realizing the capital value of the enterprises, privatization would put those valuable properties on the tax rolls; as private enterprises, they would pay whatever corporate and property taxes other private firms must pay.

But as noted above, there are additional good reasons for changing the ownership of those enterprises. Managers answerable to investors are far more likely to charge market prices than are government managers subject to political pressures. Thus, for energy and water utilities, there will be price incentives for users to conserve. Likewise, market pricing of waste disposal facilities will encourage waste reduction and recycling. And market pricing of highways and airports will encourage shifting of trips out of congested peak periods, thus making better use of the facilities.

Capital investment decisions, either for expansion of existing infrastructure or for creation of new facilities, will be based on sound return-on-investment criteria when the capital must be raised from private sources. That will serve as a powerful restraint on devoting scarce capital to projects that are politically attractive but economically unwise.

Privatization will also make more capital available for badly needed modernization of airports, highways (e.g., nonstop electronic toll collection and other "smart highway" features), and environmental infrastructure. Freed from arbitrary governmental budget constraints, those vital systems will get the modernization they badly need.

Furthermore, when building new projects or rebuilding existing ones, private firms are not bound by cumbersome, time-consuming

221

public-bidding and procurement regulations, which drive up costs and add extensive delays. On privatized infrastructure projects, firms today typically use a technique called Design/Build, in which the designers and construction contractors work as a team from the outset. That leads to a more buildable design and minimizes costly and delay-causing modifications during the construction process. Thus, the new capacity is likely to come into service significantly sooner under privatization.

Finally, the National Commission on Public Works Improvement called attention to the serious problem of "deferred maintenance" in much public-sector infrastructure. There are strong pressures in the public sector to spend limited resources on more visible projects and needs, rather than on routine maintenance. Yet skimping on maintenance is very costly in the long run. Under private ownership, deferred maintenance is reflected in reduced asset value, which leads to strong incentives for proper maintenance. (In addition, covenants in bond agreements generally require specified levels of maintenance to protect the bondholders' investments.)

The potential for improving the nation's infrastructure by privatization, and simultaneously giving state and municipal finances a strong boost, is quite large. But the extent and nature of the federal agencies' compliance with the executive order will be critical to the outcome. In the first few months after issuance of the order in 1992, the Environmental Protection Agency took a positive, pro-active stance, holding a workshop and planning pilot projects dealing with wastewater treatment plants. By contrast, the Federal Aviation Administration took no action, deciding simply to wait and see if it received requests from airport operators.

The new administration should appoint agency heads who are committed to privatization and will work enthusiastically to implement both the letter and the spirit of the executive order. In addition, it should reestablish the position of "privatization czar" within the Office of Management and Budget. The czar would serve as a kind of ombudsman for cities and states (and the private sector) in dealing with the agencies charged with implementing the order.

Conclusion

During the 1960s and 1970s, America's big businesses went on an acquisition spree. The "conglomerate" craze was based on the idea that bigger was better, and that patching together dozens of unrelated businesses into a corporate giant would somehow lead to synergy and economies of scale. In fact, it generally led to costly central offices, high overhead, and excessive layers of management. The corporate restructuring of the 1980s and 1990s, as painful as it can be, has been a necessary corrective to mindless growth.

Government in the 1990s resembles the conglomerates of the business world. Over the decades, government at all levels—local, state, and federal—has taken on function after function, program after program, getting into numerous areas in which it has no comparative advantage—and adding numerous layers of bureaucracy and costly overhead in the process. It is time for government to downsize, shedding functions that the private sector can handle. That is the meaning of today's privatization revolution.

PART IV

INTERNATIONAL AFFAIRS

13. Taking the Offensive in Trade Policy

Brink Lindsey

In the current trade policy debate, support for free trade generally means support for negotiated liberalization. In other words, the United States should lower its trade barriers, but only if other countries agree to do the same. At present, free-trade credentials are established by favoring regional liberalization through the North American Free Trade Agreement (NAFTA) and multilateral liberalization through the Uruguay round of General Agreement on Tariffs and Trade (GATT) talks.

Unfortunately, pursuing free trade through negotiations is a deeply flawed strategy. Conceptually, it relies on the same fundamental premises that underlie protectionism. And in practice, its accomplishments in opening markets and keeping them open have been modest to marginal.

There is a simpler and better approach to reducing trade barriers: unilateral free trade. Supporters of open markets should give up on negotiations and instead call for the elimination of restrictions on foreign goods, services, and investment here in the United States, regardless of what other countries choose to do. That means taking the intellectual offensive; it means challenging the whole mercantilist worldview on which protectionism is based.

Two Versions of Mercantilism

For all its intensity and even acrimony, the current dispute over trade policy actually rests on a fundamental consensus. That consensus, expressed in its simplest terms, is that exports are good and imports are bad.

Of course, one expects that sort of thinking in the protectionist camp. Desire for a "favorable" balance of trade (i.e., more exports than imports) is the hallmark of mercantilism, whether in the 18th century or at the dawn of the 21st. Modern-day mercantilists, casting themselves as champions of "fair trade," rail against unfair foreign obstacles to American exports and unfair advantages enjoyed by imports. Their solution is to "level the playing field" by closing our own markets to foreign goods.

What is curious, and regrettable, is that by and large advocates of free trade accept, at least in practice, the same mercantilist assumptions. Those assumptions are implicit in the whole notion of negotiated liberalization.

In trade negotiations, countries offer to reduce import barriers in exchange for other countries' offers of equivalent reductions. What follows is long and complicated haggling designed to ensure that the final bargain is equitable, that no party gains or gives up too much. "Gains," here, means obtains improved access to foreign markets for goods from one's country; to secure that benefit, a country "gives up" some of its own restrictions on imports. The operative premise, then, is that opening its markets is the price a country must pay for improved access to markets abroad. In other words, exports are good and imports are bad. The mercantilist worldview is quite explicit in GATT negotiations; commitments to reduce tariffs are referred to in the official nomenclature as "concessions."

Furthermore, advocates of negotiated liberalization frequently justify their position on mercantilist grounds. Supporters of NAFTA argue that new opportunities to export to Mexico will more than compensate for the job losses caused by increased Mexican imports. Likewise, supporters of the Uruguay round focus on the benefits for American exporters (e.g., liberalization of services trade and greater protection of intellectual property rights) and minimize the apparent negative of greater openness to imports. President Bush reflected that line of thinking when he claimed in his 1992 nomination acceptance speech that his market-opening initiatives would help make the United States an "export superpower." Exports are bragged about; imports are downplayed or even apologized for.

Indeed, the dominant disagreement in today's trade debate centers on what might be called pessimistic and optimistic variants of mercantilism. The pessimists, the protectionists, claim that imports destroy more jobs (or good jobs) than exports create; therefore, current liberalization initiatives should be abandoned and new import barriers erected. The optimists, the free-traders, argue the converse. Those opposing views, however, are simply two sides of the same counterfeit coin; both are based on a fundamental misunderstanding of how international trade operates within a national economy.

The Benefits of Import Competition

Protectionists generally admit that imports benefit the consumers who ultimately buy them. People who buy clothes made in Hong Kong at a low price, or a Japanese car that is of higher quality than equivalently priced domestic models, are clearly better off than if they had been forced to buy American. The problem, protectionists argue, is with the longer term consequences of that immediate benefit. They claim that imports, if unchecked, could destroy vital American industries and erode our manufacturing base, thus undermining productivity and ultimately our standard of living. Their position, then, is that it is sometimes necessary to sacrifice short-term consumer welfare for the sake of long-term economic strength. Free trade is dismissed as economic self-indulgence.

Despite the protectionists' fears, imports are not harmful in the long term. In fact, it is only in looking at the long term that the full beneficial impact of imports on our standard of living can be appreciated.

Actually, the immediate benefit of imports—lower prices or higher quality—accrues not to individual consumers but to American industries. Except for tourist purchases, all foreign goods are brought into this country by businesses. Imports allow those businesses to lower costs and improve efficiency, thereby becoming more productive. That is most obvious in the case of manufacturers who import raw materials, equipment, and components; but even imported finished consumer goods benefit importers, distributors, and retailers. Ultimately, the gains to the importing businesses are passed on to American consumers in the form of better products at lower prices.

It is thus fallacious to speak of import penetration's harming American industry generally: yes, it takes business away from industries that compete with imports, but at the same time it helps industries that use and resell imports. It should be noted that many of the imported products that arouse the fiercest calls for protectionism—for example, steel, textiles, semiconductors, and flat computer screens—are used by (and benefit) American manufacturers, thus strengthening rather than eroding our manufacturing base.

From the perspective of the overall national economy, the penetration of imported memory chips, for example, into the American market simply means that it is cheaper for us to buy them from abroad than to make them ourselves. Accordingly, as a society we are richer by the amount of those savings. Over the longer term, the manpower and resources that had been committed to making memory chips here in the United States can be shifted to making other things that people want. As a society, then, we not only get the imported semiconductors for less; we also get new goods and services produced by the people and capital that used to be tied up in domestic memory chip production.

The role of imports in the national economy is thus analogous to that of labor-saving machinery. From power looms to combines to office computers, improved tools have boosted the productivity of American labor and thus our standard of living. However, in accomplishing their salutary effect, they also eliminate jobs. Take computers, for example. Among other things, computers have eliminated large numbers of routine, clerical record-keeping and number-crunching jobs. That increased efficiency brings cost savings to the companies involved, and market competition passes those savings on to consumers. We as a society are richer by the amount of those savings. The people whose jobs were eliminated, and the capital resources that supported those inefficient operations, are ultimately redeployed in other sectors of the economy, producing new goods and services that people want. Imported goods can be viewed as a kind of labor-saving device: they free people and resources to add new value to the economy.[1]

Of course, the process of "creative destruction" is often messy and disruptive. Progress has its victims: people whose jobs are eliminated do not feel freed or liberated; they feel like their lives have been uprooted, or even wrecked. There is genuine hardship and suffering in losing a job, whether to a machine or a foreigner. But if we are to continue on the course of economic growth, those short-term and local setbacks are inevitable.

---

[1]The analogy between imports and labor-saving machinery was made in Frederic Bastiat, *Economic Sophisms* (1845) (Princeton, N.J.: Van Nostrand, 1964), series 1, chap. 20.

Protectionists see the pain and loss of boarded-up buildings in steel towns and car towns and think they are seeing "deindustrialization." A similar myopia afflicted those in the 1950s and 1960s who fretted about the rise of computers and robots and thought they saw an "automation crisis." Critics of the free market confused and continue to confuse short-term local effects (unemployment, business closings) with general long-term trends. They fail to understand that wealth-creation is a continuing process of getting more value for less effort. A necessary corollary is that businesses and jobs are eliminated as the effort they represent is no longer necessary; that eliminated effort is then refocused on new productive activities.

The beneficial effects of import penetration are only part of the story, however; one must also look at the reaction that imports provoke among domestic companies resisting import penetration. Imports' dynamic effect on the intensity of competition is perhaps the most valuable service they provide.

With the rise of trade in technologically sophisticated goods and services, international competitive advantages have less and less to do with the physical or traditional endowments of different countries. There is nothing predetermined or inevitable about the Japanese making better cars than Americans do, since the situation was once reversed. Indeed, Japanese auto companies with "transplant" factories in the United States, which hire American workers and operate under American laws and conditions, still enjoy competitive success, demonstrating conclusively that the secrets of car building are not somehow rooted in the Japanese soil. Today competitive success is frequently a matter of intangible (and fleeting) advantages in knowledge and organizational structure.

Under present conditions, international trade does far more than simply push national economies into static "comparative advantages" of specialization. Rather, it promotes dynamic cross-border rivalry to determine who is best at specializing in what. That is an ongoing process in which today's winners may be tomorrow's losers. A domestic industry may lose market share to foreign rivals selling better or cheaper products; subsequently, it may stop the erosion of its market by improving quality and efficiency, and it may even win back market share if it improves sufficiently (or if its rivals falter). Import competition thus improves American industrial productivity (and by extension the American standard of living) even when it does not displace American-made goods; it does so by forcing American producers to perform better in order to fend off foreign competition.

That effect is perhaps most visible in the case of automobiles. Americans now drive better cars than they did 20 years ago not just because many now drive Japanese cars; cars made by American companies are also much better than they once were, in large part as a response to the Japanese competitive challenge. Likewise, the efficiency of American integrated steel producers has increased dramatically in the face of foreign competition. American semiconductor manufacturers, faced with brutal Japanese competition in high-volume memory chips, have improved their manufacturing efficiency and concentrated resources on their own strengths in design-intensive logic chips. Throughout the American manufacturing sector, the presence of foreign competition has heightened the incentives to cut costs and create new value for consumers, and the effects of those increased incentives have been as dramatic as they were predictable.

Open markets are thus good on their own merits, not simply as a means to an end. Imports are not the price we pay for greater export opportunities; if anything, the ultimate value of exporting is that it allows us to import more.[2] The American economy would gain from allowing unimpeded foreign competition regardless of the policies and conditions of other countries.

The whole notion of fair trade and a level playing field misses the point of international trade, which is to improve our overall long-term standard of living. Fair-traders imagine international commerce to be a kind of game in which national teams are fielded and winners declared. If that were the case, some sort of level playing field would make sense; you wouldn't want the game to be decided unfairly, whatever that means. But the purpose of market competition, whether domestic or international, is not to pick winners; it is to produce better and cheaper goods and services. It is thus irrelevant to our economic interest *why* given foreign products

---

[2]See, for example, Ronald Krieger, "Economics and Protectionist Premises," *Cato Journal* 3, no. 3 (Winter 1983–84): 667.

are better or cheaper than domestic products; it only matters that they are.[3]

Trade Policy and the Politically Possible

Many proponents of negotiated liberalization are well aware that the benefits of open import markets do not depend on whether other countries practice fair trade, however defined. Still, they believe that the practical merits of a negotiated free-trade strategy recommend it over the purer unilateralist position.

One frequently hears that unilateral free trade is simply "unrealistic." Fully open markets in a protectionist world will never be politically sustainable, according to that line of reasoning; the cause of free trade at home can only advance if it is linked with pursuit of free trade abroad.

The simpler version of the argument is that public opinion would never accept a policy of unilateral free trade. The American people's sense of "fairness" would supposedly make them unable to tolerate such a lopsided state of affairs.[4] That is less an argument than a self-fulfilling prophecy. As long as people who know better refuse to challenge the conventional-wisdom fallacies that underlie the fair-trade worldview, the public will, of course, continue to be suspicious of unrestricted import markets. It is the business of those in the public-policy community to lead popular opinion, not to cave in to it; passive acceptance (or worse, active repetition) of prevailing misconceptions in the name of realism is an abdication of responsibility.[5]

A more sophisticated argument uses public-choice analysis to support its anti-unilateralist conclusions. The beneficiaries of protectionism—domestic producers who face import competition—are concentrated, highly visible, and easily organized. By contrast, the ultimate beneficiaries of free trade—consumers—are dispersed and anonymous. Accordingly, in the rough-and-tumble of democratic interest-group politics, there is a lobbying-power mismatch

---

[3]For an elegant demolition of the fair-trade fallacy, see Bastiat, series 1, chap. 4.

[4]For a recent example of that kind of argument, see Irwin M. Stelzer, "The New Protectionism," *National Review*, March 16, 1992, p. 30.

[5]See Leland B. Yeager and David G. Tuerck, "Realism and Free-Trade Policy," *Cato Journal* 3, no. 3 (Winter 1983–84): 645.

that favors the forces of protectionism. To counteract that imbalance, it is necessary to pursue free trade by indirection, through a regional or multilateral trade-negotiations strategy. Such a strategy enlists in support of free trade the lobbying muscle of the American exporting interests that would benefit directly from foreign liberalization.[6]

The above analysis fails to take into account the large and growing extent to which the trade policy debate pits domestic protection-seeking producers not just against American consumers but against other American producers as well. In a very real sense, all forms of protectionism—even those directed against finished consumer goods—come directly at the expense of some U.S. industry. In addition to that, the percentage of U.S. imports accounted for by capital machinery and equipment has risen dramatically over the last 20 years, even as the presence of imports in the American economy has generally been soaring. Imports as a percentage of the gross national product of the United States rose from 4 percent in 1970 to 9 percent in 1990, and during the same period, capital goods as a percentage of total imports rose from 9 to 23 percent. The competitiveness of American manufacturers depends increasingly on unimpeded access to foreign suppliers.

In addition, U.S. manufacturers are conducting more and more of their production operations outside the United States. American companies now produce an estimated 17 percent of their total output elsewhere in the world. The overseas affiliates of U.S. firms frequently ship products back to the home country; approximately 18 percent of total U.S. imports are shipments from U.S. subsidiaries located abroad.[7]

Thus, there is a powerful and growing constituency of American manufacturing interests with a direct stake in maintaining open import markets. That constituency is beginning to make itself felt in the political arena. The Coalition of American Steel Using Manufacturers, led by Caterpillar, Inc., lobbied strongly against import

[6]See, for example, Michael A. Walker, "A Canadian Vision of North American Trade Integration," Paper presented at the Cato Institute and Centro de Investigaciones Sobre la Libre Empresa conference, "Liberty in the Americas: Free Trade and Beyond," Mexico City, Mexico, May 19–22, 1992.

[7]DeAnne Julius, *Global Companies and Public Policy: The Growing Challenge of Foreign Direct Investment* (New York: Council of Foreign Relations Press, 1990).

restraints on steel and thereby helped to accelerate the demise of the so-called voluntary restraint agreements. The U.S. computer industry has had at least limited success in combatting import barriers against Japanese semiconductors and flat computer screens. A group of U.S. machine-tool manufacturers led by Hurco Companies, Inc., was being hurt, perversely enough, by import limits on Japanese and Taiwanese machine tools; their lobbying helped to cut extension of those limits from five years to two.

Regardless of what once may have been the case, there is no longer necessarily a mismatch between the lobbying power of protectionist and free-trade interests. Political leadership committed unapologetically to eliminating import barriers would no doubt face powerful opposition, but it could bring considerable muscle to the fight. And as economic globalization continues, the potential strength of the free-trade side will only increase.

It cannot be denied that, at present, unilateral free trade is politically inviable. But the current state of affairs is not immutable. Great Britain maintained a unilateral free-trade policy for a hundred years. Hong Kong maintains one today. If they could do it, so can we.

Encouraging Free Trade Abroad

The most powerful argument for negotiated liberalization (at least from a free-trade perspective) is that while unilateral free trade may be good, regional or worldwide free trade is even better. Granted, import barriers harm our economy and should come down, but why not kill two birds with one stone and get rid of other countries' protectionist policies at the same time we dismantle our own? The argument for negotiated liberalization looks good on paper, but the facts tell a different story.

Consider the record of GATT, the worldwide trade organization founded in 1947 that has been the central forum for negotiated liberalization in the postwar era. GATT is widely credited with helping to bring down tariff rates after World War II, but in more recent years its accomplishments have flagged. In 1962 tariffs on manufactured goods averaged 11.5 percent in the United States, 11.0 percent in the European Community, and 16.1 percent in Japan. Today, all of those countries have average tariffs of around 5 percent. Cutting tariff rates of the major trading countries by

5 to 10 percentage points over 30 years is not exactly dramatic progress.

Meanwhile, all kinds of new nontariff trade barriers have emerged. The Multifiber Arrangement constricts textile trade with a cobweb of quota limitations. Voluntary export restraints have curbed trade in steel, automobiles, consumer electronics, and machine tools. Anti-dumping and countervailing duty laws impose punitive duties on a wide variety of products in the name of fair trade. Health and safety regulations are used surreptitiously to block imports. And until now at least, GATT has never attempted to impose discipline on protection of agricultural and services trade.

It is, therefore, hard to argue that the major industrialized countries are less protectionist now than they were 30 years ago. Japan has liberalized significantly during that time, but the United States and the European Community are probably worse than they used to be. And while many smaller and less developed countries have slashed import barriers in the past decade, that liberalization has occurred primarily because of shifts in internal economic policy, not because of any constraints imposed by GATT. In sum, GATT has been ineffectual in promoting world free trade.

GATT supporters had pinned their hopes on the current Uruguay round of talks to change all that. Negotiators put forward bold proposals to extend GATT discipline to agriculture, textiles, services, investment, and intellectual property rights. At the time of this writing, there is still some hope that the Uruguay round will produce an agreement, but even if an agreement is reached, it will be much more modest (and loophole filled) than originally envisioned. Particularly within the industrialized world—which still accounts for nearly 75 percent of world merchandise trade— there is no discernible prospect for significant liberalization as a result of GATT negotiations.

In recent years, the United States has opened a second, regional track for negotiated liberalization. In 1988 the United States entered into a free-trade agreement with Canada, its largest single trading partner; in 1992 the Bush administration negotiated NAFTA, which expands the U.S.-Canadian agreement to include Mexico (as of this writing Congress has yet to pass the legislation needed to implement NAFTA, and it remains unclear whether Congress will do so). If NAFTA is enacted, supporters of regional liberalization hope that the United States will move to enter into free-trade agreements with countries throughout Latin America.

Free-trade agreements can significantly liberalize trade between and among the countries involved. With fewer countries involved in the process, negotiations are more manageable and real breakthroughs are possible. NAFTA, for example, would after 15 years eliminate all tariffs on trade within the region, guarantee market access in numerous service industries, and liberalize rules governing foreign investment. Of course, free-trade agreements are far from perfect: among other problems, NAFTA leaves intact the countries' anti-dumping and countervailing duty laws, and it is marred by arbitrary rules of origin that limit the products entitled to duty-free status.

The main problem with a regional free-trade strategy, though, is its diminishing returns. Canada and Mexico together account for about 28 percent of American exports and 24 percent of imports. That is a significant chunk of U.S. trade, and one could argue persuasively that pursuing regional negotiations up to the point of NAFTA has been cost-effective in terms of liberalization gained versus time and political energy expended.

Beyond NAFTA, however, there is a precipitous drop-off in the utility of additional or expanded regional agreements. The entire remainder of the Western Hemisphere accounts for only about 7 percent of U.S. exports and imports; Chile, the most logical candidate for the next agreement, absorbs only 0.4 percent of our exports and produces only 0.3 percent of our imports. While those numbers would doubtless increase under liberalized trade, it is clear that expanding NAFTA to encompass the entire hemisphere is an exceedingly modest goal.

What about negotiating free-trade agreements with our major trade partners, the European Community and Japan? Under the reigning fair-trade political culture, such negotiations would be either hopeless or exceedingly dangerous. The central issue in negotiations with the European Community would almost certainly be the Europeans' massive subsidies to industry (e.g., Airbus) and agriculture. The record of the Uruguay round has demonstrated that the European nations are not interested in seriously reforming their subsidy policies; accordingly, negotiations would be dead before they started.

American dissatisfaction with Japan has less to do with explicit protectionist policies than with the whole structure of the Japanese economy. Those issues are far beyond the scope of trade negotiations, as shown by the farcical Structural Impediments Initiative. Negotiators of a U.S.-Japanese agreement would be tempted to cut the Gordian knot and simply decide on "acceptable" import and export numbers; in the guise of a free-trade agreement, then, we would actually be saddled with a managed-trade accord that set market-share quotas for various sectors. Such an agreement would be far worse than the mess we have now.

Whatever GATT's accomplishments in its very early years, and whatever the qualified successes to date of regional free trade, the future of negotiated liberalization looks decidedly bleak. Further negotiations will at best mean marginal improvement, and they could even make matters worse. Meanwhile, all our existing protectionist barriers are frozen in place as "bargaining chips," with reform outside the negotiations process rejected as "unilateral disarmament."

Furthermore, as mentioned earlier, trade negotiations rely on and affirm the basic mercantilist assumptions that underlie protectionism. Thus, a trade-negotiations strategy helps to perpetuate a hostile political culture, one that not only makes real liberalization more difficult but also facilitates additional protectionism.

Negotiations place the focus of trade policy on the protectionism of other countries, thus keeping the fair-trade mentality stocked with an always-fresh supply of grievances. And there is no guarantee that the preferred method for settling those grievances will always be negotiated liberalization. After all, once you concede that reductions in U.S. import barriers should be conditioned on similar reductions in other countries, it is difficult to resist calls for conditioning *existing* access to U.S. markets on liberalization abroad (as in section 301 and "Super 301") or on favorable trade balances (as in various proposals by Rep. Richard A. Gephardt). Once unilateral free trade is forsaken in favor of reciprocal free trade, the principle of reciprocity can easily take on a life of its own, degenerating into ever more aggressive and dangerous manifestations.[8]

[8]For a critique of the trend in U.S. trade policy toward threatening retaliation against our trade partners unless they open their markets, see Jim Powell, "Why Trade Retaliation Closes Markets and Impoverishes People," Cato Institute Policy Analysis no. 143, November 30, 1990.

Leading by Example

If the United States were to remove its own trade barriers and convincingly renounce all future protectionism, what would be the reaction of other countries? Would they, no longer fearing loss of access to our markets, suddenly move to block American goods from their own?

Not to worry. American goods and services are vitally important and highly desired around the world. People in Japan, Germany, France, Britain, Italy, South Korea, Taiwan, Hong Kong, and Singapore all import more goods per capita from the United States than Americans import from those countries. It is really not conceivable that the governments of those and other countries would be willing—in conditions short of war—to wreak the economic dislocations and personal hardship that would result from any significant new impediments to purchasing American products.

Think of the reaction in this country if tomorrow 100 percent duties were levied on all Japanese products, and suddenly Japanese cars and televisions and radios and VCRs and computer chips and laptops were twice as expensive as they are now. Now think of Japan's doing the same to us, not in retaliation but because we had opened our markets, and remember that while we buy gadgets from them, they buy *food* from us. It just isn't in the cards.

If anything, the American adoption of a unilateral free-trade policy would inspire the opposite reaction. In the past 10 years a growing number of countries have made dramatic reforms in their trade policies, replacing the old model of import substitution with integration into the global economy. Bold moves toward freer trade have been made by countries as diverse as Australia, New Zealand, Mexico, Chile, Argentina, and India. Those countries have opened their markets and welcomed foreign goods and investment, not because of negotiating breakthroughs or U.S. threats, but because their governments finally realized that autarky was causing economic stagnation. It was not outside pressure that carried the day, but internal changes in perceived economic interest.

A U.S. policy of unilateral free trade would promote similar reevaluations around the world. Open markets would improve our economic performance and raise our standard of living, for all the world to see. Instead of haggling with and browbeating our trading partners to do what we say and not what we do, we would provide leadership by example. The power of that example would do more to encourage free trade abroad than negotiations and international organizations ever could.

Consider the European Community. Its members launched the EC 1992 initiative of internal liberalization in the mid-1980s in response to the doldrums of "Eurosclerosis." In other words, the European Community liberalized under the pressure of poor economic performance. If the United States were enjoying the benefits of free trade, and the European Community's productivity and growth were lagging behind ours, is it unreasonable to think that the European Community might find free trade preferable to becoming an economic backwater?

Getting There from Here

We do not write on a clean slate. Two major initiatives of negotiated liberalization—the Uruguay round and NAFTA—are now entering their endgame after years of slow and tortuous progress. The battle lines have been clearly drawn, and there is no sense in trying to redefine them at this late stage. Both initiatives represent true if limited progress, and both deserve the support of free-traders for the remaining few months needed to decide their fate.

After that, supporters of open markets should forget about a new round of GATT talks, as well as extending NAFTA farther south. Instead, free-traders should invest their energies and political capital in fighting trade barriers here at home. A president could stake out a position as a bold leader and a friend of consumers and economic progress by launching such an effort.

There is no shortage of inviting targets. The sugar and peanut programs probably top the list for sheer disproportion between benefit and cost. Textile quotas are a special-interest scandal: while benefiting large and profitable companies, they act as a hidden clothes tax that hits hardest those with the lowest incomes. The anti-dumping law is economic nonsense that arbitrarily and unpredictably raises the cost of doing business in this country. One could go on and on.[9]

All of those programs would, of course, be defended by the powerful and entrenched special interests that benefit from them.

[9]For a scathing attack on U.S. protectionist policies, see James Bovard, *The Fair Trade Fraud* (New York: St. Martin's, 1991).

Victories, at least in the short term, would be difficult to come by. But putting the special interests on the defensive—forcing them to explain why they deserve to profit at the expense of the rest of us—would in itself constitute a major victory. That is the immediate advantage, and the ultimate key to success, to be gained by rejecting negotiations in favor of unilateral free trade.

14. Rethinking NATO and Other Alliances in a Multipolar World

Christopher Layne

The new administration takes office at a time when international politics has been radically transformed. Because the foreign policy guideposts of the Cold War world have been swept away, the new administration's initial challenge will be conceptual: it must break away from the Cold War paradigm that still shackles American foreign policymaking and rethink from the ground up the principles that will define America's international political role in the post–Cold War world.

The collapse of the Soviet Union and America's battlefield triumph in the Persian Gulf War gave rise to a burst of optimism about the future of international politics. That attitude has been encapsulated in the so-called new world order announced by President George Bush. Accompanying the new world order was a euphoric triumphalism based on three incorrect assumptions: (1) in the post–Cold War era the United States was—and would long remain—the world's only great power (that is, the post–Cold War world is unipolar); (2) by making the export of democracy the central focus of its post–Cold War foreign policy, the United States could bring about "perpetual peace" in international politics; and (3) the Persian Gulf victory "proved" that the relative decline of American power was a myth.

Far from forcing a sweeping reconsideration of America's world role, the end of the Cold War reinforced the determination of those who believe the United States should have a muscular foreign policy—that is, a foreign policy that actively seeks to project abroad America's power and its values. The view that America is "bound to lead" the international system is deeply entrenched.

That view has precluded a reassessment of the means, as well as the ends, of American policy, as is evident in the Bush administration's defense spending plans. Rather than availing itself of the

Cold War's end to drastically reduce defense spending, U.S. officialdom conjured up new threats to justify high levels of expenditure. To replace the obsolete mission of containing the Soviet Union, the administration declared that the U.S. role now should be nothing less than preserving "peace and stability" in a post–Cold War world characterized by "uncertainty, instability, and danger."

Indeed, the foreign policy establishment believes the post–Cold War world will be more dangerous for the United States than its Cold War predecessor because of the proliferation of weapons of mass destruction in hostile states, anti-American regimes in the Third World, drug traffickers, anti-democratic insurgencies, and terrorism. In the face of those dangers, it is said, America will need to be more, not less, interventionist than it was during the Cold War era. In this uncertain new world, officials contend, the United States must maintain the same mix of forces (albeit somewhat reduced in number) and the same military commitments (to Europe, Japan, South Korea, the Philippines, Latin America, and Southwest Asia) it did during the Cold War—notwithstanding that those alliances and forces were specifically tailored to contain the Soviet Union. As Secretary of Defense Richard B. Cheney said in 1990: "America should continue to anchor its strategy to the still valid doctrines of deterrence, flexible response, forward defense [and] security alliances. . . . Even the extraordinary events of 1989 do not mean that America should abandon this strategic foundation."[1] The obvious question is, If the collapse of the Soviet Union does not provide sufficient incentive, just what would justify a fundamental reassessment of America's grand strategy?

There is a striking dissonance between the static world view of many policymakers and the objective realities that must sooner or later shape American foreign policy. Before the gulf war, a new "great debate" about America's place in the post–Cold War world was just beginning. Central to that dialogue was Yale professor Paul Kennedy's cogent thesis that, as the preeminence of other great powers in history had been lost, so America's economic strength—and hence its geopolitical primacy—was being eroded by

---

[1]Richard B. Cheney, Statement to the Senate Budget Committee, February 5, 1990, Department of Defense typescript, p. 2.

its extensive, costly overseas military commitments.[2] That debate, which was cut short by the gulf war, has not really been rejoined. The issue of America's post–Cold War world role was not a major issue in the 1992 presidential campaign, because Gov. Bill Clinton consciously sought to occupy the middle ground by advocating a world view and policies that in many respects were remarkably similar to George Bush's. Given the McGovernite political baggage carried by the Democratic party, Clinton's stance may have been politically astute. But good politics does not always make good policy. With the Cold War over, and with the gulf war's glow long since faded, there is heightened awareness that the country faces daunting challenges at home. Even some foreign policy establishment stalwarts (notably recently retired *Foreign Affairs* editor William Hyland and *New York Times* columnist Leslie Gelb) have argued that the United States should shift its priorities from foreign to domestic policy. For that to happen, however, policymakers must discard the Cold War mindset. To do that, they must understand why the United States acted as it did after 1945 and why it does not need to preserve an excessively activist strategy in the post–Cold War era.

After World War II the world was bipolar both geopolitically and ideologically. Cold War exigencies compelled the United States to focus its energies on containing the Soviet Union. Because the other pre-1939 great powers had been shattered by the war, only the United States could counterbalance Soviet power and prevent the expansion of Soviet influence. As part of its containment strategy, America assumed worldwide military responsibilities, thereby enabling the West European nations and Japan to pursue economic recovery programs. Under the circumstances prevailing after World War II, it was strategically justifiable for the United States to assume the military and economic burdens imposed by containment.

The United States need no longer bear those costs, however. Cold War constraints on the United States have been removed by (1) the Soviet Union's collapse and its successor states' preoccupation with their overwhelming internal political and economic problems, (2) the end of the Cold War in Europe following the collapse of

---

[2]Paul Kennedy, *The Rise and Fall of the Great Powers: Economic Change and Military Conflict from 1500 to 2000* (New York: Random House, 1987).

245

Soviet power in East Central Europe, (3) the political and economic recovery of Western Europe and Japan from World War II's devastating effects, and (4) the imminent emergence of Germany and Japan as great powers.

The Mirage of a Unipolar World

The world today is temporarily unipolar, and U.S. officials want to keep it that way. That was the thrust of the first draft of the Pentagon's Defense Planning Guidance document for fiscal years 1994–99. That draft explicitly stated that the basis of post–Cold War U.S. grand strategy should be nothing less than "deterring potential competitors from even aspiring to a larger regional or global role."[3] Although the initial draft of the document was revised, under pressure, to delete that language, the revision was cosmetic only. Indeed, the Bush administration repeatedly stated its belief that the world is—and should remain—unipolar. Moreover, in the late fall of 1992 the RAND Corporation and the Pentagon's joint staff were engaged in drafting a "new NSC-68"—a grand strategic charter for U.S. policy in the post–Cold War world. That document advocates a unipolar grand strategy and argues that a multipolar system would constitute the worst of all possible geopolitical worlds for the United States.

A policy of robust unipolarity, however, is not in America's interest for two reasons: (1) it will produce a backlash against the United States, and (2) it is beyond America's resources to sustain a unipolar strategy. The single superpower concept is fantasy-land foreign policy because it is based on the illusion of U.S. power and ignores the decline of America's relative power from its post–World War II zenith. The desire to be the single superpower also fails to recognize that new great powers will emerge, with or without Washington's approval.

Japan and Germany already have the potential to become great powers. To do so, they need only make a conscious political decision to translate their potential power into actual great power. It can be assumed that they will make that choice. Indeed, there is

---

[3]Patrick E. Tyler, "U.S. Strategy Plan Calls for Insuring No Rivals Develop," *New York Times*, March 8, 1992, p. A1.

plenty of evidence that they already *are* making it.[4] That development is unsurprising, because in the competitive realm of international politics, states tend to emulate their rivals. This is not the first "unipolar moment" in international history. In the 1660s France was the only superpower in world politics, and in 1860 Great Britain was the sole superpower. In both instances, other states responded to unipolarity by acquiring great power capabilities. In the late 17th century England and Austria emerged as great powers; in the late 19th century Germany, Japan, and the United States joined the ranks of the great powers. In both periods the emergence of new great powers was a direct response to unipolarity. States strive to preserve their independence and their decision-making autonomy. For that reason, states capable of doing so (and great powers always are) "balance" against the most powerful or most threatening power in the system, or both, by forming coalitions against it. States seldom "bandwagon" (go along) with the most powerful or threatening state in the system. In other words, states oppose hegemons. And by definition, the sole superpower in a unipolar system is a hegemon, even if it views its hegemony (as does the United States) as benign.

In any event, U.S. leaders will have to manage the unsettling complexities of unipolarity (and the inevitable transition to multipolarity). But the difficulty of Washington's diplomatic task is exacerbated by a policy that embraces unipolarity as a *goal* of American foreign policy. Unipolarism is accompanied by the unbridled ambition to forcibly reshape the world in America's image. Other nations find that threatening. Although Bush administration officials asserted that other nations "trust" the United States as the sole superpower, there is overwhelming evidence that they do not. Indeed, the need to counterbalance unchecked American power is a theme increasingly voiced in Europe, Japan, and the Third World. A unipolar strategy will only hasten the emergence of the very world its advocates seek to prevent. The new administration should realize that a unipolar world is unattainable and undesirable. A

---

[4]For evidence of this and fuller consideration of unipolarity's theoretical implications and policy consequences, see Christopher Layne, "Will New Great Powers Rise? A Neorealist Critique of the Unipolar Moment," *International Security*, March 1993, forthcoming.

multipolar world is inevitable. Although such a world poses certain risks for the United States, it also offers many opportunities.

The current fixation on unipolarity contrasts unfavorably with the views of the principal architects of America's post–World War II policy—Secretary of State George C. Marshall and State Department Policy Planning Staff Chief George F. Kennan. Kennan realized that in a bipolar world, the United States would be overtaxed because it would have to bear singlehandedly containment's burdens. In a multipolar world, however, there would be other power centers with which the United States could share security responsibilities. It was, therefore, Marshall's and Kennan's goal to restore a multipolar balance of power. Today, the world is on the threshold of multipolarity, but instead of reaping the benefits of that change, the United States is resisting it.

Beyond NATO

The new administration will need to cast off the old self-defeating policy, and Europe is the place to begin. The Soviet Union's collapse has left NATO with no obvious raison d'être. However, instead of writing off the alliance as a Cold War relic, the American foreign policy establishment has advanced numerous new rationales to justify it.

Washington clings to NATO because it views the alliance not only as a mechanism for American supremacy in European security affairs but also increasingly as the only means of ensuring that the United States still has a voice in Europe's diplomacy. That view overlooks an important fact: as America's power has declined, Europe's has inevitably increased. Consequently, Europe has become more assertive in defining its policies independent of Washington's tutelage. Europe is simply no longer willing to take a back seat to the United States in matters affecting its interests. Put another way, U.S. influence in European affairs will inexorably diminish, given the shift in the relative power relationship.

A second erroneous justification for keeping NATO intact is the "leverage strategy." Articulated by President Bush and Harvard professor Joseph S. Nye, Jr., among others, the leverage strategy assumes the United States can use its power to extract concessions from Western Europe and Japan in international economic and financial negotiations. The leverage strategy became official policy in the spring of 1992 when the Bush administration linked continuation of the American commitment to NATO to European Community concessions in the General Agreement on Tariff and Trade negotiations.

There are two points to be made about the leverage strategy. First, it was largely unsuccessful even during the Cold War, when Western Europe (and Japan) presumably were heavily dependent on American security guarantees. Now that the Cold War's end has devalued America's security commitments, why should it be expected that Western Europe and Japan will make economic and financial concessions to obtain (largely unneeded) American protection? Second, the leverage strategy—espoused by those who most vehemently dispute that American power has declined—is itself a damning confession of decline. The underlying assumption of the leverage theory is clear: the United States must use its military power to coerce Western Europe and Japan because its economic and financial strength alone is no longer adequate to secure acceptable outcomes in international negotiations with those two centers of power.

Another line of defense for NATO is the argument that "bad things" will happen unless the United States keeps the peace throughout Europe. For example, it has been contended that if events in Eastern Europe spiraled out of control and precipitated a general European war, the United States would be devastated economically by the disruption of transatlantic trade. In addition, NATO partisans insist that such a conflict could leap the Atlantic and draw the United States into a nuclear engagement.

A great power war in post–Cold War Europe seems unlikely but cannot be ruled out. Such a war would obviously have an adverse effect on the United States because Europe is an important export market. Nevertheless, the United States is not heavily dependent on European markets. America has a huge domestic market (which may increase if the North American Free Trade Agreement is ratified) and diversified overseas markets. Moreover, the possible loss of trade occasioned by a future European war must be measured against the likelihood that such a war would indeed occur and weighed against the very real costs of preparing for (and the anticipated costs of waging) such a war.

The fear that a European nuclear war could engulf the United States is also misplaced. If America were not party to a European great power war, and if U.S. forces were not in Europe, it is difficult to foresee how the United States could be drawn in. In fact, no one has advanced a plausible scenario to explain how a European war could "leap the Atlantic" if the United States were uninvolved in the initial conflict. Conversely, the American military presence in Europe carries with it the risk of U.S. involvement in a European conflict. Indeed, the U.S. commitment virtually ensures that the United States would be swept up into a maelstrom of spreading violence if a local European conflict did escalate into a major war. In post–Cold War Europe, military involvement, not aloofness, poses the risk to American security.

One of the most pernicious myths pervading American foreign policy is that all European wars invariably affect vital U.S. security interests. That is simply untrue. Great power wars in Europe erupted in 1792, 1803, 1854, 1866, 1871, and 1878 without having any discernible impact on U.S. interests. Only three times have Europe's major conflicts entangled the United States, and in each case there were extenuating circumstances. The first occasion was the War of 1812. Although connected tangentially to the Napoleonic Wars, the War of 1812 was rooted in long-standing Anglo-American tensions, including the desire of U.S. war hawks to conquer Canada. Indeed, the United States began hostilities by declaring war on Great Britain.

America's involvement in World War I was driven by misguided Wilsonian crusading zeal, not by any tangible threat to American security. Even if Germany had triumphed in World War I, the European balance of power would have merely been altered. It would not have been shattered, and Germany would not have been in a position to mobilize all of Europe's resources to challenge the United States. In all likelihood, however, Germany would not have won the war even in the absence of American involvement. In early 1917 the major belligerents recognized that the military deadlock was unlikely to be broken, and they began to contemplate the possibility of a negotiated peace. Ironically, the prospect of American military intervention—and with it the hope of victory—was probably the key factor that led the British government to decide against pursuing a compromise peace. Had the European powers been able to end the war diplomatically, the great upheavals of 1918–19 that destabilized East Central Europe—and sowed the seeds for Hitler's rise to power—might have been avoided. The flawed post-1918 peace treaties (largely Woodrow Wilson's handiwork) had baleful effects that still bedevil Europe, most notably Yugoslavia.

The third occasion was U.S. involvement in World War II. It would have been both difficult and risky for the United States to have remained aloof from that conflict after Germany subdued France and drove British forces from the Continent. The control of Europe's population, industrial capabilities, and resources by an aggressively expansionist state that already possessed a world-class military would have posed a serious threat to America's own security. Such circumstances, however, bear no resemblance whatsoever to present conditions in Europe.

The official rationales for preserving NATO do not hold up, but there is another reason often voiced by policymakers—though always off the record—for preserving NATO: fear of Germany.[5] As a practical matter, however, it is hard to see how NATO could be used to contain Germany, which is the alliance's most powerful and important European member. Moreover, from a policy standpoint, a U.S. policy that sought to constrain Germany would be unwise. The United States cannot prevent Germany from becoming a great power, and any attempt to thwart Germany's emergence as a great power would be resented by most Germans. Because American influence in post–Cold War Europe will hinge largely on the quality of Washington's relations with Berlin, it would be counterproductive for the United States to allow itself to be drawn into schemes that have the real—if unstated—goal of hemming in Germany.

The architects of America's post–World War II foreign policy never envisioned NATO as a permanent fixture in transatlantic relations. They wanted to protect a war-ravaged Western Europe while it regained its political, economic, and military strength—at which point Western Europe would assume responsibility for its

[5]Nongovernmental supporters of NATO are less shy about explicitly citing the containment of Germany rationale. See, for example, James Chace, *Consequences of the Peace: The New Internationalism and American Foreign Policy* (New York: Oxford University Press, 1992), pp. 68–69; William E. Odom, "The German Problem: Only Ties to the United States Provide the Answer," *Orbis* 34 (Fall 1990): 483–504; and Leslie H. Gelb, "Power in Europe," *New York Times*, October 20, 1991, p. E15.

own defense. Much of the current American foreign policy establishment has forgotten what NATO was all about. Preserving the alliance has become an end in itself.

To preserve the alliance, U.S. policymakers have acquiesced to a dangerous shift in NATO's strategic mission. Historically, the United States had one overriding security interest in Europe: preventing a single power from establishing control over the Continent. Such a power could then have conceivably threatened the United States directly. However, with the Soviet Union's collapse, the threat of a European hegemon has receded. That does not mean that post–Cold War Europe will be peaceful. Events in Yugoslavia have amply shown that in East Central Europe and the Balkans unresolved national, ethnic, and religious disputes pose a real risk of armed conflict. Such conflicts are local in nature, however, and they are unlikely to have any ramifications for the European or global balances of power. In short, they do not affect tangible American interests, notwithstanding the near hysteria of those who advance highly implausible "parade of horribles" scenarios to justify U.S. intervention in the turmoil in the Balkans.

Yet NATO has adopted as its new strategic mission the conduct of peacekeeping and peacemaking operations in such places as Bosnia-Hercegovina, Nagorno-Karabakh, and Moldova.[6] Domino-type thinking ("if we don't intervene in Bosnia, other peoples in Europe will use violence to resolve their disputes") and misguided moralism threaten to inject the United States via NATO in Europe's future quagmires. The new administration should rethink the alliance's role and not allow itself to be seduced by those arguments. The various conflicts in East Central Europe, the Balkans, and the former Soviet Union are discrete, not linked, events. NATO intervention in any one dispute is not going to have any meaningful deterrent effect on disputes elsewhere. Moreover, the conflicts in those volatile regions are not amenable to resolution by outside intervention.

---

[6]The policy adopted by the NATO foreign ministers at their June 1992 meeting in Oslo that would make alliance forces available for peacekeeping operations authorized by the Conference on Security and Cooperation in Europe certainly creates that danger. William Drozdiak, "NATO Widens Mandate on Forces," *Washington Post*, June 5, 1992, p. A41.

It is probably an illusion to believe that U.S. military involvement in the Balkans and other unstable regions could be limited. American policymakers became involved in Vietnam by gradual steps, and no one envisioned that those steps would lead ultimately to a conflict in which more than 500,000 U.S. troops would be engaged. Incremental commitments generate momentum for even greater involvement. Once a government makes a commitment, its credibility, reputation for resolve, and prestige are on the line, and it becomes increasingly difficult to disengage. Whether NATO intervention in East European ethnic conflicts would lead to another Vietnam is an open question; that such involvement would at least lead to new Lebanon-type situations is beyond dispute. Even the U.S. military exhibits little enthusiasm for performing the regional intervention tasks required of it under NATO's new strategy.[7] The prudence of the military leadership contrasts sharply with the rash interventionist sentiments expressed by many pundits and civilian analysts.

It is time to rethink America's commitment to NATO. Washington's obligations to the alliance entail significant risks. The threats in Europe are now much more diffuse than was the case during the U.S.-Soviet standoff, which at least had the virtue of being predictable. Instead of protecting vital U.S. security interests, NATO has become a means for entangling the United States in Eastern Europe's intractable internecine quarrels. The possibility of intervention in Yugoslavia underscores the danger. Aside from the cost of America's NATO obligations—at least $90 billion a year—the danger of such entanglements is reason enough to terminate the association.[8]

Terminating the East Asian Protectorates

It is also time to rethink America's other overseas alliances, especially Washington's commitments to Japan and South Korea that

---

[7] The views expressed by Chairman of the Joint Chiefs of Staff Gen. Colin Powell are an example. Michael R. Gordon, "Powell Delivers a Resounding No on Using Limited Force in Bosnia," *New York Times*, September 28, 1992, p. A1.

[8] On the cost of Washington's NATO obligations, see Earl C. Ravenal, *Designing Defense for a New World Order: The Military Budget in 1992 and Beyond* (Washington: Cato Institute, 1991), p. 51.

cost American taxpayers nearly $40 billion a year. Those two alli-
ances are vestiges of the Cold War and are irrelevant to the emerging
international security environment. Both treaties have the
unhealthy effect of trying to perpetuate the dependence of increasingly capable powers on the United States for their defense needs.

Japan has long been capable of providing for its own defense—
if it were willing to make the effort and if the United States did
not consistently discourage independent Japanese initiatives. Japan
today has the world's second largest economy as well as one of
the most dynamic and sophisticated. Yet Japan spends a mere $33
billion a year on defense while the United States spends more than
$280 billion.

A similar situation exists with regard to South Korea. When the
United States signed the "mutual" security treaty with Seoul, South
Korea had been devastated by war and faced an aggressively expansionist North Korea backed by both the Soviet Union and China.
Today, however, South Korea is an economic dynamo that com-
petes in a host of international markets. It has twice the population
and an economy nearly 11 times as large as that of North Korea.
Furthermore, Moscow and Beijing are both busy cultivating extensive diplomatic and economic ties with Seoul. Their actions are not
surprising since South Korea has much to offer both countries while
North Korea is an economic and political liability. Neither Russia
nor China shows any interest in fomenting a new war on the Korean
Peninsula; indeed, such a conflict would be utterly contrary to their
best interests. Under such conditions, South Korea no longer needs
to be a military protectorate of the United States.

U.S. relations with Japan will be crucial in coming decades.
Within the first decade of the 21st century, Japan's economy may
even overtake America's as the world's largest. As Paul Kennedy
has shown, time and again in international politics, shifts in relative
economic standing have heralded the rise of new great powers that
one day would have a decisive impact on the military and territorial
order. The shift in the relative economic power of the United States
and Japan is, therefore, of potentially enormous geopolitical sig-
nificance.

Japan's rise to great power status presages a much more difficult
relationship between Washington and Tokyo. Although skillful
diplomacy on both sides might ameliorate tensions, history suggests the existence of a "Hertz-Avis" dynamic that pushes the

two leading powers in a multipolar system into competition. The pre–World War I Anglo-German rivalry is an example of that phenomenon. For that reason, it could be argued that rather than terminating the Mutual Security Treaty with Japan, the United States should continue to protect Japan in the hope that doing so will remove incentives for Tokyo to acquire great power capabilities. Although superficially appealing, that argument is gravely flawed because (1) the United States cannot prevent Japan's emergence as a great power, and (2) an American policy that tried to do so would serve only to antagonize Japan and make it more difficult to construct a stable U.S.-Japanese relationship.[9]

Another argument against terminating U.S. military commitments in East Asia is that to do so would "destabilize" the region. In particular, many people point to the fears of other Asian countries that an American pullback would lead to increased Japanese power. No doubt, if a new U.S. strategy forces Japan to internalize its security costs and expand its military forces, regional arms races, rivalries, and "instability" may result as the other East Asian nations move to offset Japan's influence and create a regional balance of power. That would not necessarily be to America's disadvantage, however. By adopting an offshore balancer's strategy, the United States would actually reduce the likelihood of a confrontation with Tokyo, because Japan would also have to concern itself with China, Korea, and Russia. By relearning how to be a strategic balancer in a multipolar world, the United States can both protect its vital interests and dramatically lower its military expenditures. And if the new administration is serious about revitalizing the American economy, it will need to devise a new grand strategy predicated on the inevitability of much smaller defense budgets and a dramatic restructuring of overseas security commitments.

Toward a Post–Cold War Strategy

With the passing of the Cold War and the Soviet threat, there is no reason for the United States to persist in a policy that allows its allies to externalize their security costs by shifting them to this country. That underscores a fundamental point with which the

[9]For a discussion of that danger, see Ted Galen Carpenter, *A Search for Enemies: America's Alliances after the Cold War* (Washington: Cato Institute, 1992), chap. 2.

new administration will have to come to terms: at a time of declining economic competitiveness and fiscal insolvency, the opportunity costs of NATO and America's other alliances are very high. If the new administration truly wants to revitalize America, it must begin by redefining U.S. foreign policy. Foreign policy and domestic policy are interconnected. No one can reasonably doubt that America today would be more competitive economically, more prosperous, and more tranquil if, over the past 47 years, the money underpinning foreign policy had been available instead for some mix of the following: growth and investment stimulating tax reductions, inflation-reducing deficit reductions, civilian research and development, education, infrastructure restoration, and other important components of domestic economic progress. Yet few Americans in or out of government seem to understand that many of our current economic troubles are directly attributable to the costs (direct and indirect) of Washington's post–World War II foreign policy.

To adopt a radically different foreign policy, it is necessary to demolish the intellectual foundations upon which post-1945 U.S. foreign policy was based. It is also vital to understand that the key trends in world politics—especially the emergence of a multipolar system of at least four great powers—makes it possible for the United States to stop being the world's policeman without sacrificing its vital security interests. America is not *bound* to lead in world affairs, and increased "instability" (a mushy term the meaning and implications of which must be more rigorously defined) and chaos are *not* the inevitable (or even likely) alternatives to U.S. global preeminence. Unlike other great powers throughout history, the United States has the freedom to choose its security interests. Because of the interlocking factors of geography, nuclear weapons, and still impressive military and economic capabilities, the United States has choices that other nations lack. For 50 years America has opted, at considerable cost to its own domestic well-being, to put the interests of the international system first. Now it is time for a new foreign policy that puts America's interests first. A completely restructured U.S. foreign policy would include the following measures.

- A policy of strategic retrenchment that would alleviate America's foreign policy burdens by devolving security responsibilities to the emerging great powers and important regional powers.

- A new U.S. foreign policy that strives for burden *shifting*, not merely burden sharing. Direct U.S. military involvement in overseas crises would be a last, not a first, resort. Accordingly, it would be possible to make deep cuts in U.S. conventional forces. Strategic retrenchment would enable the United States to shift its resources and energies from foreign to domestic policy.
- A prompt reduction of U.S. forces in Europe to headquarters and logistics units for one corps and supporting air power. Upon the complete withdrawal of Russian forces from Germany, all American forces should also be withdrawn.
- Encouragement of initiatives, such as the formation of the Franco-German corps, to develop an independent European defense capability.
- Abrogation of the U.S.-Japanese mutual defense treaty, and return of American forces presently stationed in Japan to the United States within five years. The same policy should be adopted with regard to the U.S.–South Korean alliance.
- Immediate formation of a high-level study group tasked with reviewing U.S. foreign policy commitments and developing a grand strategic posture consistent with America's interests in the post–Cold War world.

The new administration should reject a unipolar grand strategy. Such a strategy is based on the illusion, not the reality, of American power. Simply put, the United States lacks the resources to sustain its self-appointed role as the arbiter of world affairs. America's relative economic power—the foundation of its strength as a great power—has eroded from its post–World War II apogee. Proponents of the unipolar strategy also fail to understand that new great powers will emerge regardless of Washington's wishes or its policies. Recent U.S. strategy has been based on the erroneous assumption that other states welcome American dominance in world politics. They do not, and balancing against excessive U.S. power is already occurring. The fatal paradox of the unipolar strategy is this: it will actually accelerate the emergence of new great powers and lead to increasing resistance to American policies rather than to the extension of American influence. Proponents of the unipolar strategy overlook a basic point: although the United States would be adversely affected by unipolarity, it is uniquely positioned to benefit from a multipolar world. Such a world presents the opportunity to return to a more traditional geopolitical role, to shift security burdens to others, and to turn America's focus from the illusory pursuit of world order to the imperative goal of renewal at home.

15. Learning to Live with Nuclear Proliferation

Ted Galen Carpenter

The proliferation of nuclear weapons is likely to be one of the most serious security problems for the United States in the post–Cold War era. The U.S.-led international nonproliferation system, represented by the 1968 Nuclear Nonproliferation Treaty (NPT), is showing signs of serious strain. With the breakup of the Soviet Union, at least four of the successor republics (Russia, Ukraine, Kazakhstan, and Belarus) will have nuclear weapons deployed on their territory for the next several years. Although the last three countries have agreed to ultimately become nonnuclear states, there is mounting domestic opposition to that step because it would give Russia a regional nuclear monopoly.

Even before the disintegration of the USSR, an ominous proliferation trend was evident. Israel has had an arsenal (albeit not officially acknowledged) of 100 to 300 weapons since the 1970s. Most experts believe that India and Pakistan either have small arsenals or can acquire them on short notice. Following the end of the Persian Gulf War, UN inspectors discovered Iraq's surprisingly advanced nuclear-weapons development program, and reports have surfaced that nearly a dozen nations including Iran, North Korea, and Libya have active programs.[1] True, there have also been some favorable developments—such as South Africa's decision to abandon its pursuit of an arsenal and sign the NPT and indications that North Korea may be reconsidering its options.[2] Nevertheless, it seems certain that there will be a larger number of nuclear-armed states in the future than there are at present.

[1]The best discussion of long-term proliferation trends is Leonard S. Spector with Jacqueline Smith, *Nuclear Ambitions* (Boulder, Colo.: Westview, 1990).

[2]For a cautiously optimistic assessment of such developments, see Leonard S. Spector, "Repentant Nuclear Proliferants," *Foreign Policy* 88 (Fall 1992): 21–37.

Unfortunately, U.S. officials seem to be in a state of denial about the implications of an increasingly multipolar nuclear environment; they are clinging reflexively to a nonproliferation system that is becoming less and less viable. There is an urgent need for a comprehensive reassessment of U.S. policy. Moreover, policymakers have to accept that there are no perfect solutions to the proliferation problem—only a difficult choice among unpleasant alternatives. Three options appear to be available to the United States: a "status quo plus" policy, coercive nonproliferation, and adjustment to proliferation.[3]

Status Quo Plus

Almost by intellectual default, the United States is pursuing a status quo plus policy. U.S. officials believe that the NPT has been a great success and thereby made the world a much safer place than it would have been without a concerted international strategy to prevent the spread of nuclear weapons. The operating assumption of U.S. policymakers appears to be that although the NPT system is now under siege from a variety of sources, it is still working well. They point to the recent decisions by France and China to sign the NPT, thus bringing all five of the official (declared) nuclear powers under the jurisdiction of the treaty, as evidence of success. Washington's policy, in their view, should be a redoubled diplomatic effort to strengthen the existing nonproliferation regime.

One of the most difficult tasks for statesmen is knowing when events have overtaken a successful policy and rendered it obsolete. The argument can be made that a nonproliferation strategy served American security interests effectively in the past. As the preeminent nuclear power, the United States understandably sought to prevent proliferation. Ideally, the United States would have liked to have preserved the atomic monopoly that it possessed at the end of World War II. When it proved impossible to do so after the USSR exploded an atomic device in 1949, Washington adopted the next best goal—limiting the number of nations that would have nuclear weapons. It was the emergence of both France and China

---

[3]For a more detailed discussion of those options, see Ted Galen Carpenter, "A New Proliferation Policy," *National Interest* 28 (Summer 1992): 63–72.

as uninvited members of the previously exclusive global nuclear-weapons club that impelled Washington to try to codify its nonproliferation policy in the NPT.

Given the realities of the Cold War, Washington's enthusiasm for the virtues of nonproliferation made sense. A starkly bipolar international system dominated by two nuclear-armed states imposed a stable balance of terror. Any acquisition of nuclear weapons by other actors in the international system, however, automatically weakened the ability of the superpowers to "manage" conflicts and keep the rivalry within bounds. In exchange for its allies' willingness to forgo nuclear weapons, the United States extended to them the protection of the U.S. strategic arsenal. That was the fundamental bargain underlying Washington's doctrine of extended deterrence.[4] Without such protection, even such influential nonnuclear states as West Germany and Japan would have been vulnerable to Soviet intimidation, given the USSR's nuclear trump card.

From Washington's perspective, the combination of nonproliferation and extended deterrence served American interests. True, the United States was committed to deterring a Soviet attack on various "free world" nations that had become U.S. protectorates. But an implicit set of rules gradually emerged to govern the superpower rivalry, and as time passed it seemed less and less likely that the Kremlin would ever take a reckless gamble that might plunge the world into nuclear conflict.

Because those policies succeeded in a Cold War setting, U.S. officials may have drawn some erroneous conclusions. Instead of regarding nonproliferation and extended deterrence as useful (or at least tolerable) policies under a set of conditions peculiar to a bipolar world, they assume that both policies have enduring value and are thus sacrosanct. Washington's insistence on preserving extended deterrence and strengthening the NPT in a vastly different post–Cold War era is a prime example of retrograde thinking.

There are two serious problems with pursuing a status quo plus policy. The first and most obvious is that more and more nations

---

[4]The linkages among alliance commitments, extended deterrence, and the configuration of the U.S. strategic arsenal are described in Earl C. Ravenal, "Counterforce and Alliance: The Ultimate Connection," *International Security* 6 (Spring 1982): 26–43.

have the ability to acquire, and apparently the intention of acquiring, nuclear weapons. Rudimentary nuclear technology is now nearly five decades old, and it is unrealistic to assume that only a small number of advanced industrial states will have the requisite technology or know-how to build a bomb. More than two generations of Third World scientists and engineers who have been educated at some of the finest Western (or Soviet) universities can put their expertise at the disposal of governments determined to develop nuclear weapons. Although much information on nuclear technology remains classified, there has been some leakage, and a good deal of pertinent information has legally found its way into the public domain.

And it is possible to get the fissionable material needed to build a bomb. Israel apparently built its arsenal using material it obtained illegally from U.S. and other Western sources. True, it may have been easier for Israel to engage in such surreptitious conduct because it is not a signatory to the NPT. The International Atomic Energy Agency (IAEA) does theoretically have rigorous inspection requirements to prevent the diversion of fissionable material by treaty members who build reactors for electric power or other peaceful purposes. NPT signatories with advanced nuclear technology are also supposed to make diligent efforts of their own to prevent any diversion when they assist other nations in building or operating reactors. Nevertheless, the case of Iraq demonstrates clearly that those safeguards have been ineffective. The IAEA conducted repeated inspections of Iraq's "peaceful nuclear research program" for several years before the onset of the Persian Gulf crisis without detecting the underlying nuclear-weapons effort.

The leakage of both nuclear technology and the material for weapons is likely to accelerate. There are thousands of nuclear weapons in the former Soviet Union, and the political turmoil there hardly promotes optimism about effective control. A wealthy government could conceivably acquire a fully operational small arsenal without having to go through the time-consuming process of creating its own weapons development project. Even if such an egregious leak does not take place, there are thousands of Soviet nuclear scientists and engineers whose employment prospects are uncertain in the new Commonwealth of Independent States (CIS). Governments that want to become nuclear-weapons powers are likely to offer both better job security and higher incomes than the CIS. It is reasonable to assume that at least some scientists and engineers will succumb to temptation.[5]

The nature of the post–Cold War international system also increases the incentives for various powers to acquire independent arsenals. Regional disputes that were often submerged during the long rivalry between the United States and the Soviet Union are now resurfacing. Moscow clearly no longer has the ability to keep its one-time allies and clients in line, and even Washington's ability to control its allies and clients has begun to wane. In a Cold War setting, Pakistan, for example, was hesitant to defy the United States, even though Washington's policy preferences might sometimes inhibit Islamabad's ability to deal with its principal adversary, India. No Pakistani government wanted to anger Washington to the point that it would lose U.S. protection and be vulnerable to Soviet pressure or aggression. But with the dissipation of the Soviet threat, that restraint is far weaker and the focus on the "India threat" much more pronounced. During the Cold War, the United States at least made it difficult for Pakistan to pursue its nuclear ambitions; in a post–Cold War setting, Washington does not have the same political leverage.

The likelihood of nuclear proliferation means that a status quo plus policy will not be sustainable. It also casts doubt on the wisdom of the corollary doctrine of extended deterrence. Indeed, by clinging to those two doctrines, Washington risks creating the worst of all possible situations for the United States. The nonproliferation system is producing a perverse result: the regimes that are the most determined to acquire nuclear weapons are in many cases the same ones that the United States and the world community would least like to see have them. Just as domestic gun control laws are fairly effective at taking guns out of the hands of people who would never use them for criminal purposes, while doing little to prevent hardened criminals from obtaining them, the NPT persuades the Italys, Swedens, Venezuelas, Japans, Australias, and South Koreas of the world not to acquire nuclear weapons. Unfortunately, it is

[5]Tom Clancy and Russell Seitz, "Five Minutes Past Midnight," *National Interest* 26 (Winter 1991–92): 3–13.

having progressively less ability to dissuade the Irans, Libyas, and North Koreas from doing so.

The differential impact of the NPT along with Washington's continued adherence to extended deterrence are creating a deadly combination. If U.S. policy does not change, the United States will find itself in the position of having to shield an assortment of nonnuclear allies from a rogues' gallery of nuclear-armed adversaries. That would be a more difficult and ultimately a more dangerous mission than was shielding those allies from Soviet aggression during the Cold War. Washington always operated under the assumption that although the Kremlin might be ruthless and brutal, it was rational and not unduly reckless. U.S. leaders cannot as confidently assume rationality in an adversary such as Saddam Hussein, Muammar Qadaffi, Kim Il Sung, or Iran's Shi'ite fundamentalist regime. That is especially true if the United States is attempting to deter an attack by one of those regimes on a hated regional ideological or religious opponent. By continuing to discourage allies from acquiring independent deterrents while keeping the doctrine of extended deterrence intact, the United States is placing itself on the front lines of regional disputes that could easily go nuclear, and it is attempting to deter regimes that may be undeterrable.

Coercive Nonproliferation

Some members of the foreign policy community, sensing that the old nonproliferation system with its emphasis on diplomatic cooperation and technology controls is losing its effectiveness, have begun to advocate a new, more coercive form of nonproliferation. In its extreme manifestations, that strategy is based on Washington's willingness to launch preemptive military strikes against the nuclear installations of "undesirable" regimes. Proponents see the "Osirak option"—referring to the Israeli air strikes against a reactor outside Baghdad in 1981—as the appropriate model.

More sophisticated versions of a coercive nonproliferation strategy view preemptive strikes as a last resort, preferring instead to focus on strengthening the IAEA's inspection authority—including the power to conduct unannounced inspections without the consent of the suspected government—and imposing more effective diplomatic and economic sanctions on violators of the NPT.[6] They also typically prefer an international effort directed by the UN Security Council to a unilateral policy enforced by the United States.

There are several problems with a strategy of coercive nonproliferation. In its milder incarnation, the approach does not differ materially from the status quo plus policy, and it shares most of the defects and limitations of that policy. For example, although more intrusive IAEA inspections may seem to be a worthwhile idea in the abstract, it has very little meaningful substance. The regimes that would support unimpeded inspections are not likely to be the ones pursuing clandestine nuclear-weapons programs. Proponents would still face the problem of inducing recalcitrant governments to consent. At the very least, that would require the imposition of economic sanctions. It is not an inspiring scenario, since sanctions have not had an impressive record of persuading target regimes to make concessions on important issues.

That realization leads most proponents of coercive nonproliferation back to the ultimate coercive mechanism: military force. Political scientists William H. Lewis and Christopher C. Joyner acknowledge that a willingness to use force must undergird other measures to stem the spread of nuclear weapons.

> How the international community comes out on that decision will tell much about the real prospects for international arms control. Moreover, it will clearly signal whether international arms control efforts will be backed up by serious military sanctions carrying the international consensus and a real bite, or whether such efforts will persist as sporadic, piecemeal, stop-gap measures in an increasingly complex, interdependent world order.[7]

Using military force to preserve the crumbling nonproliferation system has some serious drawbacks. One of the most basic difficulties would occur if attacks were made on operating reactors. Such

---

[6]See John Simpson and Darryl Howlett, "Nuclear Nonproliferation: The Way Forward," *Survival* 23 (November–December 1991): 491–93; Gary Milhollin and Gerard White, "Stop the Nuclear Threat at the Source," *New York Times*, August 16, 1991; and William H. Lewis and Christopher C. Joyner, "Proliferation of Unconventional Weapons: The Case for Coercive Arms Control," *Comparative Strategy* 10 (Fall 1991): 299–309.

[7]Lewis and Joyner, p. 309.

attacks could easily produce a major leak of radiation that would pose a danger not only for citizens in the target country (which would be bad enough) but for people in neighboring states as well. There are also more subtle dangers and problems. One of the lessons learned by would-be nuclear-weapons states from the Israeli raid on the Osirak reactor was the need to make their programs as clandestine as possible. The Osirak facility had been duly registered with the IAEA, was complying with the inspection requirements of that agency, and was widely known in the international community. Conversely, Iraq's post-1981 program was secretive and included several underground facilities. Even with the vaunted intelligence capabilities of the United States, most of those facilities were not discovered until after Operation Desert Storm. Other nations, including North Korea, have apparently adopted the Iraqi technique of hiding some of their installations underground.[8]

Concealment techniques mean that nations conducting preemptive strikes could never be certain that they had discovered, much less destroyed, all of the facilities—unless they were prepared to invade and occupy the offending country. If some facilities escaped destruction, the nuclear-weapons program of the target country could still go forward (probably with redoubled efforts at secrecy).

Moreover, the nation that had been attacked would have every incentive to seek revenge. Bombing North Korea's nuclear facilities, for example, could easily trigger a general war on that heavily armed peninsula. If Pyongyang decided to respond to a preemptive strike by launching an attack across the demilitarized zone, the nearly 40,000 U.S. troops deployed in the ROK—most of them directly astride the invasion routes from the DMZ to Seoul—would be immediately involved. It would be a high-stakes gamble, at best, to assume that Pyongyang would accept the humiliation of having

---

[8]One expert also notes that unlike the first generation of nuclear-armed states, the newer aspirants are not likely to announce their intentions through the test of an explosive device. Threshold states have apparently concluded that quality assurance can be obtained without testing. That change greatly complicates the process of discovering whether a state has a clandestine program. Jed C. Snyder, "Weapons Proliferation and the New Security Agenda," in *On Not Confusing Ourselves: Essays on National Security in Honor of Albert and Roberta Wohlstetter*, ed. Andrew Marshall, J. J. Martin, and Henry S. Rowen (Boulder, Colo.: Westview, 1991), pp. 272–74.

its nuclear installations destroyed without making a military response.

Even if a target regime did not resort to overt military action, there would always be the possibility of a terrorist reprisal. Proponents of the April 1986 air attacks on Libya believed that those attacks had intimidated Qadaffi and quelled Libyan-sponsored terrorism. U.S. officials persisted in that illusion until the autumn of 1991 when evidence pointed to the involvement of two high-ranking officials of Libya's intelligence service in the bombing of Pan American flight 103 over Lockerbie, Scotland, in December 1988. If that evidence proves to be accurate, Libya exacted a fierce revenge for the 1986 attacks, even though it waited nearly three years to do so.

Finally, there are significant political problems associated with a policy of coercive nonproliferation. The possibilities for double standards and hidden agendas are virtually unlimited. If the UN Security Council arrogates the right to judge proliferation matters, the fact that the five permanent members are also the five openly declared nuclear-weapons states is not going to go unnoticed by nations seeking to acquire such weapons. From their perspective it will be the verdict of a kangaroo court, however much the council may invoke noble-sounding principles. And the United States, as the leader of an international program of coercive nonproliferation, will be the principal target of their wrath, even though those nations might otherwise have no reason to regard America as an enemy.

A strategy of coercive nonproliferation might succeed in preventing some proliferation, but it is unlikely to halt the trend, and it would create a host of new risks and problems for the United States. Moreover, proponents of that strategy show no signs of regarding it as a replacement for America's Cold War policy of extended deterrence. The United States would still have the unenviable task of protecting nonnuclear allies from such declared nuclear powers as China, existing undeclared nuclear-weapons states, and any new nuclear powers that might succeed in evading the strictures of a coercive nonproliferation system.

Adjusting to Proliferation

Instead of clinging to a futile status quo plus policy or adopting the excessively dangerous coercive nonproliferation approach, the United States should adopt a strategy that adjusts to the reality of nuclear-weapons proliferation and devise ways to insulate America from its most harmful consequences. The emergence of a multipolar nuclear-weapons environment has several implications for U.S. policy. First, it underscores the need to maintain a credible deterrent despite the demise of the Soviet adversary. That is not to say that the United States cannot make sizable reductions in its strategic arsenal. The agreement reached at the June 1992 U.S.-Russian summit meeting to reduce each country's arsenal to no more than 3,500 bombs and warheads within 11 years is a promising start. Washington should go further and agree to Russian president Boris Yeltsin's original proposal for a ceiling of 2,000 weapons. Moreover, Washington can contribute to the easing of global nuclear tensions by unilaterally suspending U.S. nuclear tests for a five-year period and seeking an international agreement sharply limiting underground tests thereafter.[9] Such an agreement would be an appropriate companion to the 1963 treaty that outlawed atmospheric nuclear tests.

Nevertheless, it is essential for the United States to keep an arsenal that is sufficiently large to deter an attack on American territory by all except the most irrational regimes. Beyond a certain point, fewer is not necessarily better when it comes to nuclear weapons. An excessively small U.S. arsenal might tempt an aggressive state to assume that it could "take out" that arsenal with a sufficiently coordinated attack. Even if that assumption proved wrong—as it probably would—that would be small comfort to Americans after a nuclear exchange. There is also a more subtle danger created by excessive reductions. As the U.S. arsenal became smaller, the *relative* strength of even minor nuclear powers would become greater. That would certainly be the case if the United States cut its arsenal to 1,000 weapons—as suggested by former secretary of defense Robert McNamara and others—much less to

---

[9]Washington should not, however, sign a treaty that would forever prohibit underground nuclear tests. Changes in technology can affect nuclear weaponry as they can other components of the military, and the United States must retain the ability to keep abreast of those changes. A total ban on nuclear testing could, in time, render the U.S. arsenal obsolete. Recent congressional legislation that would restrict underground tests until 1997 and then impose a permanent ban reverses the order of the steps the United States should take.

even lower levels.[10] Creating even the impression of strategic parity between the United States and emerging nuclear powers would heighten the potential for miscalculation on their part.

A would-be aggressor must have no doubt that even the most well coordinated attack would still leave enough U.S. weapons to produce a devastating counterstroke. Given the continued existence of other significant nuclear powers, an arsenal of fewer than 2,000 bombs and warheads might undermine the credibility of the U.S. deterrent.

Maintaining an adequate deterrent would materially reduce the probability of a premeditated attack on U.S. territory, but three possible sources of danger remain. One is an accidental launch of nuclear weapons, a risk that is likely to mount with an increase in the number of nuclear-weapons states. Many of the new nuclear powers will have neither the financial resources nor the technological sophistication to establish the kinds of elaborate command and control systems that were developed by the United States and the Soviet Union.

A second source is the threat posed by the occasional undeterrable leader or regime—the so-called crazy state phenomenon. Although there may be a tendency on the part of observers in Western democratic nations to exaggerate the irrationality of mercurial dictators, the crazy state scenario cannot be ignored—especially in a multipolar nuclear environment.

The third source of danger is the possibility that a conventional conflict might spiral out of control and, through a series of miscalculations, culminate in a nuclear exchange. The emergence of a multipolar international system increases the probability of disorders and conflicts, and given the proliferation of nuclear weapons, increases the odds that one might breach the nuclear threshold. Although the United States can take steps to reduce the likelihood of becoming a party to such conflicts, it cannot guarantee that it will never be a target of a belligerent.

For all those reasons, it is essential that the United States augment a credible deterrent with effective air and missile defenses—the second adjustment that U.S. policy should make to the reality of

[10]Carl Kaysen, Robert S. McNamara, and George W. Rathjens, "Nuclear Weapons after the Cold War," *Foreign Affairs* 70 (Fall 1991): 95–110.

nuclear-weapons proliferation. An antiballistic missile (ABM) system does not require implementing President Ronald Reagan's ambitious Strategic Defense Initiative, since repelling an onslaught by the entire Soviet missile fleet is now an extremely improbable mission. A "thin layer" ABM system, however, could offer crucial protection in the case of an accidental launch of a few dozen missiles. The same would be true of a deliberate attack by a new nuclear power that had a limited arsenal.

Many of the nations that are seeking to acquire nuclear weapons also have serious programs to build ballistic missiles. Because no Third World state is likely to have intercontinental ballistic missiles (ICBMs) by the end of this decade—the goal of most existing programs appears to be confined to the development of short- or medium-range missiles capable of reaching regional adversaries—opponents of ABMs contend that the United States should delay efforts to build a defensive shield until a credible ICBM threat to U.S. territory emerges.[11]

Their conclusion is myopic. First of all, it ignores the problem of an accidental launch of existing CIS missiles. Moreover, it is not all that large a technological leap from developing shorter range missiles to having an ICBM capability. Although many of the new nuclear-weapons states may not feel the acquisition of an ICBM fleet is worth the expense, others may conclude that they must be able to threaten the U.S. homeland to prevent Washington from interfering with their regional agendas. Moreover, missile defenses cannot be built overnight. Even the single ABM installation in North Dakota, authorized by Congress in 1991, will not be operational until 1997 at the earliest. Building a nationwide system would take considerably longer. We cannot wait until hostile powers have fully operational ICBM fleets to build adequate defenses.

The other principal objection raised by critics—that ABM systems offer no protection against alternative delivery methods that enemy governments or terrorist movements might use—is also unconvincing. True, hostile forces might find other means of delivering

---

[11]For examples of that reasoning, see David C. Morrison, "Where's the Threat?" *National Journal*, October 26, 1991, p. 2629; "A Meaningful SDI Mission," editorial, *Boston Globe*, November 2, 1991, p. 18; and Matt Hansen, "Sounding Taps for Star Wars and the Stealth Bomber," *Defense Monitor* 20, no. 5 (Washington: Center for Defense Information, 1991).

nuclear weapons—using small aircraft or smuggling in "satchel bombs," for example. But the fact that a defense system would not neutralize all threats does not mean that we should refuse to use it against threats that it can thwart. Moreover, there is a crucial difference in the magnitude of the potential damage from various delivery systems. It is unlikely, for example, that a smuggling operation could successfully deploy more than a few small devices in a handful of cities. Although the detonation of such weapons would undoubtedly cause extensive damage and loss of life, America could probably recover. (The Soviet Union was able to survive the loss of more than 10 percent of its population and the destruction of many of its major cities in World War II.) Conversely, the detonation of numerous larger, more destructive missile warheads could devastate American civilization beyond recovery.

Even an imperfect shield would protect the vast majority of American population centers from that kind of massive damage. As a collateral benefit, it would reduce the likelihood of nuclear blackmail. In a world with nuclear-weapons proliferation, basic prudence dictates that U.S. leaders not leave the American people defenseless against a missile attack.

A third policy adjustment to nuclear proliferation should be the exercise of far greater caution about involving the United States in disputes that are not highly relevant to America's own vital security interests. The most important step would be to abandon the doctrine of extended deterrence. During the Cold War a plausible case could be made that the United States had to assume the risks entailed in extended deterrence to prevent Moscow from achieving global hegemony through nuclear blackmail or outright aggression, although some perceptive critics argued that the level of risk run by the United States was excessive even then.

Without the threat posed by a would-be hegemonic challenger, assuming the risk is even more unwarranted. Not only might it prove considerably more difficult to deter an assortment of small nuclear-weapons states than it did to deter the Soviet Union, but even the theoretical benefits to the United States are considerably more modest. It is difficult to imagine what interest could be important enough to justify America's defending South Korea from a nuclearized North Korea. The stakes involved are hardly of the same magnitude as those that existed during the Cold War. In a post–Cold War international system, extended deterrence is a superpower status symbol that the United States can no longer afford.

Beyond making it necessary for the United States to rescind the promises of extended deterrence to major allies, nuclear proliferation makes it imperative that Washington exercise greater caution about meddling in regional quarrels. The threshold for concluding that a vital U.S. security interest is involved in such disputes should be extremely high. The only thing worse than needlessly becoming entangled in a conflict between belligerents armed with conventional weapons would be to do so when one or more of the parties are armed with nuclear weapons. That level of risk should never be undertaken unless a vital American interest is in imminent jeopardy.

The final needed adjustment is to change the focus of Washington's nonproliferation policy. U.S. policymakers must rid themselves of the attitude that all forms of proliferation are equally bad. It ought to make a substantial difference to Americans whether nuclear weapons are acquired by a stable, democratic state with which the United States has had a lengthy record of good relations or by an unstable or brutal anti-American dictatorship. Yet the provisions of the NPT permit no such distinction. Moreover, U.S. proponents of the NPT have been as determined to prevent such stable democratic nations as Japan and Germany from developing nuclear weapons as they have Third World states—indeed, they frequently have seemed *more* determined.

Those priorities must change. It is not that Washington should encourage its major West European and East Asian allies to develop their own arsenals. Encouragement would probably be superfluous in any case. A decision by the United States to rescind the doctrine of extended deterrence would impel each of those nations to reassess its policy toward nuclear weapons in light of its own circumstances and security requirements. Some might decide to take the risk of remaining nonnuclear in an increasingly nuclear world or conclude that they can neutralize the danger through sufficiently sophisticated conventional weapons. (The U.S. performance in Operation Desert Storm demonstrated that a considerable amount of damage can be inflicted on the infrastructure of an adversary with such weapons.) Most beneficiaries of the U.S. nuclear umbrella throughout the Cold War, however, would probably conclude that they now need independent deterrents. What is required from Washington is not overt encouragement but merely acceptance of that change. U.S. leaders need not be accomplices in facilitating the acquisition of nuclear arsenals by other Western democratic states, but they must abandon the policy of obstructionism.

To do so, the United States will need to move beyond the "one size fits all" philosophy embodied in the NPT. Indeed, Washington should decline to support an extension of the NPT when it comes up for renewal in 1995. To the extent that Washington wishes to continue pursuing a nonproliferation strategy, it should concentrate on making it difficult for aggressive or unstable regimes to acquire the technology needed to become nuclear powers. And U.S. policymakers must adopt a realistic attitude toward the limitations of even that more tightly focused nonproliferation policy. At best, U.S. actions will only delay, not prevent, such states from joining the nuclear-weapons club.

But delay can provide some important benefits. It may give the United States time to develop adequate strategic defenses and other Western nations time to build their own deterrents or strategic defense systems, or both. A delay of only a few years may significantly reduce the likelihood that an aggressive power with a new nuclear-weapons capability will have a regional monopoly and be able to blackmail nonnuclear states. In some cases, the knowledge that the achievement of regional nuclear hegemony is impossible may even discourage a would-be aggressor from making the effort. At the very least, it could cause such a power to configure its new arsenal for deterrence rather than for intimidating neighboring countries for political gain.

There are other steps the United States can take to limit some of the harmful effects of proliferation. One of the most worrisome prospects is that many of the new nuclear states will lack the financial resources or the technical expertise to establish reliable command and control systems or to guard their arsenals from theft or terrorism. Inadequate safeguards greatly increase the danger of an accidental or unauthorized launch. Beyond that problem is the more subtle danger that some of those nuclear powers may fail to develop coherent strategic doctrines that would let adversaries know the circumstances under which the aggrieved party might use nuclear weapons.

Washington can help minimize such problems by disseminating command and control technology and assisting in the creation of crisis management hot lines and other confidence-building measures among emerging nuclear powers. The United States can also encourage potential adversaries to engage in strategic dialogues to delineate the kinds of provocations that might cause them to contemplate using nuclear weapons and outline the doctrines that would govern their use. Such a dialogue helped stabilize the dangerous superpower rivalry and might have a similar effect on regional confrontations. At the very least, it would reduce the chances of a nuclear conflict erupting because of miscalculation or misunderstanding.

A policy of adjusting to proliferation is not a panacea. It is, however, superior to the status quo plus policy—an ostrichlike response based on the assumptions that proliferation can be prevented indefinitely and that all forms of proliferation are equally undesirable from the standpoint of U.S. security interests. It is also superior to the dangerous and provocative alternative of coercive nonproliferation. The United States cannot prevent the spread of nuclear weapons, but a strategy of adjustment offers the most prudent method of minimizing its negative consequences for the American people.

The new administration's action plan on nuclear-weapons policy should include the following steps.

- Issue a formal notice that the United States will no longer participate in the Nuclear Nonproliferation Treaty when it comes up for extension in 1995.
- Accept Boris Yeltsin's original proposal to reduce the U.S. and Russian strategic arsenals to 2,000 weapons each.
- Accelerate the ABM program with the goal of deploying a nationwide system within 10 years.
- Suspend all U.S. nuclear tests for five years and commence negotiations for an international treaty to strictly limit underground nuclear tests as a supplement to the 1963 atmospheric test ban treaty.
- Rescind the doctrine of extended deterrence and affirm that the U.S. nuclear arsenal will exist solely to deter attacks on vital American security interests.

- Indicate to major democratic capitalist nations in Western Europe and East Asia that the United States will no longer seek to block them from creating independent strategic deterrents.
- Seek ways to help emerging nuclear powers create reliable control systems to prevent accidental or unauthorized launches and assist those countries to articulate defensive nuclear doctrines.

16. A Post–Cold War Military Budget

Jeffrey R. Gerlach

The end of the Cold War offers the United States a rare opportunity to fundamentally recast its national security policy. The collapse of the Soviet Union and the utter failure of communism as a viable political system have drastically altered America's place in the world. With no reason to "pay any price, bear any burden" to oppose the Soviets and their surrogates, the United States can return to the foreign policy posture designed by the Founding Fathers that guided the nation for most of its history. Such a policy would forgo aggressive pursuit of utopian goals, such as global stability or universal democracy, and focus instead on the defense of American territory, sovereignty, and liberty. U.S. military forces would be used solely to defend America against threats to her vital interests. A restrained foreign policy, based on the principle of avoiding unnecessary foreign entanglements, would allow a dramatic paring of America's defense expenditures. The United States would maintain extensive economic, social, cultural, and diplomatic links with other nations, but military relations would be substantially curtailed. The resulting savings could be returned to the American people.

The Base Force Concept

The Pentagon responded to the disintegration of the communist threat by developing plans for a Base Force designed to meet America's defense needs. From its post-Vietnam peak of 2.2 million in 1987, the active duty force would fall to 1.6 million by 1995, a reduction of about 25 percent. Reserve and civilian personnel would be reduced by about 20 percent. A number of major weapons programs—including the B-2 bomber, the Minuteman III intercontinental ballistic missile, the Seawolf submarine, the Comanche helicopter, and the air defense anti-tank system—would be scaled back or eliminated. The new security structure, though hailed as a dramatic reduction in U.S. military spending, would only modestly reduce expenditures for the next several years.

The proposed fiscal year 1993 defense budget called for spending $281 billion. Under that scenario, military spending would remain roughly constant through 1995, then rise to $290.6 billion in 1997, the final year considered. The House and Senate agreed on an FY93 military budget of $274.3 billion, some $7 billion less than the Department of Defense requested, and made a number of changes. Congress reduced funding for the Strategic Defense Initiative, operations and maintenance programs, and sealift capabilities and ordered changes in inventory management and overseas basing costs. Those changes are expected to save billions. Congress also funded a number of programs that were not in the DOD's original budget, including the V-22 tiltrotor aircraft, the Comanche helicopter, and the LHD amphibious assault ship, and increased funding for a number of defense conversion projects.

Though it lowered overall defense spending marginally, Congress basically approved the Pentagon's plan. The DOD is reducing military spending in real terms by about 4 percent per year through 1997 instead of the 3 percent it originally projected after the fall of the Berlin Wall in 1989. The revised budget figures represent a cumulative real decline of 35 percent between 1985 and 1997. Pentagon statistics show that defense spending as a share of the nation's gross national product has also declined. That figure, currently around 5 percent, is scheduled to fall to 3.5 percent in 1997.

Despite attempts by the Pentagon to characterize the cuts as substantial, they are actually quite modest. The DOD does not present what is perhaps the most useful indicator of the size of the current military budget. According to the Congressional Budget Office, measured in real terms, defense spending is roughly the same now as it was in the early 1960s, at the height of the Cold War. If approximately $280 billion (in constant dollars) was sufficient when the United States faced an adversary of great size and strength, it surely exceeds U.S. security needs now that the Soviet Union has collapsed.

Defense spending as a percentage of GNP reveals only the burden placed on the U.S. economy by military spending; it tells nothing about the amount of money that should be spent on defense. Proper levels of spending can be determined only by examining America's security interests, evaluating the potential threats to those interests, and striking a balance between the nation's resources and commitments. Under some conditions, the United States might need to devote a large percentage of its GNP to ensuring its security. Under other conditions, a small percentage would suffice. Thus, it is irrelevant that military spending as a percentage of GNP is falling. A military budget must be developed on the basis of the nation's security needs, not the size of its economy.

Furthermore, the decline of military spending as a percentage of GNP reflects primarily the tremendous growth of the American economy since 1960. The GNP of the United States in 1960 was $1,985.1 billion (1987 dollars) compared to a 1991 GNP of $4,836.4 billion. Given that economic expansion, it is not at all surprising that military spending has fallen as a percentage of GNP. Indeed, it would have been astonishing if such a decline had not occurred—despite the spending appetites of Pentagon officials.

Another flaw in the DOD statistics is that the analysis on which they are based covers a time period that was carefully chosen by the Pentagon. To demonstrate that the defense budget is indeed falling, the DOD uses either FY85 or FY87 as the base year for most of the raw numbers. That is inherently misleading since the early and middle 1980s witnessed a tremendous increase in military spending. Spending for defense and international programs rose from $146.7 billion in 1980 to $293.6 billion in 1987 (current dollars). In real terms, the Reagan administration's defense budget for FY87 represented more than the United States had previously spent in any one year since the end of World War II. As military spending moves to more "normal" levels, the appearance is created that drastic cuts are being made. In essence, however, the United States is simply returning to business-as-usual Cold War figures.

The statistics are skewed at the other end of the time period as well. DOD projections end in 1997, when the defense budget would be $274.6 billion (1992 dollars), but the Congressional Budget Office has released a study that examines probable military spending through the year 2010, and its analysis shows a very different outcome. The CBO estimates the amount of money that will be needed to maintain the Base Force concept, which will serve as the guide for future defense spending. It assumes that military manpower will remain roughly constant and that weapons systems will be maintained and modernized. The study concludes that "substantial increases in funding could be required in the years beyond 1997 to maintain and modernize the Base Force under the administration's plans."[1] According to the CBO, by the middle of the next decade, annual military spending (1992 dollars) will exceed 1997 levels by $20 billion to $65 billion.

The main reason for the increases will be the need to replace aging equipment. Much of the savings in the 1993–97 period is derived by postponing modernization and replacement. During the next decade, the CBO argues quite convincingly, both modernization and replacement must occur. The $20 billion estimate assumes that acquisition costs will be similar to those of the recent past. The $65 billion estimate, on the other hand, assumes that costs of weapons research and development will rise. The CBO suggests that the latter is the more likely because increasingly sophisticated weapons tend to be increasingly expensive. According to the *New York Times*, Pentagon officials realize that "projected military spending simply will not cover the costs required to equip, train and maintain the troops and accompanying ships, aircraft and ground units called for in the long-range budgets."[2]

Thus, even the meager peace dividend outlined in current budgetary projections is likely to be very short-lived. If the Base Force concept is maintained, costs will rise significantly after 1997. The result is likely to be military budgets similar to those of the 1980s— during a period in which the United States will have no serious military competitors.

National Military Strategy

Though pressure from various interest groups can often distort defense spending, the overall budget reflects the nation's perception of its security needs. As defense analyst Earl C. Ravenal points out, "A defense budget represents a view of the world and of the place and role of a nation in that world."[3] Thus, it is important to

---

[1]"Fiscal Implications of the Administration's Proposed Base Force," Congressional Budget Office Staff Memorandum, December 1991, p. 11.

[2]Eric Schmitt, "Military Planning Deep Budget Cuts," *New York Times*, August 30, 1992, p. A1.

[3]Earl C. Ravenal, *Designing Defense for a New World Order: The Military Budget in 1992 and Beyond* (Washington: Cato Institute, 1991), p. 7.

examine the assumptions underlying U.S. military expenditures. Washington's military strategy merely replaces the global focus of the Cold War with a new, but equally expansive, regional emphasis that assumes the United States must be prepared to counter a variety of local threats instead of a worldwide communist enemy. According to the Joint Chiefs of Staff's "National Military Strategy" (1992), "The United States must maintain the strength necessary to influence world events, deter would-be aggressors, guarantee free access to global markets, and encourage continued democratic and economic progress in an atmosphere of enhanced stability."[4] Maintaining stability is the overwhelming theme of the new doctrine. "The threat is instability and being unprepared to handle a crisis or war that no one predicted or expected."[5]

Two of the components outlined in the "National Military Strategy" emphasize the open-ended nature of proposed U.S. missions in the post–Cold War era. Forward Presence refers to the need to continue deploying U.S. troops in key regions of the world, allowing the United States to respond to threats to stability from any area of the globe. Crisis Response is an even broader mission that suggests that the United States must be prepared to respond to any contingency anywhere in the world. In addition, the DOD recognizes that aggression might not be limited to just one area of the planet; thus, the United States must have adequate forces to counter a number of potential adversaries simultaneously.

Crisis Response and Forward Presence highlight the goal of maintaining stability in a dangerous world. There are, however, a number of fundamental problems with the new regional outlook. One of the more significant flaws is the loose definition of areas that are "vital" U.S. interests. The regional strategy appears destined to lead the United States into conflicts that clearly involve no more than peripheral U.S. interests. The DOD is generally quite vague about areas of possible conflict. In classified documents leaked to the media, however, Pentagon planners detailed seven scenarios for regional conflicts.[6] Perhaps the most dangerous involved a

---

[4]Joint Chiefs of Staff, "National Military Strategy," 1992, p. 2.

[5]Ibid., p. 4.

[6]Patrick E. Tyler, "Seven Hypothetical Conflicts Foreseen by the Pentagon," *New York Times*, February 17, 1992, p. A8.

resurgent Russia's invading Lithuania and being repulsed by a U.S.-led NATO counterattack. The clear implication is that Lithuania is an area of vital interest to the United States. That assumption is extremely dubious when one considers that Lithuania was totally dominated by the Soviet Union for 50 years—a tragic situation for the Lithuanian people, but one that did not seem to impair vital U.S. interests. Although it is certainly preferable that Lithuania be a free and independent state, that objective is not central to the security of the United States. Lithuanian independence is not worth the risk of a major conflict between states heavily armed with nuclear weapons. Taking such a risk would be both illogical and dangerous.

"Defense Planning Guidance for the Fiscal Years 1994–1999," another document leaked to the media in the spring of 1992, further clarifies DOD intentions. That study asserts that the U.S. role in the new world order should be to ensure that no rival superpower emerges. The key to achieving that goal is to "sufficiently account for the interests of the advanced industrial nations to discourage them from challenging our leadership or seeking to overturn the established political and economic order."[7] The two main objectives inherent in the plan are to prevent the emergence of a new global rival and to address "sources of regional conflict and instability in such a way as to promote increasing respect for international law, limit international violence, and encourage the spread of democratic forms of government and open economic systems."

The first objective—preventing the emergence of a global rival—is easily achieved for the near future since the powers that have the industrial base to challenge the United States militarily are in disarray or uninterested in territorial expansion. Any resurgent threat would take years to develop, thus allowing America time to react. The first objective clearly does not require nearly $300 billion a year in military expenditures. Achieving the second objective—preventing regional conflicts—requires much more effort. Although the planners explicitly state that the United States will not be the "world's policeman," the document outlines precisely that role. The elaborate system of alliances and military guarantees

---

[7]Patrick E. Tyler, "U.S. Strategy Plan Calls for Insuring No Rivals Develop," *New York Times*, March 8, 1992, p. 1.

built up over the last four decades to combat communism sets the stage for U.S. involvement in virtually every area of the world. Indeed, the DOD argues that threats "are likely to arise in regions critical to the security of the United States and its allies, including Europe, East Asia, the Middle East and Southwest Asia, and the territory of the former Soviet Union. We also have important interests at stake in Latin America, Oceania, and Sub-Saharan Africa."[8] In other words, potential challenges await the U.S. military on every continent with the exception of Antarctica.

The central problem with linking defense spending to a quest to deter instability is that there is almost no limit to the number of potentially destabilizing situations in which the United States might feel obligated to intervene. During the Cold War, the intelligence agencies provided estimates (of questionable accuracy) of the strength of the Soviet Union and its client states. Those estimates, however flawed, allowed military planners to come up with specific requirements for countering the Soviet threat. Under the regional strategy, the only limit to sources of potential instability is the imagination of Pentagon officials.

By making stability a major goal of U.S. security policy, U.S. officials seem to be suggesting that change in the international arena may occur only on American terms. If change does not occur on U.S. terms, Washington will presumably seek to prevent or reverse particular developments. Throughout history, however, the international system has been turbulent, and there is no reason to believe the system will be any different in the future. Turbulence tends to increase in the years following the collapse of empires (e.g., the Habsburg, Ottoman, British and French, and now the Soviet). U.S. foreign policy must have the flexibility to accommodate various transformations in international politics. A policy based on an obsession with stability is particularly ironic in an era of transition. In the new international system, it will be impossible to maintain order throughout all regions. Furthermore, instability already reigns in many areas of the globe where ethnic conflicts, border disputes, insurgencies, terrorist threats, and other potentially destabilizing forces persist. The U.S. commitment to stability

---

[8]"Excerpts from Pentagon's Plan: Prevent the Emergence of a New Rival," *New York Times*, March 8, 1992, p. A14.

suggests that the nation must be prepared to intervene in many instances to maintain the status quo even though change of one kind or another is inevitable. That is a dangerously short-sighted policy.

The temptation to intervene in areas of crisis is particularly evident in recent media debates. Over the past year, editorial writers have urged the United States to intervene with force in such disparate regions as Yugoslavia, Somalia, Haiti, and parts of the former Soviet Union. Imposing just solutions to those crises would be an enormous task, but it is the tip of the iceberg of the potential for regional violence in the post–Cold War era. Fighting is currently occurring in Armenia and Azerbaijan, Georgia, Afghanistan, Tajikistan, Turkey, Indonesia, India, Liberia, Sudan, Peru, and a host of other places; that list does not include areas, in virtually every corner of the globe, where violence is apt to break out. To achieve stability throughout the world, the United States must be prepared to intervene repeatedly to halt conflict and maintain the status quo. That is a task that goes well beyond legitimate American security requirements.

Jobs, Jobs, Jobs

Pork-barrel politics has always played a role in determining military expenditures. During the Cold War, the presence of a formidable enemy provided at least some rationale for continuing programs of dubious value. However, in an era when significant threats to the United States have virtually disappeared, it is intolerable to continue to justify defense spending on the basis of its alleged economic benefits to particular groups or regions. In 1992 the November elections and a continuing recession, amid general doubts about America's economic competitiveness, made jobs a critical political issue. Paralyzed by fears that reductions in military expenditures would raise unemployment, politicians of all political stripes rallied to support defense spending. As a result, significant national security issues were decided on the basis of economic concerns, not military considerations.

The Pentagon's decision to cancel the $2 billion Seawolf submarine, a weapon designed to counter the now-defunct Soviet threat, is an excellent example. Sen. Christopher J. Dodd and Rep. Sam Gejdenson, both Democrats from Connecticut and opponents of the Reagan defense build-up, fought desperately to override the administration's decision. Both argued that the submarine is vital to America's defense needs. A more plausible explanation of their support for the Seawolf was their desire to save thousands of jobs in Groton, Connecticut. Gejdenson attempted to justify his position in a *New York Times* article. "There are better things to choose to build (than the Seawolf), but the worst thing to do is to choose not to build anything."[9] It does not take a Ph.D. in economics to realize that building obsolete submarines is not the most efficient use of scarce American resources.

Connecticut's other senator, Joseph Lieberman, also a Democrat, joined Dodd in proposing a loan guarantee program for countries that want to buy directly from U.S. weapons makers. Thus, Americans could subsidize such products twice, in the production phase and again in the sales phase. Connecticut, of course, is not the only state whose legislators are more concerned about local jobs than national defense requirements. Numerous commentators have noted that the best way to convert congressional doves to hawks is to try to cancel defense contracts in their districts. Rep. Julian Dixon of California, a Democrat who has in the past sponsored plans to reduce defense spending, provides a succinct explanation of the politics of defense pork. "The bottom line is, what is it going to do to my community's economy?"[10] Contrast that with the view that the nation's defense spending should be based on a sober calculation of its security needs.

Even members of Congress who have previously taken a strong stand against using the defense budget for programs not related to national security have been guilty. Last year, for example, Sen. John Warner (R-Va.) stated, "At a time when declining defense budgets are forcing the administration and the Congress to make difficult choices . . . I find it completely unacceptable that defense dollars are diverted to projects that have not been reviewed or requested by (the Defense Department)."[11] Yet in last-minute negotiations, against administration wishes and without debate, he

[9]Clifford Krauss, "In Battle of Budget, Democrats Defend Military Hardware," *New York Times*, March 17, 1992.

[10]Jackie Calmes, "Guns for Butter; Ardor to Trim Defense Hits Political Obstacle: The Fear of Job Losses," *New York Times*, May 7, 1992, p. A1.

[11]John Lancaster, "Senators Take Care of Own in Pentagon's Budget Bill," *Washington Post*, September 23, 1992, p. A1.

added $60 million to the defense budget for night-vision goggles, manufactured in his home state, for the National Guard. In explaining his actions, Warner commented: "Look, any lawmaker thinks in terms of his state and his industrial base. Obviously that influenced my thinking."[12]

The blame for such indiscriminate spending should not be placed solely on Congress, however. Despite Secretary of Defense Richard Cheney's firm pledge that the defense budget would not be a jobs program, the executive branch has been guilty of using defense funds to shore up political support. During the election campaign, the Bush administration announced a $250 million plan to upgrade the M-1 tank, even though White House officials had previously argued that the end of the Cold War made the improved version unnecessary. The V-22 Osprey tiltrotor aircraft, another weapon that the Pentagon had determined was unnecessary, was also saved by the president. While visiting hurricane-ravaged Florida, Bush promised to rebuild Homestead Air Force base, despite the facts that it had been a candidate for closure and that many other bases must be closed. On a trip to Fort Worth, Texas, where the F-16 is made by General Dynamics, he approved the sale of 150 aircraft (worth $4 billion) to Taiwan. He followed that with an agreement to sell Saudi Arabia 72 F-15s ($5 billion). Bush also contended that the modest cuts Bill Clinton supported would cost a million defense-related jobs. The writers of campaign rhetoric neglected to consider the jobs that would be created by channeling resources to more efficient sectors of the economy. Such moves were clearly divorced from national security considerations and reflected a desire to avoid layoffs during an election campaign.

Clinton, despite his pledge to trim defense by $60 billion (over a five-year period) more than the Bush administration would, gave few indications that he was any more immune to domestic considerations than Bush. Campaigning in Connecticut during the Democratic primary, for example, Clinton made his support of the Seawolf submarine a major issue. Perhaps even more indicative, he suggested maintaining larger National Guard and Reserve forces than did President Bush. The Guard and Reserve are powerful lobbies that have resisted budget cuts. They provide jobs in local

[12]Ibid.

communities and tremendous support to politicians who earn their favor.

If anything, Clinton appeared to favor expanding the role of the military well beyond that of national security. In a major foreign policy address, he described the Pentagon as "America's best youth training program, our most potent research center and the most fully integrated institution in American life. It's time to put those assets to work at home. . . . There ought to be some other work for military forces and the National Guard in solving the problems of infrastructure, education, and rural health—offering the possibility to our military personnel to serve as role models here at home, all the while maintaining their consistent obligation to fulfill their primary military mission."[13] Such plans reflect an extremely broad definition of the nation's security.

The temptation to develop new roles for the military must be resisted. As threats recede, spending should decline correspondingly. National security, not social welfare concerns, should dictate the level of defense spending. Health, education, and America's infrastructure are all legitimate issues, but they should not be within the purview of the Pentagon. The best prospect for military personnel and defense workers displaced by budget cuts is a healthy and growing economy that will produce jobs. After World War II, the military budget was slashed and defense and defense-related employment fell by more than 10 million in just two years. Yet by 1948, in a labor market half the size of today's, most of those people had been absorbed into the economy with little government assistance. That the period after the war was one of impressive growth in the U.S. economy certainly provides a lesson that policymakers in Washington should remember.

The short-term problem of dislocation of workers is best met by offering incentives for voluntary separation, much as the Pentagon has already done. Voluntary separation bonuses allow an individual to determine how best to plan for the future, such as moving to another region to seek work, returning to school for further education or training, or opening a business. Bonuses do not continue open-ended funding of programs that are unnecessary. The

[13]Bill Clinton, "Remarks of Governor Bill Clinton," to the Los Angeles World Affairs Council, August 13, 1992 (transcript).

worst solution is to continue employing people in useless industries, thus draining the economy of funds that could be spent on
productive enterprises. Another alternative proposed by both parties, government-funded defense conversion programs, has proven
noticeably unsuccessful in the past. Defense industries are designed
to produce military products, and their track record in converting
to civilian products is dismal.

A Real Alternative

Though pork-barrel politics distorts defense spending, the underlying reason for profligate U.S military spending is a national security strategy that commits the United States to maintaining stability
throughout the world. Once that premise is accepted, large military
expenditures must inevitably follow. One might be able to pare
defense spending by eliminating inefficiencies and waste, but the
current national security strategy requires a large, far-flung military.
Most alternative proposals put forth by political leaders, think
tanks, academics, and others decrease projected budgets somewhat
more than the DOD intends but accept the basic strategy outlined
by the Pentagon.

In some respects that approach can be more dangerous than
the current strategy. Ravenal, for example, has stressed that the
funding levels suggested in many recent proposals will not support
the forces they are meant to. Such military plans are apt to leave
the United States with substantial commitments but a hollow force
incapable of carrying out its mission. If the United States is to enjoy
a significant peace dividend, the current strategic vision must be
revised. A revision would not only provide substantial savings, it
would eliminate the risk of becoming involved in peripheral conflicts for which U.S. forces are not prepared.

A fundamental feature of a new security policy should be renunci-
ation of the reflexive desire to intervene militarily whenever crises
arise. The policy of intervening in areas of dubious value to the
United States has been costly and often counterproductive, as
events in Vietnam and Iran (the CIA-directed coup that restored
the shah to power) demonstrated. The alternative to that approach
is to strictly define the security interests of the United States. To
be a threat to a vital interest, an external development must be
truly life threatening to the Republic. The emergence of a global

military power with an expansionist ideology would constitute such a threat. A threat to vital interests could also take other forms, but currently such a challenge could come only from hostile states armed with nuclear weapons. However, that menace is best met through development of an anti-ballistic missile (ABM) system and multilateral efforts to control nuclear technology and weapons proliferation. An enormous standing army or an excessively large navy will do little to provide a credible deterrent to a renegade party armed with nuclear weapons.

A strategy based on a rigorous definition of vital interests would mean that the American military would intervene only where critical threats to vital U.S. interests developed. If such a policy were adopted, the United States could reduce its security commitments throughout the world. The U.S. military would not be charged with defending other countries. Since threats to the United States are receding, it is unlikely that major challenges will develop in the near future. Commenting on the lack of potential American enemies, Chairman of the Joint Chiefs of Staff Gen. Colin Powell has stated: "I'm running out of demons. I'm running out of villains. I'm down to Castro and Kim Il Sung."[14] That assessment concedes the paucity of real threats to the United States.

A more appropriate strategy would allow military spending levels, designed to counter a global enemy, to be significantly reduced. The United States could reduce defense spending by about one-half over the next several years and more than adequately protect national security interests.[15] Military expenditures of approximately

[14]*Newsweek*, April 22, 1991, p. 19.

[15]The numbers given here are drawn from Ravenal's *Designing Defense for a New World Order* and Ted Galen Carpenter and Rosemary Fiscarelli, "America's Peace Dividend," Cato Institute White Paper, August 7, 1990. A number of other studies have advocated cuts of a similar magnitude. William W. Kaufman and John Steinbruner suggest a "cooperative security" system that would require a military budget of $146.8 billion in *Decisions for Defense: Prospects for a New Order* (Washington: Brookings Institution, 1991), pp. 67–76. Their preferred option would consist of a multilateral agreement among the major powers to limit military capabilities and regulate arms exports. Kaufman and Steinbruner believe such an agreement would eliminate many of the dangers inherent in the international system. The Center for Defense Information argues that all of the goals of the Pentagon's National Military Strategy can be met for $212 billion ("Defending America: A Force Structure for 1995," Center for Defense Information, February 21, 1992). Even the DOD has prepared to deal with a lower budget than that envisioned for the Base Force concept (Eric Schmitt, "Military Planning Deep Budget Cuts," *New York Times*, August 30,

$150 billion (1993 dollars) would support a force of 1 million personnel including 6 Army divisions, 2 Marine divisions, 11 Air Force tactical air wings, and 6 carrier groups with 5 air wings. A military of that size would consist primarily of air and naval power and would focus on rapid response deployments, not large-scale missions designed to counter the former Soviet Union. The United States will not need massive numbers of ground troops since it is faced with no imminent global military challenge. With a scaled-down military, the United States would not only have capable conventional forces; it could afford to maintain a credible nuclear deterrent and continue funding for an ABM system and other research programs. A force of the suggested size could serve as a base from which to reconstitute a larger military if the United States were threatened in the future. An appropriate budget would also include funds for the intelligence services, albeit at reduced levels. Their mission would be to ensure that, should major threats develop, Washington would have the time to prepare accordingly. A $150 billion U.S. military budget would still be over four times larger than that of any other industrial power. It would allow the United States to guarantee its territorial integrity, maintain its place as the world's dominant naval power, and continue the development of new technology as a hedge against a resurgent global threat.

The proposed reduction would require disengaging from many of our overseas commitments and demobilizing U.S.-based forces designed specifically to fight Soviet aggression on foreign soil. Deployment of massive numbers of American personnel in Europe and East Asia to counter an enemy that has disappeared is an obsolete tactic. Weapons developed to counter the Soviet threat, such as the Seawolf submarine and the B-2 bomber, would also be eliminated. The resulting peace dividend could be returned to those who paid for the U.S. share of the Cold War in the first place, the American people. Dollars not spent on obsolete submarines or missiles, items that do not contribute to further economic development, would go to economically productive areas such as civilian investment or consumption. The result of a reallocation would be

---

1992, p. A1). A senior Army official predicted that future defense budgets would be in the $240 billion to $250 billion range.

a dramatic upsurge in the U.S. economy, the true foundation of American power.

Conclusion

The United States has no legitimate reason to continue spending more money on defense than all of the other G-7 industrial powers (Japan, Germany, France, Italy, the United Kingdom, and Canada) combined. One must seriously question the wisdom of asking Americans to pay, on a per capita basis, hundreds of dollars more for defense than do citizens of Britain, Germany, or Japan. Changes in the international environment present the opportunity to achieve a real peace dividend if America is willing to adopt a new vision of defense strategy. Washington must curtail its reflexive desire to intervene with force in disputes that do not threaten vital interests of the United States. Military expenditures will have to remain roughly constant if the nation intends to play the role of world policeman. If spending is cut dramatically while commitments remain the same, the United States runs a serious risk of becoming involved in costly conflicts for which it is not adequately prepared.

There is a real alternative. The United States can reformulate its national military strategy to reflect the demise of the Soviet threat. To implement that security policy, Washington should take the following steps.

- Over the next several years, reduce defense spending from its current level of nearly $300 billion to $150 billion (1993 dollars). That amount would support a force of 1 million personnel including 6 Army divisions, 2 Marine divisions, 11 air wings, and 6 carrier groups.
- Emphasize defense of the United States, not the Cold War goal of fighting Soviet armies across the globe. Reduce infantry forces and focus on rapid response deployments and air and naval power.
- Adjust the national military strategy to reflect the new budget by withdrawing from overseas commitments that are not directly related to vital U.S. security interests. That should be done gradually to allow allies ample time to adjust their own defense policies.
- Reject security strategies that tie large U.S. defense budgets to quixotic goals such as global democracy or stability.

- Encourage extensive economic, cultural, diplomatic, and social links with other nations. A restrained foreign policy is *not* a policy of "Fortress America."
- Reject proposals to maintain a large defense budget for economic, social, or political purposes. Civil concerns are most effectively addressed through other institutions.
- Return the money saved by defense reductions to the American people. Moving scarce resources away from inefficient and unnecessary military programs into the private sector would stimulate the U.S. economy.

The end of the Cold War should be a time of celebration and relief since the United States no longer faces a global military threat. It should not be a time when the nation looks abroad "in search of enemies," as Ted Galen Carpenter puts it. An appropriate post–Cold War military strategy would produce a significant peace dividend, thus fueling the stagnant U.S. economy and vastly reducing the chances that the country would be drawn into a conflict that was peripheral to its national interests.

17. Dangerous Panacea: A Stronger United Nations

Doug Bandow

The collapse of the Soviet Union and the end of the Cold War have forced a long-overdue reevaluation of American security policy. Traditional containment is dead, since there is no longer an opposing, hegemonic power to contain. What new strategy, then, should replace containment?

One increasingly touted alternative strategy is collective security through both regional organizations and a revitalized United Nations. At its extreme, such a system would seek to control every conflict everywhere. Writes Anthony Arend of Georgetown University, "Although a conflict may seem quite removed, the theory of collective security holds that if an act of aggression anywhere goes unchallenged, the security of all states is threatened."[1] That approach, or even one committed to responding only to the most serious conflicts, is inherently interventionist.

A diluted form of collective security has long been an important aspect of American foreign policy. For instance, the United States is a member of several regional security organizations, including the North Atlantic Treaty Organization (NATO), through which collective military action can be undertaken. Washington obtained the United Nations' imprimatur for combat in South Korea and, more recently, in the Persian Gulf and has long supported UN peacekeeping efforts in various parts of the globe.

Collective security is being advanced today under the rubric of President George Bush's "new world order," but its roots go back to Woodrow Wilson's crusade for democracy and his successful campaign to pull the nation into World War I. As the world enters a period during which the international environment may grow

[1]Anthony Arend, *Pursuing a Just and Durable Peace: John Foster Dulles and International Organizations* (New York: Greenwood, 1988), p. 39.

more chaotic even as threats to U.S. security decline, the question is whether it would be wise for the United States to "strengthen" collective security, particularly by granting the United Nations more authority to mount military operations to punish aggressors and perhaps even settle civil wars.

Collective Security: The United Nations

The most idealistic version of the collective security strategy today is grounded in reliance on the United Nations. The allied success in World War II led to a widespread desire for an international regime to achieve what Woodrow Wilson had expected his ill-fated League of Nations to deliver: an international order collectively policed by the nations of the world.

In theory the United Nations has enormous authority. The UN Charter explicitly vests the Security Council with primary responsibility for the maintenance of international peace and security. Article 42 empowers the Security Council to use armed force "as may be necessary to maintain or restore international peace and security." Article 45 orders member states to make available national air force contingents for combined international enforcement measures so that the United Nations can "take urgent action." Plans for military actions are to be drafted by a Military Staff Committee (MSC). Article 43 even outlines procedures for the United Nations to follow in raising a military. Most of those provisions have never been used, however, largely because the Cold War disrupted the expected continued allied cooperation as the Soviet Union used its veto to deadlock the Security Council.

With the end of the Cold War and Moscow's cooperation in the Persian Gulf War, some observers wish once again to embrace the original promise of the United Nations. When he appeared before the that body in October 1990, Bush declared, "Not since 1945 have we seen the real possibility of using the United Nations as it was designed, as a center for international collective security."[2] Others have echoed Bush's idea. Yale's Bruce Russett and former UN official James Sutterlin wrote, "The use of military force by the United Nations for both of these purposes—enforcement and

[2]"Transcript of President's Address to U.N. General Assembly," *New York Times*, October 2, 1992, p. A12.

peacekeeping—is surely essential to a world order in which international security is heavily dependent on the Security Council."[3]

Little more was heard about rejuvenating the collective security role of the United Nations until months after the Yugoslavian crisis began in 1991. Former secretary of state Cyrus Vance, who had been the UN special envoy to Yugoslavia, urged the United States to strengthen its participation in the international organization's peacekeeping process. Soon thereafter Bush advocated an expansion of UN peacekeeping. "Because of peacekeeping's growing importance as a mission for the United States military, we will emphasize training of combat, engineering and logistical units for the full range of peacekeeping and humanitarian activities," he told the United Nations.[4]

Secretary General Boutros Boutros-Ghali of the United Nations went much further. He issued a report, "Agenda for Peace," that advocates fulfilling Article 43 by giving the United Nations increased military capabilities. In September 1992 the European Community endorsed several of his proposals, including the dispatch of UN troops to nations threatened by invasion, and the Security Council established a working group to review his proposals.

Several suggestions for expanding the United Nations' collective security role have been advanced by other analysts and public officials. In early 1991 French president François Mitterrand proposed revitalizing the MSC, after which his country would put 1,000 soldiers at the disposal of the United Nations on 48 hours' notice and another 1,000 within a week. Former UN under secretary general for political affairs Brian Urquhart suggested using Article 43 to provide the United Nations with sufficient forces to intervene in Yugoslavia and Somalia, as well as other nations where "sovereignty is dissolving into anarchy."[5] Harvard political scientist Joseph Nye proposed the creation of a UN "rapid deployment force" of 60,000 soldiers, with a core of 5,000 troops who would

[3]Bruce Russett and James Sutterlin, "The U.N. in a New World Order," *Foreign Affairs* 70 (Spring 1991): 70.

[4]Thomas Friedman, "Bush, in Address to U.N., Urges More Vigor in Keeping the Peace," *New York Times*, September 22, 1992, p. A14.

[5]Brian Urquhart, "Who Can Stop Civil Wars?" *New York Times*, December 12, 1991, p. E9.

train regularly. The rapid deployment force would not be adequate to contain large-scale aggression, such as that against Kuwait, or a major civil war, such as the one in Yugoslavia, Nye admits. In those cases an American-led coalition would be necessary.

Plenty of people seem to believe that ambitious UN military operations will be necessary in various regions. Columnist Jim Hoagland, for example, envisions a UN operation backed, but not led, by the United States to suppress the Yugoslavian conflict. Columnist Charles Krauthammer, among others, has proposed turning Somalia into a UN protectorate, and Russian foreign minister Andrei Kozyrev has suggested creating UN trusteeships for some former Soviet republics. The potential targets of military action do not end there. Argues David Scheffer of the Carnegie Endowment for International Peace, "The number of candidates for humanitarian intervention," including forcible action under the aegis of the United Nations "continues to grow as the new world disorder takes hold."[6]

Of greatest potential impact on Americans was the willingness of both presidential candidates in the 1992 elections to edge the United States toward involvement, through the United Nations, in the conflicts in both Yugoslavia and Armenia-Azerbaijan. Bill Clinton, for instance, suggested American participation in air attacks on positions from which the Serbs were besieging Sarjevo and advocated that Washington work in concert with the United Nations to peacefully settle the conflict over Nagorno-Karabakh. The Bush administration agreed to the positioning of 5,000 NATO troops (though no American forces) in Yugoslavia to safeguard UN relief convoys and seriously considered helping bar the flight of Serbian aircraft over Bosnia-Herzegovina.

Models for UN-Organized Collective Security

Two different models have been offered for expanding the United Nations' collective security responsibilities. The first is that of the organization's traditional peacekeeping activities. The second is that of the organization's involvement in the major wars in Korea and Iraq.

---

[6]David Scheffer, "Toward a Modern Doctrine of Humanitarian Intervention," *University of Toledo Law Review* 23, no. 2 (Winter 1992): 274.

Peacekeeping

The United Nations is currently undertaking 13 different peace-keeping operations that involve nearly 51,000 soldiers, all volunteered by their respective governments. The enterprises vary dramatically in scope, ranging from 40 observers in Kashmir to a projected 22,000 participants in Cambodia. Other UN forces are stationed in Angola, Bosnia, Croatia, Cyprus, El Salvador, the Mideast, Somalia, and the Western Sahara. And proposals have been made to establish UN peacekeeping forces elsewhere.

The major controversy surrounding UN peacekeeping today is cost. Under antiquated rules, the United States is to provide 30 percent of the funding, and the recent rapid expansion of UN activities caused the Bush administration to request a $350 million supplemental appropriation in addition to the $107 million originally approved in 1992, as well as $460 million more for 1993. Those funds are by no means certain to be allocated by Congress, since the United States is currently $208.7 million in arrears on its peacekeeping assessments. Nevertheless, Secretary of State James A. Baker III called the outlays "a pretty good buy,"[7] and other UN supporters express similar views. A report from the Henry L. Stimson Center, for example, contends that "the U.N. is our cheapest alternative for containing and resolving conflict."[8]

Major Wars

Quite different from the UN peacekeeping operations were the two large-scale conflicts undertaken under the authority of the Security Council. In 1950, with the Soviet delegate boycotting the Security Council to protest the failure to seat China's new revolutionary government, the Security Council authorized the creation of a multinational force to repel North Korean aggression against the Republic of Korea. Gen. Douglas MacArthur of the U.S. Army was designated commander of the UN forces, but he never reported to the Security Council, and Washington unilaterally made all of the war's major decisions—to cross the 38th parallel, for instance, and to refuse forced repatriation of prisoners.

[7]Quoted in "Paying for Peace," *U.S. News & World Report*, March 16, 1992, p. 9.

[8]George Moffett, "UN Peacekeeping Is Costly 'Bargain' to US," *Christian Science Monitor*, March 16, 1992, p. 8.

The UN forces were predominantly American forces that joined Seoul's numerically strong but qualitatively weak forces. Ninety percent of the non–South Korean troops were Americans. Casualties showed a similar distribution. Some 47,000 Korean and 36,823 non–Korean servicemen died. Of the UN contingent, 33,629, or 91 percent, were Americans.

The Security Council didn't create a UN joint command for the Persian Gulf War. Although the United States formally observed the conditions of the Security Council's resolutions, Washington had considerable latitude in deciding how to implement them. Once again America provided the bulk of the UN forces—510,000, or 80 percent, of roughly 652,600 combat troops. The U.S. death toll, a mercifully low 148, also constituted the bulk of the allied casualties.

Is Collective Security Desirable?

Collective security assumes that it is in America's interest to work to eliminate international disorder and instability by preventing aggression and squelching civil conflicts. Indeed, the cornerstone of a policy of collective security is stability. Whatever the formal rhetoric of policymakers about human rights and democracy, the primary goal of collective security is to prevent unauthorized border crossings and ensure the survival of particular internal political systems. Observes Arend: "States must also be willing to act no matter how 'just' the cause of aggression may seem to be. In this system, the international community has determined that the highest goal of the system is the preservation of peace; even 'just causes' do not justify aggression."[9]

Instability in the post–Cold War world is inevitable and should not come as a surprise. For decades the two superpowers were largely successful in suppressing often severe cultural, ethnic, linguistic, nationalistic, and religious differences within allied states. Moscow, for instance, would not tolerate a conflict between Hungary and Romania over disputed Transylvania, and the threat of

[9]Arend, pp. 39–40. Obviously, his approach differs substantially from those of such "democratists" as Joshua Muravchik and Gregory Fossedal, who would focus the attention of national and multilateral institutions on encouraging the spread of political democracy. Their objectives are largely divorced from security concerns and may, in fact, undermine the goal of stability.

Soviet intervention held Yugoslavia together. The West backed Mobuto Sese Seko's rule over Zaire's disparate peoples. Many of the conflicts now surfacing around the world are entirely legitimate and long overdue.

Of course, it would be best if previous political settlements, however artificial, were not challenged violently. Even assuming that Iraq had legitimate grievances against Kuwait, the former was not justified in invading the latter. But the fundamental issue is how to best advance America's security. (Fostering respect for human rights in other nations is obviously an important moral value, but the foremost duty of the U.S. government is to protect the American people's lives, property, freedom, and constitutional system.)

The question, then, is, Does maintaining the international status quo make America more secure? The answer is that it is not in America's interest, nor is it feasible, to act as the star player on a collective security team.

It should be obvious that global disorder per se does not threaten the United States. If Washington was wrong to view every local conflict as instigated by the Soviet Union during the Cold War, at least that perspective was understandable. Given their ties to a threatening hegemonic power, Soviet surrogates could conceivably have harmed American security interests by attacking nations allied with the United States. Alas, Washington's devotion to stability led it to make many a bargain with the devil, or at least with his surrogates. American aid for Iran's shah, Nicaragua's Somoza, Zaire's Mobuto, the Philippines' Marcos, and Sudan's Nimiery placed the United States on the side of unsavory regimes and created anti-American sentiments, which still animate the Iranian and Sudanese governments, for instance.

In any case, the end of the Cold War has terminated the potentially zero-sum nature of international relations. The disintegration of Somalia, a U.S. ally, is tragic but has few security implications. Liberia's three-sided civil war threatens no important American interests.

Washington can view even the Yugoslavian civil war, in the ever-unstable Balkans, with detachment. Some people have, of course, advanced lurid scenarios involving the conflict's spreading to Albania, Greece, Turkey, and beyond, but a year has passed without the bloodshed expanding. Absent the interlocking alliances, worsening

tensions, and widespread popular support for war that characterized all of the major powers, conflict in the Balkans in 1914 would
never have spread to the rest of Europe, let alone America. It is
difficult to construct an even slightly plausible chain of events that
could lead to a similar global war today. If the risk is still thought
to be serious enough to warrant action, then the Europeans, who
have the most at stake, should take action. If they do not judge
the costs of intervening to outweigh the benefits, there is certainly
no reason for Washington to act.

But what about the Persian Gulf? Many advocates of collective
security view it as proof of the need for an ongoing, formal system
for stifling aggression. Turmoil or aggression in the gulf region,
they contend, would inevitably threaten American security.

In fact, reliance on the Persian Gulf as an example of the need
for collective security demonstrates the weakness rather than
strength of the case. It is impossible to point to any other regional
conflict with as far-reaching implications for the United States.
Chaos and aggression in Africa, war between Argentina and Chile,
a bloody eruption in Kashmir, and even a North Korean invasion
of the ROK (in the absence of a U.S. security guarantee and U.S.
troops) all would be human catastrophes, but none would do more
than disrupt commercial relations and concern Americans with
relatives and friends in the affected nations. Assuming that the
United States does not plan to go to war for mercantilistic or humanitarian purposes, there is no reason for a U.S.-dominated collective
security mechanism to deal with such conflicts.

Iraq's invasion of Kuwait could also have been treated as a limited
threat best met by other regional powers. Although the issue is
too complicated to deal with in detail here, the basic case against
an American-organized response in the name of collective security
is threefold.

First, the protection of Saudi Arabia, not the liberation of Kuwait,
was the primary U.S. interest. Iraq's seizure of Kuwait alone, while
brutal, did little to change the region's balance of oil or power.
Yet to have attacked as vast a land as Saudi Arabia would have
dangerously overstretched Baghdad's forces, a fact apparently recognized by Saddam. Even as Defense Secretary Richard Cheney
was in Riyadh pressuring the Saudis to accept American intervention, the Pentagon was being told by a U.S. military official inside

Kuwait that Saddam had withdrawn his elite Republican Guard units into Iraq, hardly an indication that he intended to invade Saudi Arabia.[10]

Second, Iraq's neighbors, particularly a revenge-minded Iran, were capable of containing Saddam. Syria alone possessed nearly as many tanks as did Iraq. Had the countries surrounding Iraq, which were in the best position to judge Saddam's capabilities and intentions, feared further aggression, they could have acted to contain him.[11] Of course, such cooperation between distrustful states is neither as easy nor as effective as U.S.-orchestrated action. Intervention, however, is never cost free for the United States. Washington should attempt to develop, not the theoretically perfect response, treating expense as irrelevant, but the best one given the very real costs of different options. In the case of Iraq, the best response would have been to encourage the states with the most to lose from further Iraqi expansion to forge a defensive alliance.

Indeed, regional arrangements are an obvious solution to many disputes. In November 1990 five nations—Gambia, Ghana, Guinea, Nigeria, and Sierra Leone—dispatched 7,000 soldiers under the aegis of the Economic Community of West African States to police a cease-fire between three competing factions in a devastating civil war in Liberia. Although real peace has not yet been attained, the multinational effort has survived severe trials and appears to be making progress in forging a settlement. In 1991 Australia, New Zealand, the Soloman Islands, and Vanuatu created a multinational supervisory team to break Papua New Guinea's blockade of the Pacific island of Bougainville. Russia has joined Georgia in attempting to establish a buffer zone in the territory of South Ossetia in Georgia. And for a time the European Community considered taking military action in Yugoslavia, in an attempt to enforce several EC-sponsored cease-fires. Although the European Community eventually encouraged the United Nations to send peacekeepers,

---

[10]Staff of *U.S. News & World Report*, *Triumph without Victory: The Unreported History of the Persian Gulf War* (New York: Random House, 1992), pp. 97–98.

[11]See, for example, Ted Galen Carpenter, "Bush Jumped the Gun in the Gulf," *New York Times*, August 18, 1990; Christopher Layne and Ted Galen Carpenter, "Arabian Nightmares: America's Persian Gulf Entanglement," Cato Institute Policy Analysis no. 142, November 9, 1990; and Christopher Layne, "Why the Gulf War Was Not in the National Interest," *Atlantic*, July 1991.

the Europeans were considering rejuvenating the heretofore moribund Western European Union (WEU), long intended to serve as a European defense organization. Although all of those efforts are small in comparison with the gulf war, they illustrate the possibility of relying on cooperative efforts among the parties most concerned about potential conflict in a region.

The nuclear question poses a particular problem for efforts at regional containment, but it did not motivate Washington's intervention in the Persian Gulf. Only after polls in the late fall of 1990 showed Iraq's atomic weapons program to be of great public concern did the Bush administration focus on that issue. Unfortunately, the spread of nuclear weapons seems inevitable, since the cost of attempting to forcibly disarm every potential atomic power (e.g., Iran, North Korea, and Pakistan) is likely to be prohibitive. The best hope may ultimately be regional power balances, with even a Saddam, should his efforts ever succeed, constrained by Israel's nuclear weapons, for instance.

Third, Saddam was never in a position to gain a "stranglehold" on the West's oil supply and thus its economy. The focus on oil reserves was misleading, since those reserves are not total geologic deposits but supplies economically recoverable at present prices. In fact, Saddam increased estimated world oil reserves by his invasion, since it raised world oil prices. The relevant measure was oil production, and even had Iraq conquered the entire gulf region, Baghdad would have controlled little more than one-fifth of the international petroleum market. Such a share would have allowed Iraq to increase oil prices, but only modestly. One detailed economic analysis estimated the maximum likely jump in America's oil bill at $29.2 billion annually, roughly one-half of 1 percent of gross national product and less than the added cost of the Clean Air Act amendments approved by Congress in 1990.[12]

But one's personal judgment of the necessity of America's intervention in the gulf is less important than recognizing that Iraq's aggression posed a worst-case scenario for the rest of the world. However compelling the case for action against Saddam, his aggression does not prove the need for some international mechanism,

[12]David Henderson, "The Myth of Saddam's Oil Stranglehold," in *America Entangled: The Persian Gulf Crisis and Its Consequences*, ed. Ted Galen Carpenter (Washington: Cato Institute, 1991), p. 43.

backed by the United States, to maintain "order." In most cases, instability poses little danger to America and can be contained by other states or ignored entirely.

What if, in the future, an international incident sufficiently serious to warrant intervention arises? Then the United States should help organize an ad hoc force, either through the United Nations or with like-minded countries, to meet the specific threat. The standard for American participation should be the same as it is for unilateral military action: a vital rather than peripheral interest is at stake (and therefore warrants the sacrifice of life, potentially huge expense, and other risks inherent to foreign intervention); there are no other powers that can meet the challenge; and no peaceful alternatives exist for resolving the issue.

Is Collective Security Feasible?

The objection to collective security is not purely theoretical. There are also a number of practical pitfalls. Given the low esteem in which most Americans held the United Nations throughout the 1970s and 1980s, the notion of using it to police the world would probably be considered a joke were it not for the Persian Gulf War, which President Bush declared had rejuvenated the United Nations' peacekeeping function.[13] But now serious commentators want to give the international body its own military.

Is such an approach feasible? "For a collective security system to work," argues Arend, "there must be an absolute commitment of all states. They must be willing to combat aggression, wherever and whenever it may occur." As impartial judges, countries "must also be willing to act no matter who the perpetrator may be. Special relationships or alliances are not allowed to interfere with the duty of states to confront aggression."[14]

Unfortunately, the United Nations has never demonstrated a capacity to impartially settle international disputes.[15] Moscow's

---

[13]Staff of *U.S. News & World Report*, p. 176.

[14]Arend, p. 39.

[15]Among the more egregious examples of the politicization of the United Nations was the multiyear campaign for a "new international economic order." See, for example, Doug Bandow, "Totalitarian Global Management: The U.N.'s War on the Liberal International Economic Order," Cato Institute Policy Analysis no. 61, October 24, 1985. More broadly, international organizations, particularly those within the UN system, have often contributed to global problems. Some people, writes Giulio Gallarotti, "have traditionally been overly optimistic about the ability of multilateral management to stabilize international relations and have generally

new willingness to cooperate should not obscure the fact that for 45 years the United Nations was merely another Cold War battleground. In fact, the failure of the UN collective security system fueled the expansion of regional alliances. Even today UN policy is at the mercy of the communist rulers in Beijing who, despite a demonstrated willingness to shoot down unarmed students and workers, possess a veto in the Security Council. And while more states are moving toward democracy, a majority of the members of the United Nations are still dictatorships. Thus, even if the growing number of free states survives, in the near future collective security is likely to be ineffective if the aggressor is a permanent member of the Security Council, a client state of a permanent member, or a country able to amass eight votes from the Security Council's 15 member countries, many of which will still be ruled by venal autocrats. Indeed, it is conceivable that even Western democracies might act to shield friendly states from UN censure and enforcement action. Consider Washington's probable attitude should Israel or South Korea launch a preemptive attack against Syria or North Korea, respectively.

The flip-side risk is that increased "peacekeeping" authority might cause the United Nations to shift toward an greater enforcement role not necessarily related to peacekeeping. That is, it might become a coercive tool in the hands of shifting international majorities that happened to control the Security Council at any given time. That would be of particular concern if the United Nations possessed its own military. Although the United States could always veto what it viewed as inappropriate intervention, it would pay a political price for doing so. Moreover, a recalcitrant Washington could then hardly count on Security Council support when it wanted UN support for military action.

The United Nations seems unsuited to the task of maintaining global order. Neither of the suggested models for UN enforcement of collective security offers much hope. True, traditional UN peacekeeping may help prevent small incidents that could spread and thereby threaten a fragile peace accord, and may give responsible

---

ignored the fact that [international organizations] can be a source of, rather than a remedy for, disorder in and across issue-areas." Giulio Gallarotti, "The Limits of International Organization: Systemic Failure in the Management of International Relations," *International Organizations* 45 (Spring 1991): 218–19.

officials an excuse to resist domestic political pressure to provoke a conflict. In the end, however, UN peacekeeping can only prevent fighting if both parties desire peace for other reasons. For instance, it is Israel's military superiority, not the presence of UN troops, that prevents Syria from attempting to reclaim the Golan Heights. The risks involved help deter India and Pakistan from waging a full-scale war over Kashmir, regardless of the activity of UN forces. UN peacekeepers arrived in Croatia only after the costs of war had compelled both Serbian and Croatian leaders to seek a respite from the fighting. And the patrons of the different combatants in Cambodia, not the United Nations, brought an end to the tragic fighting in that nation. UN forces in the Sinai did not prevent the 1967 war between Israel and its neighbors; UN troops in Lebanon today do not constrain Israeli, Palestinian, or Shi'ite military activity. In short, the United Nations cannot stop a war that is being waged by determined belligerents.

There are many other, secondary criticisms of UN peacekeeping, including that the efforts are expensive and often persist for decades with little apparent result. For example, UN peacekeeping forces have been in Cyprus for more than 16 years and have had virtually no effect on the de facto partition of that country.

The United Nations' peace-enforcement record is even less impressive. The major wars fought under the UN flag were UN operations in name only. Observes M. V. Naidu of Canada's Brandon University, "The most important factor" in the Korean action "was the preparedness of a superpower like the United States to provide everything necessary for the action and to take complete charge of conducting the operations." America's commitment to intervene, even without allied support, was also the most important factor in the Persian Gulf War. While UN authority was a convenient and politically popular patina, it was not necessary to prosecution of the war.

Nevertheless, the United States had to pay a price for the United Nations' imprimatur. Washington's desire for Soviet support forced the administration to ignore the USSR's crackdown in the Baltic states. China's abstention from the critical Security Council vote authorizing the use of force appears to have been purchased by new World Bank loans, which were approved shortly thereafter, possibly supplemented by reduced pressure on human rights issues. And consider the 10 nonpermanent members who had a voice in shaping Persian Gulf policy: Austria, Belgium, Cuba, Ecuador, India, the Ivory Coast, Romania, Yemen, Zaire, and Zimbabwe. Many of those nations were interested in gaining additional Western financial assistance, if nothing else. And the United States was not above using its aid policies to procure votes. Secretary of State Baker responded to Yemen's opposition to the resolution authorizing the use of force with a note to Yemen's ambassador stating, "That is the most expensive vote you have ever cast."[16] While such log-rolling might be expected, it hardly augurs well for the creation of an effective—much less an equitable—system of collective security.

In the future other nations might expect not only bribes but also real influence. Mitterrand, for instance, apparently advanced his proposal to rejuvenate the MSC envisioned by article 45 of the UN Charter because the committee would break America's military monopoly on UN actions. His foreign minister later argued that Europe and the United Nations should help counteract U.S. power. "American might reigns without balancing weight," he complained.[17] Increasingly wealthy and influential Germany and Japan may demand not only permanent seats on the Security Council but also a say in future military operations. Similarly, India, which possesses a potent military, may not be quiescent in the future. In fact, Brazil's foreign minister has proposed expanding Security Council membership, though without a veto, not only to Germany and Japan, but also to Brazil, Egypt, India, Nigeria, and other states.

There is nothing intrinsically wrong with the French desire to turn what has been a Potemkin collaborative security enterprise into a real one. But it is doubtful that a system subject to the vagaries to which any international organization is subject is going to either achieve its purpose or advance American interests. Not only might the United Nations be unduly restrictive when Washington felt intervention was necessary, but more important, a truly honest

---

[16]Staff of U.S. News & World Report, p. 181.

[17]"France to U.S.: Don't Rule," New York Times, September 3, 1991, p. A8. After the June 1991 NATO conference, French officials also grumbled about Washington's highhandedness in the wake of its victory in the gulf war. William Drozdiak, "U.S. Shows Arrogance to Allies, French Say," Washington Post, June 12, 1991, pp. A25, A26.

collective security system could drag the United States into conflicts that had no connection to American interests and that could be solved without Washington's assistance. What if, for instance, Germany, France, Italy, and Greece demanded Security Council military action in Yugoslavia? Or if Turkey, Russia, and Armenia proposed UN intervention in Azerbaijan? Should the United States again become the major combatant, perhaps consigning thousands of citizens to their deaths in a potentially interminable conflict with no impact on American security? To vest the United Nations with significant peacekeeping power requires that one trust a council including 14 foreign states more than one's elected government. Past experience does not warrant placing that kind of confidence in the Security Council.

The proposal to give the United Nations an independent combat force to be used at the Secretary General's discretion is even less prudent. Whatever the international body's value may be as a debating chamber within which to let off steam, it has never demonstrated principled leadership unhampered by multitudinous and arcane political pressures. Today, of course, the potential for abusing the United Nations is tempered by the role of the Security Council, but if the United Nations gained the sort of influence that would come with an independent armed force, a coalition of smaller states might attempt to move security power back to the General Assembly. In fact, the nations represented at the recent Nonaligned Movement summit agreed to create a "high-level working group" to develop proposals for the "democratization of the United Nations system." They went on to denounce "those who seek to preserve their privileged positions of power."[18] Ironically, the United States itself sought to circumvent the Soviet veto in the Security Council during the 1960–61 UN intervention in the Congo by appealing to the General Assembly's "uniting for peace resolution" and thereby set a dangerous precedent. As long as the United Nations is governed by a majority of nation-states, ruled by some of the worst people on earth, it should not be trusted with even one soldier.

Conclusion: Regional Peacekeeping without the United States

The dramatic international changes of recent years have truly yielded a "new world order" that provides America with a unique

[18]William Branigan, "North and South Stand Worlds Apart on Reform," *Washington Post*, September 23, 1992, p. A32.

opportunity to reassess its global role. For nearly five decades the United States has acted more like an empire than a republic, creating an international network of client states, establishing hundreds of military installations around the world, conscripting young people to staff those advanced outposts and fight in distant wars, and spending hundreds of billions of dollars annually on the military. Washington's globalist foreign policy has badly distorted the domestic political system by encouraging the growth of a large, expensive, repressive, secretive, and often uncontrolled state.

The justification for that interventionist military strategy, so alien to the original American design, was the threat of totalitarian communism. With that threat gone, the United States should return to its roots rather than look for other adversaries and embark on global interventionist crusades. It should become, in the words of former ambassador to the United Nations Jeane Kirkpatrick, a "normal country" again. And that requires a much more limited foreign policy with much more limited ends.

Most fundamental is the question of American interests. Put bluntly, what policy will best protect the lives, property, freedom, and constitutional system of the people of this nation? Entangling Washington in a potentially unending series of international conflicts and civil wars through the United Nations? Or remaining aloof from struggles that do not affect the United States? If our chief concern is preserving American lives and treasure, the latter position is clearly preferable.

To begin to implement a less interventionist foreign policy, the new administration should take the following steps.

- Reject all proposals to create an independent military force for the United Nations.
- Set a firm policy that the United States will not provide troops for UN peacekeeping or peace-enforcement missions unless there is a clear connection to vital American security interests.
- Initiate a concerted effort to renegotiate the agreement whereby the United States pays a disproportionate percentage of the costs of UN operations.
- Display greater willingness to use the U.S. veto power in the Security Council to block any initiatives that impinge on American security interests or economic and political values.

Today there is no Soviet Union to contain, and local and regional quarrels are no longer of vital concern since they are no longer part of the overall Cold War. Moreover, those states that were once possible victims of aggression—underdeveloped Korea, defeated Germany and Japan, war-torn France and Britain, and such smaller nations as Australia and New Zealand—have developed potent militaries and are capable of meeting any likely threats to themselves or their neighbors. Most security concerns now can be handled locally or regionally rather than globally.

Global collective security mechanisms were never desirable nor practical. A new grandiose mission for the United Nations, supported financially and militarily by the United States, has even less appeal in the post–Cold War era.

18. Time to Retire the World Bank and the International Monetary Fund

Melanie S. Tammen

> We are [in Eastern Europe] confronted with factors which
> have fully negative consequences upon the transformation
> process. . . . Technical assistance is offered by foreign gov-
> ernments or international institutions which very often
> employ people with a dirigistic or openly socialist outlook.
> The marginal product of such activities may even be
> negative. . . . [We also face] the procedures, charters,
> instructions and obligations connected with membership in
> international organizations—with an almost forced partici-
> pation. They were created in a different world and time and
> they bring back approaches we are trying to get rid of.
>
> —Vaclav Klaus

In July 1944, at the invitation of the United States, representatives
of 44 nations met at Bretton Woods, New Hampshire, to lay the
foundations for reinvigorating postwar economic relations. Under
the particular urging of British delegate John Maynard Keynes,
they created two sister institutions: The International Monetary
Fund was to oversee a global regime of fixed exchange rates. The
International Bank for Reconstruction and Development (now
known as the World Bank) was to provide financial assistance to
the European governments to help them rebuild their shattered
economies.

By the late 1950s Europe was back on its feet and the bank's
mission was complete. Just over a decade later, in 1971, the global
system of fixed exchange rates broke down and the IMF's mission
disappeared. Yet as so often happens with bureaucracies whose
missions are complete (or discredited), the World Bank and the IMF
crafted for themselves—with the help of political and intellectual
supporters—new sets of global exigencies that purportedly rendered them indispensable.

311

In the decades since, those institutions have extended hundreds of billions of dollars in subsidized loans to the governments of developing nations in Africa, Asia, Latin America, and Eastern Europe (an average of 75 nations each year during the 1980s). That protracted massive intervention—and the seal of approval that it gave to those governments' destructive, socialist economic policies—encouraged the governments of developed nations (directly) and private lenders (indirectly) to extend tens of billions of dollars more in credit.

In large measure because of the flagship role played by the IMF and the World Bank between 1956 and 1986, the *net* transfer of capital from the developed world to the developing world (adjusted for inflation) amounted to some $1.8 trillion.[1]

The verdict on centralized, planned economies is now in. They brought ruin to Eastern Europe, a $450 billion noose of foreign debt to Latin America, and to sub-Saharan Africa per capita incomes that are lower today than they were in 1970.

The new refrain from World Bank and IMF officials is that reform will not come for nothing. They argue that large sums of aid are required to encourage and sustain "market-opening" reforms in the developing nations and Eastern Europe and that without such aid, reform governments might fall. That rhetoric rings hollow. The unquestioned success of countries such as South Korea, Taiwan, Singapore, Malaysia, Chile, and Mexico has clearly demonstrated, for all to see, the basic elements of reform that are required to turn economies around.

Today, as in the past, World Bank and IMF lending perpetuates a larger role for government and planning—and a slower pace of reform—than nations could otherwise afford. Just as important, the continued escalation of World Bank and IMF lending programs is transferring bad debts to Western taxpayers. That escalation is apparent in Eastern Europe, to which the IMF and the World Bank have extended about $10 billion in loans over the past three years. Since 1988, for example, the World Bank has raised its annual lending rate to the region from $300 million to about $2.2 billion—

---

[1]Nicholas Eberstadt, "Foreign Aid's Industrialized Poverty," *Wall Street Journal*, November 8, 1990. Original source given is the Organization for Economic Cooperation and Development in Paris. Figure is net of profit repatriation and loan repayments and does not include private charity or military aid.

an increase of more than sevenfold. At the same time the nations of Eastern Europe are trying to move away from centrally controlled economies, the IMF and the World Bank are enticing them to get "hooked" on subsidized loans.

With the verdict on central planning so clear, the United States and other Western nations should dismantle the international lending institutions that counsel and finance it—the IMF, the World Bank, and the related regional development banks.

The Evolving World Bank: A Brief Review

In 1961, when prominent development economists were promoting the virtues of Soviet-style central planning and John F. Kennedy launched a large aid program for Latin America (the Alliance for Progress), the World Bank shifted its attention to the least creditworthy nations. It founded the International Development Association (IDA)—a concessional lending window that would offer loans with 50-year maturities at zero interest. (In the late 1980s maturities were cut to 35 and 40 years.) The World Bank continued to lend for infrastructure, and it also placed new emphasis on lending for industry, agriculture, and education.

Under Robert McNamara, president from 1968 to 1981, the World Bank emphasized alleviating poverty, particularly through loans for rural agricultural development and population control. Annual lending expanded 14-fold, to over $12 billion, during that time.

During the 1980s the bank added a new emphasis on lending to "support market-oriented reforms" to its continued emphasis on loans for social programs aimed at "poverty reduction." Such policy-based lending grew swiftly after the advent of the debt crisis in 1982, in response to pressure from Washington to increase "fast-disbursing" loans to help keep developing nations from defaulting on their foreign debts. Since the mid-1980s loans in return for promises of reform (rather than tangible projects) have constituted between one-fourth and one-third of total World Bank lending.

The World Bank's Legacy

The World Bank has created a legacy of industrialization without prosperity and investment without growth. Since the 1960s the bank has lent the governments of developing nations some $300 billion for public-sector investments in all manner of projects—including roads, bridges, dams, railroads, telephone companies,

steel mills, housing projects, electricity concerns, educational programs, agricultural mechanization, and government-run banks, to
name only a few. The shared wisdom of the leaders of developing
countries, Western development economists, and World Bank officials held that World Bank loans could transform low-income countries by funding government industrialization and social programs.
As economist and population specialist Nicholas Eberstadt argues,
it worked—if one accepts the perverse standards of the World
Bank. According to recent bank statistics on industry's share of
gross output, sub-Saharan Africa currently looks more "industrialized" than Denmark. Eberstadt writes:

> As for the relative share of investment, World Bank esti-
> mates suggest this to be lower in West Germany than in
> such countries as Togo, Nepal, Egypt and Costa Rica. Recent
> estimates put the investment ratio in Rwanda well above
> that in Belgium; Mali's appears to be higher than France's
> [and] the investment ratio appears to be higher today in the
> People's Democratic Republic of the Congo than in Japan.[2]

To be sure, in some developing countries, such as Singapore,
Korea, and Indonesia, high rates of investment have coincided with
and been followed by rapid rates of measured increase in national
output. But in quite a few other countries, high rates of investment
have been accompanied by economic stagnation or decline. Eberstadt points out:

> In the mid-1960s, according to World Bank estimates,
> the ratio of gross domestic investment in such countries as
> Nicaragua, Bolivia, the Central African Republic, Zambia
> and Jamaica was higher than in the United States. During
> the following two decades, however, per capita output in
> these countries registered a decline. The per capita growth
> rate, in other words, was negative.[3]

When investment produces such low, and even negative, rates
of return year after year, one would expect competitive economic

---

[2]Ibid.

[3]Nicholas Eberstadt, "Investment without Growth, Industrialization without
Prosperity," *Journal of Economic Growth* 3, no. 4 (Summer 1989): 20.

forces to reduce the amount of capital that went to such unproductive ends. But concessional loans from the World Bank to the governments of developing nations have *increased* in recent decades (and continue to increase), while the productivity of government investment has *decreased*. Free-market rhetoric aside, there is no getting around the inherent structural failure of the World Bank: according to its charter, it must lend to governments, and aid to governments will always result in investment *by* governments. Thus, World Bank loans designed to "underpin policy dialogues on market-oriented reform" are used by governments to expand or initiate other government investment schemes.

Global Privatization Trend Catches Up with World Bank

In 1991 the U.S. Department of the Treasury proposed a revision to the World Bank's charter that would have allowed it to extend fully half of its loans to the private sector by 1995. Treasury under secretary David Mulford explained before the Senate Foreign Relations Committee that the reform was necessary, lest the bank be left without a role to play as its borrower nations increasingly privatize their state firms.

Indeed, privatization efforts in developing countries are extending even into infrastructure—long considered a "public good" that must be delivered by government, and an important sector of World Bank lending since its founding. From 1990 to 1991, 12 nations, including Mexico, Venezuela, Argentina, Guyana, and Jamaica, sold part or all of their telecommunications systems. In 1992 Malaysia, Singapore, Argentina, and Venezuela were moving ahead with plans to privatize their postal services; and Argentina, Malaysia, and Thailand had either embarked on railway privatizations or had new, privately financed railway systems under way. Also in 1992 the privatization of ports was completed or under way in Argentina, Mexico, Panama, Venezuela, Brazil, Malaysia, and Singapore; and private tollways were initiated in Mexico, Colombia, Venezuela, Argentina, Malaysia, Hong Kong, China, Hungary, Poland, and Czechoslovakia.[4]

The Treasury abandoned its proposal barely three months after making it—in the face of stiff opposition from the World Bank itself

[4]See Reason Foundation, *Privatization 1992: Sixth Annual Report on Privatization* (Los Angeles: Reason Foundation, 1992).

and lack of support from any other major member of the bank. The suggested reform was misguided in any case, since the World Bank has for decades had a record of botched lending for private enterprise. Consequently, the U.S. administration should not confine itself to proposing to "privatize" the lending side of the World Bank. It should propose to privatize the bank's funding side as well.

Since the 1970s the World Bank has lent more than $30 billion to private-sector borrowers. But because its charter permits it to lend only to governments, it has had to create lending intermediaries— development finance institutions (DFIs)—run by local governments, to relend World Bank funds to private borrowers. During the mid-1980s World Bank officials began documenting the sorry state of its DFIs. A 1985 report concluded, "Few DFIs have become financially viable, autonomous institutions capable of mobilizing resources from commercial markets at home or abroad." Another report, issued in 1989, found that an average of 50 percent of DFI loans worldwide were in arrears. That report concluded:

> It is clear [that DFIs] have damaged financial systems. . . .
> Acquiring subsidized credit could sometimes add more to profits than producing goods. . . .
>   The ability to borrow at cheap rates encouraged less productive investment. . . . DFIs, by encouraging firms to borrow from [government-run] banks, have impeded the development of capital markets. . . . Equity finance is a more appropriate way to finance risky ventures than bank loans. If governments establish the conditions necessary for equity finance, intervention will not be necessary.[5]

The 1991 Treasury proposal was an attempt to move beyond the discredited DFI model by having the World Bank lend directly to the private sector. The proposal would have entailed not only a renegotiation of the World Bank's charter, but a total reconfiguration of the complex dynamics that allow the World Bank to combine donor government guarantees (of the money it borrows in international markets) with borrower government guarantees (when it lends that money in developing nations) to maintain its AAA credit

---

[5]World Bank, *World Development Report 1989: Financial Systems and Development* (Washington: World Bank, 1989), pp. 58–60.

rating and keep the whole exercise rolling. It would be just as easy, and a far more sensible reform, to privatize the World Bank entirely.

Privatize the World Bank

U.S. taxpayers support the World Bank with billions of dollars of unfunded guarantees in the same way they unwittingly backed the savings-and-loan insurance fund. The World Bank raises most of the money it lends by issuing bonds in international capital markets. Each year the bank floats about $12 billion in new bond issues supported by about $12 billion in new unfunded "callable capital" pledges from the United States and other industrial nations. Privatizing the fund-raising side of the World Bank would mean cutting it loose from U.S. taxpayers' annual cash infusions and their $30 billion in accumulated guarantees.

Is that a pie-in-the-sky scenario? Not if the World Bank would begin to distribute some of its annual net earnings of around $1 billion to its shareholder governments (rather than retaining the earnings). Once a track record of declaring and delivering dividends was established, the bank's member governments could credibly craft a plan to privatize the bank by selling its shares in the private marketplace.

An alternative privatization scenario—which could be called Plan B in the event that a public offering flopped because of investor distrust of the health of the bank's loan portfolio—was proposed by former Treasury official Paul Craig Roberts in the *Wall Street Journal* in 1989. The World Bank would swap all its outstanding loans for equity in enterprises in the borrower nations, then resell those equity holdings to private investors, domestic or foreign. The funds raised from the sale of equity would be used to redeem outstanding World Bank bonds. To the extent that the World Bank could not fully retire all its outstanding bonds with the funds raised, the rich member countries would assume the liability by exchanging the residual bonds for their own government bonds. Thus, the scheme might involve some further expenditures on the part of the industrial nations, but it would be worth it to clear away what Roberts rightly termed the "entrenched institutional debris" of the World Bank.

The Resilient IMF: A Brief Review

The IMF was established in 1944, under a system of fixed exchange rates, as a mechanism for the international conversion of all members' currencies—in effect, by establishing the U.S. dollar as the medium of international exchange. In short, the IMF served as a mediator between central banks attempting to maintain fixed par values for their currencies. The essential objective of the IMF was the revival and expansion of international trade through the promotion of exchange stability and the elimination of the destructive exchange practices (competitive devaluations) that had inhibited trade before World War II.

In 1971 President Nixon ended the U.S. Treasury's commitment to convert U.S. dollars into gold, and a system of floating exchange rates followed. That development stripped the IMF of its reason for being. A country with a balance-of-payment deficit could reduce demand at home, finance the deficit on the growing international capital market, or simply let its currency depreciate. Still, no one proposed closing down the IMF. Instead, the IMF's charter was revised to legitimize the new floating rate system. In the 1970s the institution defined for itself two entirely new missions: easing the adjustment for countries with balance-of-payment deficits and providing financing on especially easy terms to low-income countries through three new credit facilities. New IMF loans increased sixfold by 1974.

When the Mexican government defaulted on its foreign loans in 1982, the unprecedented bailout package devised by U.S. Federal Reserve chairman Paul Volcker and IMF managing director Jacques de Larosierre thrust the IMF to the center of a U.S.-led strategy to mobilize new loans to keep developing nations from defaulting on old loans. Thus, in 1982 the IMF's primary mission became that of "managing" developing nations' foreign debt "crises." The result has been unprecedented wide and protracted IMF intervention throughout the world.

In 1990, with nearly 50 nations under IMF lending programs, George Bush pledged another $12 billion from the United States to help the IMF further expand its lending. In late 1992 Congress approved the funds, which represented the U.S. share of a 50 percent boost in IMF resources—from $130 billion to $195 billion. "Failure of the United States to support [the $12 billion for the IMF] would seriously erode the effectiveness and credibility of the IMF," Treasury Secretary Nicholas Brady told a Senate panel while promoting congressional approval of the U.S. infusion. As evidence of "effectiveness and credibility," however, Brady spoke only of the IMF's resource transfers, noting more than once that the IMF was "providing vast amounts of resources in Eastern Europe, Latin America, Africa and Asia."

As Cato Institute senior fellow Doug Bandow argues, the best test of the effectiveness of the IMF is whether any troubled developing nation has ever "graduated" from reliance on emergency IMF loans. Success stories seem to be nonexistent. South Korea borrowed from the IMF once, but that was in 1974 after its economic miracle was well under way.

The IMF has been subsidizing the world's economic basket cases for years, without any apparent success. Egypt has not been off the IMF dole since 1959. Ghana took its first loans in 1962 and remained a borrower for all but three months over the next 27 years. India was one of the IMF's first loan recipients and, except for short intervals, has been on an IMF program for more than 40 years. Mali has been an IMF borrower for more than 25 years. Since 1959 the Sudan has been in debt to the IMF in all but two years. Bangladesh, Uganda, Zaire, and Zambia all started borrowing in the early 1970s and have yet to stop.[6]

Failed Recipe for Devaluation and Austerity

A track record like that prompts the question: what is the nature and effect of the package of economic policy reforms, or "conditionality," that accompanies most IMF loans?[7] The IMF never makes public the "letter of intent" signed by a borrower nation, which outlines the conditionality to which the nation agrees. But elements of standard IMF conditionality programs are frequently leaked— usually to journalists reporting from the borrowing countries. From such reports, it is clear that IMF conditionality typically includes an anti-growth package of currency devaluation, new taxes or tax-rate hikes, and sometimes even hikes in import taxes. In general, IMF programs concentrate on setting macroeconomic targets. The most central tenet is that a nation's trade or current account, or both, should never be in deficit.

[6]"The IMF: Foreign Aid Addiction," *National Review*, June 8, 1992, p. 16.

[7]This section is excerpted from Alan Reynolds, "The IMF's Destructive Recipe of Devaluation and Austerity," Hudson Institute, May 1992, which the author helped to prepare.

That doctrine is a discredited holdover from 17th-century mercantilism. As a rule, world capital flows toward superior investment opportunities. As the Swiss economist Jurg Niehans put it, "Countries are debtors if their investment opportunities exceed their wealth and are creditors when their wealth exceeds their investment opportunities." A deficit on current account, with one major exception, simply means that domestic investment opportunities are superior to those elsewhere, which causes capital to remain in the country and attracts foreign capital as well. (The exception occurs when governments borrow from institutions such as the IMF; such borrowing is motivated by considerations other than profitable production and thus does not represent superior investment opportunities.)

Developing countries can clearly benefit by exploiting investment opportunities beyond those that can be financed by their own accumulations of wealth. Therefore, it is not inherently sinful for growing economies to remain debtor nations—that is, run current account deficits—for many years, as Japan and South Korea did. If current-account deficits are financed by voluntary, private capital inflows, they reflect improved opportunities for profitable investment and production and make improved production possible (for example, by financing imports of high-technology equipment).

Hudson Institute economist Alan Reynolds argues that all reforms that have been truly successful in launching a major surge in economic activity and wealth have been accompanied by at least a decade of current-account deficits. For example, from 1976 to 1985 Chile had an average current-account deficit of 7 percent; Singapore's deficit was 6.6 percent; Thailand's, 5.3 percent; South Korea's, 3.3 percent; and Colombia's 2.5 percent.[8]

With today's nearly fully integrated global capital market, it is quite possible to finance new capital projects and any related current-account deficits with *private* equity and *private* debt from both domestic and foreign sources (as opposed to the *public* debts represented by IMF, World Bank, and commercial bank loans to governments). To do that requires combining an attractive tax, regulatory, and monetary environment with greater development of a nation's own capital market.

[8]Ibid., p. 18.

Encouraging Tax Hikes Still Common

The IMF's devaluation theory, then, is closely related to its austerity theory, which holds that nations should close budget deficits at any cost. According to the IMF's model, fiscal deficits cause monetary expansion, which in turn causes a deterioration in the balance of payments. "Curing" current-account deficits, then, requires addressing budget deficits. That is where IMF prescriptions for new or higher taxes, or both, come into play.

IMF officials have long maintained that they merely set a target for a nation's budget deficit and do not impose conditionality, explicit or implicit, regarding whether the deficit is to be reduced by raising taxes or by cutting spending—or the specific tax and spending measures involved. Governments, however, usually do not expect to satisfy powerful political constituencies by cutting spending on big-ticket, money-losing items such as civil service rolls and operating subsidies to state enterprises. Therefore, nations on IMF programs have commonly imposed new taxes or raised tax rates, or both, to meet their deficit-reduction targets. Nations also commonly increase import tariffs—not only in pursuit of added revenues but also to reinforce the currency devaluation's aim of making imports more expensive (and exports less expensive) and thereby manipulating a trade surplus.

In addition, notwithstanding the IMF's insistence that it merely sets deficit-reduction targets, accounts of IMF programs in the international financial press regularly link the institution to new or higher taxes: In January 1991 the Philippines bowed to IMF pressure and instituted a 9 percent supplemental levy on imports as a condition for a new IMF loan.[9] In March 1991 India instituted a new taxlike restriction designed to cut imports by 10 to 15 percent. A year later imports had fallen by 17.5 percent; but exports had fallen by 6 percent, chiefly as a result of the import restriction, which made raw materials, components, and capital goods scarce. Subsequently, Indian economists explained that the economy was plagued by an import-cut-induced recession.[10]

---

[9] Greg Hutchinson, "Philippines Austerity Awaits IMF Seal of Approval," *Financial Times*, February 20, 1991, p. 4.

[10] K. K. Sharma, "Big Fall in India's Trade Deficit," *Financial Times*, January 15, 1992, p. 4.

In the summer of 1991 *Business Latin America* reported that

- in Argentina the IMF "seeks to boost the country's fiscal surplus by raising the value-added tax, reintroducing export taxes and increasing fuel taxes";
- in Honduras "tax hikes necessitated by the [IMF] program are generating serious labor and social unrest"; and
- in Peru taxes "will be hiked sharply in an effort to narrow the deficit to the IMF-mandated target."[11]

The IMF's preoccupation with setting macroeconomic targets leads to a bias against structural, microeconomic reforms. If the governments of developing countries are to create the conditions necessary for those countries to prosper, they will have to adopt intelligent, market-oriented policies. IMF loans and bad advice reduce the likelihood that recipient countries will make urgently needed changes. Whatever its intentions, the IMF's actions only reduce the chances that Third World nations will emerge from poverty. Now that the statist vision of centralized economic planning is in retreat throughout the world, it is more apparent than ever that new and expanded missions for the IMF cannot be justified and that the organization should be retired.

Conclusion

Czech prime minister Vaclav Klaus notes correctly that "reform begins and ends at home and that the role of external factors is relatively small." Further, he cites several external factors that have a positive impact:

- "the rapidly growing *flow of visitors* (both tourists and businessmen) from abroad, who bring into the country market-oriented attitudes, habits, and experience;
- "the *international trade* of goods and services which undermines the long-prevailing atmosphere of semiautarchic centrally planned economies . . . and which brings into the transforming country real competition and previously nonavailable world standards; and

---

[11]Issues of June 24, June 10, and July 15, 1991, respectively.

- *"foreign real investment,* provided the country is in a situation where property rights are already clearly defined and reasonably protected."[12]

Such international exchanges require neither the International Monetary Fund nor the World Bank. In 1990, the most recent year for which figures are available, inflows of foreign direct investment to developing nations reached $32 billion, sharply reversing a decline in the late 1970s and 1980s. Those nations that offer a dynamic and secure investment climate—such as the Asian tigers, Chile, and Mexico—are attracting ever larger inflows from the world's private capital market.

The IMF and World Bank are discredited remnants of the past half century's global experiment with top-down government economic planning. Both institutions have fostered statism and dependence, with enormously destructive results. They should be abolished, and the private capital from Western nations that they absorb should be freed. Its owners would then be able to seek out the best investment opportunities throughout the developing world.

---

[12]Vaclav Klaus, "The Relative Role of Domestic vs. External Factors in the Integration of Former Communist Lands into the World Economy," Speech before the Mont Pèlerin Society, August 31, 1992, Vancouver, Canada, mimeographed, p. 3. Emphasis in original.

19. Ending Washington's International War on Drugs

Ian Vásquez

During the past decade, Washington has steadily intensified its international campaign against illegal drugs. The United States has increased spending on international narcotics control by more than 800 percent, and total federal expenditures on the drug war have risen by about 600 percent, soaring to $11.9 billion in 1992.[1] During the Bush administration alone, federal spending for the war on drugs rose by an unprecedented $5.3 billion.

In its efforts to curtail the supply of narcotics entering the country from abroad, Washington has used a series of trade and aid sanctions and rewards to coerce drug-source nations to enlist in its crusade. U.S. pressure and attention have been focused mainly on Latin America, in particular the Andean region, source of the majority of cocaine that reaches the United States. Unfortunately, U.S. policy toward those countries ignores basic economic principles and national political realities. As a result, the war on drugs in Latin America is producing political instability and economic disruption, posing a threat to the fragile democracies there. The region's leaders are put in the awkward, if not impossible, position of trying to satisfy conflicting U.S. and domestic agendas, while anti-American sentiment grows. Thus, what many Latin American nations consider primarily a U.S. problem has increasingly become their own.

Anemic Results

Progress in the supply-side anti-narcotics battle has been less than impressive, though official rhetoric would suggest otherwise.

---

[1]Lawrence J. Smith, "The US Role in the International War on Drugs," *Christian Science Monitor*, May 12, 1992, p. 20; and White House, *National Drug Control Strategy: A Nation Responds to Drug Use*, January 1992, p. 141.

Two main components of Washington's foreign war on drugs are interdiction of trafficking networks and eradication of illegal crops. As evidence of major advances in those areas, the State Department has stressed increased cocaine seizures and reductions in the cultivation of coca during 1991. Indeed, total land dedicated to coca cultivation in the Andean region fell from 211,820 hectares in 1990 to 206,240 in 1991.[2] But those figures do not constitute a threat to the illegal drug industry, much less represent "significant damage on the cocaine trafficking organizations" as suggested by the State Department's 1992 *International Narcotics Control Strategy Report*.[3] A paltry decline of less than 3 percent in the overall land area devoted to the cultivation of coca is unlikely to discourage most individuals involved in the multi-billion-dollar cocaine trade.

Even the official figures presented in the State Department report indicate that acreage eradicated, both in absolute terms and as a percentage of total cropland planted in coca, has declined, though modestly, since 1990. And in the case of Peru, the world's largest producer of raw coca, U.S. government data show that no crops were eradicated for two years in a row. Although coca cultivation in Peru has leveled off in the past few years, U.S. and Peruvian officials admit that the leveling is largely due to the spread of a fungus detrimental to coca plants, not to government efforts to control the illegal crop.

The eradication numbers may not be reliable in any case. The U.S.-coordinated anti-drug effort provides source countries with strong incentives to overstate the effectiveness of eradication programs. U.S. foreign assistance is more likely to be channeled to countries that are able to cite positive results of their anti-narcotics efforts. Conversely, countries whose eradication programs are not "successful" may be charged with lack of cooperation and consequently risk the suspension of aid and the application of trade sanctions.

The lack of progress in its supply-side campaign has led the U.S. government to assert that "national will" and commitment of drug-source countries are more important measures of success than eradication figures or other quantitative variables. By introducing the

---

[2]U.S. Department of State, *International Narcotics Control Strategy Report*, March 1992, p. 27.

[3]Ibid., p. 5.

concept of national will, Washington has not only attempted to gloss over the drug war's anemic results; it has also created an additional means, both ambiguous and arbitrary, of judging the cooperation of drug-source nations.

Emphasis on eradication efforts, total land devoted to coca cultivation, and national will is misplaced, however. Far more relevant, and more damning, are figures representing actual coca leaf production. Those figures indicate that net production of the leaf has actually increased every year since 1988—from 273,700 metric tons that year to an estimated 337,100 metric tons in 1992.[4] It should not be surprising then that *cocaine* production and importation into the United States have also increased every year since President Bush took office.[5]

That there is a growing amount of cocaine entering this country is an indictment not only of eradication efforts but also of the interdiction component of the drug war. In fact, only 5 to 15 percent of all intended drug imports are seized by U.S. authorities. Although the amounts captured may raise drug traffickers' operating costs somewhat, the U.S. price range for a kilogram of cocaine has not risen over the past few years. Indeed, the price range has dropped in major cities such as Los Angeles, Miami, Chicago, and New York.[6] Thus, Washington's interdiction strategy has clearly failed to achieve its primary goal of raising cocaine prices paid by U.S. drug users.

The failure of interdiction programs and source-country efforts to increase U.S. prices, and thereby effect a reduction in demand, reflects something more than ineffectiveness. Overseas counternarcotics strategy suffers from a fundamental flaw: it relates domestic demand for cocaine to supply reductions in drug-producing countries. Because of the price structure of the drug trade, however, that relationship is quite flimsy. The astronomically high profits of the illegal industry ensure that any losses caused by supply-reduction programs will have little impact on the traffickers' cost of doing business. As a study by the RAND Corporation indicates, smuggling expenses represent only 10 percent of the retail value

[4]Ibid., p. 28.
[5]Drug Policy Foundation, *The Bush Drug War Record*, September 5, 1992, p. 11.
[6]Ibid.

of cocaine. That is, the price of the drug substantially appreciates only after it enters the United States. That means that traffickers have every incentive to continue smuggling cocaine despite the fact that up to 15 percent of their product may be seized. Even a highly improbable 50 percent reduction in the amount of South American cocaine that enters the United States would increase the final price of the drug by only about 5 percent—leaving consumption mostly unaffected.[7]

The anemic results of Washington's anti-narcotics efforts in the Andean countries should hardly excite even the most avid drug warriors. The State Department's claim that it "has registered its most important gains in confronting the cocaine trade"[8] serves as an appropriate and sobering indicator of how much success the international war on drugs has had in general. Nevertheless, official declarations of progress continue while signs of policy change or reevaluation seem to be nonexistent. That trend is particularly worrisome given the severe economic, political, and social disruptions that the international anti-drug strategy causes in drug-source nations.

Coercion by Consent

Washington emphasizes the cooperation of drug-source nations as essential to its efforts to reduce the supply of illicit narcotics. Over the years, the United States has employed a combination of foreign aid benefits for countries deemed cooperative in those efforts and the threat of economic sanctions against nations considered uncooperative. U.S. financial assistance to Latin America increased significantly with the Bush administration's 1989 Andean Initiative. Under that program, $2.2 billion in economic and military aid is to be disbursed to South American drug-source nations over a period of five years.

Attention paid to the hemispheric drug war was further escalated by the much publicized drug summit of February 1990 in Cartagena,

---

[7]Peter Reuter, *Sealing the Borders: The Effects of Increased Military Participation in Drug Interdiction* (Santa Monica: RAND Corporation, 1988); cited in General Accounting Office, "Drug Control: Impact of DoD's Detection and Monitoring on Cocaine Flows," September 19, 1991, pp. 26–27; and Mathea Falco, "Foreign Drugs, Foreign Wars," *Daedalus* 121, no. 3 (Summer 1992): 7–8.

[8]U.S. Department of State, p. 5.

Colombia. That meeting, attended by Bush and the presidents of Peru, Bolivia, and Colombia, resulted in the formation of the so-called anti-drug cartel. Though a renewed commitment to fight the drug trade through a comprehensive multilateral strategy was expressed by all four nations, the summit did not produce major changes in the direction of anti-narcotics policy. Instead, Andean leaders tried to exploit Washington's desire to escalate the drug war by seeking pledges of increased economic assistance in return for their promise to increase efforts to discourage coca cultivation, disrupt drug trafficking, and improve control over chemicals used in the production of illicit drugs. Washington agreed to reduce domestic demand for drugs, increase assistance for supply-reduction and interdiction programs, and develop alternative sources of income for coca growers.

Although financial assistance to Andean countries has grown considerably since 1989, continuing disputes between the United States and its Latin American "partners" over a variety of drug war issues show that neither the Cartagena Summit nor the Andean Initiative has significantly harmonized the priorities of the nations involved. Peru, for example, has long been critical of the U.S.-funded counternarcotics programs there. Both former president Alan García and his successor, Alberto Fujimori, expressed dissatisfaction with the amount of economic aid provided by the United States. U.S.-Peruvian relations became especially tense in September 1990 when Fujimori refused to sign a $35.5 million military aid agreement and insisted that more funding for crop-substitution programs be made available.

Other examples of friction between Washington and the members of its anti-drug cartel include recurring disagreements with Colombia about the extradition of suspected traffickers and U.S. demands that the Bolivian and Peruvian governments dismiss officials who are not popular with the United States. Though Andean countries generally yield to U.S. pressure (as the Fujimori regime eventually did), U.S. and source-country priorities continue to differ.

While offers of U.S. economic assistance are used to entice Latin American governments into enlisting in the U.S.-directed drug war, perhaps a more effective means of "convincing" drug-producing nations to cooperate is the threat of economic sanctions. The U.S.

Anti–Drug Abuse Acts of 1986 and 1988 are designed to do just that. The acts make U.S. foreign aid and trade benefits contingent on the participation of drug-source countries (drug-producing or drug-transiting countries) in eradication and interdiction programs. The annual process of "certification" requires the U.S. president to determine whether the government of a source nation has adequately cooperated in those supply-reduction efforts.

Certification of cooperation compels the president to consider whether foreign government actions have resulted in the maximum possible reduction in the production of illegal drugs. If the president does not certify a major drug-source country, or if Congress disapproves his certification, mandatory sanctions are automatically imposed, and the application of other sanctions is left to the discretion of the president. The mandatory sanctions include

- suspension of 50 percent of U.S. assistance (except humanitarian and international narcotics control aid) for the current fiscal year;
- suspension of all U.S. assistance (again except humanitarian and international narcotics control aid) during subsequent fiscal years;
- voting against multilateral development bank loans to an offending country; and
- denial of a sugar quota.

Sanctions that may be imposed at the discretion of the president include

- denial of preferential tariff treatment for the exports of the noncertified country under the Generalized System of Preferences and the Caribbean Basin Initiative;
- duty increases of as much as 50 percent on exports to the United States;
- limits on air transportation and traffic between the United States and the noncertified country; and
- the end of U.S. participation in any preclearance customs arrangements with the noncertified country.[9]

---

[9]See Raphael Francis Perl, "Congress, International Narcotics Policy, and the Anti–Drug Abuse Act of 1988," *Journal of Inter-American Studies and World Affairs* 30 (Summer–Fall 1988): 25–26.

The combination of mandatory and discretionary sanctions provides the U.S. government a powerful economic lever with which to seek the compliance of drug-source nations. Although the withdrawal of multilateral and bilateral development aid would actually be beneficial for recipient nations—especially in light of the poor record of foreign assistance programs and Latin America's trend toward economic liberalization—it should not be surprising that source countries want to avoid any short-term disruptions that would be caused by sudden suspensions of aid. Trade sanctions represent an especially great threat to the economies of drug-producing nations, many of which depend heavily on access to the U.S. market. Restrictions on trade with Colombia, 46 percent of whose exports go to the United States, would cripple that country's economy. Similarly, 17 percent of Bolivia's exports are destined for the United States, and Peru's export figure is 22 percent. The prospect of losing foreign aid and the possibility of facing trade sanctions offer powerful incentives for drug-source countries to participate in anti-drug efforts even when they have grave misgivings about the wisdom of the policy.

Source Country Gestures and Economic Reality

Commitments from source nations to destroy the drug trade are tempered by the fact that the narcotics industry represents a major pillar of those countries' economies. The cocaine business in South America provides direct employment for 500,000 to 1 million people. In Bolivia the illicit drug trade employs 20 percent of the working population and provides $700 million in export revenues[10] compared to the approximately $1 billion earned from legal exports. In Peru cocaine accounts for at least 35 to 45 percent of export earnings and its production employs about 15 percent of the national workforce.[11] Moreover, the Peruvian central bank takes in $4 million to $6 million in narcodollars every day. The cocaine industry is by far Peru's largest generator of foreign exchange earnings. According to one expert, hard currency entering Peru through the illegitimate channels of the drug trade equals 20 percent of that nation's GNP,

[10]"Doped," *The Economist*, August 29, 1992, p. 36.

[11]Stephen J. Trujillo, "Peru's Maoist Drug Dealers," *New York Times*, April 8, 1992, p. A24; and Peter R. Andreas et al., "Dead-End Drug Wars," *Foreign Policy* 85 (Winter 1991–92): 113.

while Peru's largest legal export, copper, produces foreign exchange earnings of only 1.4 percent of GNP.[12] The illicit drug trade is also of vital importance to the economy of Colombia. Estimates of annual income generated by the cocaine industry generally range from $4 billion to $5 billion, whereas legal exports generate about $7 billion. One expert estimates that revenues from the narcotics business equal about 36 percent of GNP and represent Colombia's largest source of foreign income.[13]

It is naive to think that leaders of drug-source nations would seriously act to shut down an industry central to their economies. Bolivian president Jaime Paz Zamora, for instance, has compared the effect of eradicating his country's coca business to that of putting 50 million Americans out of work.[14] Yet U.S. pressure to close down the illicit drug industry continues despite the obvious incentives for source nations to comply with counternarcotics strategy in only a perfunctory manner.

In light of the relatively high profits that illegal cultivation of coca (and to a lesser extent, marijuana) can offer, U.S. and Latin American officials have tried to produce legal alternatives that growers might consider economically appealing. Thus, the governments involved have attempted to attack the drug industry in ways that might be considered less destructive. Crop-substitution programs are the most significant of those efforts.

An assortment of crops, including cotton, tea, cocoa, bananas, coffee, (oil) palms, and corn, has been proposed as substitutes for drug plants. Here again, economic realities seriously hamper the chances of reducing the supplies of coca or marijuana at their source. Both drug plants can be grown in areas and under conditions in which alternative crops cannot easily be cultivated. The Upper Huallaga Valley in Peru and Bolivia's Chapare region, two areas in which much South American coca is grown, are good examples. The remoteness and poor soil quality of those regions render substitution efforts economically unfeasible. Still more

---

[12]Gabriela Tarazona-Sevillano and John B. Reuter, *Sendero Luminoso and the Threat of Narcoterrorism* (New York: Praeger, 1990), p. 113.

[13]Brian Freemantle, *The Fix: Inside the World Drug Trade* (New York: Tom Doherty Associates, 1986), p. 211; cited in Scott B. MacDonald, *Dancing on a Volcano: The Latin American Drug Trade* (New York: Praeger, 1988), p. 45.

[14]Andreas et al., pp. 113–14.

important in considering the economic viability of legal crops is the fact that peasants can earn up to 10 times more from planting coca than they can from growing alternative crops. In addition, coca can be harvested 18 months after planting, requires little care, and can yield three to four harvests per year when mature. By contrast, many legal crops require much attention and take four or more years to yield returns.

Some substitution programs emphasize deregulation of agriculture in recognition that coca is traded in a free (though illegal) market while legal crops are traded in overregulated markets. Removing the bureaucratic and economic barriers to agricultural production and trade should be welcomed and will do much to simplify economic transactions in that sector. Nevertheless, crop-substitution programs insist on overlooking the economics underlying the cocaine industry. As long as drugs remain illegal in consuming countries—thus artificially raising their final price—and demand for those drugs persists, the enormous profit potential will provide a sufficient incentive for producers to supply market demands. Only if the sale and consumption of drugs are legalized in the United States and other narcotics-consuming countries will the cultivation of alternative crops become economically feasible.

Nevertheless, the U.S. and source-nation governments provide funds to coca farmers to encourage them to switch crops. The perverse effect of promoting substitution in that way has already been observed. Peasants often accept the money and continue cultivating drug crops elsewhere. Thus, U.S. foreign aid has actually subsidized the production of coca.

One of the most positive ways of encouraging legal agricultural production would be to reduce U.S. trade barriers. Latin American nations have long viewed U.S. protectionist policies as an impediment to the creation of a healthy, legal agricultural sector. For example, Peru's exports of cotton apparel and other textiles to the United States have been severely limited by U.S. quotas in recent years.[15] And although the 1991 Andean Trade Preference Act, which provides duty-free treatment of imports from Colombia, Ecuador, Peru, and Bolivia, is a step in the right direction, Andean

---

[15]Melanie S. Tammen, "The Drug War vs. Land Reform in Peru," Cato Institute Policy Analysis no. 156, July 10, 1991, p. 9.

leaders have reason not to be overenthused about its benefits. The legislation denies duty-free treatment to many products, including most textiles and apparel. Even official crop-substitution efforts are hindered by U.S. industries' desire to protect their market shares. A study by the General Accounting Office in October 1991 found, for example, that the American Soybean Association was effective in preventing U.S. assistance for growing soybeans in Bolivia as a substitute for coca.[16] Colombia, too, has been frustrated by its inability to get Washington to lower its tariffs on cut flowers and coffee, two of its major exports. Washington further complicated Colombia's efforts to promote legal exports by its 1990 decision to impose additional countervailing duties on Colombian cut flowers.

The Disruption of Latin American Societies

U.S. counternarcotics strategy in Latin America is undermining the region's democracies, causing societal disruptions, and producing hostile anti-U.S. sentiments among native populations.

One of the greatest threats of the international drug war to the stability of Latin American democracies has been the U.S. insistence on greater participation by the military. Obvious examples of Washington's desire to militarize the drug war include the 1989 U.S. invasion of Panama, the deployment of battleships off the coast of Colombia without that country's consent, and the construction of military bases for drug operations in the Upper Huallaga Valley of Peru.[17] Although the profile of the U.S. armed forces has been lowered since those episodes, Washington still considers military intervention in the drug war a high priority. In fact, U.S. military aid to Andean nations has increased substantially, from $3 million in 1988 to $203.5 million during 1990 and 1991.[18]

Although the military establishments of Andean countries do not identify the drug industry as the number-one threat to national

[16]General Accounting Office, "Drug Policy and Agriculture: U.S. Trade Impacts of Alternative Crops to Andean Coca," October 1991.

[17]Bruce Michael Bagley, *Myths of Militarization: The Role of the Military in the War on Drugs in the Americas* (Coral Gables, Fla.: University of Miami North-South Center, 1990), p. 15.

[18]White House, p. 169; Andreas et al. report that "the Andean region has now replaced Central America as the leading recipient of U.S. military aid in the hemisphere" (p. 106).

security and cite counterinsurgency or the defense of national borders as their primary missions, the drug war serves as a credible pretext for increasing military involvement in domestic affairs. By strengthening the armed forces of various Latin American nations, U.S. aid promotes the traditional interventionist role of the military in civil and economic affairs. Washington's attempt to apply a military solution to what is primarily an economic problem threatens to weaken fragile democratic institutions and even reverse the past decade's trend toward democratization.

Washington's policies have also sent the drug industry into areas that might otherwise have remained unaffected by the business. Eradication and interdiction campaigns simply force trafficking organizations to move their operations to other locations. Thus, drug operations spread to the central and lower parts of Peru's Huallaga Valley when officials intensified their anti-narcotics efforts in the Upper Huallaga. Similarly, when Colombia clamped down on the Medellín cartel in 1989, the Cali cartel increased its market share of cocaine from 30 to 70 percent in less than a year.[19] The dispersal of the drug trade has led to a significant rise in drug-related activity in Brazil, Venezuela, Guatemala, Argentina, and Suriname. That "push down, pop up" effect has also resulted in a sharp increase in drug trafficking in Chile. Since Chile emerged from dictatorship only a few years ago, the reluctance of Chilean officials to involve the military in fighting the drug problem is understandable.[20]

Another problem with U.S. counternarcotics strategy is that it places drug-source governments in untenable positions and heightens anti-U.S. sentiments. The Colombian government's quarrels with the United States over the extradition of drug traffickers illustrate that point. Washington's demand that suspected traffickers be extradited to the United States is highly unpopular with most Colombians who view it as an expression of Yankee imperialism. Rather than continue its bloody battle against the cartels, Colombia has resisted U.S. pressure and, under President César Gaviria, has sought to recover the political and economic stability the country

[19]Andreas et al., p. 111.

[20]Sara Isaac, "Chile Wary of Growing Drug Trade," *Orlando Sentinel*, March 1, 1992, p. G2.

had been losing. In 1991 Gaviria successfully convinced cartel leaders to surrender in exchange for reduced sentences, guarantees against extradition, and other concessions. Although that move was popular with Colombians, Washington was not fully satisfied.

Cartel leader Pablo Escobar's July 1992 escape from prison undeniably confirmed Washington's suspicion that Colombia's criminal justice system could be easily corrupted by the drug bosses. Nevertheless, the use of U.S. military planes over the city of Medellín to search for Escobar triggered renewed protests against U.S. violations of national sovereignty. Although Gaviria defended the flights, Colombians remained suspicious of U.S. motives. A June 1992 U.S. Supreme Court ruling that the United States could kidnap suspects abroad and bring them to trial in the United States had not been quickly forgotten. Colombians' suspicions gained credibility when both Rep. Robert G. Torricelli (D-N.J.), chairman of the House Subcommittee on Western Hemispheric Affairs, and Rep. Charles E. Schumer (D-N.Y.), chairman of the House Subcommittee on Crime and Criminal Justice, agreed that a U.S. expedition to capture Escobar was "an option that has to be considered."[21] Although Washington has not taken such dramatic steps, those events are indicative of the conflicting demands, of both their own citizenry and the U.S. government, with which governments of drug-source countries must contend.

Peru perhaps provides the best example of how Washington's drug policy disrupts Latin American societies. As the U.S.-orchestrated war against coca steadily escalated in Peru's Upper Huallaga Valley during the 1980s, the Shining Path guerrilla movement, which had previously had a minimal presence there, gained control of about 90 percent of the region.[22] The guerrillas have expanded their base of popular support by exploiting the *cocaleros'* hostility toward eradication programs. With over 200,000 Peruvian peasant families directly dependant on coca cultivation for their livelihood, eradication efforts play into the hands of the Shining Path, and coca growers are not reluctant to accept the guerrillas' offers of protection from drug enforcement officials.

---

[21]Joseph B. Treaster, "Frustration in Washington," *New York Times*, July 24, 1992, p. A9.

[22]Tammen, p. 14.

Anti-drug efforts have also produced a source of substantial financial support for the Shining Path. As drug traffickers sought to protect their businesses, they too entered a marriage of convenience with the guerrillas. Estimates of annual income earned by the Shining Path range from $15 million to $100 million. U.S. counternarcotics assistance actually creates the conditions under which the Shining Path's services become necessary. That point has led Harvard economist Robert J. Barro to conclude, "The U.S. government could achieve pretty much the same results if it gave the aid money directly to the terrorists."[23]

Peruvian president Fujimori's April 1992 abrogation of the constitution and military-backed suspension of democracy were largely the results of factors created by Washington's war on drugs. Although U.S. anti-narcotics assistance increased the militarization of Peruvian society, the demise of democracy was due more to Fujimori's attempt to more effectively fight the growing presence of the Shining Path. Both the expanded role of the military in Peru's domestic affairs and the increased economic and popular support enjoyed by the Shining Path resulted from Washington's obsession with fighting the drug problem at its source. Unfortunately for Peru, its fledgling democracy was irreparably undermined.

Conclusion

Washington's international war on drugs has not only failed to achieve its stated objectives; it has also caused severe economic, political, and social disruptions in source nations. Increased efforts to fight the drug war will only aggravate those conditions. The worldwide, and especially the hemispheric, trend toward political and economic liberalization should facilitate Washington's urgently needed radical departure from its foreign drug policy of recent years. The United States should recognize the economic realities of its anti-narcotics campaign and end its futile experiment in prohibition. The legalization of drugs would bring an end to narcotics-related violence both in the United States and abroad by bringing

---

[23]Robert J. Barro, "To Avoid Repeats of Peru, Legalize Drugs," *Wall Street Journal*, April 27, 1992, p. A14. The Defense Intelligence Agency estimates that Colombia's largest guerrilla group, *Fuerzas Armadas Revolucionarias de Colombia*, earned up to $40 million in 1988 through its involvement in the drug industry. See Charles Lane et al., "The Newest War," *Newsweek*, January 6, 1992, p. 22.

the drug industry into the legal framework of the market. In countries such as Peru or Colombia, legalization would be the single most powerful tool for undermining the legitimacy of guerrilla groups because it would remove both economic and popular support. Legalization would also reduce the enormous profits of the drug trade, thus making the cultivation of alternative crops economically viable.

Short of legalization, Washington should take the following steps.

- End the *international* war on drugs. Enlisting other countries to fight what is primarily a U.S. domestic problem is poor foreign policy. Theoretical and practical analyses of efforts to curtail drug supplies at their source suggest that even impressive results in those efforts would have little impact on domestic consumption.
- Repeal legislation requiring the certification of drug-source countries. That type of coercion has succeeded only in worsening U.S. relations with drug-producing countries. It has not been effective in getting source nations to implement policies that are contrary to their best interests.
- Substantially reduce trade protectionism and all stipulations that trade privileges be tied to cooperation in the drug war. That step would make legal export goods more appealing as alternatives to the cultivation and production of illicit commodities. The establishment of free-trade agreements with Latin American nations, for example, would be a step in the right direction. Such agreements, however, must minimize both tariff and nontariff barriers.

PART V

ECOLOGY

20. Global Warming: Facts vs. the Popular Vision

Patrick J. Michaels

Virtually all scientists directly involved in research on climatic change believe that the earth will undergo some warming as a result of the increase in manmade emissions that absorb infrared radiation, or enhance the "greenhouse effect."

However, within certain broad limits, how *much* the world warms is irrelevant. The critical policy question is *how* the world will warm, because the real effect of warming will be expressed by its regionality, seasonality, and distribution within the day-night cycle. There are now several compelling lines of evidence that indicate that, when those three factors are taken into account, the odds on the earth's experiencing an ecologically or economically disastrous global warming, either in magnitude or in time, are long indeed.

Those findings are at considerable variance with what might be referred to as the "Popular Vision" of global warming: a doubling of carbon dioxide in the earth's atmosphere resulting in a temperature increase of approximately 4°C, a pronounced rise in sea level due to the melting of major areas of land ice and thermal expansion of water, and starvation and civil strife as the consequences of ecological chaos.[1]

Although proponents of the Popular Vision cite the *Policymakers Summary* of the recent report of the United Nations' Intergovernmental Panel on Climate Change (IPCC) in support of their position,[2] the

---

[1]That vision also appears in the refereed scientific literature; for example, R. Rind, J. Goldberg, J. Hansen, et al., "Potential Evaporation and the Likelihood of Future Drought, *Journal of Geophysical Research* 95 (1990): 9983–10004, projected a 1,000 percent increase in the frequency of severe drought by the year 2050.

[2]United Nations' Intergovernmental Panel on Climate Change, *Policymakers Summary of the Scientific Assessment of Climate Change* (World Meteorological Organization, UN Environmental Programme, 1990).

median range of the climate impacts suggested in the report as a whole does not suggest that apocalyptic change is imminent.

The Popular Vision became prominent as the result of two synergistic events. The first was the publication in the middle to late 1980s of several computer climate simulation models that predicted that a doubling of atmospheric carbon dioxide would cause a mean global warming of 4.2°C with winter warming of as much as 18°C in the north polar region. The second was the June 23, 1988, congressional testimony of James E. Hansen of the National Aeronautics and Space Administration that there was a "high degree of cause and effect" between current temperatures and human greenhouse alterations.[3]

Nowhere in that testimony nor, to the best of my knowledge, anywhere else did Hansen ever state that the anomalously warm summer of 1988 in the United States was caused by an enhanced greenhouse effect. Nonetheless, the press and the public concluded otherwise: 70 percent of the respondents to a subsequent CNN poll agreed with the statement that the 1988 drought was in fact caused by "the greenhouse effect." That response obviously reflects the Popular Vision.

Trace Gas Concentrations and Temperature Histories

The earth naturally radiates infrared (low-energy) wavelengths, which warm primarily the lower atmosphere. Several natural molecules, notably water and carbon dioxide, absorb the infrared radiation and redirect some of it back toward the earth's surface, which has the effect of warming the lower levels of the atmosphere even further. That is the greenhouse effect. The most significant greenhouse-enhancing chemical species whose concentrations have been increased by human activity are, in descending order, carbon dioxide (CO_2), methane, nitrous oxide, and chlorofluorocarbons.

Because of the total change in atmospheric greenhouse gases, the current effective CO_2 concentration is approximately 420 parts per million (ppm), or 50 to 60 percent greater than the preindustrial background range of 260 to 279 ppm. The IPCC corroborated that view when it stated, "Greenhouse gases have increased since preindustrial times . . . by an amount that is radiatively equivalent to

---

[3]James E. Hansen, Testimony before the U.S. Senate Committee on Energy and Natural Resources, June 23, 1988.

about a 50 percent increase in carbon dioxide," which gives a current effective value of 390 to 420 ppm. Thus, we have already proceeded more than halfway to an effective doubling of the background CO_2 concentration.

The computer models of the mid-1980s predicted that a 50 percent increase in the relevant trace gases would lead to a warming of more than 2.0°C, but the earth has actually warmed only about half a degree in the last 100 years.[4] If greenhouse enhancement invariably leads to an increase in surface temperature, why has such an increase not been observed?

Ground-Based Temperature Records

Figure 20.1 shows the ground-based temperature records of the Northern and Southern Hemispheres from 1860 to the present. It is clear that virtually all of the warming of the Northern Hemisphere occurred before 1945 when the major industrial emissions of greenhouse-enhancing trace gases began. A linear trend through the data since 1935 is statistically indistinguishable from zero. Figure 20.2 shows the results of a trend analysis of *global* temperature records. That figure also demonstrates that, in a statistical sense, much of the observed warming had already taken place before 1945 and that there has been very little additional warming during the period in which a majority of the emissions have occurred.

It should be noted that the longest standing ground-based temperature records are frequently biased by the effects of urbanization. Most of those records originated at 19th-century points of commerce, which means that temperatures were initially recorded at low-lying sites near rivers (sources of waterpower). Those sites, in which cold air pools at night, then showed artificial local warming years later as the cities grew up around the weather stations. Thus, those weather stations were initially shielded from a true climatic warming, and then they exaggerated one that may not have occurred. The artificial upward bias of temperature readings taken at those stations has nothing to do with global or enhanced greenhouse warming. Rather, it has to do with the urban infrastructure— pavement that retains heat and buildings that impede ventilating winds—that goes with growth of economic activity.

[4]R. C. Balling, Jr., and S. B. Idso, "100 Years of Global Warming?" *Environmental Conservation* 17 (1990): 165.

343

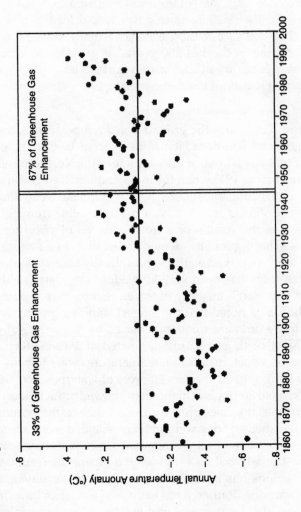

Figure 20.1
GROUND-BASED TEMPERATURE RECORDS

A: Northern Hemisphere

B: Southern Hemisphere

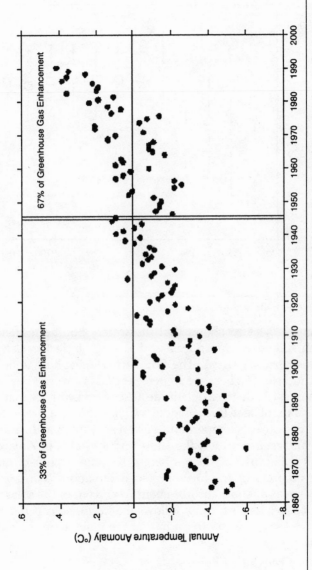

NOTE: This record, compiled by Phil Jones and Tom Wigley of the University of East Anglia, is the one most cited by scientists. The vertical bars indicate when the majority of greenhouse emissions began.

Figure 20.2
TRENDS IN GROUND-BASED TEMPERATURES SINCE 1920

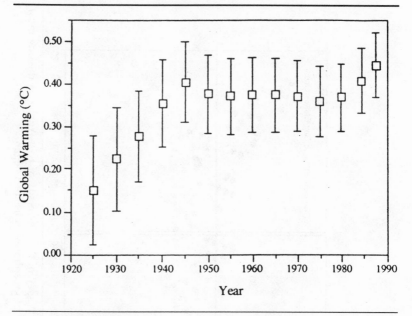

SOURCE: Balling and Idso.

Figure 20.1 also shows that the watery Southern Hemisphere, which should warm up least and slowest, in fact *exhibits the more "greenhouse-like" signal.* The Southern Hemisphere should warm least and slowest because 90 percent of it is covered by water, and the highest 20 degrees of latitude are covered with ice that averages thousands of feet thick. Liquid water requires a great deal more energy to raise its temperature a given amount than does an equivalent land area. Further, the snow and ice fields of Antarctica and vicinity, because of their inherent brightness, reflect more than three-quarters of the incoming solar radiation. (For comparison, the earth as a whole absorbs about 75 percent of the solar radiation that reaches its surface.) It follows that *temperature variations should be much less* in the southern half of the globe than they are in the north.

Satellite Temperature Records

In 1979 the first of a series of weather satellites capable of measuring the temperature of the lower layer of the atmosphere with an accuracy of ± 0.01°C was launched. Satellite coverage is virtually global, and there can be no urban effect on satellite data. Figure 20.3 shows the temperatures recorded from satellite platforms for both the Northern and the Southern Hemisphere.[5]

It is immediately apparent that there is no significant warming trend in either hemisphere over the period of record. Moreover, the fairly rapid warming between 1979 and the present that appears in the ground-based data (Figure 20.1B) for the Southern Hemisphere is absent from the satellite data.

Thus, the temperature history of the planet supports neither the Popular Vision nor the mid-1980s computer model forecasts of global warming, either in pattern or in magnitude.

In his excellent book, *The Heated Debate*, Robert Balling, after convincingly demonstrating that observed warming of the planet has been far less than even the most conservative projections of the early computer models,[6] indicates that other industrial by-products, such as sulfate aerosol (the chemical associated with acid rain), may be in large part responsible for the observed lack of warming. And several calculations indicate that the magnitude of compensatory cooling could be sufficient to have canceled all the expected greenhouse warming to date.[7]

I do not believe that the hypothesis of sulfate cooling alone provides a sufficient explanation of the observed data. Rather, there is evidence that a concurrent increase in cloudiness, which is not related to that aerosol and may, in fact, be a result of the greenhouse enhancement itself, is mitigating the expected warming.

The Importance of Increasing Cloudiness

The importance of increasing cloudiness in a world with an enhanced greenhouse effect cannot be overstated. Instead of the Popular Vision of climate apocalypse, it would mean a pleasant world with warmer nights and little change in daytime temperatures.

[5]R. W. Spencer and J. R. Christy, "Precise Monitoring of Global Temperature Trends from Satellite," *Science* 247 (1990): 1558–62.

[6]Robert C. Balling, Jr., *The Heated Debate* (San Francisco: Pacific Research Institute, 1992).

[7]James E. Hansen and A. A. Lacis, "Sun and Dust versus Greenhouse Gases: An Assessment of Their Relative Roles in Global Climate Change," *Nature* 346 (1990): 713–18.

Figure 20.3
SATELLITE TEMPERATURE RECORDS

A: Northern Hemisphere

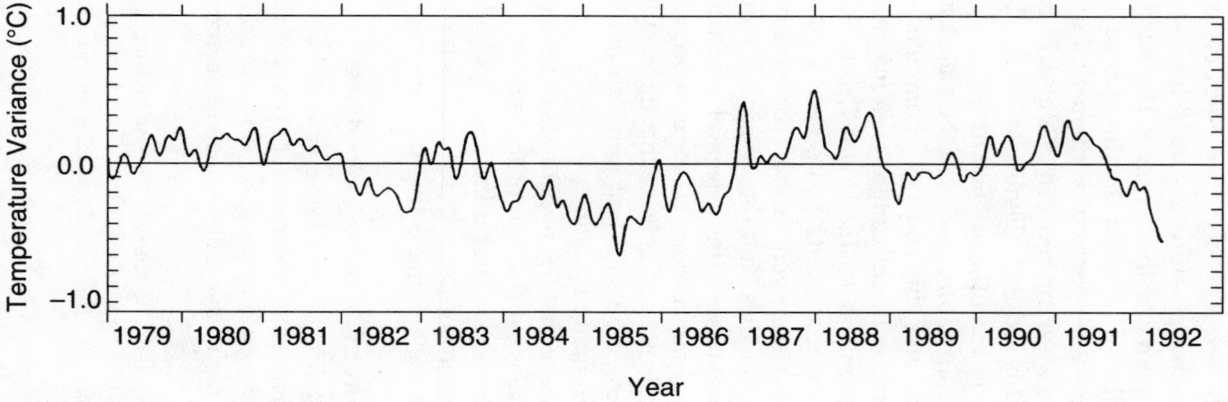

B: Southern Hemisphere

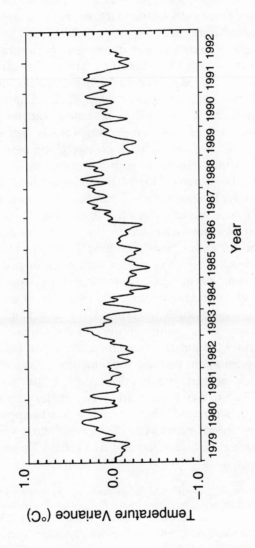

The Popular Vision of global warming entails three major threats: (1) major reductions in crop yields, (2) a rapid and disastrous rise in sea level caused by the melting of large areas of land ice, and (3) ecological disequilibrium and loss of plant species. Each of those threats is dramatically lessened if the greenhouse effect is mitigated by increased cloudiness.

First, the primary cause of decreased agricultural yields is moisture stress, which can result in plant death, caused by lack of sufficient water. Moisture stress is maximized during daytime, especially on hot, sunny afternoons. If cloudiness increases, daytime temperature rises will be lessened, and moisture stress on plants reduced. Further, temperatures reach their lowest values at the end of clear winter nights. Increased cloudiness will warm those nights and thus lengthen the growing season.

Second, large areas of high-latitude (polar) land ice—which must melt in order to raise sea level significantly—melt during summer. Yet all climate models, from the 1896 calculations of the Swedish physicist Svante Arrhenius to the most recent version of the Princeton computer model,[8] confine the greatest warming to high-latitude winter, which coincides with night or twilight. If the projected warming is modified by an increase in cloudiness, the warming in high-latitude summer could be canceled entirely.

An increase in air temperature over Greenland and Antarctica would allow the moisture content of the atmosphere to increase (the warmer the air, the more moisture it can hold) and result in more precipitation. Because the temperature is so far below freezing, all the moisture would fall as snow. It may seem paradoxical, but the way to make the world's two major ice fields grow is to warm things up a bit. That, in fact, is what happened during the last warm period, from 4,000 to 7,000 years ago, according to studies by Domack et al. and Miller and de Vernal.[9] Those authors argued

[8]S. Manabe, R. J. Stouffer, M. J. Spelman, and K. Bryan, "Transient Responses of a Coupled Ocean-Atmosphere Model to Gradual Changes of Atmospheric CO_2: Part 1, Annual Mean Response," *Journal of Climate* 4 (1991): 785–818.

[9]E. W. Domack, A. J. Jull, and S. Nakao, "Advance of East Antarctic Outlet Glaciers during the Hypsithermal: Implications for the Volume State of the Antarctic Ice-Sheet under Global Warming," *Geology* 19 (1991): 1059–62; and G. H. Miller and A. de Vernal, "Will Greenhouse Warming Lead to Northern Hemisphere Ice-Sheet Growth? *Nature* 355 (1992).

that warming would increase the ice volume and thus mitigate a rise in sea level.

Indeed, satellite measurements indicate that snow cover in the Northern Hemisphere increased by 18 percent between 1966 and the late 1970s (see Figure 20.4).[10] In addition, the history of a worldwide sample of mountain glaciers from 1964 to 1980 indicated that the number of advancing glaciers increased dramatically and the number of receding ones dropped by an equivalent value. Those trends did not reverse in the first half of the 1980s (see Figure 20.5).[11]

The third negative prospect from climatic change—ecological disequilibrium and loss of species—is also profoundly affected by a cloud-mitigated greenhouse, because the main cause of plant death remains moisture stress, which occurs primarily during the day. In addition, temperature changes of 5°C in less than 50 years—values that exceed those of the direst computer model projections—have been common in the deglaciation of the last 18,000 years.[12] Those observed climatic changes, more rapid than the ones forecast, were insufficient to promote ecological disaster.

Furthermore, throughout most of the past billion years, the concentration of atmospheric CO_2 has been greater than it is today. The same is true of the past 100 million years, which is the period during which most of our food and fiber crops evolved. Only since the beginning of the ice ages, some 5 million years ago, have temperatures and atmospheric CO_2 fallen to current levels. When it was really cold, at the height of the ice ages (the last advance terminated only 18,000 years ago), the concentration of CO_2 fell to values that were within 100 million ppm of being unable to support life. Thus, from the perspective of both geological and evolutionary history, the atmosphere is currently impoverished in CO_2. An additional historical peculiarity is that gas bubbles trapped in Antarctic ice tell us that the temperature dropped *before* the CO_2 concentration changed, not after.

[10]Donald Wiesnet and Michael Matson, *Environmental Data and Information Service Report* 11, no. 1 (U.S. Department of Commerce, 1980).

[11]Fred B. Wood, "Global Alpine Glacier Trends, 1960s to 1980s," *Arctic and Alpine Research* 20 (1988): 404–13.

[12]S. J. Lehmen and L. D. Keigwin, "Sudden Changes in North Atlantic Circulation during the Last Deglaciation," *Nature* 356 (1992): 747–62.

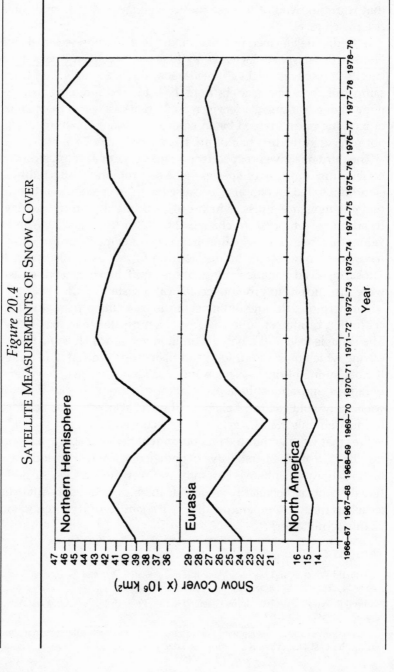

Figure 20.4
SATELLITE MEASUREMENTS OF SNOW COVER

Northern Hemisphere

Eurasia

North America

Snow Cover (x 10⁶ km²)

Year

Figure 20.5
WOOD'S GLACIER HISTORY

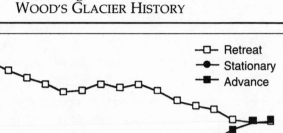

Evidence of Increasing Cloudiness

Cloudiness increased 3.5 percent across the United States between 1950–68 and 1970–88.[13] Sunshine declined in Germany, and the effect is greatest in the mountains. S. G. Warren and his colleagues at the University of Washington have studied millions of shipboard observations and found that global cloudiness has increased (most notably in the Northern Hemisphere).[14]

If those findings are correct and clouds—from any source, including sulfates—are increasing, the following should be observed:

1. Nights should be warmed by both the increase in greenhouse gases and the increase in cloudiness.
2. Daytime warming should be counteracted by cloud reflectivity.
3. There should be a consequent decline in the daily temperature range (difference between day and night).
4. The greatest warming (night effect) of clouds should occur on (long) winter nights.

[13]J. K. Angell, "Variation in United States Cloudiness and Sunshine Duration between 1950 and the Drought Year of 1988," *Journal of Climate* 3 (1990): 296–306.

[14]S. G. Warren, C. J. Hahn, J. London, et al., "Global Distribution of Total Cloud Cover and Cloud Type Amounts over the Ocean," U.S. Department of Energy, 1988.

5. The greatest counteraction of warming (day effect) should occur on (long) summer days.
6. The least warming (night effect) should occur on (short) summer nights.
7. The least cooling (day effect) should occur on (short) winter days.

Each of those hypothetical effects is confirmed by the data.

Tom Karl and his colleagues have created a Historical Climate Network (HCN) of 492 weather stations that are not affected by urban growth.[15] As shown in Figure 20.6A, daily high temperatures across the United States have actually been declining since the early 1930s. The behavior of night temperatures (Figure 20.6B) began to change after 1950. Since then, while day temperatures have declined slightly, night temperatures have risen.

Figure 20.7 details the change in daily temperature range (difference between high and low) in Karl's HCN. It is apparent that the difference began to decrease around 1950.

In addition to the U.S. HCN, Karl and colleagues examined day and night temperatures, in another urbanization-adjusted record, for mainland China and the former Soviet Union.[16] Although their results are presented nationally, a composite table (Table 20.1) demonstrates the ubiquitous nature of night warming and the lack of day warming in the Northern Hemisphere.[17] Table 20.1 is broken down into seasons, and it is evident that summer daytime temperatures—the ones that must rise to create a climate catastrophe—have actually fallen across the hemisphere, while the 100-year trend shows that there has been a dramatic rise in winter night temperatures of 1.8°C.

Since each of the six implicative hypotheses about temperature and cloudiness is supported by the data, only the question of causation remains: is the mitigation of the greenhouse effect a result of an increase in sulfate aerosol, and therefore merely the screening

[15]Tom R. Karl, R. G. Baldwin, and M. G. Burgin, *Historical Climatology Series 4–5* (Asheville, N.C.: National Climatic Data Center, 1988).

[16]Tom R. Karl, G. Kukla, V. N. Razuavayev, et al., "Global Warming: Evidence for Asymmetric Diurnal Temperature Change," *Geophysical Research Letters* 18 (1991): 2252–56.

[17]Patrick J. Michaels and D. E. Stooksbury, "Global Warming: A Reduced Threat?" *Bulletin of the American Meteorological Society* 73 (1992): 15-63–15-77.

Figure 20.6
AVERAGE DAILY MAXIMUM (DAYTIME) AND MINIMUM (NIGHTTIME) TEMPERATURES IN KARL'S HISTORICAL CLIMATE NETWORK

A: Maximum Temperatures

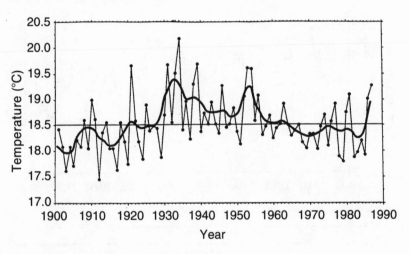

B: Minimum Temperatures

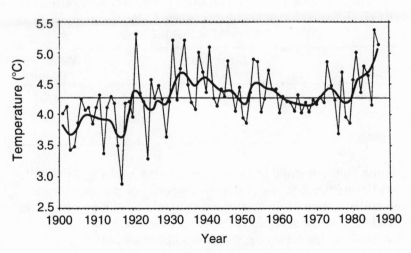

Figure 20.7
AVERAGE DAILY TEMPERATURE RANGE, OR THE DIFFERENCE BETWEEN DAYTIME AND NIGHTTIME TEMPERATURES, IN KARL'S HISTORICAL CLIMATE NETWORK

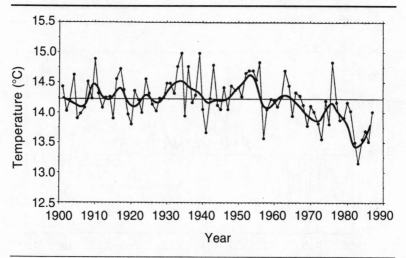

Table 20.1
AREA-WEIGHTED AGGREGATE TEMPERATURE TRENDS (°C/100 YR) FOR THE UNITED STATES, CONTINENTAL CHINA, AND THE FORMER SOVIET UNION

Season	Mean Max. (Day)	Mean Min. (Night)
Winter	+0.6	+1.8
Summer	-0.4	+0.4
Annual	+0.05	+1.1

of one environmental problem (greenhouse warming) by another (acid rain)? Or is it also a natural response of the atmosphere to an enhancement of the greenhouse effect? If it is in part the latter, in addition to the seven hypotheses noted above, which are verified by the data, the following should also be observed:

1. Night, day, and seasonal changes in temperatures recorded at high-elevation land stations (such as those on mountaintops)

should be similar in character to those observed at low elevations.
2. There should be disproportionate night warming in the Southern as well as in the Northern Hemisphere.

Theoretical calculations all agree that surface warming should be accompanied by some cooling of the upper layers of the atmosphere, and most computer models confine that cooling to regions above the earth's active weather zone, or approximately 45,000 feet in the midlatitudes. But J. K. Angell has demonstrated that cooling has been observed from approximately 25,000 feet upward.[18] That altitude is easily within the active weather zone and, everything else being equal, should result in increased cloudiness. Thus, the natural atmospheric response to greenhouse enhancement may be an increase in midlevel and high-level cloudiness.

Almost all sulfate aerosol—along with other particulates—tends to be confined to the bottom 7,000 feet of the atmosphere. If the cloud increases were primarily a result of sulfate aerosol, high-elevation stations should not show night warming (accentuated in winter) and counteraction of daytime warming (especially in summer).

Figure 20.8 shows maximum (day) and minimum (night) temperatures for winter and summer from the Pic du Midi Observatory in the French Pyrenees.[19] Pic du Midi is a particularly important weather station inasmuch as the surrounding terrain is exceedingly difficult, which minimizes human interference, and the station is above timberline, which means that growing trees cannot artificially warm the nights and cool the days. Perhaps most important, at 9,400 feet, it is above almost all the sulfate aerosol.

Yet its temperature record is similar to that of the low-elevation stations detailed in Table 20.1. The rise in nighttime temperature (for both summer and winter) is highly significant, as is the decline in summer daytime temperature. The magnitude of those changes is striking and clearly out of proportion to the minuscule amount of sulfate aerosol residing at or above 9,400 feet. Thus, it would

[18]J. K. Angell, "Variation in Global Tropospheric Temperature after Adjustment for the El Niño Influence, 1958–89," *Geophysical Research Letters* 17 (1991): 1093–96.

[19]A Bucher and J. Dessens, "Secular Trend of Surface Temperature at an Elevated Observatory in the Pyrenees," *Journal of Climate* 4 (1991): 859–68.

Figure 20.8
TEMPERATURES AT PIC DU MIDI OBSERVATORY

A: Winter Temperatures

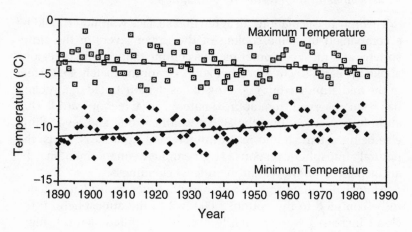

B: Summer Temperatures

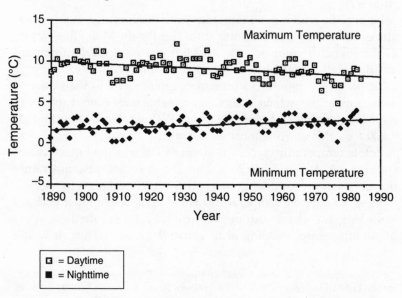

□ = Daytime
■ = Nighttime

seem that mitigation of greenhouse warming is due primarily to the high-altitude cooling noted by Angell.

Additional evidence for that conclusion is provided by P. A. Jones's study that indicates that night warming in Australia (in the Southern Hemisphere) also exceeds day warming, in this case by a factor of 2 (0.12°C/decade vs. 0.06°C/decade).[20] (Note that observed warming is still far less than that projected by the computer models.) And Warren and his colleagues also found significant increases in cirrus (high-altitude) clouds around Australia but no concomitant increase in low-level stratocumulus, the type of cloud one would expect to be enhanced by sulfate aerosol.

Second-Generation Computer Models

The first computer models were especially primitive in their handling of oceanic heat transfer, both within the ocean and to the atmosphere, and in their formulation of clouds. Those models predicted an average surface warming of 4.2°C after an effective doubling of atmospheric CO_2.

The early models have been changed and improved. By using a modified ice-water interaction within clouds, the United Kingdom model projects a mean warming of 1.9°C, considerably less than its earlier projection of 5.2°C. The National Center for Atmospheric Research (NCAR) model, which uses a coupled ocean and atmosphere, projects warming of 1.6°C for 30 years after an "instantaneous" doubling of CO_2, compared to 3.7°C projected by an earlier model with a more primitive ocean. A slightly different version of that model, in which the greenhouse effect increases at a rate commensurate with industrial emissions, implies that the global temperature should have risen by 0.7°C since 1950; the measured trend of 0.33°C is less than half of what was projected.

Manabe et al. still calculate a net equilibrium warming of 4.0°C in their coupled ocean-atmosphere model, but comparison of observed behavior of the Northern Hemisphere and that predicted by the model suggests that, to date, it has overpredicted warming by at least a factor of 2.

Even though the new simulations still appear to be too warm, they do predict most warming will occur in high-latitude winter of

[20]P. A. Jones, "Historical Records of Cloud Cover and Climate for Australia," *Australian Meteorological Magazine* 39 (1991): 181–89.

the Northern Hemisphere. In the new NCAR version (Figure 20.9), the area of projected warming of more than 4°C is less than 5 percent of the planetary surface, but more important, because almost all of it is confined to latitudes higher than 60° in Northern Hemisphere winter, *virtually all of the major warming is projected for either twilight*

Figure 20.9
FOUR 1989 NCAR MODEL PROJECTIONS FOR WINTER

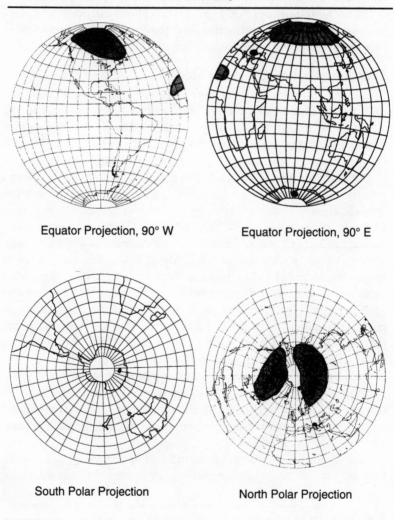

Equator Projection, 90° W   Equator Projection, 90° E

South Polar Projection   North Polar Projection

or nighttime, similar to what has been observed in the climate record. (Note that compensatory cooling by sulfate aerosol is not included in those calculations.)

Enhancement of Plant Growth

It has long been known that many plants grow faster in the presence of elevated concentrations of carbon dioxide, which shouldn't be surprising: CO_2 is the prime reactant in the overall equation of photosynthesis. An examination of the scientific literature reveals that 1,087 individual experiments reported in 324 scientific papers, or 93 percent of the studies, found an increase in plant productivity with an increase in the CO_2 content of the air, while only 2 percent documented a decrease.[21] P. E. Kauppi and his colleagues have demonstrated that European forests have increased in biomass during the last two decades; according to those researchers, "The fertilization effect of pollutants overrides the adverse affects, at least for the time being."[22] Further, if warming caused by an enhanced greenhouse effect occurs primarily during winter and nighttime, then the growing season will lengthen, increasing the time during which plants can capture CO_2.

Several real-world surveys indicate an acceleration in vegetative growth. According to Sherwood Idso,[23] the effect has been noted in montane species in the western United States, in a carefully monitored virgin forest plot at the Oak Ridge National Laboratory, and in the northern forests of Scandinavia.

If plant growth is indeed accelerating, it is doing so at a time when forest growth is ostensibly being retarded by acid precipitation. If sulfate aerosol is one (insufficient) factor involved in mitigating prospective warming, then its negative effects are being countered in part by enhanced carbon dioxide. An additional factor of environmental importance is that enhanced cloudiness serves to block incoming solar radiation, mitigating effects of a stratospheric ozone decline. A combination of those factors is probably responsible for

[21]K. E. Idso, *Plant Responses to Rising Levels of Atmospheric Carbon Dioxide* (Tempe, Ariz.: Institute for Biospheric Research, 1992).

[22]P. E. Kauppi, K. Mielikainen, and K. Kuusela, "Biomass and Carbon Budget of European Forests," *Science* 256 (1992): 70–74.

[23]Sherwood B. Idso, *Carbon Dioxide and Global Change: Earth in Transition* (Tempe, Ariz.: Institute for Biospheric Research, 1989).

the fact that ultraviolet B radiation—the casual agent for basal cell skin cancer—is actually *declining* across the United States and much of the Northern Hemisphere's landmass.[24]

Conclusion

The best scientific data available indicate that greenhouse warming is less than predicted and that its prevalence at night in high-latitude winter rather than on summer days means that any rise in sea level will be mitigated and the world's food supply could increase. Those findings suggest only one thing: *the Popular Vision of climate apocalypse is wrong.*

Nonetheless, there have been and there will be excessive pressures for economically important mitigation of the Popular Vision. They should be resisted. The consensus of data indicates that acquiescing to such pressures will result in an impoverished nation attempting to fight a problem that never existed. Our policy should be commensurate with our science.

[24]J. Scotto, G. Cotton, F. Urbach, et al., "Biologically Effective Ultraviolet Radiation: Surface Measurements in the United States," *Science* 293 (1988): 762–63.

21. The Growing Abundance of Natural Resources

Jerry Taylor

> One of the most serious problems now facing the planet
> is that associated with historical patterns of unsustainable
> consumption and production, leading to environmental
> degradation, aggravation of poverty, and imbalances in the
> development of countries.
>
> —*Agenda 21*, presented at 1992 UN Conference on
> Environment and Development

The most fundamental axiom of economics is the objective reality
of scarcity. Productive resources are limited, yet human desires are
virtually unbounded. Resources have thus been scarce since time
immemorial and will continue to be so for all eternity.

From that simple, self-evident fact a corollary hypothesis has
arisen: as population and economies grow, resource depletion
accelerates until physical limits are reached and resource exhaustion
occurs. Such a corollary would hardly strike one as radical. After
all, if resources are fundamentally scarce, it stands to reason that
increased demand for them hastens the day when they will disap-
pear from the planet.

Warnings of impending catastrophe, which have been around
for almost 200 years, have arisen with increasing frequency in the
20th century. The population explosion in the Third World, coupled
with the dramatic postwar growth of the global economy since
1950, has increased the volume, pitch, and urgency of warnings
that civilization is living on borrowed time. The gasoline lines and
inflation of the 1970s brought warning voices from the intellectual
wilderness squarely into the center of public debate. International
best sellers such as Paul Ehrlich's *The Population Bomb*, the Club of
Rome's *Limits to Growth*, and the Carter administration's *Global 2000*

363

Report all helped convince millions of people that civilization as they knew it was on the verge of collapse.

Although the boom years of the 1980s temporarily quieted the voices of doom, the "conservation ethic" has become an institutionalized element of American politics. Both political parties agree that government must intervene in the economy to protect us from potentially catastrophic overexploitation of natural resources. The debate tends to be over "how much" intervention is necessary, not whether intervention is justified in the first place.

Today, government planners, having been judged incompetent when it comes to overseeing economic production, are firmly entrenched in the United States with a new mandate: to eliminate resource waste in virtually every industry while strictly regulating the use of our supposedly dwindling stock of natural resources.

Many people still believe that conservation is simply not enough, that it will only temporarily stall our slide into crisis. Indeed, the authors of *Limits to Growth*, in their recently published sequel *Beyond the Limits*, argue that "even with much more efficient institutions and technologies, the limits of the earth's ability to support population and capital are close at hand."[1] The only way out of "civilizational collapse," they contend, is to radically reform all elements of society. "We are talking about a revolution here, not in the political sense, like the French revolution, but in the much more profound sense of the Agricultural or Industrial Revolution."[2] And just what kind of reconstituted American civilization do the "revolutionaries" envision? Theirs is the same tired vision that has hypnotized communitarians for decades: socialism, but this time with a happy green face.[3]

Taking Inventory

So is it true, then, that civilization is teetering on the precipice of collapse due to resource exhaustion? Just how far down have we drawn earth's material abundance?

---

[1] Donella Meadows, Dennis Meadows, and Jorgen Randers, *Beyond the Limits* (Post Mills, Vt.: Chelsea Green, 1992), p. 47.

[2] Ibid., p. 219.

[3] See ibid., pp. 209–36, for a rather vague but militantly communalistic view of how a sustainable society might look.

There are three means by which to judge the extent of our resource base: proven reserves, price data, and ultimately recoverable stock.

Proven reserves measure the amount of a given resource that has been discovered and can be extracted profitably given current prices and technologies. Thus, proven reserves are a function of economics, not geological abundance. When resource prices are low, there is little incentive to invest in exploration or development. Dropping resource prices also make uneconomical exploitation of certain resources that were economically viable under higher prices. Although those reserves are moved off the books, so to speak, they will still be available when prices increase at some point in the future. Likewise, low resource prices provide little incentive to invest in research and development efforts for new extraction technologies that often allow previously uneconomical resource fields to be mined profitably. Only when inventories begin to dwindle and resource prices begin to rise do commercial enterprises find it necessary to invest in resource exploration and development.

Thus, proven reserves, although providing useful information to industry, tell us little about ultimately available resources. As economists Ronald Ridker and Elizabeth Cecelski noted, "Since exploration and development are costly, little effort is made to find proof of new resources if what is already known is considered adequate to meet demands for the next ten to twenty years."[4]

Price data are a far more accurate means by which to evaluate relative resource scarcity. Basic economics tells us that, in a free market, prices rise when demand for a resource is greater than current supply. Likewise, prices fall when the supply of a given resource is greater than consumer demand. Because prices reflect the accumulated knowledge of millions of economic actors who daily put their own money at risk, the market is far more likely to accurately judge resource scarcity than are noneconomic actors.

Moreover, the needs of future generations are fully considered in the pricing mechanism. An asset's value is determined by the projected value of its future returns. Resource owners are thus

[4]Ronald Ridker and Elizabeth Cecelski, "Resources and Population," in *International Encyclopedia of Population*, ed. John Ross (New York: Free Press, 1980), p. 595. Cited in David Osterfeld, *Prosperity versus Planning* (New York: Oxford University Press, 1992), p. 93.

fully encouraged to consider the long-term implications of their management decisions. Resource degradation and depletion are costly; as soon as the market anticipates future problems with a commodity, the value of that commodity falls and the owner's wealth depreciates immediately. Likewise, the maintenance of a strong resource base increases both the value of a holding and the wealth of the owner.

Producers of resource materials have an incentive to maintain adequate stocks for the future simply because potential shortages in the years ahead will lead to higher prices and thus greater returns on the sale of commercial resources. The rapid emergence of futures markets for most resources allows speculators to purchase the rights to various resources and hold them off the market for resale at higher prices in the future. If future supply of and demand for a resource are poorly reflected by its market price, enterprises that know better have every incentive to act on their superior knowledge to garner large future profits.

The third means of examining resource abundance is by reference to ultimately recoverable stock, defined as a mere 1 percent of a given resource estimated to be in the top kilometer of the earth's crust. Although advances in extraction technologies and adjustments in resource prices will perhaps allow us to economically mine a greater proportion of the earth's abundance, it is historically reasonable (and perhaps even a bit conservative) to assume that man can use about 1 percent of the earth's mineral and fossil fuel deposits.[5]

If we examine the earth's resource base using those three yardsticks, we do indeed come to a jarring conclusion: at the very time that the conservation lobby was convincing millions of Americans and legislatures everywhere that resource shortages were lurking just around the corner, the global economy witnessed the greatest explosion of resource abundance in the history of mankind.

If there are indeed "physical limits to the sources of materials and energy that sustain the human population and the economy," as is contended in Beyond the Limits, it appears that those limits are

---

[5]William Nordhaus, "Resources as Constraint on Growth?" American Economic Review, May 1974, pp. 22–26.

so far beyond the human horizon that they are for all intents and purposes nonexistent.

Energy

Contrary to popular belief, energy stocks of all kinds, both fossil and nonfossil, have been increasing steadily and dropping in price. We face unprecedented abundance, not scarcity.

As noted by MIT professor Morris Adelman, one of America's foremost energy experts, "The great oil shortage is like the horizon, always receding as one moves toward it."[6] The world has nearly 10 times the amount of proven oil reserves that it had in 1950 and almost twice the known reserves of 1970. In fact, proven oil reserves are greater today than at any other time in recorded history.

Oil prices have dropped 35 percent in constant dollars since 1980. When indexed to U.S. wages, oil prices have dropped 43 percent since 1980 and show steady and continuing declines in price from as far back as 1870.[7] The decline in oil prices has been reflected in the price of gasoline at the pump. Fuel prices in constant dollars are 6 percent lower today than they were in 1972 (just before the OPEC oil embargo), 25 percent lower than in 1963, and 30 percent lower than in 1947.[8] Whereas 3.2 percent of total household expenditures were devoted to gasoline in 1972 (the lowest such rate since 1952), American households today devote but 2.6 percent of total expenditures to gasoline purchases.[9]

Proven natural gas reserves have also shown dramatic increases in the past 20 years; they have increased by 84 percent since 1974. At current rates of consumption, proven gas reserves alone will be sufficient for approximately 58 years.[10] The fact that natural gas prices, after adjusting for inflation, have dropped only 3 percent since 1980 is largely a function of price and production controls

[6]Morris Adelman, "Oil Fallacies," *Foreign Policy* 82 (Spring 1991): 10.

[7]Stephen Moore, "Doomsday Delayed: America's Surprisingly Bright Natural Resource Future," Institute for Policy Innovation Policy Report no. 118, July 1992, pp. 35–40.

[8]Daniel Yergin, "Gasoline and the American People," Cambridge Energy Research Associates, June 1991, p. 15.

[9]Ibid., p. 17.

[10]"Energy and the Environment: A Power for Good, a Power for Ill," *The Economist*, August 31, 1991, survey, p. 4.

that lingered into the 1980s and discouraged optimum production levels.

Likewise, between 1979 and 1989 proven coal reserves grew by 84 percent, an amount sufficient for 238 years given current levels of consumption.[11] On an energy equivalent basis, proven reserves of coal are 43 percent greater than the world's combined total of proven oil and natural gas reserves.[12] Since 1980 the price of coal has dropped 91 percent when adjusted for inflation and 243 percent when indexed to U.S. wages.[13]

Economist William Nordhaus concludes from U.S. Geological Survey data that the world has enough ultimately recoverable fossil fuel reserves to last approximately 520 years given projected rates of demand, although others have pegged that figure as high as 650 years.[14] If historic rates of productivity increase and technological advances are considered, then we have every reason to believe that the 1,000-year trend of falling energy prices will continue for generations to come.

Remember, the figures cited above are for fossil fuel reserves only. Current nuclear technology ensures that the world has 8,400 years of energy for the future at current rates of consumption.[15] Advances in nuclear breeder and fusion technologies would ensure vast supplies of energy for tens of thousands of years, and geothermal resources and the potential of solar energy also promise virtually limitless supplies of energy as technology improves and those sources become more economically competitive.

Mineral Deposits

Back in 1980, during the height of the Carter-era resource depletion scare, economist Julian Simon bet conservationist Paul Ehrlich $1,000 that the real price of any group of natural resources of Ehrlich's choice would be less at any given date in the future than in 1980. Ehrlich chose five minerals—copper, chrome, nickel, tin, and tungsten—and set the payoff date for 10 years hence. As Simon

[11]Ibid.

[12]National Coal Council, "The Long-Range Role of Coal in the Future Energy Strategy of the United States," June 1990, p. 3.

[13]Moore, pp. 35–40.

[14]See Nordhaus and "Energy and the Environment."

[15]Nordhaus, p. 25.

expected, the real price of those five resources dropped by 24 percent, 40 percent, 8 percent, 68 percent, and 78 percent, respectively. Ehrlich sent Simon a check—but no admission of error—in 1990.

No matter which minerals Ehrlich chose, it was a sucker's bet. All but two strategic minerals (manganese and zinc) declined in price during the 1980s, reflecting the dramatic increase in mineral abundance that has occurred globally since the beginning of time. Simon renewed his offer to any and all comers in 1992, but to date there have been no takers. As the data in Table 1 indicate, proven reserves of virtually all important minerals have skyrocketed since 1950.

An examination of the price of 13 metals and minerals (aluminum, antimony, copper, lead, magnesium, manganese, mercury, nickel, platinum, silver, tin, tungsten, and zinc) shows a net 31 percent decline in real prices from 1980 to 1990. When indexed to wages, those price declines are even more dramatic. "Most of the minerals and metals at the turn of the century were five to ten times more

Table 21.1
PROVEN RESERVES OF VARIOUS RESOURCES, 1950–90
(MILLION METRIC TONS)

Resource	1950	1990	Change (%)
Bauxite	1,400	21,500	1,436
Chromium	70	420	500
Copper	100	350	250
Iron ore	19,000	145,000	663
Lead	40	70	75
Manganese	500	980	96
Nickel	17	59	247
Oil[a]	104	1,002	863
Tin	6.0	4.2	−30
Zinc	70	145	107

SOURCE: Kahn, Brown, and Martel, p. 92; U.S. Bureau of Mines, *Mineral Commodities Summary*, January 1990; *Resources for Freedom*, Report of the President's Materials Policy Commission, 1952, vol. 2, p. 27; and *Energy Statistics Source Book* (New York: PennWell, 1991), pp. 143, 151.

NOTE: Information on proven reserves of coal, magnesium, natural gas, and titanium in 1950 is unavailable.

[a]Billion barrels.

expensive than they are today in terms of numbers of hours of work needed to purchase them."[16]

Declines in metal and mineral prices are reflected in the equally dramatic declines in raw material costs. From 1980 to 1990 the real price of glass fell 33 percent, cement prices fell 40 percent, metal prices dropped 18 percent, and rubber prices declined by 40 percent.[17]

Examination of ultimately recoverable mineral resources indicates that we have only begun to tap the rich veins of the earth's abundance. U.S. Geological Survey data reveal that, if current consumption trends continue, recoverable mineral resources will last for hundreds and in many cases thousands and even tens of thousands of years.[18] Physicist Herman Kahn and several colleagues concluded in 1976 that "over 95 percent of the world demand [for minerals] is for five metals (iron, aluminum/bauxite, silicon, magnesium, and titanium), which are not considered exhaustible." Another 4.85 percent of world mineral demand is for seven metals (copper, zinc, manganese, chromium, lead, nickel, and tin) that are "probably inexhaustible." Thus, 99.9 percent of all mineral demand is for metals virtually inexhaustible over any conceivable time horizon.[19]

Agricultural Resources

The disturbing, ongoing pattern of famine and drought in Africa and Asia has added credibility to the argument that the earth is approaching a point at which it will not be able to continue to feed the "teeming masses" of the planet. Yet by any analysis, this is a time of agricultural abundance unprecedented in the history of the world. Economist Thomas De Gregori observes that "if there is hunger in the world—and so there is, in abundance, even in wealthy countries—it is because of maldistribution of food, not insufficient global production."[20] Ten times as many people died of famine in the last quarter of the 19th century as have died of

[16]Moore, pp. 25–31.

[17]Moore, p. 32.

[18]Nordhaus, p. 23.

[19]Herman Kahn, William Brown, and Leon Martel, *The Next 200 Years* (New York: William Morrow, 1976) p. 102.

[20]Thomas De Gregori, "Resources Are Not; They Become: An Institutional Theory," *Journal of Economic Issues* 21, no. 3 (September 1987): 1252.

famine in the third quarter of the 20th century, despite our much larger present population and the massive engineered famines in Cambodia during the 1970s.[21]

An examination of 15 representative agricultural commodities (barley, broilers, carrots, cattle, corn, cotton, eggs, milk, oats, oranges, rice, sorghum, soybeans, wheat, and wool) reveals that real prices in the United States dropped by an average of 38 percent from 1980 to 1990. When indexed to wages, the price of those foodstuffs has declined 83 percent since 1950.[22] Clearly, if the earth's agricultural productivity were being outpaced by voracious demand for food as a result of the population explosion, agricultural prices would be rising sharply rather than falling dramatically as the data indicate.

Likewise, it is clear that the agricultural output of the planet has increased exponentially over the past several centuries. Since 1960 technological advances in farm equipment, pesticides, fertilizers, irrigation techniques, bioengineering, and soil management have led to a doubling of world food production and 30 percent increases in farmland productivity.[23] Technological advances have more than kept pace with the explosion in global population. Since 1948 world food production has surpassed population increases by about 1 percent a year.[24] Although global population has doubled since World War II, world grain production has tripled.

The dramatic increase in the availability of foodstuffs occurred without any appreciable global increase in land committed to agricultural uses over the last 30 years. Since 1950, in fact, 200 million acres of U.S. farmland have been retired as a result of the unprecedented glut of agricultural commodities on the world market.

Agricultural abundance has translated into improved health for even the poorest in the Third World. Whereas only 42 percent of all countries reported that average daily caloric consumption

---

[21]Julian Simon, *Population Matters* (New Brunswick, N.J.: Transaction Books, 1990), pp. 43–45.

[22]Moore, pp. 12, 16–19.

[23]Dennis Avery, "Sustainable and Beneficial Agriculture," Paper presented at Cato Institute conference on "Global Environmental Crises: Science or Politics?" June 1991, p. 1.

[24]Osterfeld, p. 61.

reached 100 percent of recommended levels in the mid-1960s, 66 percent of all nations reported caloric intake at those levels by the mid-1980s, a 56 percent increase in less than 20 years. Fully 81 percent of the world's countries, including China and India, now report average caloric intake of at least 90 percent of recommended levels.[25]

Moreover, there is good reason to believe that the planet can feed tens of billions of people for many generations to come. Suitable agricultural land makes up 24 percent of the total ice-free landmass of the globe, well over twice the amount cultivated in recent decades and more than triple the acreage cultivated in any given year.[26] Moreover, a great deal of the world's cropland is underused or cultivated using low-yield technologies and practices similar to those used in this country in 1910. Obviously, agricultural productivity will skyrocket as high-yield technologies continue to advance throughout the developing world.

Yet even those expansive limits are not fixed. Agricultural history is largely defined as the transformation of land unsuited for cultivation into productive cropland. Nobel laureate Theodore Schultz observes that "the original soils of western Europe, except for the Po Valley and some parts of England and France, were in general very poor in quality. As farmland, these soils are now highly productive. A substantial part of the productivity of farmland is manmade by investments in land improvements."[27] Political economist David Osterfeld points out that "much of the American Midwest was forest and swampland. No account of arable land in, say, 1800 would have included it. Now, after it has been cleared and drained, it is among the most fertile lands in the world. And the elimination of the tsetse fly would open up to cultivation about 200 million hectares of African land, an area larger than the total cropland in the United States."[28] Productive farmland is not some sort of finite

[25]World Resources Institute, *World Resources 1987* (New York: Basic Books), pp. 252–53.

[26]Roger Revelle, "The World Supply of Agricultural Land," *The Resourceful Earth*, ed. Julian Simon and Herman Kahn (New York: Basil Blackwell, 1984), pp. 184–201.

[27]Theodore Schultz, in *Lectures in Agricultural Economics* (Washington: Economic Services Bicentennial Lecture Series Committee, 1977), pp. 16–17. Cited in De Gregori, p. 1254.

[28]Osterfeld, p. 66.

given; it is, instead, a function of agricultural skill and technology, two "resources" that have been expanding rapidly over the centuries and exponentially over the past 80 years.

Simply increasing the efficiency of water use in developing nations could provide enough advances in productivity to support a global population of 35 billion to 40 billion people, between seven and eight times the current population of the world.[29] And then there is the coming revolution in biotechnology, a science well on its way to producing crops that are able to resist drought, insects, disease, and salinity and thrive in the harshest soils and previously inhospitable environments. Because of the projected low costs of those new products, biotechnology will probably have its greatest impact in the developing world, enabling poor farmers to take full advantage of the agricultural revolution and to afford the relatively costly inputs required to make high-yield farming economical.

Although conservationists argue that accelerating soil erosion will make those productivity gains short-lived and illusory, the facts speak otherwise. Most of the world's worst soil erosion problems are the result, not of modern high-yield farming, but of attempts to use low-yield, traditional agricultural techniques on fragile soils.[30]

Studies by the U.S Department of Agriculture, the University of Minnesota's Soil Sciences Department, and economist Pierre Crosson of Resources for the Future all conclude that, at current erosion rates, heavily farmed soils in the United States might lose 3 to 10 percent of their inherent fertility over the next 100 years. Such small losses are sure to be more than offset by continued improvements in agricultural productivity even if no new conservation techniques are adopted. As Crosson noted:

> The success of the new [high-yield] technologies strongly suggests that erosion damage to soils in the main crop-producing regions of the country was not and is not as severe as is sometimes claimed. Soil scientists have acknowledged that even severely eroded soil can be restored to high productivity with investments of human skill and other resources, even though they may seem to forget this when

[29]Ibid., pp. 67, 83.
[30]Dennis Avery, *Global Food Progress 1991* (Indianapolis: Hudson Institute, 1991), pp. 78–79, 81, 224.

they make pronouncements about the erosion threat. Continuation of present rates of erosion throughout most of the next century would pose no serious threat to the productivity of the nation's soils.[31]

Timber Products

The fear that mankind is rapidly deforesting the globe has arisen on and off ever since the 18th century. Yet precious little evidence, other than anecdotes, has ever been advanced to support that lamentably widespread belief.

According to the most recent UN data, the most authoritive figures at our disposal, world forestland today covers 4 billion hectares, more than 30 percent of the total global land area. That figure has not changed appreciably since 1950, even in the midst of the population explosion, massive economic growth, and urbanization of the globe. Today forestland occupies about one-third of the United States, and that proportion has been expanding steadily for over 70 years. According to the U.S. Forest Service, 22 million new cubic feet of wood are grown annually in the United States, while only 16.5 million cubic feet are harvested. Net annual growth exceeds annual harvests in commercial forests by 27 percent.

Since 1920 U.S. forests have expanded by 57 percent, a remarkable fact given that during the same period the U.S. population doubled, the economy grew by a factor of 6, and per capita output increased by a factor of 3. Forestland has increased by 27 percent since 1952.[32] Although demand for wood products today is at an all-time high, the United States is still able not only to meet demand with currently available timber stock but to continue adding to forest reserves. In fact, there is only one-third less forestland in the United States today than there was in the 1600s when European settlers first encountered it.

An example of the striking increase in U.S. forest reserves is found in New England, where logging thrived in the 19th century. From the mid-1800s to 1980 the amount of land covered by forests

---

[31]Pierre Crosson, "Cropland and Soils: Past Performance and Policy Challenges," in *America's Renewable Resources*, ed. Kenneth Frederick and Roger Sedjo (Washington: Resources for the Future, 1991), pp. 190, 191, 196.

[32]Roger Sedjo, "Forest Resources: Resilient and Serviceable," in *America's Renewable Resources*, pp. 81–115.

increased from 74 to 90 percent in Maine; from 50 to 86 percent in New Hampshire; from 35 to 76 percent in Vermont; and from 35 to 59 percent in Connecticut, Massachusetts, and Rhode Island.[33]

That growth in forest reserves is reflected in the price of various wood commodities. The real prices of lumber and paper have fallen by 10 and 25 percent, respectively, since 1980. When indexed to wages, lumber prices today are one-third those of 1950, one-sixth those of 1900, and one-tenth those of 1800. Likewise, the cost of paper when indexed to wages is less than half that of 1930.[34]

The increased supply of wood has not come at the expense of rugged, pristine nature preserves. From 1980 to 1989 land classified as wilderness increased by 29 percent. Although environmentalists argue that the second-growth forests of today are ecologically inferior to the old-growth forests that the colonists encountered three centuries ago, Roger Sedjo of Resources for the Future points out:

> In the United States, the forest estate consists of a wide array of forest types and ages. In this regard it is not too different from the mosaic of forest types present during the time of early settlement. The species found in these stands are usually similar to those that would have existed there at settlement. Even in most forest plantations in the United States the species composition mimics the forest that would have naturally regenerated there. By most criteria, U.S. forests are in excellent condition. U.S. forests have shown the potential to deliver large volumes of wood on a sustainable level into the indefinite future.[35]

Market Liberalism and Resource Creation

So how does one explain the unprecedented abundance of natural resources today, an explosion of plenty in the very midst of record demands for resources?

One school of thought holds that the world's economic growth since World War II is historically atypical and that our half century of prosperity since then is the result of "a fortuitous confluence of

---

[33]John Barrett, "The Northeast Region," in *Regional Silviculture of the United States,* ed. John Barrett (New York: John Wiley & Sons, 1980), pp. 25, 37. Cited in Sedjo, p. 109.

[34]Moore, pp. 21–24.

[35]Sedjo, pp. 111–14.

favorable events" that cannot be counted on again. The revolution of high-yield agriculture, favorable weather, massive petroleum finds in the Middle East, the exploitation of the last hectares of virgin land, and countless other events are one-time gains that have shielded man from the true reality of his condition. As those events run their course in the 1990s, we are due for a jarring return to global reality.

Yet declining resource scarcity is a long-term trend, evident from the beginning of human society. Without exception, every material resource imaginable has become more abundant during the course of civilization. Whether measured in terms of proven reserves or prices relative to income, a graph of the relative abundance of virtually every resource looks like the population graphs we have seen so many times before: long-term, steady growth in resources with an exploding, exponential increase in resource availability over the last 200 years. The record of the last 50 years, then, is not atypical but perfectly consistent with the observable data on increasing resource availability since the beginning of time.

Another view holds that we are a world in "overshoot," living off our resource capital and not our income, irresponsibly and rapidly drawing down precious stocks of resources that have taken eons for the earth to accumulate. The authors of *Beyond the Limits* argue that "overshoot comes from delays in feedback—from the fact that decisionmakers in the system do not get, or believe, or act upon information that limits have been exceeded until long after they have been exceeded. Overshoot is only possible because there are accumulated resource stocks that can be drawn down."[36]

That argument, however, is in direct contradiction to every possible measurement of resource scarcity and the march of recorded history. If overshoot occurs when we use resources faster than they are created by nature, then the world has been in accelerating "overshoot" for the last 10,000 years, or ever since the development of agriculture. Moreover, our best "feedback" on scarcity—market prices—tells us that resources are expanding, not contracting (Table 2).

Virtually every year since 1800 a book, study, report, or commission has pronounced the imminent depletion of this or that resource

---

[36]Meadows, Meadows, and Randers, p. 137.

Table 21.2
RESOURCE PRICES INDEXED TO WAGES, 1950–90
(RELATIVE TO 1990 BASELINE)

Resource	1950	1960	1970	1980	1990	Change (%) 1950–90
Food[a]	386	210	145	161	100	−74
Lumber	170	114	95	126	100	−41
Paper	139	121	97	104	100	−28
Minerals[b]	194	147	179	217	100	−48
Energy[c]	184	126	74	138	100	−46

SOURCE: Moore, pp. 18–19, 23, 30–31, 40.

[a]Includes barley, broilers, carrots, cattle, corn, cotton, eggs, milk, oats, oranges, rice, sorghum, soybeans, wheat, and wool.

[b]Includes aluminum, antimony, copper, lead, magnesium, manganese, mercury, nickel, platinum, silver, tin, tungsten, and zinc.

[c]Includes coal, electricity, natural gas, and oil.

on the basis of indices that examine current trends and known reserves. Yet every one of those pronouncements has been not only wrong but spectacularly and embarrassingly wrong.[37] More efficient technologies that require fewer resource inputs, advanced extraction and harvesting technologies that allow far greater access to resource deposits, and material substitutions that replace scarce resources with far more abundant resources are just a few of the routine advances that mark the entire march of human civilization.

The fundamental flaw in the conservationist paradigm is the premise that global resources are created by nature and thus fixed

---

[37]As noted by Nobel laureate Friedrich Hayek, "Industrial development would have been greatly retarded if sixty or eighty years ago the warning of the conservationists about the threatened exhaustion of the supply of coal had been heeded; and the internal combustion engine would never have revolutionized transport if its use had been limited to the known supplies of oil . . . though it is important that on all these matters the opinion of the experts about the physical facts should be heard, the result in most instances would have been very detrimental if they had had the power to enforce their views on policy." Friedrich Hayek, *The Constitution of Liberty* (Chicago: University of Chicago Press, 1960), pp. 369–70.

See further James Bennett and Thomas DiLorenzo, *Official Lies* (Alexandria, Va.: Groom Books, 1992), pp. 132–56; Ronald Bailey, *ECO-SCAM: The False Prophets of Ecological Apocalypse* (New York: St. Martin's, 1993), pp. 40–78; and Osterfeld, pp. 85, 103.

and finite. Not a single material resource has ever been created by "nature." Human knowledge and technology are the resources that turn "stuff" into useful commodities. What we think of as resources are actually certain sets of capabilities. As De Gregori points out, "Humans are the active agent, having ideas that they use to transform the environment for human purposes. . . . Resources are not fixed and finite because they are not natural. They are a product of human ingenuity resulting from the creation of technology and science."[38]

Two hundred years ago petroleum was just a useless ooze that actually drove down property values. Human creative endeavor, knowledge, and technology, however, turned the ooze into a valuable resource. Likewise, sand has never been considered a resource, but the revolution in telecommunications and man's expanding technological capacity have turned sand into a valuable commodity—the basic resource from which computer chips and fiber-optic telecommunication devices are made.

"Since resources are a function of human knowledge, and since our stock of knowledge has increased over time, it should come as no surprise that the stock of physical resources has also been expanding," observes Osterfeld.[39]

The free, competitive marketplace is the most efficient engine of resource creation and conservation because it is the most explosive engine for intellectual and technological advance. Technological advance, the heart of resource creation, depends heavily on the competitive free exchange of ideas, entrepreneurial activity, investments in capital and labor, and a profit mechanism.

The size of our resource pie is determined not by nature but by the social and economic institutions that set the boundaries of technological advance. Closed societies and economies under the heavy hand of central economic planners are doomed to live within the confines of dwindling resource bases and eventually experience the very collapse feared by the conservationists. Liberal societies, built on free markets and open inquiry, create resources and expand the possibilities of mankind.

[38]De Gregori, pp. 1243, 1247.
[39]Osterfeld, p. 99.

22. Why Health and Safety Are Products of Competitive Institutions

Aaron Wildavsky

Why is richer safer, if I may presume upon old titles, and wealthier healthier?[1] For one thing, health and safety are collective products. No one does it alone. No one. The most physically fit person who follows all the admonitions for the healthy life might not last a minute in the former Yugoslavia. Kings and nobles in other times and poorer societies lived notoriously uncomfortable and unhealthy lives, even though they had more than anyone else. But those examples are too dramatic. In some neighborhoods, it is reasonably safe to go to and return from work, and to walk the streets; in other neighborhoods, it is not. The chance of being run over by irresponsible drivers or inhaling fumes from untuned cars varies greatly from place to place. We already know that by far the most dangerous thing a man can do is stay unmarried, and though women are better able to live alone, unmarried women have far worse health than married women. (It is possible that long-lived same-sex liaisons would show the same results, not least because of the reduction in the probability of getting AIDS, but I have not seen relevant research.) The point is that if safety depends on others as well as on ourselves, the quality of the institutions that relate us to those others matters.

Safety Is a Social Phenomenon

The care we give and get goes to and comes from others. The resources we use to promote and protect ourselves involve others. Indeed, our health and safety are far more a product of collective construction than of what any single individual can do. Nowhere

---

[1] Aaron Wildavsky, "Richer Is Safer," *Public Interest* 60 (Summer 1980): 23–29; and Aaron Wildavsky, "Wealthier Is Healthier," *Regulation*, January–February 1980, pp. 10–12, 55.

is that more evident than in natural disasters. What happens may be a product of natural forces, but the human response depends on societal capacities. Hurricanes and tidal surges of great magnitude recently struck the American states of Florida, Louisiana, and Hawaii. Although there were large losses of property, reflecting the wealth of those areas, little or no life was lost. That is remarkable. Soon thereafter, huge floods struck Pakistan. Thousands died. Why the difference?

It is hardly that Americans care more about each other or, more to the point, are better able to figure out and carry out individual strategies of preservation. True, Americans are considerably richer, and a few with the highest incomes might be able to fly out of harm's way, but the vast majority, even if they take recommended precautions, such as boarding their windows and stocking food and water, are limited in how far they alone can protect themselves. It is not wealth per se but what it stands for that helps secure safety—early warning; better (not perfect) housing construction; better transportation; more of everything, including organizational capacity and expertise, to ward off the worst and provide assistance where it is needed. There is chaos too, but comparatively speaking, the rich have the resources to move, as we used to say, the fastest with the mostest. It is the quality of our institutions, our ways of relating to each other, that improves health and safety in society as a whole.

Health and safety are functions of genetic inheritance, personal habits, and the accumulation of flexible social resources that can be used to ameliorate difficulties as they arise. Genetic inheritance is, of course, personal, and there is not much we can do about it, although biotechnology is beginning to open up prospects of ameliorating the worst defects. Good personal habits, which may be summed up as moderation in eating, drinking, sleeping, and worrying, but no smoking, are known to exert great influence on health. The poor person with good personal habits is likely to be healthier than the rich person who overeats or eats irregularly, sleeps fitfully, worries too much, and otherwise leads a disorderly life. (Yet it is easier for rich people to lead regular lives.) The accumulation of societal resources that fills in the cracks of individual differences in genetic inheritance and personal habits has produced the consistent decline in morbidity and mortality that has occurred everywhere in the Western world. What is it, I ask, along with countless others, that nations with the healthiest people have in common? The answers, known to everyone but not heretofore directed to health and safety, are democracy, science, and capitalism. There is no getting away from it: if you want your children to be healthier, see that they are born in scientifically strong capitalist democracies. Because health and safety are part and parcel of the standard of living in a given society (another way of saying that richer is safer), to become safer a society also has to become richer. Why, I ask again, do wealth and health go together? What is the institutional connection among wealth, health, democracy, capitalism, and science?

If we think of science as competition in ideas, democracy as competition for office, and capitalism as competition for resources, it is clear that institutions that facilitate competition are the key. The common experience of collapsed command economies shows us that uncompetitive institutions can make people not only poor but sick; the indicators of health and safety for command economies are much worse than those for capitalist democracies. Yet the ex-communist countries deliberately set out to improve public health, whereas science, democracy, and capitalism are institutional processes by which individuals and groups compete, not to achieve any particular purpose such as enhancing safety and health, but to improve themselves.

Why Markets Are Safer Than Hierarchies

If capitalism is bad for our health, how can we support it? How do we face ourselves in the mirror, knowing that in our insatiable desire for profit we have eaten out the substance of numerous unsuspecting individuals, despoiled the natural environment, and corrupted the moral climate?

That would not necessarily be an important question if there were not a worldwide movement attempting to convict corporate capitalism of causing cancer. If Joe and Paul have grocery stores on opposite sides of the street, and if Joe wants to drive Paul out of business, do you suppose he can convince residents of the neighborhood that if they buy from Paul they will get cancer?

In America you can hardly pick up a newspaper without finding numerous discussions of insidious external contamination, coming

381

from industry and technology, that poisons people. Nuclear waste is not the only hazard fingered; the foods we eat, the air we breathe, the water we drink, and the land we live on are also suspect. Do you suppose a civilization would survive if it could not abide its own waste products? What better way to counter despised social forms than by showing that they are unhealthy?

What are the facts? People in capitalist democracies are the richest, longest lived, and healthiest people in world history. In the last decade, life expectancy has increased substantially. Accident rates are down, indices of health are up. Even cancer rates are declining: If you will allow me to kill off everybody at age 35, the age at which people used to die, then I would immediately reduce cancer rates, since cancer is a disease of old age. If we control for age and cigarette smoking, the incidence of most forms of cancer is down. It would make more sense for us to worry about how we are going to live as we all get old and fall all over one another, as happens in the marvelous science fiction movie *Soylent Green.* Longevity is also associated with competitive institutions.

If we are living longer rather than shorter lives, how do we explain the anomaly of the immense concern about danger, which is exactly contrary to the evidence? If you believe that social relations should be egalitarian, you want to ream out the economic markets that support the opposing way of life. If you are interested in the facts, you accept certain conclusions that were the staples of every social reformer of the 1930s and 1940s—for one, richer is safer. If you rank the countries of the world, is it the poorer people or the richer who are healthier and whose environment is better?

Why is it, then, that through all sorts of regulatory and risk-aversion measures we want to make ourselves poorer in order to make ourselves healthier? Behind risk aversion is the idea that if you slow down technological development, you make people healthier. Three reasons are usually given to explain why capitalism is bad for our health: risks are hidden—we are not told about them; involuntary—we would not accept them if we knew them; and irreversible—there is no recovery. In 30 years our health will deteriorate. What philosopher, I ask, said the opposite, namely, that the benefits are hidden—you don't know you're getting them; involuntary—you get them whether you want them or not; and irreversible—if you play by the rules of the game, you always get

382

the same result. Of course, that is a rather abstract version of Adam Smith's *Wealth of Nations*. Which paradigm is correct? Do you get healthier by making yourself poorer or by making yourself richer?

Amazingly enough, I cannot find a single article in the economic literature, including literature by libertarians and objectivists, on the relation between capitalism and health and safety. It seems to be a topic not covered; either the relation is assumed or it is totally neglected. I see in a few newspapers that when asked about the "richer is safer" thesis, economists say it is part of their mainstream. Good. But there is no literature that explains why, as industrial capitalism developed, people got healthier.

We know that as wealth diffused in society, people became more valuable and there were more resources with which to do things such as invest in science and undertake public health measures. As individuals gained greater command over resources, they were able to purchase more of their own health. I do not mean merely that they were able to purchase more medical care, which has rapidly diminishing returns, but vacations, baby sitters, labor-saving devices, beauty aids, anything that an individual believes will enhance health. Because no central authority can know as well as individuals what will make them feel better, the diffusion of wealth is as important as its accumulation. Wealth, it should be understood, is a proxy for the capacity to accumulate other flexible resources—energy, knowledge, communications, organizational capacity—that enable individuals to do for themselves. We also know that the spread of technological innovation led to an agricultural revolution, which provided a lot more calories to go around, and calories (up to a point, of course) are good for your health, as you discover when you are hungry. The agricultural innovators were not necessarily motivated by the desire to do good for mankind. They had the usual sorts of motivations—lust for power, greed, envy—as well as that of meeting other people's needs. Thus, we can begin to sketch out a little bit of a theory of how capitalism, by indirectly spurring production and wealth, created opportunities for better health.

Here we must go back to the Smithean premise and ask, How did we became healthier, since that was not anyone's avowed intention? Indeed, what stops capitalists from making people sicker to make money? On a systemic level, we understand: if you kill your customers, they will not buy from you again. That gives us a moment of pause, but not too great a moment. We also know that it is not worthwhile making people sick. They sue you. And those who do make people sick do not do as well as others who keep them healthy.

People are harmed by technology; there is no denying it. The use of coal to generate electricity, for example, is known to have caused millions of deaths over the years. Practically everything that is good—love, children, food, friendship—also harms us. The axiom of connectedness[2] states that the good and the bad effects of virtually everything are intertwined; you can't have one without the other. The purpose of institutions, insofar as they have a common purpose, is to develop processes that provide more of what is desired and less of what is not. I call this the Los Angeles problem: if you go there for the sunshine, you also have to take some of the smog. Life comes wrapped in bundles of good and bad; what is interesting is how one grows in comparison with the other.

One possibility is that, as alternative products are tried, some turn out to be just as profitable as others and a little better for your health. And over time they get selected out. A clue is provided in Schumpeter's notion of creative destruction. As capitalism develops, it both extinguishes forms that used to exist and creates new forms. If the major problem is that life is too complicated to anticipate and therefore protect against evils, we need to be in a position to cope with the unexpected. Two things follow. One is that the old forms of variety that were good for their time are not good for this time; if they were good for this time, the unexpected would not occur. The other is that, in order to deal with future ills of a magnitude and kind we know nothing about, we need to be able to take numerous, diverse, and independent forms of action.

This, I believe, is exactly what capitalism does. It makes room for the new by extinguishing some of the old; it creates all sorts of variety that cannot be justified entirely on the basis of its contribution to some specific good. Nothing that we now know we need copes with the unexpected, because it is precisely our inability to anticipate the unexpected that is the difficulty.

---

[2]For the full argument, see Aaron Wildavsky, *Searching for Safety* (New Brunswick, N.J.: Transaction Books, 1988).

How, I ask, might we sample the truly unexpected? The problem is not merely that we do not know the probability of events' occurring, but that we may be surprised (think of AIDS) by wholly new classes of events. Should governments conduct studies of the unknown? No doubt. But records of predictions are poor. However, the existence of independent centers of decision, each, within broad limits, allowed to go its own way, is a partial solution to the problem. For each organization (or firm) samples the environment differently. Absence of central direction, allowance for peculiarity and failure, and incentives to act differently so as to profit from innovation make possible a broader scan of the potential universe, albeit not by a single decisionmaker at a single time.

Under competitive capitalism (excuse the redundancy), anticipation is decentralized. Not everyone, by any means, anticipates the same sort of thing. The probability of being both exactly right and precisely wrong declines. But the likelihood that someone will anticipate the unexpected and learn to cope with it is much greater than under central control.

Risk-Risk or Health-Health Analysis

If health and safety are indeed functions of a society's standard of living, it follows that seeking safety without considering how it is produced is counterproductive. Instead, every proposal or activity designed to improve health and safety should be subject to a risk-risk (sometimes called a health-health) analysis. When people say that you care only about money whereas they care only about health, the contest is unequal. Instead, invoking the richer-is-safer thesis, I have proposed comparing health to health by going risk to risk—comparing the consequences for both health and safety of government regulations with the consequences in the absence of such regulation. There are those, to be sure, who believe that declarations of love are forever; that if you promise safety, safety is what you get; and that only noble feelings are aroused in the name of liberty. But if there are still people from Missouri who like to be shown, a risk-risk analysis is appropriate. It requires two steps: (1) From whatever health and safety benefits are postulated, *subtract the harm done, if any, by the remedial effort.* All construction and destruction, transportation, dirt moving, ladder climbing involves a low but palpable level of danger. To alter the adage slightly, there is no such thing (recall the axiom of connectedness) as riskless health and safety. (2) *Subtract again the adverse consequences* for health and safety of *lowering the standard of living*.

Rather than repeat what I have said elsewhere, I would like to quote directly from Ralph Keeney's quantitative model of "Mortality Risks Induced by Economic Expenditure."

> Existing evidence shows that lower incomes are associated with higher mortality risks. . . . A model is developed for estimating the number of fatalities possibly induced by economic expenditures. . . . These results suggest that some expensive regulations and programs intended to save lives may actually lead to increased fatalities. . . . Health and safety are improved via social mechanisms, such as education and "upgraded" associations, both of which are positively influenced by more disposable income, as well as directly by individual actions. . . . A general increase in the standard of living influences societal structure. A wealthier society leads to the development of a better and more diverse medical research establishment, to larger markets to stimulate creation of safer products, to an infrastructure of health clubs and many opportunities for exercise, and to the societal resilience to rapidly and efficiently attack new unforeseen problems threatening our collective health and safety. . . . For example, using Kitigawa and Hauser data and allocating costs proportional to income, there is an induced fatality for every $7.25 million spent if all the assumptions in the model are felt to be reasonable. However, again, it is important to stress that calculations in this paper are illustrative only.[3]

The principle, not the precise number that emerges from Keeney's risk-risk model, is the important thing: spending tax resources to

---

[3]Ralph L. Keeney, "Mortality Risks Induced by Economic Expenditures," *Risk Analysis* 10 (December 1990): 147–48, 155. A number of newspaper articles and a report of the General Accounting Office ("Risk-Risk Analysis: OMB's Review of a Proposed OSHA Rule," July 1992) criticize Keeney's model on the grounds that it is not conclusive. Of course not. It is preliminary, being the first of its kind, and exploratory. The GAO report especially is misleading in that it evaluates Keeney's model against an absolute standard. Compared with the models the Occupational Health and Safety Administration uses, it stands up very well. A model to test regulations should be judged by the models used to regulate. But that is another story.

improve safety may be counterproductive if the physical effort and cost involved do more harm to health than the good intended.

Conclusion

All of us like to think we are helping, not harming, others. The so-called helping professions are aptly named, not because mental health practitioners never do harm, but to accentuate their good intentions. For instance, I do not doubt the good intentions of the people employed by the Occupational Safety and Health Administration. They are persuaded that their mission is to improve safety, and their disbelief and anger when some fool professor (perhaps that's an oxymoron) tells them that they may be doing harm is understandable. But their consternation is unwise. All of us must take the risk that what we do may have unintended and harmful consequences. Just as it is the temptation of the powerful to abuse their power, so it is the temptation of safety advocates to believe that whatever they do can do no harm. Life teaches otherwise. If I am not committing lese majesty by suggesting that expenditures designed to reduce risk may actually increase it, then research on the conditions under which richer is safer should be undertaken.

Health and safety, to reiterate, are collective achievements. Immense quantities of evidence correlate both with competitive capitalist institutions, and there are intriguing rationales that suggest the mechanisms through which competition improves health and safety. When we know enough and are rich enough, we should adopt protective public health measures. But that degree of knowledge is relatively rare. When we are partially or wholly ignorant of what lies in store, we should not rely on futile anticipation but rather on competition to separate the harmful from the healthful.

23. A Free-Market Environmental Vision

Fred L. Smith, Jr., and Kent Jeffreys

There is one environmental vision, and only one, that is compatible with all other human values. Only a vision that recognizes and responds to universal human traits will be successful in the long run. Only a vision that accounts for the reality of individual self-interest can be applied in the real world. Only a vision that sees value in *human* diversity as well as ecological diversity can capture the entrepreneurial potential of the human race. That vision is free-market environmentalism.

America has long been known as a nation where private homes and backyards are beautiful but politically managed parks and streets are a mess. For some the answer is to raise taxes to better support the "cash starved" public sector. For others the answer will be found in stringent regulations covering every aspect of modern society. A better approach would be to discover what makes homes and backyards beautiful and apply the lessons to problem areas. Rather than bureaucratize the environment, we should privatize our efforts to protect the environment. In other words, environmental values must be fully integrated into the free-enterprise system. One might say that trees should not have legal standing, but behind every tree should stand a private steward, a private owner, willing and legally enabled to protect that resource.

This vision of an America engaged in creative ecological privatization may be radical, but it offers great promise of lasting success in dealing with the ever-changing circumstances of human interaction with the natural world. Not only is this vision applicable to environmental protection, it is compatible with the traditional American respect for individual liberty.

Myth vs. Reality

Current environmental policies reflect the false assumptions of the recent past: that the natural environment is benign, that the

389

economy can grow without using resources, that once mankind has touched a wilderness it is forever ruined, and that political actors can best protect environmental amenities. Of the many erroneous assumptions, the most widespread has been that stringent government regulations could eliminate pollution without significant economic cost. One result of basing policy on that myth has been the growth of special-interest environmental politics. Special-interest bees will always find the political honey, and the average citizen will usually get stung. For example, tremendous profits are available to corporations that capture the regulatory process and turn it into a barrier to competitors.[1]

For similar reasons, a strong incentive exists for environmental groups to find a crisis within each issue, from the nonexistent health risk to children from pesticide residues on vegetables to the greatly exaggerated effects of so-called acid rain on forests and lakes. By constantly claiming that the sky is falling, the environmentalist Chicken Littles have become geese that lay golden eggs. Contributions from philanthropic foundations and sincerely concerned individuals are used to purchase political power and to support massive bureaucratic empires. A mutually beneficial arrangement has been created among some industries and the environmental lobbying elite. Presiding over it all is the permanent political class.

Free-market environmentalism seeks to break that triangle by returning to the principles of self-government and self-reliance upon which America was founded. The free-market vision is based on a merger of individual responsibility with individual rights. Unfortunately, free-market proponents carry the burden of a widespread misunderstanding of the history of capitalism. The image of an uncaring, unresponsive, and ecologically destructive corporation is set against an enlightened and altruistic state that is seen as the protector of the environment. Capitalism, we are told, causes pollution.[2] Yet for all its problems, capitalism has created a Garden

---

[1]See, for example, *Environmental Politics: Public Costs, Private Rewards*, ed. Fred L. Smith, Jr., and Michael Greve (New York: Praeger, 1992).

[2]See, for example, Barry Commoner, *Making Peace with the Planet* (New York: Pantheon Books, 1990). For a rebuttal, see Thomas DiLorenzo, "Does Capitalism Cause Pollution?" Center for the Study of American Business, Washington University, St. Louis, August 1990.

of Eden in comparison with what the socialist economies of the former Soviet bloc created.

The reasons for the socialist failure in the ecological realm are the same as for socialism's economic disasters. Key aspects included the state ownership of resources, the bureaucratic decisionmaking processes, and the denial of private property rights (among other important liberties). The original (economic) socialists argued that people would be better off under socialism than they had been under the previous regime. Although history has proved the opposite to be true, many socialist economic tools are being promoted as the answer to America's environmental problems.

Market Socialism

Because today the victory of market freedom over state tyranny is a metaphor embraced by all, almost every environmental position is defended as being "market oriented." Unfortunately, the rhetoric does not reflect the reality. For example, the multi-billion-dollar Clean Air Act amendments of 1990 contain only a few, almost insignificant provisions that even touch on market-style arrangements for dealing with pollution. Yet those tiny concessions are eviscerated by simultaneous declarations to the effect that no property rights will arise from the operation of the act and that federal confiscation of the fruits of pollution-reducing investment is specifically permitted. That version of market socialism displays the same flaws detected by Ludwig von Mises and F. A. Hayek in their debate with the socialist economist Oskar Lange in the 1930s. Neither side argued that a Soviet-style economy could succeed, but Lange asserted that tradeable production quotas and state pricing systems could replicate market efficiencies. Although it is generally conceded that Hayek and von Mises won that particular debate, Lange's arguments still strike a responsive chord with government planners.

To be fair, ecological market socialists also have a vision. It bears various names, such as "sustainable development" or "ecological economics." Oddly enough, proponents of those approaches claim to seek the same goal as free-market environmentalism, that is, a reconciliation of man and nature. It is more likely, given their heavy reliance on state-controlled economies, that those approaches would result in greatly reduced economic performance, reduced standards of living, and, eventually, a political backlash. The recent UN-sponsored Earth Summit in Rio de Janeiro was a perfect example of how the advocates of the market-socialist approach are becoming more detached from the average citizen as they spend more and more of their time meeting and talking with one another at world-renowned resorts. Little was said in Rio about the real problems confronting the people of the world: unsafe drinking water, lack of respect for property rights, government distortion of markets for food and other commodities, and a "tragedy of the commons" in forests and oceans. Instead, world "leaders" shared a platform with Fidel Castro, who was welcomed as an honestly concerned ecologist.

Regardless of the nomenclature employed by the market socialists, the goal remains the same: to direct human behavior through state action. The justification of a centralized decisionmaking process is the assumption that individual humans will often make "wrong" choices, which will eventually create widespread ecological catastrophe. That argument more accurately applies to the governments of the world. Only governments possess the coercive force necessary to collect revenues for money-losing "development" schemes. Thus, capitalism has scarcely touched the great river systems of the world. Most major hydropower projects have been state sponsored. Even the pollution that flows into rivers has been the result of the state's neglect of its duty to defend private rights. Similarly, capitalists mostly ignored the tropical rain forests until state subsidies for clearing them were introduced. In fact, in those nations with secure property rights, capitalism plants far more trees than it cuts. The oceans' living marine resources are at risk precisely because governments deny private property rights to wildlife and fish. Those are not examples of the failure of existing markets; they are examples of the failure to allow markets to exist.

Despite its inherent limitations, market socialism remains (at least rhetorically) attractive to many because of its emotional appeal. The forces of "good" government will repel or punish the forces of "evil" polluters. Unfortunately, real life is rarely so conveniently black and white. Whenever reality is so clear-cut, free-market environmentalism detects, deters, and deals with polluters or other environmental transgressors at least as well as market socialism does. Free-market environmentalism, like capitalism itself, has not received full and open consideration in the policy arena, in large part because, in the political world, utopian lies are often more useful than realistic assessments of the truth. Absurd accusations leveled against free-market environmental approaches take on mythic proportions. One common claim, for example, is that without universal government controls, the poor would be buried under the toxic wastes generated by the wealthy. The irony of state monopolies' dumping municipal waste in the poorest areas is apparently lost on the adherents to that myth. The fact is that enforcing the property rights of the poor would do far more to protect them from pollution (or crime or any number of other problems) than has, for example, the federal government's $15 billion hazardous waste cleanup program known as Superfund. Superfund benefits lawyers, bureaucrats, Environmental Protection Agency contractors, and environmental lobbyists. Free-market environmentalism would empower the poor, not profit from—and then leave them in—their plight.

Using Children as Shields

Perhaps the most pernicious aspersion cast on capitalism is the claim that it will leave a desolate world as an inheritance for today's children. That assertion is breathtaking in its boldness. Any rational assessment of history would declare capitalism the savior of the world's children. Present, and future, generations have benefited, not merely in the material goods provided by capitalism, but in every category of health care and in quality of life. The only subtle aspect of the depleted-inheritance myth arises when its proponents occasionally admit that capitalism has improved the situation *too much*. World population is growing because far more children live to adulthood and bear offspring of their own. Eventually, it is claimed, capitalism will run out of "natural" resources to "deplete," and the whole system will come crashing down in cataclysmic fashion. That view is as inaccurate as it is apocalyptic. The most important "natural" resource is the human mind. As long as a liberal society exists, that resource is inexhaustible and can readily replace or find substitutes for all other "natural" resources.

The incredible ingenuity of the human mind is the solution, not the problem. Rather than shackle it, we must free it to create new miracles. A revealing moment occurred during the brief publicity of so-called cold fusion, which potentially offered limitless, inexpensive, clean energy to mankind. When asked about the prospects for future generations if cold fusion turned into a reality, ecological guru Paul Ehrlich said it would be "like giving a machine gun to an idiot child," and environmental radical Jeremy Rifkin claimed, "It's the worst thing that could happen to our planet."[3]

It is not much of an exaggeration to say that if human ingenuity were supplied with unlimited energy, *anything* would be possible. Little wonder, then, that the strongest push of the market socialists is against the increased production or use of energy. "We are running out of fossil fuels" has been a government refrain for over a century, yet supplies are more plentiful today than ever before, as Jerry Taylor points out in chapter 21. That inconvenient fact is rarely admitted in public. No matter, higher taxes will fulfill the prophecy by creating an artificial scarcity. Thus are our hopes and aspirations held hostage to environmental extremism.

Capitalism: Beyond Economics

Fortunately, free-market environmentalism is not limited to a sterile discussion of economic efficiency, contracts, or private property rights. In essence, free-market environmentalism is a reconciliation of man and nature. Rather than practice ecological apartheid—the separation of man from nature—political policy should rely on the natural incentives of private individuals cooperating through voluntary associations. Policy should empower millions of individuals to protect their environment, rather than thousands of bureaucrats to protect their political turf. It is beyond question that if the billions of individuals on the earth do not desire to protect it, the planet is beyond hope. No amount of coercion will save the planet if the average person truly wants to destroy it. The simple fact is that people everywhere desire a better life, and a better life includes a sound and safe environment.

The universal desire for a livable environment is often translated into an excuse for political action. Because everyone agrees that something should be done, for example, to reduce pollution, politicians feel justified in taking exclusive control of the issue. Yet granting a monopoly on pollution control to the state is like granting

[3]Both quotes are from Paul Ciotti, "Fear of Fusion: What if It Works?" *Los Angeles Times*, April 19, 1989.

government a monopoly on the delivery of mail. Like those of the government-controlled postal service, the environment-protecting services provided will generally be slow and unable to respond to changing circumstances. The costs will generally be high and extremely resistant to economizing reforms. Important niches will be either ignored or heavily subsidized. While a basic level of protection may be available under a state ecological monopoly, the rich diversity of the biosphere cannot be reflected in the dull mirror of a centralized political system.

In an important regard, today's moral opposition to pollution can be compared with the anti-slavery movement of the 19th century. The abolitionists were not opposed to work itself; they were fighting against involuntary servitude. Forced labor was considered a violation of an individual's rights, but freely contracted labor (even if it consisted of the identical tasks) was clearly legitimate. In similar fashion, pollution should be seen as the violation of an individual's right to be free from trespass rather than an evil in and of itself. The situation could be contemplated in advance and adequate contractual arrangements developed to avoid the *involuntary* introduction of a foreign substance to the property of another. As long as the parties to the agreement properly manage the by-products of their activities, there is no reason for the state to become a senior partner in every business. The goal of state intervention should be to prevent or correct coercion of innocent parties. Under appropriate circumstances, pollution may become a valid concern of the state, but it is illegitimate for the state to initially sanction pollution (or slavery) and then condemn capitalism as the source of the problem.

One of the major criticisms of free-market policies is that the private sector will never protect the diversity found in nature. In fact, there are numerous examples of successful private efforts to preserve environmental amenities, and they deserve far greater attention than they have received to date.[4] The argument against private-sector protection of natural diversity is also weakened by the fact that few governments have displayed an ability to balance their fiscal budgets. It would seem that balancing the ecology is an

[4]See, for example, Robert J. Smith, *15th Annual Report of the Council on Environmental Quality* (Washington: CEQ, 1984), chap. 9, "Special Report: The Public Benefits of Private Conservation."

even more complex undertaking. However, if the state performs its proper role and protects the private liberties we all hold individually, the environment will greatly benefit. Whenever one individual succeeds in protecting his property (with its associated environmental aspects), a precedent is established. Those precedents strongly influence the subsequent actions of others, even of parties unrelated to the original dispute. Relying on centralized government to address environmental problems may also establish precedents, but they are likely to be bad ones. Election year politics, budgetary constraints, conflicting agency agendas, special-interest influences, and political selection of priorities all work to make centralized environmental policy ineffective.

Perhaps the most significant obstacle to the adoption of alternatives to centralized control over the environment is a widely held, if greatly exaggerated, fear of impending ecological catastrophe. In a crisis, real or perceived, people have a natural tendency to demand emergency accommodations. As mentioned earlier, preying upon the natural concern that parents have for their children has become a major preoccupation of the environmental movement in recent years, from the Alar-treated apple hoax to the end-of-the-world global-warming fantasies. In each case, the concern is not so much for the present as it is for some indeterminate future. Because it is extremely difficult to refute vague assertions of far-off disaster, new panics can be manufactured much faster than old ones can be laid to rest. The result is a layer cake of half-baked state policies made according to a market-socialist recipe.

Popular myths are perpetuated by many who know better, and free-market environmentalists must continue to rebut those science fiction scenarios. Widespread concern for the environment is being used to move large segments of the population to action. If that action is limited to the voting booth, casting a ballot for the "greenest" candidate, little more than market socialism can be expected to result. But if the same people were encouraged to accept responsibility for their own backyards, a tremendous number of diverse improvements could be made. Even if it could be shown that a flood of biblical proportions was likely, we should avoid building a huge state "ark" to shelter politically preferred environmental amenities. Instead, America should become a land of millions of small arks, each tended by individuals or voluntary organizations and thus better able to preserve and protect the diversity of the natural world.

For public agencies to deal with the full range of ecological niches and changing circumstances found in nature, constant fine-tuning of the bureaucratic mechanism is needed, yet bureaucracies are notoriously difficult to fine tune. In contrast, free markets are naturally self-correcting and every transaction is an act of fine-tuning. Unfortunately, because of the prevalent myths, the actual results of capitalism are compared with the stated intentions of government policies. The risks to future generations arise not from exposure *to* capitalism but from exclusion *from* it.

Property Rights

Free-market environmentalism, like capitalism itself, is dependent on private property rights. Those rights must be well defined, well defended, and voluntarily transferable. When those prerequisites exist, competitive capitalism becomes a remarkable efficiency generator. The desire for profit leads directly to the elimination of waste. Pollution is generally some form of waste, but even if pollution were unavoidable in certain manufacturing processes, strongly enforced property rights would force polluters to either clean up or close shop. By definition, pollution is a trespass against someone's property or person. If the trespass is so minor that it creates no impact or inconvenience for the property owner, it will normally be tolerated, even under common law rules. Today's pollution dilemma is the result of what is essentially a universal "easement" granted by the state to polluters, even producers of significant and damaging pollution. The debate now revolves around how best to gradually restore their original right (to be free of the trespass of pollution) to citizens. The first question that should be asked is not, Why does capitalism destroy the environment? It is, Why isn't everything already polluted or destroyed? The answer is that the same private property rights that form the basis for capitalism also stand as a bulwark against environmental degradation.

It should be remembered that property rights are basically a voluntary ordering system for resources in a human society. Whenever private property rights have been respected within a society, the ecological outcome has been superior to that under state ownership of resources. Even vaunted state "successes," such as Yellowstone National Park, are rarely as successful as claimed. Consider that state policies led directly to the disastrous forest fires of 1988 and the quiet devastation of continuing management practices.[5]

In contrast, the successes of capitalism are so ubiquitous and taken for granted that they are rarely acknowledged. Efficiencies and improvements in resource use, dramatic increases in life spans and living standards, and the vast private wealth that undergirds the massive governmental structure are key examples. Unfortunately, many of the accomplishments of capitalism are touted as the results of state manipulation of the economy. Failure to recognize the primary importance of capitalism is not of interest only to historians. Unless it is understood that capitalism must come first, other nations may adopt American-style environmental policies—with disastrous consequences. Some, especially the nations of Eastern Europe, are already being encouraged to do so. Yet the U.S. approach to environmental policy cannot possibly be exported to most countries. It relies on legions of experienced management personnel and tremendous amounts of capital to meet the high costs of the mandated technologies. In addition, a highly trained and fairly honest bureaucracy must be in place. Watchdogging the entire apparatus are nongovernmental organizations, especially environmental lobbying groups and the print and broadcast media. If that is to be the initial paradigm for the developing countries, they may have to wait decades to deal successfully with ecological questions. However, they are unlikely to wait that long before they implement environmental programs. Thus, it is vitally important that accurate information and workable solutions, tailored to local conditions, be made available to policymakers. The current sense of urgency created by the constant barrage of environmental scare stories is likely to produce the same types of inappropriate policies across the globe that it has here at home.

Risks

The fact is that most of the urgency imparted to environmental policy is unnecessary. Where there is a serious problem, a chemical

---

[5]For a discussion of the general failure of federal policies in Yellowstone, see *The Yellowstone Primer: Land and Resource Management in the Greater Yellowstone Ecosystem*, ed. John A. Baden and Donald Leal (San Francisco: Pacific Research Institute, 1990). See also Alston Chase, *Playing God in Yellowstone: The Destruction of America's First National Park* (Boston: Atlantic Monthly Press, 1986).

spill, for example, there really is no debate over whether a problem exists. However, environmental policy today has shifted its focus from risks with immediate and measurable impacts to those with small (if any) impacts that are, at the very least, far off in the future.

Bureaucrats and their political bosses have powerful incentives to regulate highly visible or publicized risks, even when few individuals are actually exposed to the risk and the costs of regulation are high. Such regulation often results in shifting greater risks to unseen, or unpublicized, segments of society. Society as a whole is no better off; generally, it is worse off.

Many people are enticed (or even required) to dedicate excessive resources to risk avoidance because of the fashion in which the options are presented. If the choice is between saving a life and spending money, almost everyone would vote to save the life. Yet the truth, in many cases, is that focusing too many resources on a small risk factor necessarily reduces other, equally important risk-avoidance efforts. Thus, the real choice is between reducing *this* risk or reducing *that* risk. Lives may be at stake on each side of the equation, as Aaron Wildavsky points out in chapter 22.

Furthermore, in some situations, the only lives at stake are those put at risk by the environmental policy itself. The anti-asbestos hysteria whipped up by assertions that a single asbestos fiber could cause lung cancer led to many unnecessary and even dangerous asbestos removal efforts. Recently, a federal court declared that the fuel efficiency requirement for automobiles was directly related to increased highway injuries and fatalities because it resulted in the production of smaller, lighter vehicles that are inherently less safe than larger, heavier models.[6] In such situations, individuals have a paramount right to make critical personal choices for themselves and their families.

Conclusion

We have seen that pollution is not a failure of markets but a failure of government to permit private individuals to protect their property and persons against trespass. Free-market environmentalism offers a solution to the problem. Also, when government

[6]*Competitive Enterprise Institute v. National Highway Traffic Safety Administration,* 956 F.2d 321 (D.C. Cir. 1992).

imposes a single risk standard on society in general, many individuals in particular may be harmed. Again, free-market environmentalism would enable individuals to assume (or reject) certain risks without imposing additional risks on other individuals.

Some argue that free-market environmentalism entails excessive transaction costs, that is, the costs of time and resources dedicated to negotiating specific arrangements between parties. Therefore, it is claimed, government should step in and impose uniform standards. Efficiency is an important consideration, especially when costs are being imposed against the will of the people who will bear them. However, efficiency is not the only consideration. The best example may be the court system, which is anything but efficient. Society recognizes that human liberty is an overriding concern and, therefore, accepts lowered efficiency in order to preserve a greater good. Some environmentalists have tried to raise a similar argument with the claim that the intrinsic value of an ecological asset can override the liberty of the individual. That argument is a dangerous weapon to place in the hands of any state, for it is as likely to be abused as it is to be applied carefully. Fortunately, that line of thinking is inappropriate in light of the fact that modern technologies are constantly reducing the transaction costs involved in negotiating, monitoring, and enforcing environmental arrangements.

If free-market environmentalism is to be widely accepted, it must occupy the moral high ground. To a certain degree it has already done so, although often by default on the part of its detractors. However, merely paying lip service to the efficiency of markets is not enough. Free-market environmentalists must strive to demonstrate the superiority of voluntary markets in a host of ecological niches. Because most of the threatened resources, from wildlife to wetlands, from airsheds to oceans, are held and managed by political bureaucracies, they remain at risk. It will be necessary to move more of those resources, along with the direct responsibilities of stewardship, into private hands before clear-cut examples become commonplace.

Some environmentalists see limits to free markets at every turn. Yet those same individuals see no limits to government. Past environmental policies have been designed as if politically directed resources automatically become unlimited. Those environmentalists' excessive faith in government is as unwarranted as their visceral opposition to private ownership of resources. The free-market environmental vision does not purport to eliminate the state (or state involvement); it merely limits it to an appropriate role.

America needs to take several steps to develop an effective and sustainable environmental policy. First and foremost, Congress and the new administration should begin to restore private property rights in and to environmental resources. Critical ecological amenities should be removed from public hands and conserved through private stewardship arrangements. The details will vary among, and even within, resources. For example, one end of a coral reef might be managed by recreational fishermen while another portion was managed by a diving club. Particular stretches of rivers might be leased to fishing clubs while tracts of forest could be owned by hiking, hunting, or camping organizations. Any harm to the rivers or forests from external forces could be dealt with through contractual obligations and, if necessary, tort law.

Although strong incentives to conserve resources will be generated through private ownership, it is also important to eliminate perverse incentives. The federal government provides subsidies to many activities through direct transfers as well as through the provision of free or below-cost access. For example, recreational activities in the national forests and parks are heavily subsidized; most users pay low (or no) fees. Such subsidies encourage people to "consume" more of those public resources than they would be likely to in a market system. In addition, subsidies for favored providers of environmental amenities tend to squeeze out private alternatives. Other well-known subsidies that can unintentionally degrade the environment include agricultural subsidies, grazing subsidies, and water and hydropower project subsidies, among others. Unfortunately, the political process finds it almost impossible to deal honestly with the issue of subsidies. Only free markets are able to assess the full costs of resource use. Until property rights–based policies are instituted, environmental issues—from waste disposal to wetlands protection—will be poorly managed.

For most Americans, environmentalism is an important value, but it is not the only one. Jobs, housing, health care, education, national defense, and other values make demands on the resources

401

of the individuals who constitute society. Like it or not, ecological purity must compete with other objectives. Therefore, a responsible policy must allow individuals to make choices for themselves, consistent with the rights of others. In the final analysis, to be compatible with the full array of individual values, environmental policy must adopt a free-market approach.

Contributors

Doug Bandow is a senior fellow at the Cato Institute.

David Boaz is executive vice president of the Cato Institute.

Ted Galen Carpenter is director of foreign policy studies at the Cato Institute.

Edward H. Crane is president of the Cato Institute.

Bert Ely is the principal of Ely & Company, a financial institutions consulting company.

Jeffrey R. Gerlach is a foreign policy analyst at the Cato Institute.

Thomas W. Hazlett teaches economics and public policy at the University of California, Davis, and in 1991–92 was visiting chief economist at the Federal Communications Commission.

Kent Jeffreys is director of environmental studies at the Competitive Enterprise Institute.

Christopher Layne teaches international relations at UCLA and is a senior fellow of the Cato Institute.

Brink Lindsey is director of regulatory studies at the Cato Institute.

Stephen Moore is director of fiscal policy studies at the Cato Institute.

Patrick J. Michaels is associate professor of environmental sciences at the University of Virginia, senior fellow in environmental studies at the Cato Institute, and author of *Sound and Fury: The Science and Politics of Global Warming*.

William A. Niskanen is chairman of the Cato Institute and editor of *Regulation* magazine.

Lewis J. Perelman is a senior fellow at the Discovery Institute and author of *School's Out: Hyperlearning, the New Technology, and the End of Education*.

Roger Pilon is director of the Cato Institute's Center for Constitutional Studies.

Robert W. Poole, Jr., is president of the Reason Foundation.

A. Haeworth Robertson is president of the Retirement Policy Institute, former chief actuary of the Social Security Administration, and author of *Social Security: What Every Taxpayer Should Know.*

Fred L. Smith, Jr., is president of the Competitive Enterprise Institute.

Melanie S. Tammen is an adjunct scholar of the Cato Institute.

Michael Tanner is director of research at the Georgia Public Policy Foundation.

Jerry Taylor is director of natural resource studies at the Cato Institute.

Ian Vásquez is assistant director of the Cato Institute's Project on Global Economic Liberty.

Aaron Wildavsky is Class of 1940 Professor of Political Science and Public Policy at the University of California, Berkeley.

Cato Institute

Founded in 1977, the Cato Institute is a public policy research foundation dedicated to broadening the parameters of policy debate to allow consideration of more options that are consistent with the traditional American principles of limited government, individual liberty, and peace. To that end, the Institute strives to achieve greater involvement of the intelligent, concerned lay public in questions of policy and the proper role of government.

The Institute is named for *Cato's Letters*, libertarian pamphlets that were widely read in the American Colonies in the early 18th century and played a major role in laying the philosophical foundation for the American Revolution.

Despite the achievement of the nation's Founders, today virtually no aspect of life is free from government encroachment. A pervasive intolerance for individual rights is shown by government's arbitrary intrusions into private economic transactions and its disregard for civil liberties.

To counter that trend, the Cato Institute undertakes an extensive publications program that addresses the complete spectrum of policy issues. Books, monographs, and shorter studies are commissioned to examine the federal budget, Social Security, regulation, military spending, international trade, and myriad other issues. Major policy conferences are held throughout the year, from which papers are published thrice yearly in the *Cato Journal*. The Institute also publishes the quarterly magazine *Regulation*.

In order to maintain its independence, the Cato Institute accepts no government funding. Contributions are received from foundations, corporations, and individuals, and other revenue is generated from the sale of publications. The Institute is a nonprofit, tax-exempt, educational foundation under Section 501(c)3 of the Internal Revenue Code.

CATO INSTITUTE
1000 Massachusetts Ave., N.W.
Washington, D.C. 20001